Street by Street

BRADFORD
HALIFAX
BRIGHOUSE, KEIGHLEY

Bingley, Calverley, Hipperholme, Northowram, Queensbury, Saltaire, Shipley, Wyke

Ist edition May 2001

© Automobile Association Developments Limited 2001

This product includes map data licensed from Ordnance Survey® with the permission of the Controller of Her Majesty's Stationery Office. © Crown copyright 2000. All rights reserved. Licence No: 399221.

Published by AA Publishing (a trading name of Automobile Association Developments Limited, whose registered office is Norfolk House, Priestley Road, Basingstoke, Hampshire, RG24 9NY. Registered number 1878835).

Mapping produced by the Cartographic Department of The Automobile Association.

A CIP Catalogue record for this book is available from the British Library.

Printed by GRAFIASA S.A., Porto, Portugal

The contents of this atlas are believed to be correct at the time of the latest revision. However, the publishers cannot be held responsible for loss occasioned to any person acting or refraining from action as a result of any material in this atlas, nor for any errors, omissions or changes in such material. The publishers would welcome information to correct any errors or omissions and to keep this atlas up to date. Please write to Publishing, The Automobile Association, Fanum House, Basing View, Basingstoke, Hampshire, RG21 4EA.

Ref: ML013

Key to map pages	ii-iii
Key to map symbols	iv-1
Enlarged scale pages	2-5
Street by Street	6-53
Index – towns & villages	54
Index – streets	55-77
Index – featured places	78-80

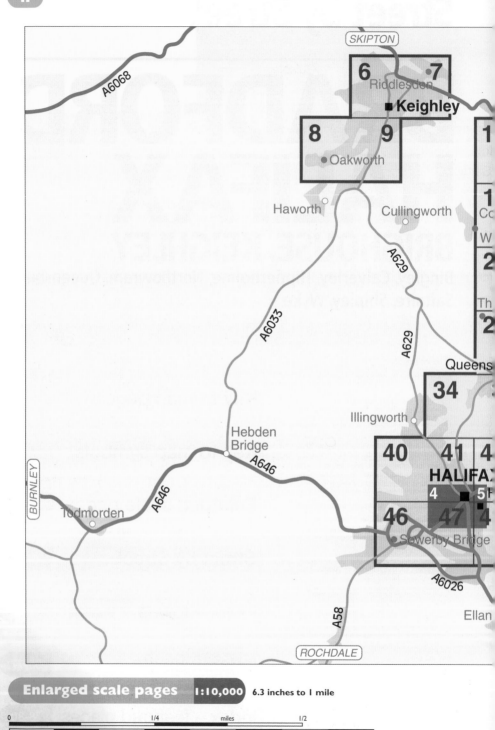

SKIPTON

A6068

6
·7

Riddlesden

■ **Keighley**

8
9

·Oakworth

1

Haworth

Cullingworth

Co

W

A629

2

A6033

A629

Th

2

Queens

34

Illingworth

Hebden
Bridge

A646

40
41
4

HALIFAX

BURNLEY

A646

4
5

Todmorden

46
47
4

·Sowerby Bridge

A6026

A58

Ellan

ROCHDALE

Enlarged scale pages **1:10,000** 6.3 inches to 1 mile

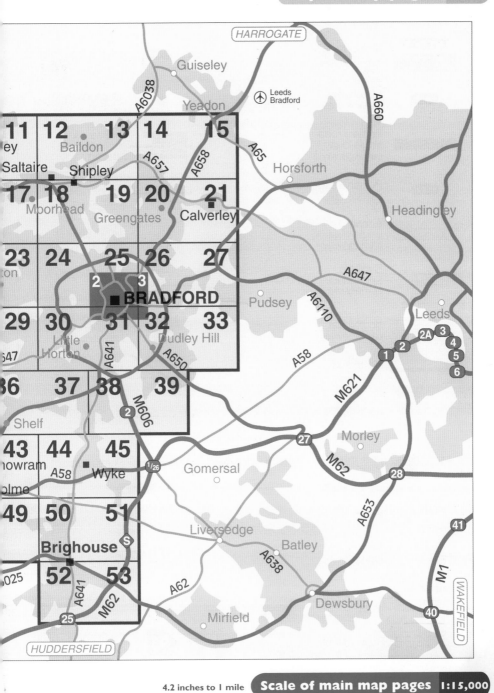

iv

Symbol	Description	Symbol	Description
Junction 9	Motorway & junction	P+	Park & Ride
Services	Motorway service area		Bus/Coach station
	Primary road single/dual carriageway		Railway & main railway station
Services	Primary road service area		Railway & minor railway station
	A road single/dual carriageway		Underground station
	B road single/dual carriageway		Light Railway & station
	Other road single/dual carriageway	+++++++	Preserved private railway
	Restricted road	LC	Level crossing
	Private road		Tramway
← ←	One way street	----------	Ferry route
	Pedestrian street	············	Airport runway
	Track/ footpath	— · — · —	Boundaries- borough/ district
	Road under construction		Mounds
	Road tunnel	93	Page continuation 1:15,000
P	Parking	7	Page continuation to enlarged scale 1:10,000

	River/canal, lake, pier		Toilet with disabled facilities
	Aqueduct, lock, weir		Petrol station
465 ▲ Winter Hill	Peak (with height in metres)	PH	Public house
	Beach	PO	Post Office
	Coniferous woodland		Public library
	Broadleaved woodland	*i*	Tourist Information Centre
	Mixed woodland		Castle
	Park		Historic house/ building
	Cemetery	Wakehurst Place NT	National Trust property
	Built-up area	M	Museum/ art gallery
	Featured building	†	Church/chapel
	City wall		Country park
A&E	Accident & Emergency hospital		Theatre/ performing arts
	Toilet		Cinema

BRADFORD
BD1

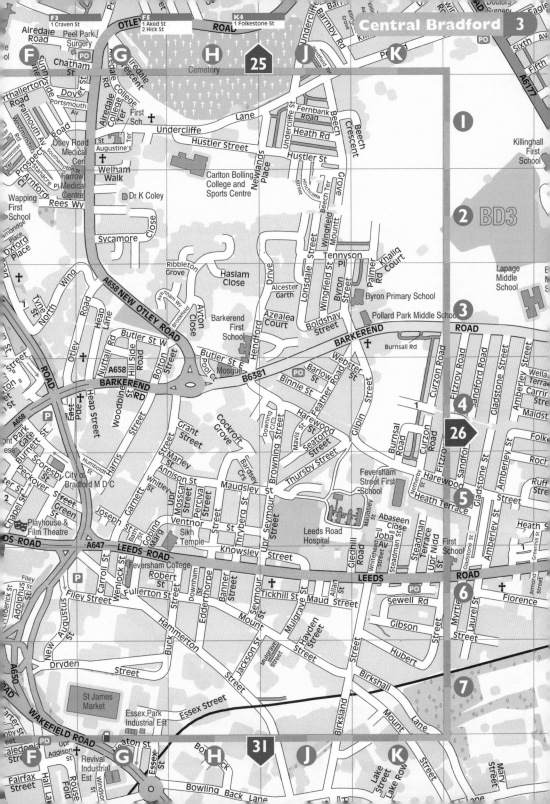

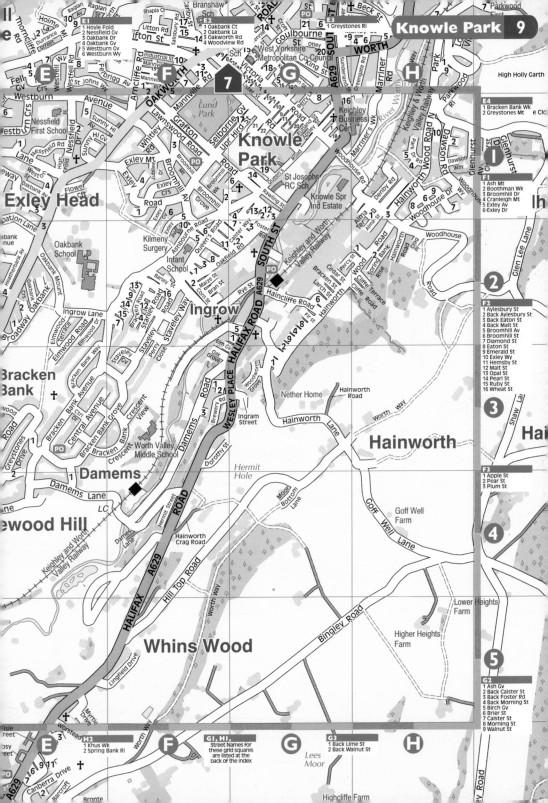

High Holly Garth

E1
1 Hoyle Fold
2 Nessfield Gv
3 Oakbank Dr
4 Oakbank Gv
5 Westburn Gv
6 Westburn Wy

E2
1 Oakbank Ct
2 Oakbank La
3 Oakworth Rd
4 Woodview Rd

E4
1 Bracken Bank Wk
2 Greystones Mt   e Clc

F1
1 Ash Mt
2 Boothman Wk
3 Broomhill Dr
4 Cranleigh Mt
5 Exley Av
6 Exley Dr

F2
1 Aylesbury St
2 Back Aylesbury St
3 Back Eaton St
4 Back Malt St
5 Broomhill Av
6 Broomhill St
7 Diamond St
8 Eaton St
9 Emerald St
10 Exley Wy
11 Hemsby St
12 Malt St
13 Opal St
14 Pearl St
15 Ruby St
16 Wheat St

F3
1 Apple St
2 Pear St
3 Plum St

G2
1 Ash Gv
2 Back Caister St
3 Back Foster Rd
4 Back Morning St
5 Birch Gv
6 Brier St
7 Caister St
8 Morning St
9 Walnut St

H2
1 Khus Wk
2 Spring Bank Ri

G1, H1
Street Names for these grid squares are listed at the back of the index

G3
1 Back Lime St
2 Back Walnut St

Exley Head

Bracken Bank

Knowle Park

Ingrow

Damems

Hainworth

Whins Wood

Lees Moor

Nessfield First School

Oakbank School

Worth Valley Middle School

Lund Park

Kilmeny Surgery

Infant School

West Yorkshire Metropolitan Co-Council

Keighley Business Cen

St Josephs RC Sch

Knowle Spr Ind Estate

Nether Home

Hermit Hole

Goff Well Farm

Lower Heights Farm

Higher Heights Farm

Highcliffe Farm

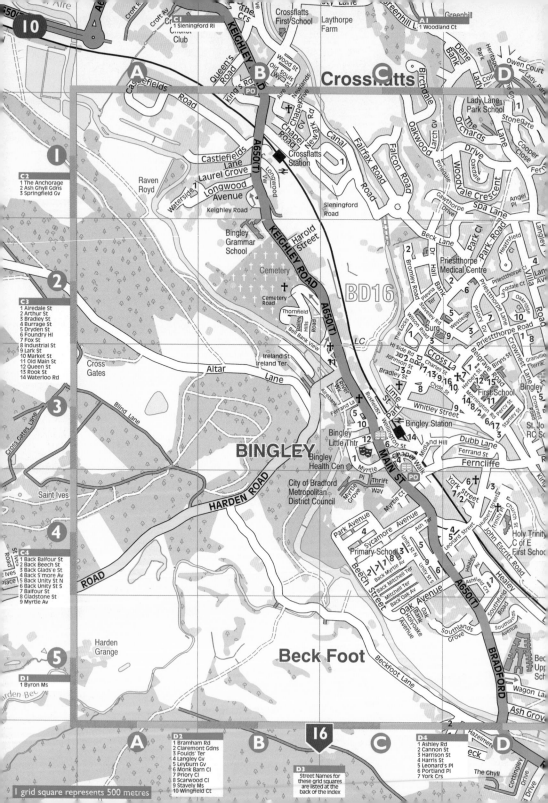

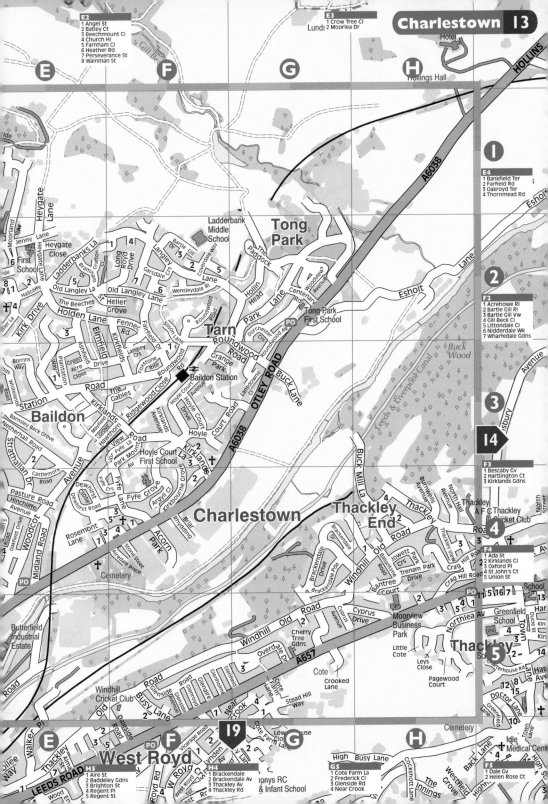

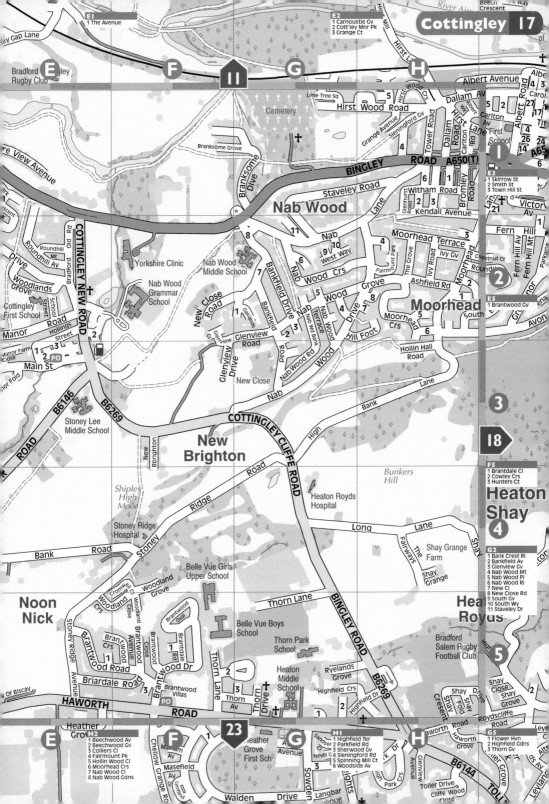

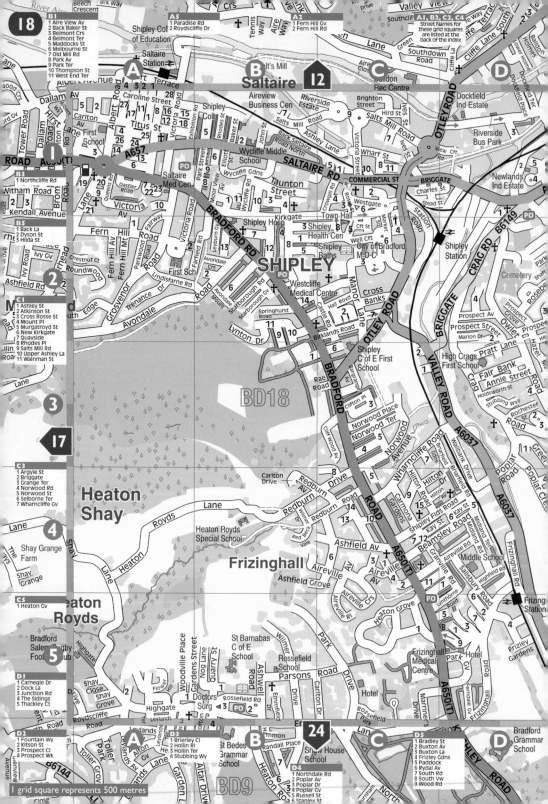

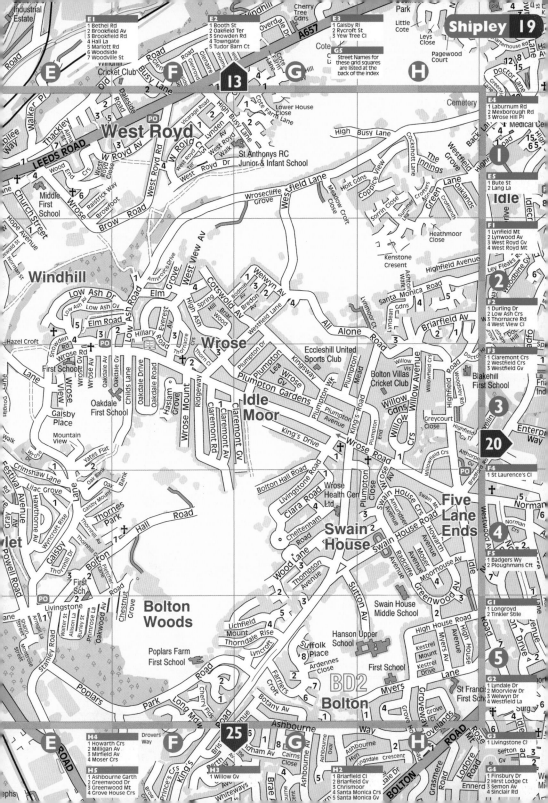

Map labels and areas

West Royd

Windhill

Wrose

Idle Moor

Idle

Five Lane Ends

Swain House

Bolton Woods

Bolton

Poplars Farm First School

BD2

E F 15 G H

Woodlands Close

✝
Woodhouse Grove School

E1
1 Brookhouse Gdns
2 Waterloo Crs

F3
1 Carr Hill Nook

Leeds Country Way

Leeds Co Way

Dr

Drive

Way

Leeds Way

I

G3
1 Back Thornhill St
2 Capel Ct
3 Chestnut Gv

Thornhill Drive

Thornhill Drive

Calverley Wood

Lodge Wood

West Wood

Calverley Cutting

Clara Drive

Drive

Drive

Clara

Manor Way

Way

2

Pearson St
St Wilfred's Street
Lydgate St
Lydgate Place
Wood La
Thornhill Cl
Thornhill La

Calverley C of E Primary School
✝

Calverley House Farm

Calverley

CARR ROAD

Crowther Avenue

Carr Rd
Fraser Rd
Rd
St Stephen's Rd
Carr Wd Gdns
Clover
Clover Crs
Woodland Vw
Salisbury Pl
Salisbury St
Chapel Street
PO
Thornhill Gv
Blackett St
W End Rd
Portman St
Rushton St
Clarke St
Town Gate
Town Wls Dr

Carr Hill Av

Carr Hill Road

Carr Hill Dr
Carr Hill Ri
Grove
Carr Hi Ri
1
Hollin Pk Rd

Infant School
Victoria Street

Parkwood St
Parkwood Gdns
1
2
Capel St
Monson Av

A657

3

RODLEY LANE

Brookfield Av
Brookfield Gdns

Upper Carr La

Calverley Medical Centre

Hollin Pk Ct
Hollin Pk Drive
Woodhall Ct
Woodhall Pk
Woodhall Road
Foxhole
Foxholes
Foxholes Crs
Foxhole La

Shell Lane

CALVERLEY LANE

4

Wood Hill

B6156

FARSLEY

Round Wood

Woodhall Road

Priesthorpe Rd

5

CALVERLEY LANE DR

Beech
Lees
Lees Lane
Bryan St
Bryan St N

Woodhall Hills Golf Club

Priesthorpe

Priesthorpe Rd
✝
Wadlands Rd
Wadlands Gv
Wadlands Cl
Wadlands

E F 27 G H

Woodhall Hills

Woodhall Rd

RING

ROAD

Red Lane
Low Bank St
Broad St
Stony Royd
Gladstone St
Charles St
Waterla
Farfield Gv
Alma Ct
Westway
Paradise St
Edroyd Pl
Edroyd St
Wadlands Drive

22

Lingb[]

B6144

Shay Gate

Meadow Green

A   **B**   **16**   **C**   **D**

WILSDEN   ROAD

Sandy Lane

COTTINGLEY ROAD

Acacia Dr

Hornbeam Close

Sandy Lane First School

B6144

I

BD15

Gazeby Hall

Back Lane

Prune Park Lane

Stony Lane

Crasleigh Way

Ollerdale Av

Craisdale Court

Burnsdale

Avenue

Deanwood Crs

2

Harron

Stephenson Road

Shay House Farm

Mutton Lane

Bailey Fold

High Ash Park

Crasleigh Way

Dale Croft

Cliffe View

Ryedale Way

Rudding Av

Rudding Crs

3

Ten Road

Dean Lane Head Farms

Dean Lane

Allerton Road

Long Lane

Rosedale Avenue

Allerton Road

Byland Grove

Ivy Grove

North Parade

Egerton Grove

Kildare Crs

Cote Lane

Hill Top Lane

Hill Cl

4

Bell Dean

Heights Road

Upper Pikeley

Long Lane

Yew Tree Lane

Aldersley Farm

Upper Allerton Lane

Sandal Farm

Woodford Cl

Weymouth Avenue

Merr Roa

Heights Road

Pitty Beck

Bracewell

Chevet Mount

Ayrecome Ov

Ormo Driv

Hill Top

5

Spring Holes Lane

Salt Pie

Cliffe Lane

Allerton Lane

Windy Ridge

Wicken Lane

West Lane

Hill Crest Road

Leaside

Valentine Ct

Back Lane

Hill Cft

N Cliffe Lane

Harcourt

James Street

Alpine Rise

Wold Lane

High Street

Havelock Street

Sapgate Lane

N Cliffe Av

Wembley Avenue

Watkin Av

West Street

HighWicken St

George Street

A   **B**   **28**   **C**   **D**   School

Bede's Cl

Firth St

Westville Way

Church School

Spring Head

N Cliffe Road

E4, F5
Street Names for these grid squares are listed at the back of the index

First School

Wensley Bank (West)

Wensley Bank Ter

Market Street

Bronte Old Road

THORNTON

Thorpe Avenue

Hughendon

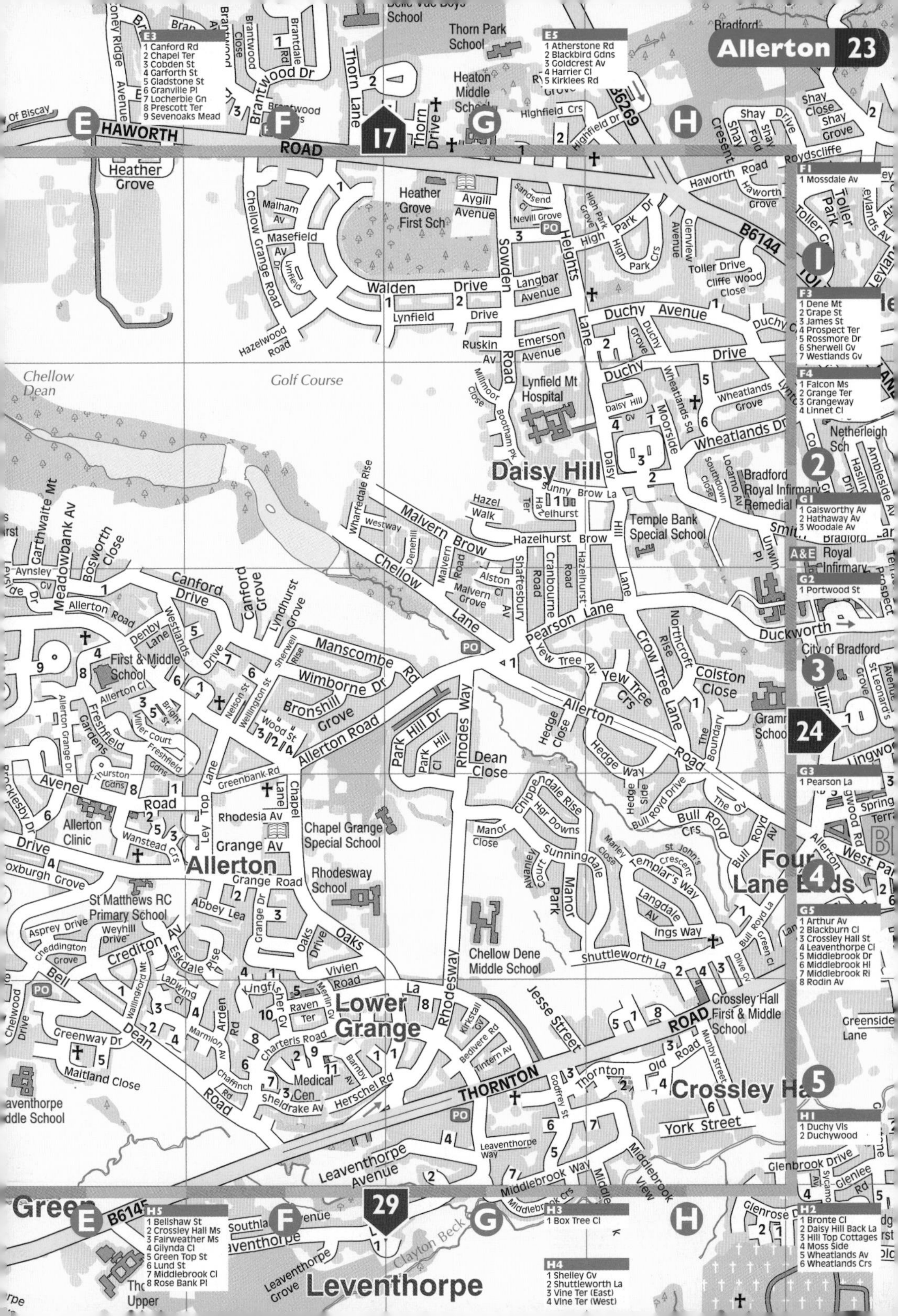
E3
1 Canford Rd
2 Chapel Ter
3 Cobden St
4 Garforth St
5 Gladstone St
6 Granville Pl
7 Locherbie Gn
8 Prescott Ter
9 Sevenoaks Mead
E5
1 Atherstone Rd
2 Blackbird Gdns
3 Goldcrest Av
4 Harrier Cl
5 Kirklees Rd
F1
1 Mossdale Av
F3
1 Dene Mt
2 Grape St
3 James St
4 Prospect Ter
5 Rossmore Dr
6 Sherwell Gv
7 Westlands Gv
F4
1 Falcon Ms
2 Grange Ter
3 Grangeway
4 Linnet Cl
G1
1 Galsworthy Av
2 Hathaway Av
3 Woodale Av
G2
1 Portwood St
G3
1 Pearson La
G5
1 Arthur Av
2 Blackburn Cl
3 Crossley Hall St
4 Leaventhorpe Cl
5 Middlebrook Dr
6 Middlebrook Hl
7 Middlebrook Ri
8 Rodin Av
H1
1 Duchy Vls
2 Duchywood
H2
1 Bronte Cl
2 Daisy Hill Back La
3 Hill Top Cottages
4 Moss Side
5 Wheatlands Av
6 Wheatlands Crs
H3
1 Box Tree Cl
H4
1 Shelley Gv
2 Shuttleworth La
3 Vine Ter (East)
4 Vine Ter (West)
H5
1 Bellshaw St
2 Crossley Hall Ms
3 Fairweather Ms
4 Gilynda Cl
5 Green Top St
6 Lund St
7 Middlebrook Cl
8 Rose Bank Pl
HAWORTH ROAD
Heather Grove
Heather Grove First Sch
Thorn Park School
Heaton Middle School
Golf Course
Chellow Dean
Daisy Hill
Lynfield Mt Hospital
Temple Bank Special School
Bradford Royal Infirmary
City of Bradford Grammar School
Allerton
Chapel Grange Special School
Rhodesway School
St Matthews RC Primary School
Allerton Clinic
Chellow Dene Middle School
Lower Grange
Crossley Hall
Crossley Hall First & Middle School
Four Lane Ends
Leventhorpe
THORNTON ROAD
Clayton Beck
17
24
29

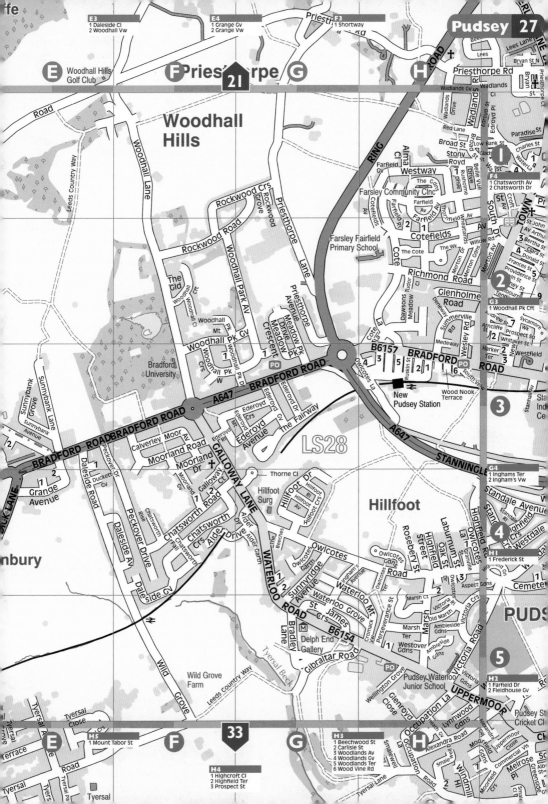

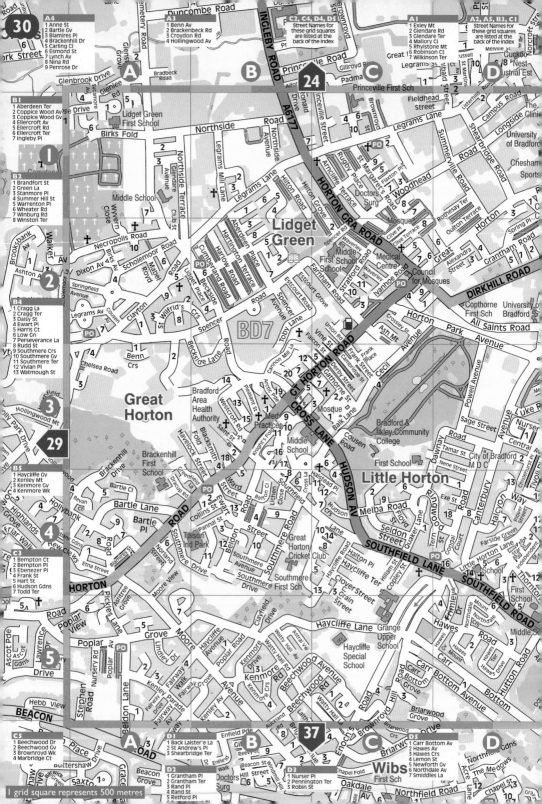

E1
1 Tyersal Garth

E

Wild Grove
Farm

Leeds Country Way

F

Tyersal Beck

Gibralta

Delph End
Gallery

Hadley

G

B6154
Cross

Ter
Westover
Gdns

Ambleside

Westover
Gdns

E4
1 Wenborough La
2 Woodgarth Gdns

PO

Wellington Grove

Pudsey Waterloo
Junior School

W Parks

Tofts

Holme 33

UPPERMOOR

H

Pudsey
Cricket C

27

Tyersal Crs
Tyersal
Close

Tyersal Avenue

Tyersal
Road

Terrace

Tyersal
Grove

Tyersal
Green

Tyersal
Court

Tyersal Walk

Tyersal Drive

Tyersal
Park

Tyersal
Family
Clinic

Pudsey Tyersal
Primary School

Tyersal

Occupation Road

Glenroyd Close

Lynnwood
Gdns

New
Occupation
Road

Alexandra Road

Smalewell
Gdns

Smalewell

Smalewell Lane

Smalewell
Gdns

Smale

Windmill Hill

Uppermoor
Close

Commercial Vls

Moorfield
Gdns

Moor Field

Melrose
Pl

Smale
Ct

Greenside

I

E5
1 Ardsley Cl
2 Bankholme Ct
3 Barthorpe Cl
4 Bowater Ct
5 Craigmore Ct
6 Greenholme Ct
7 Heybeck Wk
8 Kesteven Cl
9 Landsholme Ct
10 Lansdale Ct
11 Lynwood Ms
12 Simon Cl
13 Wenborough La

Tyersal Lane

Black Hey
Farm

Westroyd Av

Westroyd Gdns

Westroyd
Crs

Westroyd

Westroyd
Crs

Leeds Country Way

2

H1
1 Moorfield Gv
2 Smalewell Dr

Tyersal Lane

Tyersal
Hall

Leeds

Bradford

Black Hey
Farm

Black
Carr

Bankhouse

Scholebrook Lane

Tyersal Lane

Tyersal
Gate

Ned

Lane

Holmefield
First
School

Holme

Scholebrook Lane

3

BD4

Holme
Wood

Heysham

Drive

Heysham
Drive

Holme La

Maythorne Farm

Scholebrook Farm

Park
Wood

4

13

Royd
Road

3

Thorn Royd Drive

12

11

4

1

steven

5

Avenue

iel Court

Argent
Way

10

6

Eggleston Drive

9

2

Raikes Lane

New Lane

5

Howden
Close

E

F

G

H

Ryecroft Farm

Denbrook Wn

Denbrook
Road

Denbrook
Walk

7

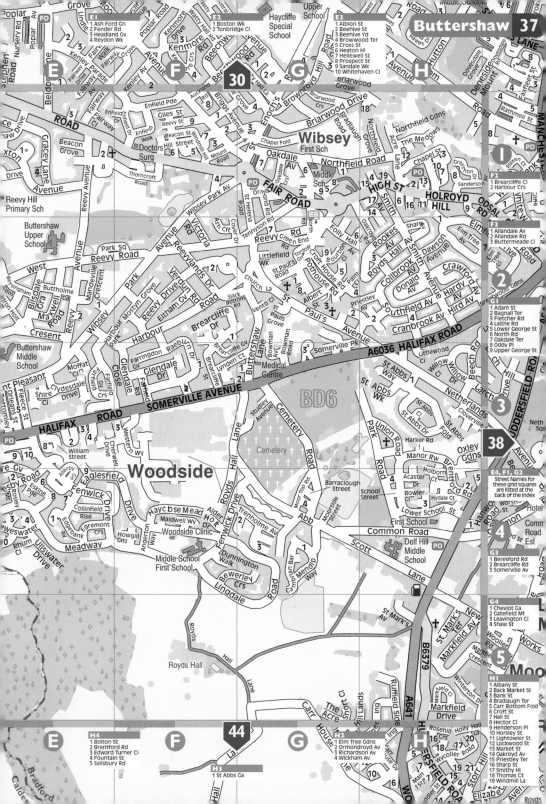

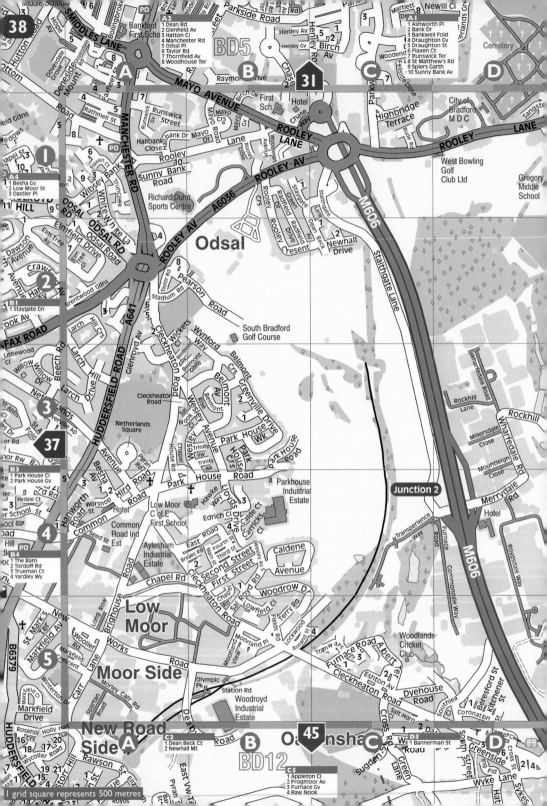

E1
1 Bannockburn Ct
2 Bell House Av
3 Crestwood Cl
4 Hopefield Wy
5 Mill House Rd
6 Newhall Rd

E2
1 Armadale Av
2 Ashmore Gdns
3 Daffels Wood Cl
4 Danby Av
5 De Lacy Av
6 Middlegate Ct
7 School St

St Columbas
RC Primary
School

Venlo
Industrial
Estate

32

Tong
Street

BIERLEY

Broomwood
Middle
School

E3
1 Parkmere Cl

I

Toftshaw

Meadowcroft
Rise

E5
1 Hollowfield Cft
2 New Cross St

2

**East
Bierle**

Bradford
Kirklees

Raikes
Wood
Drive

Club
House

3
Verity St

F1
1 Fallowfield Gdns

Cliff Hollins Lane

East Bierley
Cricket Club

South
Way

4

F2
1 Harmon Cl
2 Hopkinson Dr

Copley House
Farm

Lower Lane

Heritage Trail

Spen Valley

5

E   H2
1 Thorverton Dr   **F**   H1
Street Names for
these grid squares
are listed at the
back of the index   **G**   G1
1 Glenhurst
2 William St   **H**

M62

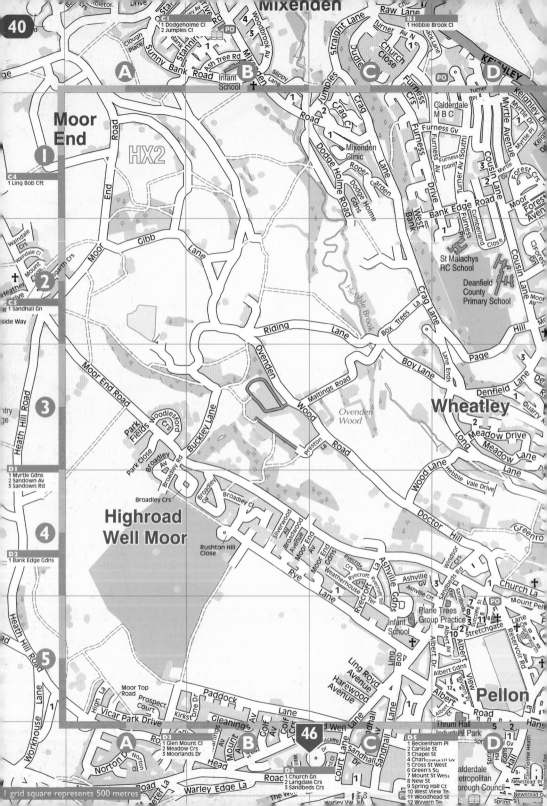

Stone Chair

Northowram

Coley

Norwood Green

Priestley Green

Hipperholme

E F G H

36

44

49

HALIFAX ROAD

A644

BRIGHOUSE AND DENHOLME GATE ROAD

DENHOLME GATE ROAD

Coley Road

Coley Hall Lane

Shutts Lane

Northedge Lane

Syke Lane

Soaper House Lane

Westercroft Lane

Holme Lane

Bird

Wood Lane

LEEDS ROAD

Sutherland Road

Knowle Top Drive

Halifax Old Road

Tanhouse Hill

Westfield Drive

Coach Road

C3
1 St Mary's Mt

C1
1 The Coppies

Royds Hall

A   B   37   C   D

I

C4
1 Cameron Av

Bradford Calderdale

wood Green

2

Watford Avenue

Village

Norwood

Queen's Rd
Green Hill

Shut Lane

3

43

D2
1 Carr Rd
2 Gannerthorpe Cl
3 Hanson Fold

Hill End Close

Street

Rookes Lane

Station

Road

4

D3
1 Aysgarth Cl
2 Gayle Cl
3 Griffe Head Crs
4 Wilkinson Fold

Leeds Rd

A58(T)

A641

5

Cecil Avenue

Knowle Top Road

Knowle Top Drive

Valley Av

Cath Lane

PO

Lightcliffe C of E Primary School

Park Cl

Coach Road

Lightcliffe

A

AFIELD

D4
1 Greengates Av
2 Kirkley Av
3 Methuen Ov
4 Rushdene Ct
5 Woodkirk Gv

B

ROAD

A649

Acacia Drive

West Av

East Stre

Bailiff Brid

50

Victoria Road

Primary School

C

D1 G5
Street Names for these grid squares are listed at the back of the index

holme rial

D

Carr House Lane

Royds Hall Lane

High Fernley Road

High Fernley

Carr Hall Road

Hannah Ct
The Hudson

Acomb Ter

Hind St

Clare Rd

Hanson Mt

St Mary's Crs

St Mary's Dr

Shirley Crs

Whitehall Av

Crest Av

Shirley Pl

Angus Av

Shirley Avenue

Tor

Meadow

Paddock Cl

B6379

Ruffield Side
Markfield Drive

HUDDERSFIELD ROAD

Rosehill Crs

Holly

Woodside Road

A641

Main St

Saddler St

18
17

15

14

13

9

8

11

19

Wroe Crs
Wroe Ter
Wroe Pl

High Fernley First School

Wyke Middle School

The Surgery

PO
West

Oakensha Court

Cft

HUDDERSFIELD ROAD

TOWNGATE

Green Lane

Vicarage Close

St Mary's

Griffe Head Road

Griffe Road

Griffe Dr

Villa Mt

Wyk

Avenue

Blackstone Av

Fearns Av

Lwr Wyke Green

Lower

Capel

Wyke

Lower Wy

Mayfield Gv

Mayfield Av

Highfield Av

Bronte Way

A641

A58(T)

grid square represents 500 metres

Woodlands
Cres

Moor Side

New
Fold

Woodlands
C of E
First
School

Furnace Road Abert

1 Bentley St
2 Mayfield Ter
3 Pearson Rw
4 Worthing Head Cl

E

New Road Side

F

38

G

Dyehouse
Road

H

Wyke Manor
Upper
School

Worthinghead
First School

Cow   Close   Lane

Whitehall
Road

A58(T)   WHITEHALL ROAD

2

E4
1 Sellerdale Wy

3

F4
1 Providence St

Langdale Av

Kentmere
Av

Thirlmere Av

Grasmere Rd

Greenton
Avenue

Westfield
Place

Meadowlands

Wickham St

Whitechapel Gv

Cemetery

4

F5
1 Foldings Ct

WESTFIELD   LANE
B6379

Brookfields
Rd

Tabbs
Lane

Tabbs Ct

Branch Road

Greenfield
Drive

WHITECHAPEL ROAD

Old Popplewell La

NEW ROAD EAST

Temperance

Town Gate

Oddfellows St

Wellands   Lane

5

G1
1 Armitage Rd
2 Illingworth Rd

Foldings Pde

New
Popplewell
Lane

SCHOLES   LANE

Scholes

E

H1
1 Back North St
2 Back Rich'son St
3 North St
4 Richardson St
5 St Andrew's Crs
6 School St

F

51

**Hartshead
Moor Top**

G

G4
1 Brighton Ter
2 Springfield Ter

H

Wes

Wellands Lane

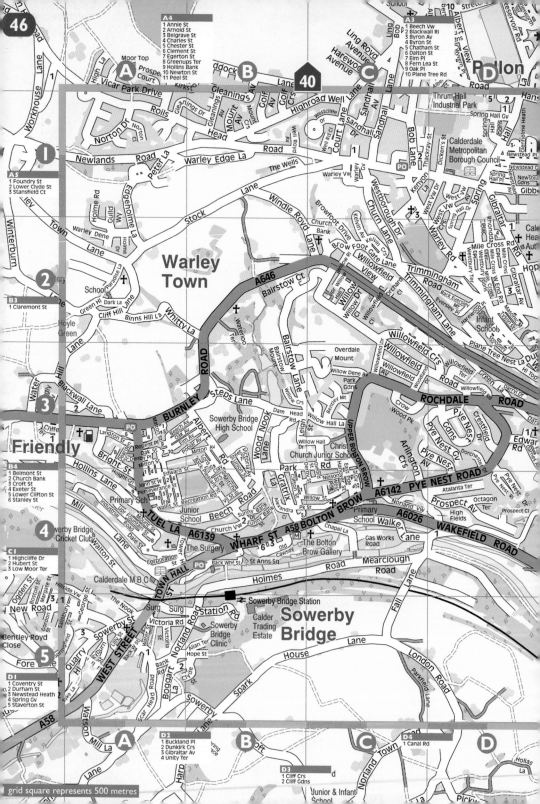

40

P**D**lon

Warley Town

Friendly

Sowerby Bridge

A4
1 Annie St
2 Arnold St
3 Belgrave St
4 Charles St
5 Chester St
6 Clement St
7 Egerton St
8 Greenups Ter
9 Hollins Bank
10 Newton St
11 Peel St

A3
1 Beech Vw
2 Blackwall Ri
3 Byron St
4 Byron St
5 Chatham St
6 Dalton St
7 Elm Pl
8 Fern Lea St
9 Oak Pl
10 Plane Tree Rd

A5
1 Foundry St
2 Lower Clyde St
3 Stansfield Ct

B3
1 Claremont St

B4
1 Belmont St
2 Church Bank
3 Croft St
4 Exeter St
5 Lower Clifton St
6 Stanley St

C1
1 Highcliffe Dr
2 Hubert St
3 Low Moor Ter

D1
1 Coventry St
2 Durham St
3 Newstead Heath
4 Spring Gv
5 Staverton St

D2
1 Buckland Pl
2 Dunkirk Crs
3 Gibraltar Av
4 Unity Ter

D3
1 Cliff Crs
2 Cliff Gdns

D4
1 Canal Rd

Calderdale
Metropolitan
Borough Council

Thrum Hall
Industrial Park

Sowerby Bridge
High School

Sowerby Bridge
Station

Calder
Trading
Estate

Sowerby
Bridge
Clinic

ROCHDALE ROAD

PYE NEST ROAD

WAKEFIELD ROAD

BURNLEY ROAD

WEST STREET

A58

A646

A6139

A6142

A6026

F1 1 Moorfield Wy

Foldings Close

Oddfellows St 1 Scholes La

Wellands Lane

E F 45 New Applewell Lane G Scholes H

Spen Whit Mour.

Wes

I

Hartshead Moor Top

Scholes Lane

Field Mt Hillcrest St

Hurst

The Copse

Moorfield Av

B6120

LANE A649 HALIFAX ROAD

Sunnybank Close

Manor Street

Wellands

Lark Hill

VCamo Lwr Lark Hill

Lark Av Lark St Park St

Moo

Hartshead Moor Side

House La

Lane

Brier Hill

East Vw

Pearson Street

MOORSIDE

Thornton St

A643

New Lane

Stonefield Street

2

Pits Lane

WALTON LANE

B6119 Tanner St 7 6 2 3 Sixth A 4

Highmoor Lane

Windy Bank La

Highba School

3

Highmoor

Lane

A643 LANE

Clough Lane

Jay House Lane

M62

Fifth Av West Secor 4

5

WINDY

4

Hartshead Moor Service Area

Bronte Way

HIGHMOOR LANE

Cam Lane

Gills

Calderdale Kirklees

5

K'th Fo H

A643

Birdswell Av Highmoor Crescent

Towngate Av Blake Law Drive

Savile Cl Savile La

Towngate

Highley Hall Cft Highley Park

Green Lane

Vine Garth

E New Cl Vine Court F 53 G Blake Law Lane H Freakfield

Cannon Hall Dr

PO Cemetery

Robin Hood Way Primary School

Grange Towngate

Vine Street

Vine Grove

Well Lane

Clifton

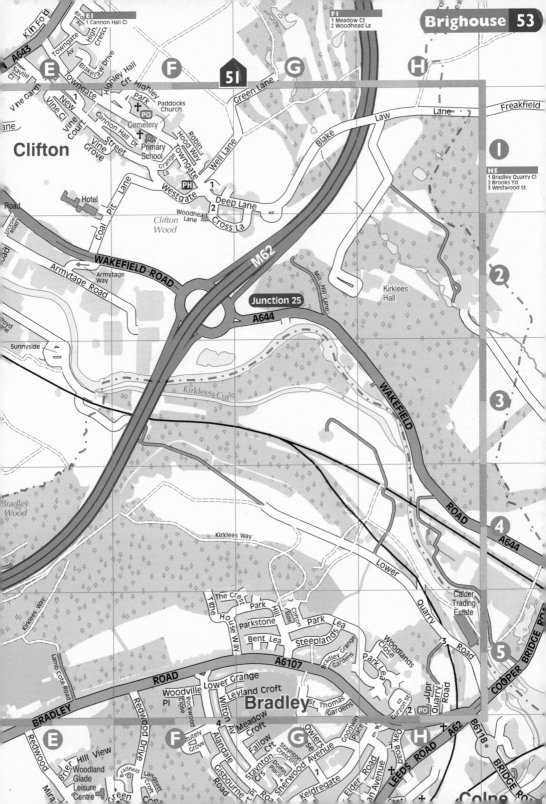

Allerton 23 F4	Dockroyd 8 B5	Long Lee 7 F5	Siddal 48 B5
Ambler Thorn 34 C2	Dudley Hill 32 B5	Lower Grange 23 F5	Southowram 48 C4
Apperley Bridge 14 D5	Eccleshill 20 A4	Lower Wyke 44 D5	Sowerby Bridge 46 B5
Baildon 13 E3	Eldwick 11 G1	Low Green 15 H3	Stockbridge 7 E1
Baildon Green 12 B4	Esholt 14 B1	Low Moor 38 A5	Stone Chair 43 F1
Bailiff Bridge 44 B5	Exley Head 9 E1	Manningham 24 D2	Stoney Royd 5 H6
Bank Top 20 B4	Fagley 26 C1	Moorhead 17 H2	Stump Cross 42 B4
Bank Top 48 C3	Five Lane Ends 19 H4	Moor Side 38 A5	Swain House 19 G4
Beck Foot 10 B5	Four Lane Ends 23 H4	Nab Wood 17 G1	Sympson Green 14 B5
Beechcliffe 7 E2	Frizinghall 18 B4	Nether Yeadon 15 F1	Tarn 13 F2
Bierley 39 E1	Gilstead 11 F3	New Brighton 17 F3	Thackley 13 H5
Bingley 10 B3	Girlington 24 B3	New Road Side 45 E1	Thackley End 13 G4
Birkhouse 50 D2	Great Horton 30 A3	Noon Nick 17 E5	Thornbury 26 D4
Black Hill 6 A3	Greengates 20 C3	Norr 16 A4	Thornhills 50 D4
Bogthorn 8 D2	Hainworth 9 H3	Northowram 43 E3	Thornton 28 B1
Bolton 19 G5	Halifax 5 H4	Norwood Green 43 H2	Thorpe Edge 20 A3
Bolton Woods 19 F5	Harewood Hill 8 D4	Oakenshaw 45 F1	Thwaites 7 G4
Boothtown 41 F3	Hartshead Moor Side 51 H2	Oakworth 8 A5	Thwaites Brow 7 G5
Bowling 32 A3	Hartshead Moor Top 51 F1	Odsal 38 B2	Toftshaw 39 F2
Bracken Bank 9 E3	Heaton 24 A1	Old Dolphin 28 D5	Tong Park 13 G2
Bradford 2 B5	Heaton Royds 17 H5	Ovenden 41 E3	Tong Street 39 G1
Bradley 53 G5	Heaton Shay 18 A4	Owlet 18 D4	Toothill 52 B5
Bradshaw 34 A1	Henshaw 15 F1	Pellon 40 D5	Tyersal 33 E2
Brighouse 52 A1	Highroad Well Moor 40 A4	Pepper Hill 36 A4	Undercliffe 25 H2
Brookfoot 49 H5	Hillfoot 27 H4	Priesthorpe 21 F5	Utley 6 C1
Buttershaw 36 C2	Hipperholme 43 E5	Priestley Green 43 G4	Warley Town 46 A2
Cackleshaw 8 C4	Holdsworth 34 C4	Priestthorpe 10 D2	West Bowling 31 G4
Calverley 21 H3	Holme 33 E3	Pule Hill 41 H2	Westfield 14 D1
Catherine Slack 34 D4	Holme Wood 33 E4	Queensbury 34 D1	West Morton 7 H1
Charlestown 13 F4	Holmfield 34 A5	Rastrick 52 A3	West Royd 19 E1
Chat Hill 28 D2	Hove Edge 49 H3	Ravenscliffe 20 D5	West Scholes 28 A4
Claremount 5 H1	Idle 20 A1	Rawdon 15 H3	Wheatley 40 C3
Clayton 29 F3	Idle Moor 19 G3	Riddlesden 7 H2	Whins Wood 9 F5
Clayton Heights 29 F5	Ingrow 9 F2	Saltaire 12 B5	Wibsey 37 G1
Clifton 53 E1	Keighley 6 D3	Sandy Lane 22 C1	Windhill 19 E2
Coley 43 G3	Knowle Park 9 G1	Savile Park 47 F4	Woodhall Hills 27 F1
Cottingley 16 D2	Laisterdyke 32 C1	Scholemoor 29 H2	Woodhouse 52 D3
Crossley Hall 23 H5	Leventhorpe 29 F1	Scholes 45 G5	Woodlands 41 H3
Cross Roads 8 D5	Lidget Green 30 B2	School Green 28 D1	Woodside 37 F4
Crow Nest 11 E3	Lightcliffe 50 A1	Shay Gate 16 B5	Wrose 19 F3
Daisy Hill 23 G2	Lingbob 16 A5	Shelf 36 C4	Wyke 44 D3
Damems 9 E4	Little Horton 30 C4	Shibden Head 35 E4	Yeadon 15 G1
Dam Head 42 C2	Little London 15 F3	Shipley 18 B2	

USING THE STREET INDEX

Street names are listed alphabetically. Each street name is followed by its postal town or area locality, the Postcode District, the page number, and the reference to the square in which the name is found.

Example: **Abbotside CI** *IDLE* BD10 .... **20** B3 **1**

Some entries are followed by a number in a blue box. This number indicates the location of the street within the referenced grid square. The full street name is listed at the side of the map page.

GENERAL ABBREVIATIONS

ACC ....ACCESS	CPS ....COPSE	FY ....FERRY	LA....................LANE
ALY ....ALLEY	CR ....CREEK	GA ....GATE	LDG....................LODGE
AP ....APPROACH	CREM ....CREMATORIUM	GAL ....GALLERY	LGT....................LIGHT
AR ....ARCADE	CRS ....CRESCENT	GDN ....GARDEN	LK....................LOCK
ASS ....ASSOCIATION	CSWY ....CAUSEWAY	GDNS ....GARDENS	LKS....................LAKES
AV ....AVENUE	CT ....COURT	GLD ....GLADE	LNDG....................LANDING
BCH....................BEACH	CTRL ....CENTRAL	GLN ....GLEN	LTL....................LITTLE
BLDS....................BUILDINGS	CTS ....COURTS	GN ....GREEN	LWR....................LOWER
BND....................BEND	CTYD ....COURTYARD	GND ....GROUND	MAG....................MAGISTRATE
BNK....................BANK	CUTT ....CUTTINGS	GRA ....GRANGE	MAN....................MANSIONS
BR....................BRIDGE	CV ....COVE	GRG ....GARAGE	MD....................MEAD
BRK....................BROOK	CYN ....CANYON	GT ....GREAT	MDW....................MEADOWS
BTM....................BOTTOM	DEPT ....DEPARTMENT	GTWY ....GATEWAY	MEM....................MEMORIAL
BUS....................BUSINESS	DL....................DALE	GV ....GROVE	MKT....................MARKET
BVD....................BOULEVARD	DM ....DAM	HGR ....HIGHER	MKTS....................MARKETS
BY....................BYPASS	DR ....DRIVE	HL ....HILL	ML....................MALL
CATH....................CATHEDRAL	DRO ....DROVE	HLS ....HILLS	ML....................MILL
CEM....................CEMETERY	DRY ....DRIVEWAY	HO ....HOUSE	MNR....................MANOR
CEN....................CENTRE	DWGS ....DWELLINGS	HOL ....HOLLOW	MS....................MEWS
CFT....................CROFT	E....................EAST	HOSP ....HOSPITAL	MSN....................MISSION
CH....................CHURCH	EMB....................EMBANKMENT	HRB ....HARBOUR	MT....................MOUNT
CHA....................CHASE	EMBY ....EMBASSY	HTH ....HEATH	MTN....................MOUNTAIN
CHYD....................CHURCHYARD	ESP ....ESPLANADE	HTS ....HEIGHTS	MTS....................MOUNTAINS
CIR....................CIRCLE	EST ....ESTATE	HVN ....HAVEN	MUS....................MUSEUM
CIRC....................CIRCUS	EX ....EXCHANGE	HWY ....HIGHWAY	MWY....................MOTORWAY
CL....................CLOSE	EXPY ....EXPRESSWAY	IMP ....IMPERIAL	N....................NORTH
CLFS....................CLIFFS	EXT ....EXTENSION	IN ....INLET	NE....................NORTH EAST
CMP....................CAMP	F/O ....FLYOVER	IND EST ....INDUSTRIAL ESTATE	NW....................NORTH WEST
CNR....................CORNER	FC ....FOOTBALL CLUB	INF ....INFIRMARY	O/P....................OVERPASS
CO....................COUNTY	FK ....FORK	INFO ....INFORMATION	OFF....................OFFICE
COLL....................COLLEGE	FLD ....FIELD	INT ....INTERCHANGE	ORCH....................ORCHARD
COM....................COMMON	FLDS ....FIELDS	IS ....ISLAND	OV....................OVAL
COMM....................COMMISSION	FLS ....FALLS	JCT ....JUNCTION	PAL....................PALACE
CON....................CONVENT	FLS ....FLATS	JTY ....JETTY	PAS....................PASSAGE
COT....................COTTAGE	FM ....FARM	KG ....KING	PAV....................PAVILION
COTS....................COTTAGES	FT....................FORT	KNL ....KNOLL	PDE....................PARADE
CP....................CAPE	FWY ....FREEWAY	L ....LAKE	PH....................PUBLIC HOUSE

PK	PARK	R	RIVER	SPR	SPRING	VA	VALLEY
PKWY	PARKWAY	RBT	ROUNDABOUT	SQ	SQUARE	VIAD	VIADUCT
PL	PLACE	RD	ROAD	ST	STREET	VIL	VILLA
PLN	PLAIN	RDG	RIDGE	STN	STATION	VIS	VISTA
PLNS	PLAINS	REP	REPUBLIC	STR	STREAM	VLG	VILLAGE
PLZ	PLAZA	RES	RESERVOIR	STRD	STRAND	VLS	VILLAS
POL	POLICE STATION	RFC	RUGBY FOOTBALL CLUB	SW	SOUTH WEST	VW	VIEW
PR	PRINCE	RI	RISE	TDG	TRADING	W	WEST
PREC	PRECINCT	RP	RAMP	TER	TERRACE	WD	WOOD
PREP	PREPARATORY	RW	ROW	THWY	THROUGHWAY	WHF	WHARF
PRIM	PRIMARY	S	SOUTH	TNL	TUNNEL	WK	WALK
PROM	PROMENADE	SCH	SCHOOL	TOLL	TOLLWAY	WKS	WALKS
PRS	PRINCESS	SE	SOUTH EAST	TPK	TURNPIKE	WLS	WELLS
PRT	PORT	SER	SERVICE AREA	TR	TRACK	WY	WAY
PT	POINT	SH	SHORE	TRL	TRAIL	YD	YARD
PTH	PATH	SHOP	SHOPPING	TWR	TOWER	YHA	YOUTH HOSTEL
PZ	PIAZZA	SKWY	SKYWAY	U/P	UNDERPASS		
QD	QUADRANT	SMT	SUMMIT	UNI	UNIVERSITY		
QU	QUEEN	SOC	SOCIETY	UPR	UPPER		
QY	QUAY	SP	SPUR	V	VALE		

POSTCODE TOWNS AND AREA ABBREVIATIONS

AIRE	Airedale	CLAY	Clayton	HIPP	Hipperholme	PDSY/CALV	Pudsey/Calverley
BAIL	Baildon	CLECK	Cleckheaton	HTON	Heaton	RPDN/SBR	Ripponden/Sowerby Bridge
BFD	Bradford	CUL/QBY	Cullingworth/Queensbury	HUDN	Huddersfield north	SHPY	Shipley
BFDE	Bradford east	ECHL	Eccleshill	HWTH	Haworth	WBOW	West Bowling
BGLY	Bingley	GIR	Girlington	IDLE	Idle	WBSY	Wibsey
BIRK/DRI	Birkenshaw/Drighlington	GSLY	Guiseley	KGHY	Keighley	WIL/AL	Wilsden/Allerton
BOW	Bowling	GTHN	Great Horton	LM/WK	Low Moor/Wyke	YEA	Yeadon
BRIG	Brighouse	HFAX	Halifax	LUD/ILL	Luddenden/Illingworth		

Index - streets

A

Aachen Wy HFAX HX1	4	C7
Abaseen Cl BFDE BD3	3	K5
Abbey Lea WIL/AL BD15	23	F4
Abbey Wk HIPP HX3	47	H4
Abbey Wk South HIPP HX3	47	H4
Abbotside Cl IDLE BD10	20	B3 🖫
Abb Scott La LM/WK BD12	37	G4
Abelia Mt GTHN BD7	29	H1 🖫
Abel St LM/WK BD12	44	D1 🖫
Aberdeen Pl GTHN BD7	30	B2
Aberdeen Ter CLAY BD14	29	G3
GTHN BD7	30	B1 🖫
Aberford Rd GIR BD8	24	C3
Abingdon St GIR BD8	24	C3
Acacia Dr BRIG HD6	50	B1
WIL/AL BD15	16	D5
Acacia Park Crs IDLE BD10	15	E4
Acacia Park Dr IDLE BD10	15	E4
Acacia Park Ter IDLE BD10	15	E4
Acaster Dr LM/WK BD12	37	H4
Acer Wy CLECK BD19	45	G5 🖫
Ackroyd Ct CUL/QBY BD13	28	A1 🖫
Ackworth St WBOW BD5	31	F3
Acorn Cl WBSY BD6	36	D4 🖫
Acorn Pk BAIL BD17	13	F4
Acorn St HFAX HX1	4	C3
Acre Av ECHL BD2	20	A4
Acre Cl ECHL BD2	20	A4
Acre Crs ECHL BD2	20	A4
Acre Dr ECHL BD2	20	A4
Acre Gv ECHL BD2	20	A4 🖫
Acrehowe Ri BAIL BD17	13	F2 🖫
Acre La ECHL BD2	20	A5
WBSY BD6	37	H1
Acre Ri BAIL BD17	12	D2
Acre St KGHY BD20	6	C5 🖫
The Acre LM/WK BD12	37	G5
Acton St BFDE BD3	26	B5
Adam St WBSY BD6	37	G1 🖫
Ada St HFAX HX1	13	F4 🖫
CUL/QBY BD13	35	E1 🖫
HIPP HX3	41	H4
KGHY BD21	6	B4
SHPY BD18	18	A1 🖫
Addison Av BFDE BD3	26	C3 🖫
Addi St BOW BD4	32	B4
Adelaide St HFAX HX1	4	B4
WBOW BD5	31	F2 🖫
Adgil Crs HIPP HX3	48	D3 🖫
Adolphus St BFD BD1	3	F6
Adwalton Gv CUL/QBY BD13	35	G1
Agar St GIR BD8	24	A4
Agar Ter GIR BD8	24	A4 🖫
Agnes St KGHY BD21	6	D2
Ainsbury Av IDLE BD10	14	A3
Airebank BGLY BD16	10	C3
Aire Cl BAIL BD17	12	C5

Airedale Av BGLY BD16	16	D3
Airedale College Rd BFDE BD3	25	H3
Airedale College Ter BFDE BD3	3	G1
Airedale Crs BFDE BD3	25	H3
Airedale Dr HIPP HX3	36	A3
Airedale Pl BAIL BD17	13	F4
Airedale Rd BFDE BD3	25	G3
KGHY BD21	7	G3
Airedale St BGLY BD16	10	C3 🖫
ECHL BD2	26	A1 🖫
KGHY BD21	7	F3
Aire St BGLY BD16	10	B1
BRIG HD6	52	C2
IDLE BD10	13	H5 🖫
KGHY BD21	7	E3 🖫
Airevalley Rd KGHY BD21	7	E3 🖫
Aire Vw AIRE BD20	7	G1
Aire View Av BGLY BD16	17	E1
SHPY BD18	18	B1 🖫
Aireview Crs BAIL BD17	12	B5
Aireville Av SHPY BD18	18	B4
Aireville Cl AIRE BD20	6	B1
SHPY BD18	18	C4 🖫
Aireville Crs HTON BD9	18	C4
Aireville Dr SHPY BD18	18	C4
Aireville Gra SHPY BD18	18	C4 🖫
Aireville Gv HTON BD9	18	C4 🖫
Aireville Ri HTON BD9	18	C5
Aireville Rd HTON BD9	18	D4
Aireville St AIRE BD20	6	B1 🖫
Airey Wy BAIL BD17	12	B5
Aireworth Cl KGHY BD21	7	F3 🖫
Aireworth Gv KGHY BD21	7	F3
Aireworth Rd KGHY BD21	7	F2
Aireworth St KGHY BD21	6	D4
Airey St KGHY BD21	6	B4
Akam Rd BFD BD1	2	A4
Aked's Rd HFAX HX1	4	E5
Aked St BFD BD1	3	F5 🖫
Akroyd Pl HFAX HX1	5	G2
Akroyd Ter LUD/ILL HX2	47	E3 🖫
Alabama St HFAX HX1	4	B3 🖫
Alban St BOW BD4	32	A3 🖫
Albany Ct KGHY BD21	6	B3 🖫
Albany St HIPP HX3	5	K7
WBOW BD5	31	F3 🖫
WBSY BD6	37	H1 🖫
Albert Av IDLE BD10	20	B1
LUD/ILL HX2	40	D5
SHPY BD18	11	H5
Albert Crs CUL/QBY BD13	35	F1 🖫
Albert Ct LUD/ILL HX2	40	D5
Albert Dr LUD/ILL HX2	40	D5
Albert Gdns LUD/ILL HX2	40	D5
Albert Pl BFDE BD3	26	D4
Albert Prom HIPP HX3	47	F4
Albert Rd CUL/QBY BD13	28	A5
CUL/QBY BD13	35	F1
LUD/ILL HX2	40	D5
RPDN/SBR HX6	46	B3
SHPY BD18	18	A1

Albert St BAIL BD17	12	D5 🖫
BRIG HD6	50	D5
CUL/QBY BD13	28	A1
CUL/QBY BD13	35	G1 🖫
HFAX HX1	4	E3
IDLE BD10	20	A3
KGHY BD21	6	C4
LM/WK BD12	44	D3
WBSY BD6	37	G2
Albert Ter LM/WK BD12	38	C5
SHPY BD18	12	A5
Albert Vw LUD/ILL HX2	40	D5
Albert Wk SHPY BD18	17	H1
Albion Rd IDLE BD10	20	B1
Albion St BRIG HD6	50	B5
CUL/QBY BD13	35	E1
HFAX HX1	5	H4
WBSY BD6	37	E3 🖫
Alcester Garth BFDE BD3	3	J3
Alder Carr BAIL BD17	12	C3
Alder Garth PDSY/CALV LS28	27	G4
Alder Garth PDSY/CALV LS28	27	G4
Alder Holt Dr WBSY BD6	37	F4
Aldermanbury BFD BD1	2	C6
Alderscholes Cl		
CUL/QBY BD13	28	A1 🖫
Alderson St WBSY BD6	36	D3 🖫
Alegar St BRIG HD6	52	D1 🖫
Alexander Sq CLAY BD14	29	E3 🖫
Alexander St WBSY BD6	37	G2 🖫
Alexander Ter HFAX HX1	4	B3
Alexandra Cl RPDN/SBR HX6	46	B4
Alexandra Gv PDSY/CALV LS28	27	H5
Alexandra Rd ECHL BD2	20	B4
PDSY/CALV LS28	33	H1
SHPY BD18	18	B2 🖫
Alexandra St CUL/QBY BD13	35	F1 🖫
GTHN BD7	30	D2
HFAX HX1	5	G5
Alexandra Ter ECHL BD2	26	B4
Alford Ter HIPP HX3	24	B5
Alfred St East HFAX HX1	5	J4 🖫
Alfred St BRIG HD6	50	C5 🖫
HFAX HX1	4	B3
Alice St GIR BD8	2	A2
KGHY BD21	6	C5
Alkincote St KGHY BD21	19	G2
All Alone Rd IDLE BD10	19	G2
Allanbridge Cl IDLE BD10	20	B2 🖫
Allandale Av WBSY BD6	37	F3 🖫
Allandale Rd WBSY BD6	37	F3 🖫
Allan St BFDE BD3	3	J6
Allan Ter RPDN/SBR HX6	46	B5
Allerby Gn WBSY BD6	37	E4
Allerton Cl WIL/AL BD15	23	E3
Allerton Grange Dr		
WIL/AL BD15	23	E3
Allerton La WIL/AL BD15	22	D5
Allerton Pl HFAX HX1	4	C1
Allerton Rd GIR BD8	23	G3
WIL/AL BD15	22	A3

Aac - Ann

Allison La ECHL BD2	19	E5
All Saints Rd GTHN BD7	30	D2
All Souls' Rd HIPP HX3	41	H4
All Souls' St HIPP HX3	41	H4 🖫
Alma Cl PDSY/CALV LS28	27	H1
Alma Pl KGHY BD21	9	H1 🖫
Alma St BOW BD4	32	C3
BOW BD4	32	B2
CUL/QBY BD13	35	E1
KGHY BD21	9	H2
SHPY BD18	19	E1
Alma Ter KGHY BD21	9	H2
Almond St BFDE BD3	32	B1 🖫
Alpha St KGHY BD21	7	E4 🖫
Alpine Ri CUL/QBY BD13	22	A5
Alston Cl HTON BD9	23	G3
Alston Rd KGHY BD21	7	E2
Altar Dr AIRE BD20	7	H2
HTON BD9	24	B1
Altar La BGLY BD16	10	B3
Althorpe Gv IDLE BD10	19	H3
Alton Gv HTON BD9	24	A1
SHPY BD18	18	C4 🖫
Alum Ct HTON BD9	24	B1 🖫
Alum Dr HTON BD9	24	B1
Alvanley Ct GIR BD8	23	G4
Amberley Ct BFDE BD3	26	B5
BFDE BD3	32	B1
Ambers Cft IDLE BD10	14	A4
Amblers Ter HIPP HX3	41	H4 🖫
Ambler St GIR BD8	24	D2
KGHY BD21	7	E4 🖫
Ambler Wy CUL/QBY BD13	34	D3
Ambleside Av HTON BD9	24	A2
Ambleside Gdns		
PDSY/CALV LS28	27	H5
Ambleton Wy CUL/QBY BD13	34	D2
Amelia St SHPY BD18	12	A5 🖫
America La BRIG HD6	52	D1
Amisfield Rd HIPP HX3	43	G5
Amos St HFAX HX1	4	B3
Amport Cl BRIG HD6	52	C2
Amundsen Av ECHL BD2	19	H4
Amyroyce Dr SHPY BD18	19	F2
Amy St BGLY BD16	10	D3 🖫
HIPP HX3	41	F3 🖫
The Anchorage BGLY BD16	10	C2 🖫
Anderson St GIR BD8	24	D3 🖫
Andover Gn BOW BD4	32	D3 🖫
Andrew Cl HIPP HX3	48	D4 🖫
Angel Rd HFAX HX1	4	D2
Angel St BAIL BD17	13	E2 🖫
GIR BD8	2	A5
Angerton Wy WBSY BD6	37	F4
Angus Av LM/WK BD12	44	D4
Anlaby St BOW BD4	32	C2
Annes Ct HIPP HX3	48	D4
Anne St KGHY BD21	6	D2 🖫
RPDN/SBR HX6	46	A4 🖫

SHPY BD18 .... **18** D3
Annison St *BFDE* BD3 .... **3** C5
Ann Pl *WBOW* BD5 .... **31** F2
Ann St *KGHY* BD21 .... **6** C5
Anson Gv *GTHN* BD7 .... **30** A5
Anvil St *BRIC* HD6 .... **50** B5
GIR BD8 .... **24** C3
Apperley Gdns *IDLE* BD10 ...... **20** D1
Apperley La *IDLE* BD10 .... **15** E4
IDLE BD10 .... **20** D1
YEA LS19 .... **15** F3
Apperley Rd *IDLE* BD10 .... **20** B1
Apple St *HWTH* BD22 .... **9** F5
Appleton Cl *BGLY* BD16 .... **11** E1
LM/WK BD12 .... **38** C5
Apsley Crs *GIR* BD8 .... **24** D3
Apsley St *HWTH* BD22 .... **8** C3
KGHY BD21 .... **9** G1
Arcadia St *KGHY* BD21 .... **9** G1
Archbell Av *BRIC* HD6 .... **52** C3
Archer Rd *BRIC* HD6 .... **53** E2
Arches St *HFAX* HX1 .... **5** F5
Archibald St *GTHN* BD7 .... **24** D5
Arctic Pde *GTHN* BD7 .... **30** D5
Arctic St *KGHY* BD21 .... **6** C2
Ardennes Cl *ECHL* BD2 .... **19** G5
Arden Rd *GIR* BD8 .... **23** F5
HFAX HX1 .... **4** D7
Ardsley Cl *BOW* BD4 .... **33** E5
Argent Wy *BOW* BD4 .... **33** E5
Argyle St *BOW* BD4 .... **32** A3
KGHY BD21 .... **6** C4
SHPY BD18 .... **18** C3
Argyll Cl *BAIL* BD17 .... **12** D1
Arkendale Ms *GTHN* BD7 .... **29** H4
Arkwright St *BOW* BD4 .... **32** D1
CLAY BD14 .... **29** E3
Arlesford Rd *BOW* BD4 .... **32** D5
Arlington Crs *LUD/ILL* HX2 .... **46** C3
Armadale Av *BOW* BD4 .... **39** E2
Armgill La *SHPY* BD18 .... **19** E5
Armidale Wy *ECHL* BD2 .... **25** G1
Armitage Av *HWTH* BD22 .... **6** B5
Armitage Rd *BRIC* HD6 .... **52** C3
Armitage Rd *HFAX* HX1 .... **4** A7
LM/WK BD12 .... **45** G1
Armstrong St *BOW* BD4 .... **32** C1
Armytage Rd *BRIC* HD6 .... **52** C3
Armytage Rd *BRIC* HD6 .... **53** E2
Arncliffe Av *HWTH* BD22 .... **6** B5
Arncliffe Gv *HWTH* BD22 .... **6** B5
Arncliffe Rd *HWTH* BD22 .... **9** F1
Arnford Cl *BFDE* BD3 .... **3** F2
Arnold Pl *GIR* BD8 .... **24** C4
Arnold St *GIR* BD8 .... **24** D3
HFAX HX1 .... **4** C4
Arnside Av *AIRE* BD20 .... **7** F2
Arnside Rd *WBOW* BD5 .... **31** E5
Arthington St *GIR* BD8 .... **24** D3
Arthur Av *GIR* BD8 .... **23** C5
Arthur St *BGLY* BD16 .... **10** C3
BRIG HD6 .... **52** D1
HWTH BD22 .... **8** A4
IDLE BD10 .... **20** A3
Arum St *WBOW* BD5 .... **30** D4
Arundel St *HFAX* HX1 .... **4** B3
Ascot Av *GTHN* BD7 .... **29** H5
Ascot Dr *WBSY* BD6 .... **29** H5
Ascot Gdns *GTHN* BD7 .... **29** H5
Ascot Pde *GTHN* BD7 .... **29** H5
Ashbourne Av *ECHL* BD2 .... **25** G1
Ashbourne Bank *ECHL* BD2 ...... **25** G1
Ashbourne Cl *ECHL* BD2 .... **19** G5
Ashbourne Crs *CUL/QBY* BD13 ... **35** E1
ECHL BD2 .... **25** G1
Ashbourne Dr *ECHL* BD2 .... **25** G1
Ashbourne Gdns *ECHL* BD2 ...... **25** G1
Ashbourne Garth *ECHL* BD2 ..... **25** G1
Ashbourne Gv *ECHL* BD2 .... **25** G1
HFAX HX1 .... **4** A4
Ashbourne Hvn *ECHL* BD2 .... **25** G1
Ashbourne Mt *ECHL* BD2 .... **25** G1
Ashbourne Ov *ECHL* BD2 .... **25** G1
Ashbourne Ri *ECHL* BD2 .... **25** G1
Ashbourne Rd *ECHL* BD2 .... **25** G1
HWTH BD22 .... **9** F2
Ashbourne Wy *ECHL* BD2 .... **25** G1
Ashburn Gv *BAIL* BD17 .... **12** D2
Ashburnham Gv *HTON* BD9 .... **24** C1
Ashby St *BOW* BD4 .... **31** H3
Ash Cl *HIPP* HX3 .... **43** G5
Ash Ct *CLECK* BD19 .... **45** G5
Ash Cft *BFDE* BD3 .... **3** C3
Ashfield *BOW* BD4 .... **39** G1
Ashfield Av *SHPY* BD18 .... **18** C4
Ashfield Cl *HIPP* HX3 .... **43** G5

Ashfield Crs *BGLY* BD16 .... **10** D4
Ashfield Dr *BAIL* BD17 .... **13** E2
HIPP HX3 .... **41** E3
SHPY BD18 .... **18** C4
Ashfield Gv *SHPY* BD18 .... **18** B4
Ashfield Pl *ECHL* BD2 .... **26** C2
Ashfield Rd *CUL/QBY* BD13 ..... **28** A1
IDLE BD10 .... **14** A5
IDLE BD10 .... **14** B5
SHPY BD18 .... **17** H2
Ash Ford Gn *WBSY* BD6 .... **37** E1
Ash Ghyll Gdns *BGLY* BD16 ..... **10** C2
Ash Gv *BGLY* BD16 .... **10** D5
BRIC HD6 .... **50** D5
GTHN BD7 .... **2** A7
Ashgrove *ECHL* BD2 .... **26** B1
GTHN BD7 .... **2** A7
Ashgrove *IDLE* BD10 .... **20** D2
Ashgrove Av *HIPP* HX3 .... **48** B4
Ashgrove Rd *AIRE* BD20 .... **7** H2
Ashington Cl *ECHL* BD2 .... **26** C1
Ashlar Gv *CUL/QBY* BD13 .... **35** E3
Ashlea Av *BRIC* HD6 .... **52** C3
Ashlea Cl *BRIC* HD6 .... **52** C3
Ashlea Dr *BRIC* HD6 .... **52** C3
Ashleigh St *KGHY* BD21 .... **6** D3
Ashley La *BAIL* BD17 .... **18** B1
Ashley Rd *BGLY* BD16 .... **10** D4
LM/WK BD12 .... **44** D3
Ashley St *HFAX* HX1 .... **4** B4
SHPY BD18 .... **18** C1
Ashmews *IDLE* BD10 .... **20** D2
Ashmore *BOW* BD4 .... **39** E2
Ashmount *CLAY* BD14 .... **29** G5
Ash Mt *GTHN* BD7 .... **30** C2
KGHY BD21 .... **9** F1
Ash Ter *BGLY* BD16 .... **10** C4
Ashton Av *GTHN* BD7 .... **29** H2
Ashton St *BFD* BD1 .... **2** A4
Ashton Wk *IDLE* BD10 .... **19** H2
Ashtree Gv *GTHN* BD7 .... **30** A5
Ashville Cft *LUD/ILL* HX2 ..... **40** C4
Ashville Gdns *LUD/ILL* HX2 .... **40** C4
Ashville Gv *LUD/ILL* HX2 ...... **40** C4
Ashville St *HIPP* HX3 .... **41** F4
Ashwell Rd *GIR* BD8 .... **24** C3
HTON BD9 .... **18** B5
Ashwell St *GIR* BD8 .... **24** C3
Ashwood Dr *AIRE* BD20 .... **7** H2
Ashwood St *BOW* BD4 .... **39** G1
Ashworth Pl *WBSY* BD6 .... **38** A1
Aspect Gdns *PDSY/CALV* LS28 ... **27** H4
Aspen Ri *WIL/AL* BD15 .... **16** C5
Aspinall St *HFAX* HX1 .... **4** B6
Asprey Dr *WIL/AL* BD15 .... **23** E4
Aston Rd *WBOW* BD5 .... **31** F4
Astral Av *HIPP* HX3 .... **43** G5
Astral Cl *HIPP* HX3 .... **43** G5
Astral Vw *WBSY* BD6 .... **30** B5
Atalanta Ter *LUD/ILL* HX2 ..... **46** D4
Atherstone Rd *WIL/AL* BD15 .... **23** E5
Atherton La *BRIC* HD6 .... **52** C3
Athol Crs *HIPP* HX3 .... **41** F2
Athol Gdns *HIPP* HX3 .... **41** F2
Athol Gn *HIPP* HX3 .... **41** F2
Athol Rd *HIPP* HX3 .... **41** F2
HTON BD9 .... **24** C2
Athol St *HIPP* HX3 .... **41** F2
KGHY BD21 .... **7** F2
Atkinson St *SHPY* BD18 .... **18** C1
Atlas Mill Rd *BRIC* HD6 .... **52** B1
Atlas St *GIR* BD8 .... **24** C3
Auckland Rd *WBSY* BD6 .... **37** F1
Austin Av *BRIC* HD6 .... **50** A4
Austin St *KGHY* BD21 .... **7** E3
Autumn St *HFAX* HX1 .... **4** B7
Avenel Rd *WIL/AL* BD15 .... **23** E4
Avenel Ter *WIL/AL* BD15 .... **23** E4
Avenham Wy *BFDE* BD3 .... **3** G3
Avenue No 2 *BRIC* HD6 .... **52** B2
Avenue Rd *WBOW* BD5 .... **31** G4
Avenue St *BOW* BD4 .... **39** G1
The Avenue *BGLY* BD16 .... **17** E1
CLAY BD14 .... **29** E3
HIPP HX5 .... **43** G5
IDLE BD10 .... **14** D3
Averingcliffe Rd *IDLE* BD10 ... **20** C3
Avondale *KGHY* BD21 .... **6** B3
Avondale Crs *SHPY* BD18 .... **18** B2
Avondale Gv *SHPY* BD18 .... **18** B2
Avondale Mt *SHPY* BD18 .... **18** B2
Avondale Pl *HIPP* HX3 .... **47** G4
Avondale Rd *SHPY* BD18 .... **18** A2
Aydon Wy *WBSY* BD6 .... **36** D3
Aygill Av *HTON* BD9 .... **23** G1
Aylesbury St *HWTH* BD22 .... **9** F2
Aynsley Gv *WIL/AL* BD15 .... **23** E4
Ayresome Ov *WIL/AL* BD15 ...... **22** D5

Aysgarth Av *BRIG* HD6 .... **50** B2
Aysgarth Cl *LM/WK* BD12 .... **44** D3
Ayton Cl *BFDE* BD3 .... **3** H3
Azealea Ct *BFDE* BD3 .... **3** J3

B

Back Ada St *KGHY* BD21 .... **6** B4
Back Aireview Ter *KGHY* BD21 .. **7** F5
Back Aireville St *AIRE* BD20 .. **6** B1
Back Ashgrove (West) *GTHN* BD7 . **2** A7
Back Aylesbury St *HWTH* BD22 .. **9** F2
Back Baker St *SHPY* BD18 ...... **18** B1
Back Balfour St *BGLY* BD16 .... **10** C4
KGHY BD21 .... **6** C5
Back Beech St *BGLY* BD16 ...... **10** C4
Back Blackwood Gv *HFAX* HX1 ... **4** A1
Back Blenheim Mt *GIR* BD8 ..... **24** D2
Back Broomfield Rd
KGHY BD21 .... **6** C4
Back Broomfield St *KGHY* BD21 . **6** C4
Back Buxton St *KGHY* BD21 ..... **7** E4
Back Byrl St *KGHY* BD21 .... **7** E4
Back Caister St *KGHY* BD21 .... **9** G2
Back Caledonia Rd *KGHY* BD21 .. **7** E2
Back Cartmel Rd *KGHY* BD21 .... **6** B4
Back Castle Rd *KGHY* BD21 ..... **6** C5
Back Cavendish Rd *IDLE* BD10 .. **20** A2
Back Cavendish St *KGHY* BD21 .. **6** D4
Back Cavendish Ter *HFAX* HX1 .. **4** D3
Back Charles St *BRIC* HD6 ..... **50** B5
Back Clarence St *HFAX* HX1 .... **4** E4
Back Clarendon Pl *HFAX* HX1 ... **4** C4
Back Clock View St *KGHY* BD21 . **6** C1
Back Clough *HIPP* HX3 .... **42** D3
Back Colenso Rd *KGHY* BD21 .... **7** F2
Back Compton St *KGHY* BD21 .... **7** E3
Back Croft House La *AIRE* BD20 . **6** B1
Back Cromer Av *KGHY* BD21 ..... **9** G1
Back Cromer Gv *KGHY* BD21 ..... **9** G1
Back Cromwell Ter *HFAX* HX1 ... **4** E3
Back Dudley Hill Rd *ECHL* BD2 . **26** A2
Back Eaton St *HWTH* BD22 ...... **9** F2
Back Edensor Rd *KGHY* BD21 .... **6** B4
Back Elizabeth St *WBOW* BD5 ... **31** F2
Back Elmfield Ter *HFAX* HX1 ... **47** F3
Back Eric St *KGHY* BD21 .... **6** D3
Back Eversley Mt *LUD/ILL* HX2 . **46** D2
Back Ferguson St *HFAX* HX1 .... **5** G5
Back Fld *CUL/QBY* BD13 .... **28** A1
Back Field Ct *CUL/QBY* BD13 ... **28** A1
Back Florist St *KGHY* BD21 .... **7** F2
Back Fold *CLAY* BD14 .... **29** E2
Back Foster Rd *KGHY* BD21 ..... **9** G1
KGHY BD21 .... **9** G2
Back Gerrard St *HFAX* HX1 ..... **4** E4
Back Giles St North
WBOW BD5 .... **31** E2
Back Giles St South
WBOW BD5 .... **31** E2
Back Girlington Rd *GIR* BD8 ... **24** B4
Back Gladstone St *KGHY* BD21 .. **10** C4
Back Gooder La *BRIC* HD6 ...... **52** C3
Back Grant St *HWTH* BD22 ...... **6** B4
Back Great Russell St
GTHN BD7 .... **24** D5
Back Greaves Streen
WBOW BD5 .... **31** E4
Back Grosvenor Ter *HFAX* HX1 .. **4** D4
Back Grouse St *KGHY* BD21 ..... **7** E3
Back High St *CUL/QBY* BD13 .... **28** A1
Back Hird St *KGHY* BD21 .... **6** C5
Back Hyde Gv *KGHY* BD21 .... **7** E3
Back Irwell St *BOW* BD4 .... **31** H2
Back John St *CUL/QBY* BD13 .... **28** A1
Back Kensington St *GIR* BD8 ... **24** B4
Back Kirby St *KGHY* BD21 ...... **7** E3
Back Kirkgate *SHPY* BD18 ...... **18** B2
Back Laisteridge La *GTHN* BD7 . **30** D1
Back La *CUL/QBY* BD13 .... **22** B5
CUL/QBY BD13 .... **29** E5
HTON BD9 .... **18** B5
WIL/AL BD15 .... **16** B5
YEA LS19 .... **15** F1
Back Lime St *KGHY* BD21 .... **9** G3
Back Lindum St *GIR* BD8 .... **24** D2
Back Lombard St *YEA* LS19 ..... **15** F2
Back Lord St *HFAX* HX1 .... **5** F4
Back Lyon St *CUL/QBY* BD13 .... **35** G1
Back Malt St *HWTH* BD22 .... **9** F2
Back Mannville Rd *KGHY* BD21 .. **6** B5
Back Manor St *ECHL* BD2 .... **26** A1
Back Market St *WBSY* BD6 ...... **37** H3

Back Minnie St *KGHY* BD21 ..... **6** C5
Back Mitchell Ter *BGLY* BD16 .. **10** C4
Back Moorfield St *HFAX* HX1 ... **4** C7
Back Morning St *KGHY* BD21 .... **9** G2
Back Muff St *BOW* BD4 .... **32** A2
Back Myrtle Gv *HFAX* HX1 ...... **10** C4
Back North St *LM/WK* BD12 ..... **45** H1
Back Oak Av *BGLY* BD16 .... **10** C5
Back Otterburn St *KGHY* BD21 .. **6** D3
Back Paget St *KGHY* BD21 ...... **6** B4
Back Park Ter *HFAX* HX1 .... **4** C4
Back Pleasant St
RPDN/SBR HX6 .... **46** B3
Back Prospect Pl *KGHY* BD21 ... **6** C5
Back Rhodes St *HFAX* HX1 ...... **4** E4
Back Ribble St *KGHY* BD21 ..... **7** G3
Back Richardson St
LM/WK BD12 .... **45** H1
Back Ripley St *AIRE* BD20 ..... **7** G2
Back Ripon Ter *HIPP* HX3 ...... **41** G4
Back Rd *LM/WK* BD12 .... **44** D1
Back Rowsley St *KGHY* BD21 .... **7** E4
Back Rupert St *KGHY* BD21 ..... **6** D3
Back Russell St *WBOW* BD5 ..... **31** E2
Back Rydal St *KGHY* BD21 ...... **6** B5
Back Rylstone St *KGHY* BD21 ... **7** F3
Back St Paul's Rd *SHPY* BD18 .. **18** B2
Back Saltaire Rd North
SHPY BD18 .... **18** B1
Back Savile Pde *HFAX* HX1 ..... **47** G3
Back Simpson St *KGHY* BD21 .... **6** B4
Back Sladen St *KGHY* BD21 ..... **6** B4
Back Smith Rw *WBOW* BD5 .... **30** D4
Back Stone Hill Rd *ECHL* BD2 .. **20** A5
Back Swinton St *HFAX* HX1 ..... **4** A6
Back Sycamore Av *BGLY* BD16 ... **10** C4
Back Tamworth St *BOW* BD4 ..... **32** D1
Back Thornhill St
PDSY/CALV LS28 .... **21** G3
Back Trinity Ter *WBOW* BD5 .... **31** E2
Back Unity St North
BGLY BD16 .... **10** C4
Back Unity St South
BGLY BD16 .... **10** C4
Back Victoria St *HFAX* HX1 .... **5** G3
Back Victor Ter *HFAX* HX1 ..... **4** C1
Back Walnut St *KGHY* BD21 ..... **9** G3
Back West St *RPDN/SBR* HX6 .... **46** A5
Back Wharf St *RPDN/SBR* HX6 ... **46** B4
Back Winterburn St
KGHY BD21 .... **6** D3
Back Wood St *GIR* BD8 .... **24** D4
Back Wright Av *HWTH* BD22 ..... **8** C3
Baddeley Gdns *IDLE* BD10 ...... **13** H3
Badger La *HIPP* HX3 .... **49** E1
Badgers Wy *ECHL* BD2 .... **19** F5
Bagnall Ter *WBSY* BD6 .... **37** G1
Baildon Holmes *BAIL* BD17 .... **12** D5
Baildon Rd *BAIL* BD17 .... **12** D4
Baildon Wood Ct *BAIL* BD17 ... **12** D5
Bailey Hall Bank *HIPP* HX3 .... **5** K4
Bailey Hall Rd *HIPP* HX3 ...... **5** K2
Bailey Hills Rd *BGLY* BD16 .... **10** B3
Bailey St *BOW* BD4 .... **31** G2
Bailey Wells Av *WBOW* BD5 ..... **30** D4
Baines St *HFAX* HX1 .... **4** C2
Baird St *WBOW* BD5 .... **31** F5
Bairstow Ct *LUD/ILL* HX2 ...... **46** B2
Bairstow La *LUD/ILL* HX2 ...... **46** B2
Bairstow Mt *LUD/ILL* HX2 ...... **46** B3
Bairstow St *WIL/AL* BD15 ...... **22** D1
Baker St *ECHL* BD2 .... **26** A2
SHPY BD18 .... **18** B1
Baker St North *LUD/ILL* HX2 ... **34** B5
Bakes St *GTHN* BD7 .... **30** B3
Baldwin La *CLAY* BD14 .... **28** D4
Balfour St *BGLY* BD16 .... **10** C4
BOW BD4 .... **31** H3
KGHY BD21 .... **6** C5
Balk La *GTHN* BD7 .... **30** C3
Ballantyne Rd *IDLE* BD10 ...... **13** H4
Ball St *CUL/QBY* BD13 .... **28** B1
Balme La *LM/WK* BD12 .... **45** E2
Balme St *BFD* BD1 .... **2** E4
LM/WK BD12 .... **44** D2
Balmoral Pl *HFAX* HX1 .... **5** F5
Bank *IDLE* BD10 .... **20** C3
Bank Bottom *HFAX* HX1 .... **5** K4
Bank Cl *IDLE* BD10 .... **20** B4
Bank Crest *BAIL* BD17 .... **12** D3
Bank Crest Ri *SHPY* BD18 ...... **17** G2
Bank Dr *WBSY* BD6 .... **38** A1
Bank Edge Gdns *LUD/ILL* HX2 ... **40** D2
Bank Edge Rd *LUD/ILL* HX2 ..... **40** C2
Bankfield Av *SHPY* BD18 .... **17** G2
Bankfield Dr *SHPY* BD18 .... **17** G2
Bankfield Gdns *HIPP* HX3 ...... **48** C2
Bankfield Rd *SHPY* BD18 .... **17** G2

Bankfield Ter *BAIL* BD17 .... 13 E4 ▫
Bankfield Vw *BAIL* BD17 .... 41 G4
Bankholme Ct *BOW* BD4 .... 33 E5 ▫
Bank Rd *RPDN/SBR* HX6 .... 46 A5
Banks La *AIRE* BD20 .... 7 G1
Bank St *BFD* BD1 .... 2 D5
BRIG HD6 .... 52 B1
SHPY BD18 .... 18 C2 ▫
WBSY BD6 .... 37 H1 ▫
Bank Top *HIPP* HX3 .... 48 B2
Bank Top Dr *AIRE* BD20 .... 7 G1
Bank Top Wy *KGHY* BD21 .... 7 G5
Bankwell Fold *WBSY* BD6 .... 38 A1 ▫
Bankwell Vw *BAIL* BD17 .... 12 C4
Banner St *BFDE* BD3 .... 3 H6
Bannockburn Ct *BOW* BD4 .... 39 E1 ▫
Bantree Ct *IDLE* BD10 .... 13 H5
Baptist Fold *CUL/QBY* BD13 .... 35 F1 ▫
Baptist Fold *BFD* BD1 .... 2 B4
Barberry Av *BFDE* BD3 .... 26 D4 ▫
Barber St *BRIG* HD6 .... 50 C4 ▫
Barden Av *WBSY* BD6 .... 36 C1 ▫
Barden Dr *BGLY* BD16 .... 11 F2
Barden St *GIR* BD8 .... 24 C3 ▫
Bardsey Crs *BFDE* BD3 .... 26 D4 ▫
Bare Head La *HIPP* HX3 .... 35 E4
Barfield Rd *HIPP* HX3 .... 49 F1
Bargrange Av *SHPY* BD18 .... 18 C3
Barham Ter *IDLE* BD10 .... 20 C5
Baring Av *BFDE* BD3 .... 26 C4
Barker Cl *HIPP* HX3 .... 48 B5
Barkerend Rd *BFDE* BD3 .... 3 F4
Bar La *AIRE* BD20 .... 7 G2
Barley Cote Av *AIRE* BD20 .... 7 H1 ▫
Barley Cote Gv *AIRE* BD20 .... 7 H1 ▫
Barley Cote Rd *AIRE* BD20 .... 7 H1 ▫
Barley St *HWTH* BD22 .... 9 F2
Barlow Rd *KGHY* BD21 .... 7 F3
Barlow St *BFDE* BD3 .... 3 J4
Barmby Pl *ECHL* BD2 .... 26 A3
Barmby Rd *ECHL* BD2 .... 26 A3
Barmby St *LM/WK* BD12 .... 45 E1
Barmouth Ter *BFDE* BD3 .... 25 G3
Barnaby Rd *BGLY* BD16 .... 11 F2
Barnard Rd *BOW* BD4 .... 31 H2
Barnby Av *GIR* BD8 .... 23 F5
Barnes Rd *GIR* BD8 .... 24 A5 ▫
Barnsley Beck Gv *BAIL* BD17 .... 13 E3
The Barn *LM/WK* BD12 .... 38 B4 ▫
Barraclough Sq *LM/WK* BD12 .... 44 D1 ▫
Barraclough St *LM/WK* BD12 .... 37 G5 ▫
Barran St *BGLY* BD16 .... 10 D3 ▫
Barrington Cl *HIPP* HX3 .... 48 D4 ▫
Barrowclough La *HIPP* HX3 .... 48 C1
Barry St *BFD* BD1 .... 2 C5
Barthorpe Ct *BOW* BD4 .... 33 E5 ▫
Bartle Cl *GTHN* BD7 .... 30 A4
Bartle Fold *GTHN* BD7 .... 30 B3 ▫
Bartle Gill Dr *BAIL* BD17 .... 13 F2
Bartle Gill Ri *BAIL* BD17 .... 13 F2 ▫
Bartle Gill Vw *BAIL* BD17 .... 13 F2 ▫
Bartle Gv *GTHN* BD7 .... 30 A4 ▫
Bartle Pl *GTHN* BD7 .... 30 A4
Bartle Sq *GTHN* BD7 .... 30 B3 ▫
Barton St *BRIG* HD6 .... 50 B5 ▫
WBOW BD5 .... 30 C4 ▫
Barwick Gn *WBSY* BD6 .... 36 D1
Basil St *WBOW* BD5 .... 30 C4 ▫
Baslow Gv *HTON* BD9 .... 24 A2
Bateman St *GIR* BD8 .... 25 E3
Bateson St *IDLE* BD10 .... 20 D2
Bath Pl *HIPP* HX3 .... 41 G4
Bath Rd *HIPP* HX3 .... 47 H4
Bath St *BFDE* BD3 .... 3 G5
HFAX HX1 .... 5 J5 ▫
KGHY BD21 .... 6 C4 ▫
Batley Ct *BAIL* BD17 .... 13 E2 ▫
Batley St *HIPP* HX3 .... 41 F4 ▫
Batter La *YEA* LS19 .... 15 H2
Battinson Rd *HFAX* HX1 .... 4 A2
Battinson St *HIPP* HX3 .... 48 B3
Battye St *BOW* BD4 .... 32 B1
Bavaria Pl *GIR* BD8 .... 24 C3
Baxandall St *WBOW* BD5 .... 31 E4 ▫
Baxter La *HIPP* HX3 .... 42 D2
Bayne Dr *BOW* BD4 .... 39 E2
Bay of Biscay *WIL/AL* BD15 .... 17 E5
Bayswater Gv *ECHL* BD2 .... 26 C2
Bayswater Ter *HIPP* HX3 .... 47 H5
Beacon Brow *WBSY* BD6 .... 29 G5 ▫
Beacon Cl *BGLY* BD16 .... 11 E3
Beacon Gv *WBSY* BD6 .... 37 E1
Beacon Hill Rd *HIPP* HX3 .... 5 J2
HIPP HX3 .... 48 B1
Beacon Pl *WBSY* BD6 .... 36 D1

Beacon Rd *WBSY* BD6 .... 29 H5
Beaconsfield Rd *CLAY* BD14 .... 29 F3
Beaconsfield St *HIPP* HX3 .... 48 B2
Beacon St *BD7* BD7 .... 29 H5 ▫
WBSY BD6 .... 37 F1
Beamsley Gv *BGLY* BD16 .... 11 E3 ▫
Beamsley Rd *HTON* BD9 .... 18 C4
HTON BD9 .... 24 C2
Beatrice St *KGHY* BD21 .... 6 D2 ▫
Beaufort Gv *ECHL* BD2 .... 25 H1
Beaumont St *GIR* BD8 .... 24 C3
Beck Bottom *PDSY/CALV* LS28 .... 20 D3 ▫
Beckenham Pl *HFAX* HX1 .... 40 D5 ▫
Beckfield Rd *BGLY* BD16 .... 10 C2
Beckfoot La *BGLY* BD16 .... 10 C5
Beck Hl *WBSY* BD6 .... 36 D3
Beck La *BGLY* BD16 .... 10 C2
Beck Side *KGHY* BD21 .... 6 D5
Beckside La *GTHN* BD7 .... 30 A2
Beckside Rd *GTHN* BD7 .... 30 B2
Becks Rd *HWTH* BD22 .... 6 B5
Beck St *KGHY* BD21 .... 6 C5 ▫
Beckwith Dr *IDLE* BD10 .... 20 C4
Bedale Dr *WBSY* BD6 .... 36 D1
Bede's Cl *CUL/QBY* BD13 .... 28 A1
Bedford St *BOW* BD4 .... 2 E7
HFAX HX1 .... 5 F4
KGHY BD21 .... 6 C4
Bedford St North *HFAX* HX1 .... 5 F5
Bedivere Rd *GIR* BD8 .... 23 C5
Beech Av *RPDN/SBR* HX6 .... 46 A3
Beech Cl *HIPP* HX3 .... 5 J5
IDLE BD10 .... 14 A4 ▫
Beech Crs *BAIL* BD17 .... 12 A5
BFDE BD3 .... 3 K1
Beecher St *HIPP* HX3 .... 41 G3 ▫
KGHY BD21 .... 7 F2
Beeches Rd *KGHY* BD21 .... 7 F3 ▫
The Beeches *BAIL* BD17 .... 13 E2
PDSY/CALV LS28 .... 27 G4
Beech Gv *BFDE* BD3 .... 3 J1
BGLY BD16 .... 11 F1
CLAY BD14 .... 29 F3
HIPP HX3 .... 50 B1
Beech Lees *PDSY/CALV* LS28 .... 21 H5
Beechmount Cl *BAIL* BD17 .... 13 E2 ▫
Beech Rd *RPDN/SBR* HX6 .... 46 A4
WBSY BD6 .... 37 H3
Beech Sq *CLAY* BD14 .... 29 F3 ▫
Beech St *BGLY* BD16 .... 10 C4
HFAX HX1 .... 5 H3
KGHY BD21 .... 7 F3
Beech Ter *BFDE* BD3 .... 3 J2
Beech Vw *RPDN/SBR* HX6 .... 46 A3 ▫
Beechwood Av *AIRE* BD20 .... 7 G2
HIPP HX3 .... 36 A5
LUD/ILL HX2 .... 34 B5
SHPY BD18 .... 17 H2 ▫
WBSY BD6 .... 30 B5
Beechwood Cl *LUD/ILL* HX2 .... 41 E1
Beechwood Dr *LUD/ILL* HX2 .... 41 E1
WBSY BD6 .... 30 C5 ▫
Beechwood Gv *LUD/ILL* HX2 .... 41 E1 ▫
SHPY BD18 .... 17 H2 ▫
WBSY BD6 .... 30 C5 ▫
Beechwood Rd *LUD/ILL* HX2 .... 41 E1
WBSY BD6 .... 30 B5
Beechwood St
PDSY/CALV LS28 .... 27 H3 ▫
Beecroft St *KGHY* BD21 .... 7 E4 ▫
Beehive St *WBSY* BD6 .... 37 E3 ▫
Beehive Yd *WBSY* BD6 .... 37 E3 ▫
Bela Av *BOW* BD4 .... 32 B4
Belcross Dr *HIPP* HX3 .... 5 J1
Beldon La *WBSY* BD6 .... 37 E1
Beldon Park Av *GTHN* BD7 .... 30 A5 ▫
Beldon Park Cl *GTHN* BD7 .... 30 A5 ▫
Beldon Pl *ECHL* BD2 .... 26 A2 ▫
Beldon Rd *GTHN* BD7 .... 30 B4
Belfast St *HFAX* HX1 .... 4 B6
Belgrave Av *HIPP* HX3 .... 5 K1
Belgrave Cl *HIPP* HX3 .... 5 K1
Belgrave Crs *HIPP* HX3 .... 42 B5 ▫
Belgrave Dr *HIPP* HX3 .... 42 B5
Belgrave Gdns *HIPP* HX3 .... 5 K1
Belgrave Gv *HIPP* HX3 .... 5 K1
Belgrave Ms *YEA* LS19 .... 15 F2 ▫
Belgrave Mt *HIPP* HX3 .... 42 A4
Belgrave Pk *HIPP* HX3 .... 5 K1
Belgrave Rd *BGLY* BD16 .... 10 D3
KGHY BD21 .... 6 C3
Belgrave Sq *RPDN/SBR* HX6 .... 46 A4 ▫
Bell Bank Vw *BGLY* BD16 .... 10 B2
Bell Dean Rd *WIL/AL* BD15 .... 23 E4
Bellerby Brow *WBSY* BD6 .... 36 C1
Belle View Ri *HIPP* HX3 .... 36 A5 ▫
Belle Vue *CUL/QBY* BD13 .... 35 F4

GIR BD8 .... 2 A1
Belle Vue Crs *HIPP* HX3 .... 36 A5
Belle Vue Dr *PDSY/CALV* LS28 .... 27 H1
Belle Vue Rd *HIPP* HX3 .... 36 A5
Bell Hall Mt *HFAX* HX1 .... 47 F3 ▫
Bell Hall Ter *HFAX* HX1 .... 47 F3 ▫
Bell House Av *BOW* BD4 .... 39 E1 ▫
Bellhouse Crs *BOW* BD4 .... 39 E2
Belloe St *WBOW* BD5 .... 31 E3 ▫
Bellshaw St *GIR* BD8 .... 23 H5 ▫
Bell St *HIPP* HX3 .... 5 J1
LM/WK BD12 .... 44 D1 ▫
Belmont Av *BAIL* BD17 .... 12 C3
LM/WK BD12 .... 38 B3
Belmont Cl *BAIL* BD17 .... 12 C3
Belmont Crs *LM/WK* BD12 .... 38 B3
SHPY BD18 .... 18 B1 ▫
Belmont Gdns *WBSY* BD6 .... 38 A3
WBSY BD6 .... 38 A3
YEA LS19 .... 15 H1
Belmont Ri *BAIL* BD17 .... 12 C3
LM/WK BD12 .... 38 B3
Belmont St *ECHL* BD2 .... 20 B4
HIPP HX3 .... 42 B5
RPDN/SBR HX6 .... 46 B4 ▫
Belmont Ter *SHPY* BD18 .... 18 B1 ▫
Belton Cl *GTHN* BD7 .... 30 B4
Belvedere Ter *GIR* BD8 .... 24 C4
Belvoir Gdns *HIPP* HX3 .... 47 H5
Bempton Cl *GTHN* BD7 .... 30 C3 ▫
Bempton Pl *GTHN* BD7 .... 30 C3 ▫
Benbow Av *IDLE* BD10 .... 20 D4
Benn Av *GTHN* BD7 .... 30 A3 ▫
Benn Crs *GTHN* BD7 .... 30 A3
Bennett St *HIPP* HX3 .... 41 F3 ▫
Bentfield Cottages *CLAY* BD14 .... 29 F2 ▫
Bent Lea *HUDN* HD2 .... 53 G5 ▫
Bentley Av *BRIG* HD6 .... 50 B1
Bentley Cl *BAIL* BD17 .... 12 C2
Bentley Mt *RPDN/SBR* HX6 .... 46 C3
Bentley St *LM/WK* BD12 .... 45 E2 ▫
Benton Park Av *YEA* LS19 .... 15 H1
Benton Park Crs *YEA* LS19 .... 15 H1
Benton Park Dr *YEA* LS19 .... 15 H1
Benton Park Rd *YEA* LS19 .... 15 H1
Beresford Rd *WBSY* BD6 .... 37 G3 ▫
Beresford St *LM/WK* BD12 .... 38 D5
Berrington Wy *HWTH* BD22 .... 8 A3
Berry La *HFAX* HX1 .... 5 K4
KGHY BD21 .... 9 G1
Berry St *KGHY* BD21 .... 7 E4 ▫
Bertie St *BOW* BD4 .... 32 B4
Bertram Dr *BAIL* BD17 .... 12 C4
Bertram Rd *GIR* BD8 .... 24 D2
Berwick St *HFAX* HX1 .... 5 J4
Bescaby Gv *BAIL* BD17 .... 13 F5 ▫
Besha Av *LM/WK* BD12 .... 38 A3
Besha Gv *LM/WK* BD12 .... 38 A4 ▫
Bessingham Gdns *WBSY* BD6 .... 37 G3 ▫
Beswick Cl *BFDE* BD3 .... 26 C5 ▫
Bethel St *SHPY* BD18 .... 19 E1 ▫
Bethel St *BRIG* HD6 .... 52 C1
HIPP HX3 .... 41 F3 ▫
Bevan Ct *GTHN* BD7 .... 30 A4
Beverley Av *LM/WK* BD12 .... 45 E3
Beverley Dr *LM/WK* BD12 .... 45 E3
Beverley Pl *HIPP* HX3 .... 41 H5 ▫
Beverley Rd *BOW* BD4 .... 32 C2
Beverley Ter *HIPP* HX3 .... 41 G4
Bewerley Crs *LM/WK* BD12 .... 37 F4
Bierley Gv *BOW* BD4 .... 39 E3
Bierley House Av *BOW* BD4 .... 39 E1
Bierley La *BOW* BD4 .... 39 E1
Bierley Vw *BOW* BD4 .... 39 F1
Billing Vw *IDLE* BD10 .... 20 B2
Bilsdale Gra *WBSY* BD6 .... 37 E2
Bilsdale Wy *BAIL* BD17 .... 12 A4
Bilton Pl *GIR* BD8 .... 24 D4
Bingley Rd *HTON* BD9 .... 17 G5
KGHY BD21 .... 9 G5
SHPY BD18 .... 17 G1
Bingley St *GIR* BD8 .... 24 B5
Binks Fold *LM/WK* BD12 .... 45 E3
Binnie St *BFDE* BD3 .... 3 J4
Binns Hill La *LUD/ILL* HX2 .... 46 A2
Binns La *GTHN* BD7 .... 30 A2 ▫
Binns St *BGLY* BD16 .... 10 D3
Binns Top La *HIPP* HX3 .... 49 E5
Birch Av *WBOW* BD5 .... 31 G5 ▫
Birch Cliff *BAIL* BD17 .... 12 C4
Birch Cl *IDLE* BD10 .... 20 D5
WBOW BD5 .... 31 G5 ▫
Birch Gv *HWTH* BD22 .... 9 G2 ▫
WBOW BD5 .... 38 B1
Birch La *WBOW* BD5 .... 31 F4
WBOW BD5 .... 31 G4 ▫

Birch St *GIR* BD8 .... 24 B4
Birch Tree Gdns *KGHY* BD21 .... 7 F5 ▫
Birch Wy *WBOW* BD5 .... 31 G5 ▫
Birchwood Av *AIRE* BD20 .... 6 C1 ▫
Birchwood Dr *AIRE* BD20 .... 6 B1 ▫
Birchwood Rd *AIRE* BD20 .... 6 B1
Birdcage Hl *HIPP* HX3 .... 47 F5
Birdcage La *HIPP* HX3 .... 47 F5
Bird Holme La *HIPP* HX3 .... 43 E4
Birds Royd La *BRIG* HD6 .... 52 C2
Birdswell Av *BRIG* HD6 .... 51 E5
Birkby Hvn *WBSY* BD6 .... 36 D2
Birkby La *BRIG* HD6 .... 50 D1
Birkby St *LM/WK* BD12 .... 45 E1
Birkdale Gv *LUD/ILL* HX2 .... 34 A3
Birkhouse La *BRIG* HD6 .... 51 E2
Birkhouse Rd *BRIG* HD6 .... 50 D1
Birklands Rd *SHPY* BD18 .... 18 B2
Birklands Ter *SHPY* BD18 .... 18 C2 ▫
Birks Av *GTHN* BD7 .... 30 A2
Birks Fold *GTHN* BD7 .... 30 A1
Birkshall La *BFDE* BD3 .... 3 K7
Birks Hall St *HFAX* HX1 .... 4 D2
Birks Hall Ter *HFAX* HX1 .... 4 D2
Birksland St *BOW* BD4 .... 32 A2
Birnam Gv *BOW* BD4 .... 31 H3
Birr Rd *HTON* BD9 .... 24 C1
Bishopdale Holme *WBSY* BD6 .... 36 D2
Bishop St *HTON* BD9 .... 24 C1
Blackbird Gdns *GIR* BD8 .... 23 E5 ▫
Blackburn Cl *GIR* BD8 .... 23 G5 ▫
HIPP HX3 .... 41 E2 ▫
Blackburn Rd *BRIG* HD6 .... 50 A4
Blackett St *PDSY/CALV* LS28 .... 21 C2
Blackledge *HFAX* HX1 .... 5 J5
Blackmires *LUD/ILL* HX2 .... 34 B5
Blackshaw Beck La *HIPP* HX3 .... 35 H3
Blackshaw Dr *WBSY* BD6 .... 36 C2
Blacksmith *GTHN* BD7 .... 30 B3 ▫
Blacksmith Fold *GTHN* BD7 .... 30 B3
Blackstone Av *LM/WK* BD12 .... 44 D3
Blackwall *HFAX* HX1 .... 5 F5
Blackwall Ri *RPDN/SBR* HX6 .... 46 A3 ▫
Blackwood Gv *HFAX* HX1 .... 4 A2
Blaithroyd La *HIPP* HX3 .... 48 B2
Blake Hl *HIPP* HX3 .... 42 B2
Blakehill Av *ECHL* BD2 .... 26 B2
Blake Hill End *HIPP* HX3 .... 42 C1
Blakehill Ter *ECHL* BD2 .... 26 B2
Blakelaw Dr *BRIG* HD6 .... 51 E5
Blake Law La *BRIG* HD6 .... 53 C1
Blamires Pl *GTHN* BD7 .... 30 A4 ▫
Blamires St *GTHN* BD7 .... 30 A4
Blanche St *BOW* BD4 .... 32 C1 ▫
Bland St *HFAX* HX1 .... 5 F4 ▫
Blenheim Mt *GIR* BD8 .... 24 D2 ▫
Blenheim Pl *IDLE* BD10 .... 14 A5 ▫
Blenheim Rd *GIR* BD8 .... 24 D3
Blind La *BGLY* BD16 .... 10 A3
Blucher St *BOW* BD4 .... 32 C1 ▫
Bluebell Cl *WIL/AL* BD15 .... 23 E4 ▫
Blythe Av *GIR* BD8 .... 24 B4
Bob La *LUD/ILL* HX2 .... 46 C1
Bodmin Av *SHPY* BD18 .... 19 F2
Boggart La *HIPP* HX3 .... 43 G4
RPDN/SBR HX6 .... 46 A5
Boland Crs *HWTH* BD22 .... 8 D3
Boldron Holt *WBSY* BD6 .... 37 E2
Boldshay St *BFDE* BD3 .... 3 J3
Bolehill Pk *BRIG* HD6 .... 49 H2 ▫
Bolingbroke St *WBOW* BD5 .... 31 E5
Bolland St *LM/WK* BD12 .... 38 B5
Bolling Rd *BOW* BD4 .... 3 F7
Boltby La *WBSY* BD6 .... 36 D2
Bolton Brow *RPDN/SBR* HX6 .... 46 B4
Bolton Dr *ECHL* BD2 .... 20 A5
Bolton Gv *ECHL* BD2 .... 20 A5 ▫
Bolton Hall Rd *ECHL* BD2 .... 19 G4
SHPY BD18 .... 19 E4
Bolton La *ECHL* BD2 .... 25 G1
Bolton Rd *BFD* BD1 .... 2 E4
BFDE BD3 .... 25 G2
ECHL BD2 .... 25 H1 ▫
Bolton St *BFDE* BD3 .... 3 G4
LM/WK BD12 .... 37 H4 ▫
Bond St *BRIG* HD6 .... 50 B5 ▫
HFAX HX1 .... 5 F5 ▫
Bonegate Av *BRIG* HD6 .... 50 C5
Bonegate Rd *BRIG* HD6 .... 50 B5
Bonn Rd *HTON* BD9 .... 24 B2
Bonwick Ml *WBSY* BD6 .... 36 D3
Bootham Pk *HTON* BD9 .... 23 G2
Boothman Wk *KGHY* BD21 .... 9 F1 ▫
Booth Royd *IDLE* BD10 .... 14 A5
Booth Royd Dr *IDLE* BD10 .... 14 A5 ▫
Booth St *IDLE* BD10 .... 20 A2 ▫
SHPY BD18 .... 19 E2 ▫

Boothtown Rd *HIPP* HX3 41 G2
Borrins Wy *BAIL* BD17 13 E3
Boston St *HFAX* HX1 4 B4
Boston Wk *WBSY* BD6 37 E2 1
Bosworth Cl *WIL/AL* BD15 23 E3
Botany Av *ECHL* BD2 19 G5
Bottomley St *BRIG* HD6 50 C4 2
WBOW BD5 31 E3 2
WBSY BD6 37 E3
Bottoms *HIPP* HX3 48 A5
The Boundary *GIR* BD8 23 H3
Bourbon Cl *WBSY* BD6 37 G2
Bourne St *IDLE* BD10 14 A5 5
Bowater Ct *BOW* BD4 33 E5 4
Bow Beck *BOW* BD4 31 H2
Bowbridge Rd *WBOW* BD5 31 F4 1
Bower Gn *BFDE* BD3 26 B5 1
Bower St *WBOW* BD5 31 F2 4
Bowes Nook *WBSY* BD6 36 D3
Bow Gn *CLAY* BD14 29 G3 2
Bowland St *GIR* BD8 2 A2
Bowler Cl *LM/WK* BD12 37 H4
Bowling Aly *BRIG* HD6 52 B3
Bowling Back La *BOW* BD4 31 H2
Bowling Ct *BRIG* HD6 50 A5
Bowling Dyke *HFAX* HX1 5 H2
Bowling Hall Rd *BOW* BD4 31 H4
Bowling Old La *WBOW* BD5 31 E5
WBOW BD5 31 F3
WBOW BD5 31 F4 2
Bowling Park Cl *BOW* BD4 31 G3
Bowling Park Dr *WBOW* BD5 31 G4
Bowman Av *WBSY* BD6 37 G3
Bowman Gv *HFAX* HX1 4 C3
Bowman Pl *HFAX* HX1 4 C3 1
Bowman Rd *WBSY* BD6 37 G3
Bowman St *HFAX* HX1 4 C3 2
Bowman Ter *HFAX* HX1 4 D3
Bowness Av *IDLE* BD10 20 C5
Bow St *KGHY* BD21 6 D4
Box Tree Cl *GIR* BD8 23 H3 1
Box Trees La *LUD/ILL* HX2 40 C2
Boyd Av *BFDE* BD3 26 D3
Boy La *BOW* BD4 39 E3
HIPP HX3 40 C3
Boyne St *HFAX* HX1 5 F4
Boynton St *WBOW* BD5 31 E4
Boynton Ter *WBOW* BD5 31 F4 3
Boys La *HIPP* HX3 48 A3
Bracewell Av *WIL/AL* BD15 22 D4
Bracewell Bank *HIPP* HX3 41 F3 3
Bracewell Dr *HIPP* HX3 41 E3
Bracewell Gv *HIPP* HX3 41 F4 3
Bracewell St *KGHY* BD21 7 F4 1
Bracken Av *BRIG* HD6 50 B3
Bracken Bank Av *HWTH* BD22 9 E3
Bracken Bank Crs *HWTH* BD22 9 E3
Bracken Bank Gv *HWTH* BD22 9 E3
Bracken Bank Wk *HWTH* BD22 9 E4 1
Bracken Bank Wy *HWTH* BD22 9 E3
Brackenbeck Rd *GTHN* BD7 30 A3 2
Brackenbed La *HFAX* HX1 41 E4
Bracken Cl *BRIG* HD6 50 B3
Brackendale *IDLE* BD10 13 H4 1
Brackendale Av *IDLE* BD10 13 H4 2
Brackendale Dr *IDLE* BD10 13 G4
Brackendale Gv *IDLE* BD10 13 G4
Brackendale Pde *IDLE* BD10 13 G4
Bracken Edge *IDLE* BD10 20 B2
Brackenhill Dr *GTHN* BD7 30 A4 4
Brackenholme Royd *WBSY* BD6 36 D2
Bracken Pk *BGLY* BD16 11 F3
Bracken Rd *BRIG* HD6 50 B3
HWTH BD22 9 F2
Brackens La *HIPP* HX3 36 A3
Bracken St *KGHY* BD21 9 G2
Bradbeck Rd *GTHN* BD7 24 A5
Bradford La *BFDE* BD3 26 C5
Bradford Old Rd *BGLY* BD16 17 E2
HIPP HX3 41 H2
Bradford Rd *BFDE* BD3 27 E3
BGLY BD16 10 D5
BRIG HD6 50 C3
BRIG HD6 52 C1
CLAY BD14 29 G2
HIPP HX3 42 C4
IDLE BD10 19 H4
KGHY BD21 7 E3
PDSY/CALV LS28 27 E3
SHPY BD18 18 B1
Bradford St *KGHY* BD21 6 D3
Bradlaugh Rd *WBSY* BD6 37 G1
Bradlaugh Ter *WBSY* BD6 37 H1 4
Bradley Grange Gdns
HUDN HD2 53 G5
Bradley La *PDSY/CALV* LS28 27 G5
Bradley Quarry Cl *HUDN* HD2 53 H5 1
Bradley St *BGLY* BD16 10 C3 3
HTON BD9 18 D5 1
Bradshaw La *LUD/ILL* HX2 34 A1
Bradshaw Vw *CUL/QBY* BD13 34 D1 1
Brae Av *ECHL* BD2 25 G1
Brafferton Arbor *WBSY* BD6 36 D2
Braithwaite Av *HWTH* BD22 6 A4
Braithwaite Crs *HWTH* BD22 6 A4
Braithwaite Dr *HWTH* BD22 6 A4
Braithwaite Gv *HWTH* BD22 6 A4
Braithwaite Wk *HWTH* BD22 6 A4
Braithwaite Wy *HWTH* BD22 6 A4 1
Bramble Cl *CLAY* BD14 29 E4
Bramham Dr *BAIL* BD17 13 E2
Bramham Rd *BGLY* BD16 10 D2 1
Bramley Cl *HWTH* BD22 8 A3
Bramley Fold *HIPP* HX3 43 G5 1
Bramley La *HIPP* HX3 43 G5
Bramley St *WBOW* BD5 31 F2 5
Bramley Vw *HIPP* HX3 43 H5
Bramston Gdns *BRIG* HD6 52 B3
Bramston St *BRIG* HD6 52 B2
Branch Rd *CLECK* BD19 45 G4
Brandfort St *GTHN* BD7 30 B2 1
Branksome Ct *HTON* BD9 24 A2 1
Branksome Crs *HTON* BD9 24 A2
Branksome Dr *SHPY* BD18 17 G1
Branksome Gv *BGLY* BD16 17 F1
Bransdale Cl *BAIL* BD17 12 B4 2
Bransdale Clough *WBSY* BD6 36 D1
Branshaw Dr *HWTH* BD22 8 D1 1
Branshaw Gv *HWTH* BD22 8 D1
Branshaw Mt *HWTH* BD22 8 D1 2
Bran St *HWTH* BD22 9 F2
Brant Av *LUD/ILL* HX2 41 E1
Brantcliffe Dr *BAIL* BD17 12 C2
Brantdale Cl *HTON* BD9 17 F5 1
Brantdale Rd *HTON* BD9 17 F5
Brantwood Av *HTON* BD9 17 F5
Brantwood Cl *HTON* BD9 17 F5
Brantwood Crs *HTON* BD9 17 E5
Brantwood Dr *HTON* BD9 17 F5
Brantwood Gv *HTON* BD9 17 E5 1
Brantwood Ov *HTON* BD9 17 F5
Brantwood Rd *HTON* BD9 17 E5
Brantwood Vls *HTON* BD9 17 F5
Brassey Rd *BOW* BD4 31 H3 2
Brassey St *HFAX* HX1 5 F6
Brassey Ter *BOW* BD4 31 H3 3
Braybrook Ct *GIR* BD8 24 D1
Bray Cl *WBSY* BD6 29 G5 2
Brayshaw Dr *GTHN* BD7 29 G5
Break Neck *HIPP* HX3 42 D5
Breaks Rd *LM/WK* BD12 38 A4
Brearcliffe Cl *WBSY* BD6 37 F2 1
Brearcliffe Dr *WBSY* BD6 37 F2
Brearcliffe Gv *WBSY* BD6 37 F3
Brearcliffe Rd *WBSY* BD6 37 G3 2
Brearcliffe St *WBSY* BD6 37 F3
Brearton St *BFD* BD1 2 C2
Brecks Rd *CLAY* BD14 29 G2
Brecon Cl *IDLE* BD10 20 A2 3
Bredon Av *SHPY* BD18 19 G2
Breighton Adown *WBSY* BD6 36 C2
Brendon Ct *BOW* BD4 32 C4 1
Brendon Wk *BOW* BD4 32 C5 1
Brentford Rd *LM/WK* BD12 37 H4 2
WBSY BD6 37 H3
Brentwood Gdns *WBSY* BD6 37 H2
Brewery La *CUL/QBY* BD13 28 A4
CUL/QBY BD13 34 D3
Brewery Rd *HWTH* BD22 9 F3
Brewery St *HIPP* HX3 41 H3 2
KGHY BD21 7 E4
Briardale Rd *HTON* BD9 17 E5
Briarfield Av *IDLE* BD10 19 H2
Briarfield Cl *IDLE* BD10 19 H2 1
Briarfield Gdns *SHPY* BD18 18 C3
Briarfield Gv *IDLE* BD10 19 H2 2
Briarfield Rd *SHPY* BD18 18 D3
Briar Rhydding *BAIL* BD17 13 F4
Briar Wd *SHPY* BD18 19 F2
Briarwood Av *KGHY* BD21 7 G2
Briarwood Crs *WBSY* BD6 37 G1
Briarwood Dr *WBSY* BD6 37 G1
Briarwood Gv *WBSY* BD6 30 C5
Brick & Tile Ter *BRIG* HD6 52 B2
Brickfield Gv *LUD/ILL* HX2 34 B5 1
Brickfield La *LUD/ILL* HX2 34 B5
Brickfield Ter *LUD/ILL* HX2 34 B5 2
Brick Rw *LM/WK* BD12 44 D2
Brick Ter *BRIG* HD6 52 C2 2
Bridge End *BRIG* HD6 52 B2
Bridgegate Wy *IDLE* BD10 20 C4 1
Bridge La *HIPP* HX3 36 A3
Bridge Rd *BRIG* HD6 52 B1
Bridge St *BFD* BD1 2 C5
HWTH BD22 8 A4
KGHY BD21 6 C5
Bridgeway *BOW* BD4 32 B5
Bridgwater Rd *HTON* BD9 24 B2
Bridle Dene *HIPP* HX3 36 B5
Bridle Stile *HIPP* HX3 36 B5
Bridle Stile La *CUL/QBY* BD13 28 B5
Brier Hill Cl *CLECK* BD19 51 H2
Brierley Cl *SHPY* BD18 18 D3 1
Brier St *HIPP* HX3 41 G3 2
KGHY BD21 9 G2 6
Briery Fld *SHPY* BD18 18 C4 7
Briggate *BAIL* BD17 18 C1
BRIG HD6 52 B1
SHPY BD18 18 C3 2
Briggs Av *WBSY* BD6 37 F1
Briggs Gv *WBSY* BD6 37 F1 1
Briggs Pl *WBSY* BD6 37 F1 2
Briggs St *CUL/QBY* BD13 35 F1 4
Brighouse & Denholme Gate
Rd *HIPP* HX3 43 F1
Brighouse Rd *CUL/QBY* BD13 35 F1
HIPP HX3 49 F1
LM/WK BD12 38 A5
Brighouse Wood La *BRIG* HD6 50 A5
Brighouse Wood Rw
BRIG HD6 50 A5 1
Brighton St *BAIL* BD17 18 C1
HIPP HX3 41 F4 4
IDLE BD10 13 H5 3
Brighton Ter *CLECK* BD19 45 G4 1
Bright St *CLAY* BD14 29 E3 3
CUL/QBY BD13 35 G1
RPDN/SBR HX6 46 A3
WIL/AL BD15 23 E3
Brindley Gv *GIR* BD8 23 F5 1
Brisbane Av *ECHL* BD2 25 F1
Bristol St *HIPP* HX3 48 A5 1
Britannia St *BGLY* BD16 10 D3 3
WBOW BD5 2 E7
Broadfield Cl *BOW* BD4 39 H1 1
Broadfolds *CLAY* BD14 29 F3
Broad Ings Wy *HIPP* HX3 36 B5
Broadlands *KGHY* BD21 6 A3
Broadlands St *BOW* BD4 32 C3 1
Broad La *BOW* BD4 32 C2
Broadlea Crs *WBOW* BD5 31 G4
Broadley Av *LUD/ILL* HX2 40 A4
Broadley Cl *LUD/ILL* HX2 40 B4
Broadley Gv *LUD/ILL* HX2 40 A4
Broadley Rd *LUD/ILL* HX2 40 A4
Broad Oak La *HIPP* HX3 49 G2
Broad Oak St *HIPP* HX3 49 G2
Broadstone Wy *BOW* BD4 32 D3 2
BOW BD4 39 H1 2
Broad St *BFD* BD1 2 D4
HFAX HX1 5 H3
PDSY/CALV LS28 27 H1
Broad Tree Rd *HIPP* HX3 41 F3 4
Broadway *BFD* BD1 2 D5
BGLY BD16 10 D3
HIPP HX3 48 B3
Broadway Av *WBOW* BD5 31 E5
Broadway Cl *WBOW* BD5 31 E5 1
Broadwood Av *LUD/ILL* HX2 40 B4
Brocklesby Dr *WIL/AL* BD15 23 E3
Brodley Cl *HIPP* HX3 43 F5
Broken Wy *WBOW* BD5 31 E5 2
Bromet Pl *ECHL* BD2 20 A5 3
Bromford Rd *BOW* BD4 31 H3 4
Bromley Gv *HWTH* BD22 8 D1
Bromley Rd *BGLY* BD16 10 C2
SHPY BD18 17 H1
Brompton Av *BOW* BD4 31 H4
Brompton Rd *BOW* BD4 31 H3
Bronshill Gv *WIL/AL* BD15 23 F3
Bronte Cl *HTON* BD9 23 H2 1
Bronte Dr *HWTH* BD22 8 D3
Bronte Old Rd *CUL/QBY* BD13 28 B1
Bronte Pl *CUL/QBY* BD13 28 B1 1
Bronte St *KGHY* BD21 7 E3
Bronte Wy *BRIG* HD6 44 C5
CUL/QBY BD13 28 C1
HIPP HX3 36 A2
Brooke St *BRIG* HD6 52 B2
Brookeville Av *HIPP* HX3 49 F1 1
Brookfield Av *SHPY* BD18 19 E1 2
Brookfield Rd *BFDE* BD3 3 H3
SHPY BD18 19 E1 3
Brookfields Av *CLECK* BD19 45 F5
Brookfields Rd *LM/WK* BD12 45 E4
Brookfoot La *HIPP* HX3 49 H5
Brook Grain Hl *BRIG* HD6 52 B3 1
Brookhouse Gdns *IDLE* BD10 21 E1 1
Brooklyn Ter *BRIG* HD6 49 H3 1
Brookroyd Av *BRIG* HD6 50 C2
Brooksbank Av *GTHN* BD7 29 H2
Brooks Ter *CUL/QBY* BD13 29 E5 1
Brook St *KGHY* BD21 9 G1 5
Brooks Yd *HUDN* HD2 53 H5 2
Broomcroft *CLAY* BD14 29 F3
Broome Av *ECHL* BD2 25 F
Broomfield *CLAY* BD14 28 D
Broomfield Av *HIPP* HX3 47 G
Broomfield Pl *CLAY* BD14 28 D4
KGHY BD21 6 C4
Broomfield Rd *KGHY* BD21 6 C4
Broomfield St *CUL/QBY* BD13 35 F1
KGHY BD21 6 C4
Broomhill Av *KGHY* BD21 9 F2
Broomhill Dr *KGHY* BD21 9 F1
Broomhill Gv *KGHY* BD21 9 F
Broomhill Mt *KGHY* BD21 9 F
Broomhill St *KGHY* BD21 9 F2
Broomhill Wk *KGHY* BD21 9 F
Broomhill Wy *KGHY* BD21 9 G1
Broom St *BOW* BD4 2 E
KGHY BD21 6 D5
Broster Av *HWTH* BD22 6 A
Brougham Rd *HIPP* HX3 41 H
Brougham St *HIPP* HX3 41 H4
Broughton Av *BOW* BD4 39 E
Browfield Vw *HWTH* BD22 8 D
Browfoot *SHPY* BD18 19 E
Browfoot Dr *LUD/ILL* HX2 46 C
Brow Foot Gate La *LUD/ILL* HX2 46 C
Browgate *BAIL* BD17 12 D
Brow La *CLAY* BD14 28 D4
HIPP HX3 36 C
HIPP HX3 42 B
LUD/ILL HX2 34 B
Brownberry Gv *HIPP* HX3 36 C
Browning Av *HIPP* HX3 48 A4
Browning St *BFDE* BD3 3 J
Brownroyd Hill Rd *WBSY* BD6 37 G
Brownroyd St *GIR* BD8 24 C
GTHN BD7 30 C
Brownroyd Wk *WBSY* BD6 30 C5
Brown St *KGHY* BD21 7 E3
Browsholme St *KGHY* BD21 6 C5
Brow St *KGHY* BD21 7 E5
Brow Wood Crs *ECHL* BD2 25 F
Brow Wood Ri *HIPP* HX3 36 C4
Brow Wood Rd *HIPP* HX3 36 C
Browwood Ter *WBSY* BD6 37 E3
Bruce St *HFAX* HX1 4 B6
Brunel Cl *HTON* BD9 24 B2 1
Brunswick Pl *IDLE* BD10 20 C2 1
Brunswick Rd *IDLE* BD10 20 C2
Brunswick St *BGLY* BD16 11 E3 2
CUL/QBY BD13 35 G
Bryanstone Rd *BOW* BD4 32 C
Bryan St *BRIG* HD6 52 B2
Buckfast Ct *IDLE* BD10 20 A2
Buckingham Crs *CLAY* BD14 29 G2
Buckland Pl *HFAX* HX1 46 D2
Buck La *BAIL* BD17 13 G
Buckley La *LUD/ILL* HX2 40 B
Buck Mill La *IDLE* BD10 13 H
Buckstone Dr *YEA* LS19 15 F
Buck St *BFDE* BD3 3 H7
Bude Rd *WBOW* BD5 38 C1
Bull Close La *HFAX* HX1 5 F5
Buller St *BOW* BD4 32 B2
Bull Gn *HFAX* HX1 5 G5
Bull Royd Av *GIR* BD8 23 H4
Bull Royd Crs *GIR* BD8 23 H4
Bull Royd Dr *GIR* BD8 23 H4
Bull Royd La *GIR* BD8 23 H4
Bunker's Hill La *HWTH* BD22 8 C1
Burberry Cl *BOW* BD4 39 F2
Burdale Pl *GTHN* BD7 30 C1 1
Burdock Wy *HFAX* HX1 5 F3
Burleigh St *HFAX* HX1 4 B7
Burley St *ECHL* BD2 19 E5
Burlington Av *BFDE* BD3 26 D3 1
Burlington St *GIR* BD8 2 B1
HFAX HX1 4 B3
Burned Gv *HIPP* HX3 36 B3
Burned Rd *HIPP* HX3 36 C3
Burneston Gdns *WBSY* BD6 36 D2 1
Burnett Av *WBOW* BD5 31 E4
Burnett Pl *WBOW* BD5 31 E4 3
Burnett Ri *CUL/QBY* BD13 34 D2
Burnett St *BFD* BD1 3 F5
Burnham Av *BOW* BD4 39 E1
Burnley Rd *RPDN/SBR* HX6 46 A3
Burnsall Rd *BFDE* BD3 3 K3
Burnsdale *WIL/AL* BD15 22 D1
Burns St *LUD/ILL* HX2 41 F1 1
Burnwells Av *IDLE* BD10 13 H4
Burrage St *BGLY* BD16 10 C3 4
Burras Rd *BOW* BD4 32 A5
Burrow St *WBOW* BD5 2 C7
Burton St *BOW* BD4 31 H3 5
KGHY BD21 6 C2
LUD/ILL HX2 34 B5
Busfield St *BGLY* BD16 10 C3

BOW BD4 .... 32 A4
usy La SHPY BD18 .... 13 F5
utcher St BFD BD1 .... 2 A6
ute Av BGLY HD6 .... 50 B3
ute St SHPY BD18 .... 19 E5
utler La BAIL BD17 .... 13 E2
utler St East BFDE BD3 .... 3 H3
utler St West BFDE BD3 .... 3 G3
uttermeade Cl WBSY BD6 .... 37 F3
uttershaw Av WBSY BD6 .... 36 D1
uttershaw La WBSY BD6 .... 37 G3
uttholme Ga WBSY BD6 .... 37 G2
utt La IDLE BD10 .... 20 A1
uxton Dr WBSY BD9 .... 18 D5
uxton La HTON BD9 .... 18 D5
uxton St HIPP HX3 .... 41 F4
  HTON BD9 .... 24 C2
  KGHY BD21 .... 7 E4
uxton Vw HIPP HX3 .... 41 E2
yril St KGHY BD21 .... 7 E2
yland Gv WIL/AL BD15 .... 22 C2
yron Av RPDN/SBR HX6 .... 46 A3
yron Ms BGLY BD16 .... 10 D1
yron St BFDE BD3 .... 3 J3
  HFAX HX1 .... 4 A3
  RPDN/SBR HX6 .... 46 A3

C

adney Cft HFAX HX1 .... 5 G5
ain La HIPP HX3 .... 48 D4
airns Cl ECHL BD2 .... 25 G1
aister St KGHY BD21 .... 9 G2
aister Wy KGHY BD21 .... 9 G2
alde Ct LM/WK BD12 .... 38 B4
aldene Av LM/WK BD12 .... 38 B4
alder Av LUD/ILL HX2 .... 47 E3
alder Banks CUL/QBY BD13 .... 35 H1
alderdale Wy BRIG HD6 .... 50 D3
  HIPP HX3 .... 35 H5
alderstone Av WBSY BD6 .... 36 C3
alder St BRIG HD6 .... 52 D2
alder Vw BRIG HD6 .... 52 A2
aledonia Rd KGHY BD21 .... 7 E3
aledonia St BOW BD4 .... 31 G2
  WBOW BD5 .... 31 G2
alpin Cl IDLE BD10 .... 20 A1
alton Gv KGHY BD21 .... 7 G5
alton Rd KGHY BD21 .... 7 F5
alton St KGHY BD21 .... 6 C5
  KGHY BD21 .... 9 G1
alver Av KGHY BD21 .... 6 A3
alver Gv KGHY BD21 .... 6 A3
alverley Av BFDE BD3 .... 26 C4
alverley Cutting IDLE BD10 .... 21 E1
alverley La PDSY/CALV LS28 .... 21 H3
alverley Moor Av
  PDSY/CALV LS28 .... 27 F3
alver Rd KGHY BD21 .... 6 A3
alversyke St HWTH BD22 .... 6 B4
amargue Fold ECHL BD2 .... 19 G5
amberley Mt WBOW BD5 .... 32 D3
amborne Wy HWTH BD22 .... 8 D1
ambrian Bar LM/WK BD12 .... 37 G4
ambridge Pl BFDE BD3 .... 3 F2
  CUL/QBY BD13 .... 35 F1
ambridge St CLAY BD14 .... 29 E3
  CUL/QBY BD13 .... 35 G1
  GTHN BD7 .... 30 C3
amellia St GTHN BD7 .... 29 H1
ameron Av LM/WK BD12 .... 44 C4
am La BRIG HD6 .... 51 E5
amm St BRIG HD6 .... 50 B5
ampbell St CUL/QBY BD13 .... 35 G1
  KGHY BD21 .... 6 D4
ampus Rd GTHN BD7 .... 30 D1
anada Crs YEA LS19 .... 15 H2
anada Dr YEA LS19 .... 15 H1
anada Rd YEA LS19 .... 15 H1
anada Ter YEA LS19 .... 15 H2
anal Rd AIRE BD20 .... 7 F1
  BFD BD1 .... 2 E4
  BFDE BD3 .... 2 E2
  BGLY BD16 .... 10 C1
  ECHL BD2 .... 18 D5
  RPDN/SBR HX6 .... 46 D4
anal St BRIG HD6 .... 52 C1
  HIPP HX3 .... 5 K6
anford Dr WIL/AL BD15 .... 23 E3
anford Gv WIL/AL BD15 .... 23 F3
anford Rd WIL/AL BD15 .... 23 E3
anker La HIPP HX3 .... 41 F2
annon Hall Cl BRIG HD6 .... 53 E1
annon Hall Dr BRIG HD6 .... 53 E1
annon Mill La GTHN BD7 .... 30 B3
annon St BGLY BD16 .... 10 D4

HFAX HX1 .... 4 B7
Canterbury Av WBOW BD5 .... 30 D4
Canterbury Crs HIPP HX3 .... 41 G4
Capel Ct PDSY/CALV LS28 .... 21 G3
Capel St BRIG HD6 .... 52 B2
  PDSY/CALV LS28 .... 21 G3
Cape St BFD BD1 .... 2 D2
Captain St BFD BD1 .... 2 E4
Carden Rd BOW BD4 .... 32 D2
Cardigan St CUL/QBY BD13 .... 35 G1
Carisbrooke Crs WBSY BD6 .... 37 G2
Cark Rd KGHY BD21 .... 6 D3
Carlby St HWTH BD22 .... 6 B5
Carleton St KGHY BD21 .... 6 D2
Carling Cl GTHN BD7 .... 30 A4
Carlisle Pl GIR BD8 .... 24 D3
Carlisle Rd GIR BD8 .... 24 C3
Carlisle St GIR BD8 .... 24 C3
  KGHY BD21 .... 7 E5
  LUD/ILL HX2 .... 40 D5
  PDSY/CALV LS28 .... 27 H3
Carlisle Ter GIR BD8 .... 24 D3
Carlton Av SHPY BD18 .... 18 A1
Carlton Dr BAIL BD17 .... 12 D2
  HTON BD9 .... 18 B5
  SHPY BD18 .... 18 B4
Carlton Gv SHPY BD18 .... 18 C4
  WBOW BD5 .... 31 E4
Carlton House Ter HFAX HX1 .... 4 D7
Carlton Pl HFAX HX1 .... 5 G5
Carlton Rd SHPY BD18 .... 17 H1
Carlton St GTHN BD7 .... 2 B6
  HFAX HX1 .... 5 G5
Carlton Ter HFAX HX1 .... 5 G5
Carlton Wk SHPY BD18 .... 18 A1
Carmel Rd HIPP HX3 .... 48 C4
Carmona Av SHPY BD18 .... 18 C4
Carmona Gdns SHPY BD18 .... 18 C4
Carnaby Rd GTHN BD7 .... 29 H5
Carnegie Dr SHPY BD18 .... 18 E1
Carnoustie Gv BGLY BD16 .... 17 E2
Caroline St SHPY BD18 .... 18 A1
Carr Bottom Av WBOW BD5 .... 30 D5
Carr Bottom Fold WBSY BD6 .... 37 H1
Carr Bottom Gv WBSY BD6 .... 30 C5
Carr Bottom Rd IDLE BD10 .... 20 D3
  WBOW BD5 .... 30 D5
Carr Green Av BRIG HD6 .... 52 A5
Carr Green Cl BRIG HD6 .... 52 A5
Carr Green Dr BRIG HD6 .... 52 A5
Carr Green La BRIG HD6 .... 52 A4
Carr Gv AIRE BD20 .... 7 H2
Carr Hall Rd LM/WK BD12 .... 44 D2
Carr Hill Av PDSY/CALV LS28 .... 21 F3
Carr Hill Dr PDSY/CALV LS28 .... 21 F3
Carr Hill Gv PDSY/CALV LS28 .... 21 F3
Carr Hill Nook PDSY/CALV LS28 .... 21 F3
Carr Hill Ri PDSY/CALV LS28 .... 21 F3
Carr Hill Rd PDSY/CALV LS28 .... 21 F3
Carr House Gv LM/WK BD12 .... 44 D1
Carr House La HIPP HX3 .... 36 D3
  LM/WK BD12 .... 37 G5
  LM/WK BD12 .... 44 D1
Carr House Mt LM/WK BD12 .... 44 D1
Carr House Rd HIPP HX3 .... 36 C4
Carricks Cl LM/WK BD12 .... 38 B4
Carrington St BFDE BD3 .... 26 B5
Carr La AIRE BD20 .... 7 H2
  LM/WK BD12 .... 38 A5
  SHPY BD18 .... 19 E2
Carroll St BFDE BD3 .... 3 G6
Carr Rd LM/WK BD12 .... 44 D2
  PDSY/CALV LS28 .... 21 F3
Carr St BRIG HD6 .... 50 B4
  KGHY BD21 .... 6 D3
  WBOW BD5 .... 31 E5
Carr Wood Gdns
  PDSY/CALV LS28 .... 21 F3
Carter La CUL/QBY BD13 .... 28 A4
Carter St BFD BD1 .... 3 F7
Cartmel Rd KGHY BD21 .... 6 B4
  KGHY BD21 .... 6 B3
Caryl Rd BOW BD4 .... 31 H4
Cashmere St HWTH BD22 .... 6 B4
Castle Av BRIG HD6 .... 52 A3
Castlefields Crs BRIG HD6 .... 52 A3
Castlefields Dr BRIG HD6 .... 52 A3
Castlefields La BGLY BD16 .... 10 B1
Castlefields Rd BGLY BD16 .... 10 A1
  BRIG HD6 .... 52 A3
Castlegate St IDLE BD10 .... 20 B3
Castle Hl BRIG HD6 .... 52 A3
Castlemore Rd BAIL BD17 .... 13 E4
Castle Rd KGHY BD21 .... 6 C3
  SHPY BD18 .... 18 B2
Castle St WBOW BD5 .... 31 F2
Cater St BFD BD1 .... 3 F5
Cathcart St HIPP HX3 .... 41 G4

Catherine Slack BRIG HD6 .... 50 A2
Catherine St BRIG HD6 .... 50 B5
  KGHY BD21 .... 9 G1
  KGHY BD21 .... 9 G1
Cauldwell Gdns WBOW BD5 .... 31 F3
Causeway HFAX HX1 .... 5 J4
Cavalier Dr IDLE BD10 .... 20 C2
Cave Hl HIPP HX3 .... 42 C1
Cavendish Dr BGLY BD16 .... 11 E1
Cavendish Rd IDLE BD10 .... 20 A2
Cavendish St HFAX HX1 .... 4 D3
Cavendish Ter HFAX HX1 .... 4 D3
  HFAX HX1 .... 4 D4
Cawcliffe Dr BRIG HD6 .... 50 B4
Cawcliffe Rd BRIG HD6 .... 50 B4
Cawood Hvn WBSY BD6 .... 36 D2
Caygill Ter HFAX HX1 .... 5 G7
Caythorne Wk IDLE BD10 .... 20 B4
Cecil Av BAIL BD17 .... 12 D2
  GTHN BD7 .... 30 D7
  HIPP HX3 .... 43 H5
Cedar Dr LM/WK BD12 .... 45 F1
Cedar St HFAX HX1 .... 4 D3
Cemetery La AIRE BD20 .... 6 C1
Cemetery Rd BGLY BD16 .... 10 B2
  GIR BD8 .... 24 A5
  WBSY BD6 .... 37 G3
Centenary Rd BAIL BD17 .... 13 G2
Central Av BAIL BD17 .... 12 C4
  HWTH BD22 .... 9 E3
  SHPY BD18 .... 18 C2
  WBOW BD5 .... 30 D3
Central Dr HWTH BD22 .... 9 E3
Central Pk HFAX HX1 .... 5 G4
Central St HFAX HX1 .... 5 F4
Centre St WBOW BD5 .... 30 D4
Century Pl GIR BD8 .... 24 D3
Chadwell Springs BGLY BD16 .... 16 D2
Chaffinch Rd GIR BD8 .... 23 F5
Chain St BFD BD1 .... 2 B4
Challenge Wy BOW BD4 .... 32 C3
Challis Gv WBOW BD5 .... 31 F4
Chandos St BOW BD4 .... 2 E7
  KGHY BD21 .... 9 G1
Channing Wy BFD BD1 .... 2 C6
Chapel Cft BRIG HD6 .... 52 A4
Chapel Fold LM/WK BD12 .... 44 D5
  WBSY BD6 .... 37 G1
Chapel Gv BGLY BD16 .... 10 B1
Chapel House Rd LM/WK BD12 .... 38 A3
Chapel La BAIL BD17 .... 14 A1
  CUL/QBY BD13 .... 29 E5
  HIPP HX3 .... 48 A5
  HIPP HX3 .... 49 E4
  KGHY BD21 .... 6 C4
  RPDN/SBR HX6 .... 46 C4
  WIL/AL BD15 .... 23 F4
Chapel Rd BGLY BD16 .... 10 B1
  LM/WK BD12 .... 38 A4
Chapel St BFD BD1 .... 3 F5
  BRIG HD6 .... 49 H3
  CUL/QBY BD13 .... 28 A1
  CUL/QBY BD13 .... 35 C1
  ECHL BD2 .... 20 C5
  LUD/ILL HX2 .... 40 D5
  PDSY/CALV LS28 .... 21 G2
  WBOW BD5 .... 31 E3
  WBSY BD6 .... 37 H1
  YEA LS19 .... 15 G2
Chapel St North HIPP HX3 .... 41 E2
Chapel Ter WIL/AL BD15 .... 23 E3
Chapeltown HFAX HX1 .... 5 F3
Chapel Wk BGLY BD16 .... 10 C3
  ECHL BD2 .... 20 C5
Chapman St BOW BD4 .... 32 C1
Charles Av BFDE BD3 .... 26 C5
  HIPP HX3 .... 48 D4
Charles St BAIL BD17 .... 13 C1
  BGLY BD16 .... 10 C3
  HFAX HX1 .... 5 J4
  RPDN/SBR HX6 .... 46 A4
Charlestown Rd HIPP HX3 .... 5 J2
Charlesworth Gv LUD/ILL HX2 .... 40 D5
Charlesworth Ter LUD/ILL HX2 .... 40 D5
Charnwood Cl ECHL BD2 .... 26 B2
Charnwood Gv ECHL BD2 .... 26 B2
Charnwood Rd ECHL BD2 .... 26 B2
Charterhouse Rd IDLE BD10 .... 14 A5
Charteris Rd GIR BD8 .... 6 A3
The Chase KGHY BD21 .... 6 A3
  YEA LS19 .... 15 F2
Chase Wy WBOW BD5 .... 31 F5
  WBOW BD5 .... 38 B1
Chassum Gv HTON BD9 .... 24 B2
Chatham St BFDE BD3 .... 25 G3
  HFAX HX1 .... 4 E3

RPDN/SBR HX6 .... 46 A3
Chat Hill Rd CUL/QBY BD13 .... 28 C2
Chatsworth Av
  PDSY/CALV LS28 .... 27 F4
Chatsworth Crs
  PDSY/CALV LS28 .... 27 F4
Chatsworth Dr
  PDSY/CALV LS28 .... 27 F4
Chatsworth Fall
  PDSY/CALV LS28 .... 27 F4
Chatsworth Pl GIR BD8 .... 24 C2
Chatsworth Ri PDSY/CALV LS28 .... 27 F4
Chatsworth Rd PDSY/CALV LS28 .... 27 F4
Chatsworth St KGHY BD21 .... 7 F4
Chatts Wood Fold LM/WK BD12 .... 39 E5
Chaucer St HFAX HX1 .... 4 A5
Cheapside BFD BD1 .... 2 D4
  HIPP HX3 .... 36 B4
Cheddington Gv WIL/AL BD15 .... 23 E4
Chellow Grange Rd HTON BD9 .... 23 F1
Chellow La HTON BD9 .... 23 F2
Chellow St WBOW BD5 .... 31 E5
Chelmsford Rd BFDE BD3 .... 26 B4
Chelmsford Ter BFDE BD3 .... 26 B5
Chelsea Man HIPP HX3 .... 42 D3
Chelsea Rd GTHN BD7 .... 30 A3
Chelsea St KGHY BD21 .... 9 G1
Cheltenham Ct HIPP HX3 .... 48 A4
Cheltenham Gdns HIPP HX3 .... 48 A4
Cheltenham Pl HIPP HX3 .... 48 A4
Cheltenham Rd ECHL BD2 .... 19 G4
Chelwood Dr WIL/AL BD15 .... 23 E5
Cheriton Dr CUL/QBY BD13 .... 35 G1
Cherry Flds ECHL BD2 .... 19 F5
Cherry Lea Ct YEA LS19 .... 15 G1
Cherry St KGHY BD21 .... 7 F3
Cherry Tree Av IDLE BD10 .... 20 C2
Cherry Tree Gdns SHPY BD18 .... 13 G5
Chervana Ct BOW BD4 .... 32 D3
Cherwell Dr WBSY BD6 .... 37 E3
Chesham St KGHY BD21 .... 7 E4
Chester Cl HIPP HX3 .... 41 G4
Chester Gv HIPP HX3 .... 41 G4
Chester Pl HIPP HX3 .... 41 G4
Chester Rd HIPP HX3 .... 41 G4
Chester St GTHN BD7 .... 2 B6
  HIPP HX3 .... 41 G4
  RPDN/SBR HX6 .... 46 A4
Chester Ter HIPP HX3 .... 41 G4
Chestnut Cl HWTH BD22 .... 6 A5
Chestnut Ct SHPY BD18 .... 17 H2
Chestnut Gv ECHL BD2 .... 19 F5
  PDSY/CALV LS28 .... 21 G3
Chestnut St HFAX HX1 .... 4 A6
Chevet Mt WIL/AL BD15 .... 22 D5
Chevington Ct YEA LS19 .... 15 F3
Cheviot Ga LM/WK BD12 .... 37 G4
Cheyne Wk KGHY BD21 .... 6 B5
Childs La SHPY BD18 .... 19 F3
Chippendale Ri GIR BD8 .... 23 G4
Chislehurst Pl WBOW BD5 .... 30 D4
Chrisharben Pk CLAY BD14 .... 29 F3
Chrismoor IDLE BD10 .... 19 H2
Christopher St WBOW BD5 .... 30 D4
Christopher Ter WBOW BD5 .... 30 D4
Church Bank BFD BD1 .... 2 E5
  LUD/ILL HX2 .... 46 C2
  RPDN/SBR HX6 .... 46 B4
Church Ct GTHN BD7 .... 30 A2
Church Flds ECHL BD2 .... 26 C2
Churchfields Rd BRIG HD6 .... 50 B5
Church Gn LUD/ILL HX2 .... 40 D4
Churchill Rd CUL/QBY BD13 .... 28 C1
Church La BAIL BD17 .... 14 B1
  BRIG HD6 .... 50 B5
  BRIG HD6 .... 52 B1
  HIPP HX3 .... 49 F4
  LUD/ILL HX2 .... 40 D4
  WBSY BD6 .... 37 G2
Church Pl HFAX HX1 .... 4 E5
Church Rd WBSY BD6 .... 37 G2
Church Side Cl HIPP HX3 .... 41 H4
Church Side Dr HIPP HX3 .... 41 H4
Church St BGLY BD16 .... 10 D4
  BRIG HD6 .... 52 A3
  GIR BD8 .... 24 D3
  HFAX HX1 .... 5 J4
  KGHY BD21 .... 6 C5
  KGHY BD21 .... 7 E4
  SHPY BD18 .... 19 E1
  WBSY BD6 .... 36 D1
Church Vw RPDN/SBR HX6 .... 46 B4
Church Wk HIPP HX3 .... 42 D3
Church Wy KGHY BD21 .... 6 D5
Churn La LUD/ILL HX2 .... 46 C1
Churn Milk La HIPP HX3 .... 41 F1
Cinderhills La HIPP HX3 .... 48 B5

City La HIPP HX3 ... 40 D4
City Rd GIR BD8 ... 24 D4
Clapton Av HFAX HX1 ... 4 D6
Clara Dr PDSY/CALV LS28 ... 21 E2
Clara Rd ECHL BD2 ... 19 G4
Clara St BRIG HD6 ... 52 B2
Clare Crs LM/WK BD12 ... 44 D3
Clare Hall La HFAX HX1 ... 5 H6
Claremont GTHN BD7 ... 2 A7
Claremont Av SHPY BD18 ... 19 F3
Claremont Crs SHPY BD18 ... 19 F3 1
Claremont Gdns BGLY BD16 ... 10 D2 2
Claremont Gv SHPY BD18 ... 19 F3
Claremont Rd SHPY BD18 ... 19 F3
Claremont St RPDN/SBR HX6 ... 46 B3 1
Claremount Rd HIPP HX3 ... 41 H3
Claremount Ter HIPP HX3 ... 41 H4 5
Clarence Rd SHPY BD18 ... 18 A1 3
Clarence St HFAX HX1 ... 5 F4
Clarendon Pl CUL/QBY BD13 ... 34 D2 1
Clarendon Rd BGLY BD16 ... 11 E2
Clarendon St KGHY BD21 ... 9 G1 11
Clare Rd HFAX HX1 ... 5 H5
LM/WK BD12 ... 44 D3
Clare St HFAX HX1 ... 5 H5
Clarges St WBOW BD5 ... 30 D4
Clarke St PDSY/CALV LS28 ... 21 G3
Clayfield Dr GTHN BD7 ... 30 B5
Clay Hill Dr LM/WK BD12 ... 45 E2
Clay Pits La HFAX HX1 ... 4 A2
Clay St HFAX HX1 ... 4 B3
RPDN/SBR HX6 ... 46 B4
Clayton La CLAY BD14 ... 29 E4
WBOW BD5 ... 31 F3 4
Clayton Ri KGHY BD21 ... 6 B3
Clayton Rd GTHN BD7 ... 29 H3
Cleckheaton Rd WBSY BD6 ... 38 A2
Cleeve Hl YEA LS19 ... 15 G2
Clement St GIR BD8 ... 24 A4 2
RPDN/SBR HX6 ... 46 A4 6
Clevedon Pl HIPP HX3 ... 41 F3 5
Cleveland Av HIPP HX3 ... 48 A4 3
Cleveland Rd HTON BD9 ... 24 C1
Cliff Crs LUD/ILL HX2 ... 46 D3 1
Cliffe Av BAIL BD17 ... 12 D3
HIPP HX3 ... 50 B1
Cliffe Dr YEA LS19 ... 15 F3
Cliffe La BAIL BD17 ... 12 D5
CUL/QBY BD13 ... 22 B5
YEA LS19 ... 15 H3
Cliffe La South BAIL BD17 ... 12 D5
Cliffe La West BAIL BD17 ... 12 D4
Cliffe Rd BFDE BD3 ... 25 G2
BRIG HD6 ... 52 B1
KGHY BD21 ... 9 H2
Cliffe Ter BAIL BD17 ... 12 D5
GIR BD8 ... 25 E3
KGHY BD21 ... 9 H2
Cliffe Vw WIL/AL BD15 ... 22 C2
Cliffe Wood Cl HTON BD9 ... 23 H1
Cliff Gdns LUD/ILL HX2 ... 46 D3 2
Cliff Hill La LUD/ILL HX2 ... 46 A2
Cliff Hollins La LM/WK BD12 ... 39 G4
Clifford Rd BAIL BD17 ... 12 D4
Clifford St WBOW BD5 ... 31 F2 7
Cliff Vale Rd SHPY BD18 ... 18 C4 10
Cliff Wood Av SHPY BD18 ... 18 C3
Clifton Av HFAX HX1 ... 4 A6
Clifton Common BRIG HD6 ... 52 D1
Clifton Pl SHPY BD18 ... 18 C3
Clifton Rd HIPP HX3 ... 47 H4
Clifton Side HUDN HD2 ... 53 G5
Clifton St GIR BD8 ... 25 E3
HIPP HX3 ... 41 F4 5
HWTH BD22 ... 6 B5
RPDN/SBR HX6 ... 46 B4
Clifton Vls GIR BD8 ... 25 E3
Clipstone St WBOW BD5 ... 31 F5 1
Clive Pl GTHN BD7 ... 30 C2
Clive Ter GTHN BD7 ... 30 C2
Clock View St KGHY BD21 ... 6 C2
Clog Sole Rd BRIG HD6 ... 50 A4
Close Lea BRIG HD6 ... 52 A2
Close Lea Av BRIG HD6 ... 52 A2
Close Lea Dr BRIG HD6 ... 52 A3
Close Lea Wy BRIG HD6 ... 52 A2
Closes Rd BRIG HD6 ... 52 B2 5
Cloudsdale Av WBOW BD5 ... 31 F3
Clough Ga HWTH BD22 ... 8 C4 1
Clough La BRIG HD6 ... 51 E3
BRIG HD6 ... 52 A5
HWTH BD22 ... 8 B3
Clough St WBOW BD5 ... 31 F4 4
Clover Ct PDSY/CALV LS28 ... 21 F3
Clover Crs PDSY/CALV LS28 ... 21 F2
Cloverdale HIPP HX3 ... 36 C3
Clover Hill Cl HFAX HX1 ... 5 F6
Clover Hill Rd HFAX HX1 ... 47 G3
Clover Hill Ter HFAX HX1 ... 47 G3
Clover Hill Vw HFAX HX1 ... 47 G3 2
Clover St GTHN BD7 ... 30 C4
Cloverville Ap WBSY BD6 ... 37 H3
Club La LUD/ILL HX2 ... 41 E2
Club St GTHN BD7 ... 30 A1
Clydesdale Dr WBSY BD6 ... 37 E3
Clyde St BGLY BD16 ... 10 C3
RPDN/SBR HX6 ... 46 A5
Coach La CUL/QBY BD13 ... 28 C1 1
Coach Rd BRIG HD6 ... 50 A2
HIPP HX3 ... 49 H1
Coal Pit La BRIG HD6 ... 53 E2
Coalpit La HIPP HX3 ... 48 B4
Coates St WBOW BD5 ... 31 E3 4
Coates Ter WBOW BD5 ... 31 E3 5
Cobden St CLAY BD14 ... 29 E3
CUL/QBY BD13 ... 35 G1
IDLE BD10 ... 20 A2 5
WIL/AL BD15 ... 23 E3 3
Cock Hill La HIPP HX3 ... 35 H4
Cockin La CLAY BD14 ... 28 B4
CUL/QBY BD13 ... 28 A4
Cockroft Gv BFDE BD3 ... 3 H4
Cockshott La IDLE BD10 ... 19 H1
Coldbeck Dr WBSY BD6 ... 36 D2
Coleman St BFDE BD3 ... 2 E1
Coleridge Gdns IDLE BD10 ... 20 B1 1
Coleridge St HFAX HX1 ... 5 H5
Coles Wy AIRE BD20 ... 7 E1
Coley Hall La HIPP HX3 ... 43 G3
Coley Rd HIPP HX3 ... 43 F2
Coley Vw HIPP HX3 ... 42 D2
Collbrook Av WBSY BD6 ... 37 H2
Collier La BAIL BD17 ... 12 C2
Colliers Cl SHPY BD18 ... 17 H2 3
Collindale Cl IDLE BD10 ... 20 D3 3
Collinfield Ri WBSY BD6 ... 37 E4
Collingham Av WBSY BD6 ... 36 C2
Collins St BOW BD4 ... 32 A2
GTHN BD7 ... 30 B4
Colne Road (Goodley)
HWTH BD22 ... 8 A4
Colston Cl GIR BD8 ... 23 H3
Columbus St HIPP HX3 ... 41 F4 6
Colyton Mt WIL/AL BD15 ... 22 D3 1
Commerce Ct BOW BD4 ... 32 C3 2
Commercial St BRIG HD6 ... 52 B1
CUL/QBY BD13 ... 28 B1 2
HFAX HX1 ... 5 G4 1
HFAX HX1 ... 5 G4 1
SHPY BD18 ... 18 C1
Commondale Wy BOW BD4 ... 38 D4
Common La HIPP HX3 ... 48 C2
Common Rd LM/WK BD12 ... 37 H4
Como Av GIR BD8 ... 24 A3
Como Dr GIR BD8 ... 24 A3
Como Gdns GIR BD8 ... 24 A4 3
Como Gv GIR BD8 ... 24 A3
Compeigne Av AIRE BD20 ... 7 G2 2
Compton St BOW BD4 ... 32 B5
Concrete St HIPP HX3 ... 41 F4 7
Conduit St GIR BD8 ... 24 D3 5
Coney La KGHY BD21 ... 6 D4
Coniston Av CUL/QBY BD13 ... 35 E1 3
Coniston Cl CUL/QBY BD13 ... 35 E1
Coniston Gv HTON BD9 ... 24 A2
Coniston Rd GTHN BD7 ... 29 H4 2
Constance St SHPY BD18 ... 18 A1 4
Constitutional St HFAX HX1 ... 4 B7
Conway St HFAX HX1 ... 4 C5
Cooke La KGHY BD21 ... 6 D4 2
Cooke St KGHY BD21 ... 6 D4 3
Cookson St BRIG HD6 ... 50 A5
Coombe Hl CUL/QBY BD13 ... 29 E5
Co-operative Buildings
BRIG HD6 ... 50 C1 1
Cooper Cl BGLY BD16 ... 10 D1
Cooper Gv WBSY BD6 ... 36 C3
Cooper La HIPP HX3 ... 36 C2
WBSY BD6 ... 36 C1
Copeland St BOW BD4 ... 32 C2
Copgrove Cl BOW BD4 ... 32 D4 1
Copgrove Ct BOW BD4 ... 32 D4 2
Copgrove Rd BOW BD4 ... 32 D4
Copley Av LUD/ILL HX2 ... 46 D3
Copley St WBOW BD5 ... 30 C4
Coplowe La WIL/AL BD15 ... 16 A2
The Coppice YEA LS19 ... 15 E1
Coppice Vw IDLE BD10 ... 19 H1
Coppice Wood Av GTHN BD7 ... 30 B1 2
Coppice Wood Gv GTHN BD7 ... 30 B1 3
The Coppies LM/WK BD12 ... 44 C1 1
Coppy Cl BGLY BD16 ... 16 D3 1
The Copse BGLY BD16 ... 11 G3
CLECK BD19 ... 51 G1
Corban St BOW BD4 ... 32 B4 1
Cordingley Cl BOW BD4 ... 39 H1 3
Cordingley St BOW BD4 ... 39 H1
Corn Mill La CLAY BD14 ... 28 C2
Corn St HWTH BD22 ... 9 F2
Cornwall Crs BAIL BD17 ... 12 C2
BRIG HD6 ... 50 C2
Cornwall Pl GIR BD8 ... 2 B1
Cornwall Rd BGLY BD16 ... 11 E4
GIR BD8 ... 2 B1
KGHY BD21 ... 7 F2 5
Cornwall Ter GIR BD8 ... 2 B1
Coronation Av IDLE BD10 ... 14 C2
Coronation Mt HWTH BD22 ... 6 A4
Coronation Rd HIPP HX3 ... 47 H4
Coronation St LM/WK BD12 ... 38 D5
Coronation Wk HWTH BD22 ... 6 A3 1
Corporal La CUL/QBY BD13 ... 35 F4
Corporation St ECHL BD2 ... 26 B1
HFAX HX1 ... 5 G2
RPDN/SBR HX6 ... 46 A4
Corrance Rd LM/WK BD12 ... 45 E4
Corrie St CUL/QBY BD13 ... 28 B1 3
Cote Farm La SHPY BD18 ... 13 G5 1
Cotefields Av PDSY/CALV LS28 ... 27 H1
Cote La PDSY/CALV LS28 ... 27 H2
WIL/AL BD15 ... 22 D3 2
The Cote PDSY/CALV LS28 ... 27 H2
Cotewall Rd WBOW BD5 ... 31 E4
Cotswold Av SHPY BD18 ... 19 F2
Cottage Rd IDLE BD10 ... 20 C2
Cottam Av GTHN BD7 ... 30 C1 2
Cottam Ter GTHN BD7 ... 30 C1 3
Cotterdale WIL/AL BD15 ... 22 D1 2
Cottingley Cliffe Rd BGLY BD16 ... 17 F3
Cottingley Dr BGLY BD16 ... 16 D1
Cottingley Manor Pk
BGLY BD16 ... 17 E2 2
Cottingley Moor Rd BGLY BD16 ... 16 D4
Cottingley New Rd BGLY BD16 ... 17 E2
Cottingley Rd WIL/AL BD15 ... 22 D1
Cottingley Ter GIR BD8 ... 2 B1 1
Courtenay Cl BFDE BD3 ... 26 D5 1
Court La LUD/ILL HX2 ... 46 C1
Courts Leet LM/WK BD12 ... 44 D1 7
Cousen Av GTHN BD7 ... 30 A2
Cousen Rd GTHN BD7 ... 30 C3
Cousin La LUD/ILL HX2 ... 40 D1
Coventry St BOW BD4 ... 32 A3 3
HFAX HX1 ... 46 D1 1
Coverdale Wy BAIL BD17 ... 13 F2
Cover Dr WBSY BD6 ... 37 F2
The Covet IDLE BD10 ... 20 C1 1
Cow Close La LM/WK BD12 ... 45 F3
Cowdray Dr CLECK BD19 ... 45 G5 3
Cowgill St GIR BD8 ... 24 D3 6
Cow Gn HFAX HX1 ... 5 G4
Cow La HIPP HX3 ... 49 G4
Cowley Crs HTON BD9 ... 17 F5 2
Cowling La HIPP HX3 ... 35 G5
Cowroyd Pl HIPP HX3 ... 5 J1
Crabtree Pl GTHN BD7 ... 30 B3 5
Crabtree St GTHN BD7 ... 30 B3 6
HFAX HX1 ... 4 A4
Crack La WIL/AL BD15 ... 16 A4
Crag Cl LUD/ILL HX2 ... 40 C1
Cragg La GTHN BD7 ... 30 B4 1
Cragg Ter GTHN BD7 ... 30 B4 2
Cragg Wood Dr YEA LS19 ... 15 F3
Crag Hill Rd IDLE BD10 ... 13 H4
Crag La LUD/ILL HX2 ... 40 C1
Crag Pl KGHY BD21 ... 9 H2
Crag Rd SHPY BD18 ... 18 D2
Crag Vw IDLE BD10 ... 20 B2
Craiglands HIPP HX3 ... 43 G5
Craiglea Dr LM/WK BD12 ... 45 E3
Craigmore Ct BOW BD4 ... 33 E5 5
Cranbourne Rd HTON BD9 ... 23 G2
Cranbrook Av WBSY BD6 ... 37 H2
Cranbrook Pl WBOW BD5 ... 31 F4 5
Cranbrook St CLAY BD14 ... 29 E3 5
WBOW BD5 ... 31 F4 6
Cranleigh Mt KGHY BD21 ... 9 F1 4
Cranmer Rd BFDE BD3 ... 25 G3
Craven Av CUL/QBY BD13 ... 28 B1 4
Craven Rd KGHY BD21 ... 7 F3 4
Craven St BFDE BD3 ... 3 F3 1
Crawford Av WBSY BD6 ... 37 H2
Crawford St BOW BD4 ... 31 H3 6
Crediton Av WIL/AL BD15 ... 23 E4
The Crescent BAIL BD17 ... 12 D4
HIPP HX3 ... 48 B2
WBSY BD6 ... 36 D2
Crescent Vw HWTH BD22 ... 9 F3
Crescent Wk CLAY BD14 ... 29 G2
The Cresent HIPP HX3 ... 43 G5
Creskeld Wy WIL/AL BD15 ... 22 C2
Cresswell Mt GTHN BD7 ... 29 H5
Cresswell Pl GTHN BD7 ... 29 H5 3
Cresswell Ter GTHN BD7 ... 29 H5 4
Crest Av LM/WK BD12 ... 44 D
Crestfield Dr LUD/ILL HX2 ... 46 D
The Crest HUDN HD2 ... 53 F
Crestville Cl CLAY BD14 ... 29 G2
Crestville Rd CLAY BD14 ... 29 F
Crestville Ter CLAY BD14 ... 29 C
Crestwood Cl BOW BD4 ... 39 E1
Crib La HFAX HX1 ... 5 C
Crimshaw La SHPY BD18 ... 19 E
Cripplegate HFAX HX1 ... 5 K
Crofters Gn IDLE BD10 ... 19 H
Croft House Cl WBSY BD6 ... 37 G2
Croft House La AIRE BD20 ... 6 B1
Croft House Rd WBSY BD6 ... 37 C
Croftlands IDLE BD10 ... 19 H
Crofton Rd HTON BD9 ... 24 E
Croft Pl BRIG HD6 ... 50 C
Croft St BRIG HD6 ... 52 B1
IDLE BD10 ... 20 B
KGHY BD21 ... 6 C
RPDN/SBR HX6 ... 46 B4
SHPY BD18 ... 18 C
WBOW BD5 ... 2 D
WBSY BD6 ... 37 H1
Cromack Vw PDSY/CALV LS28 ... 27 H
Cromer Rd KGHY BD21 ... 9 G1 1
Cromer St HFAX HX1 ... 4 A7
KGHY BD21 ... 9 G1 1
Cromwell Cl HIPP HX3 ... 48 D
Cromwell Ct BGLY BD16 ... 17 E
Cromwell Rd HIPP HX3 ... 48 D
Cromwell Ter HFAX HX1 ... 4 E4
Crooked La HIPP HX3 ... 34 C
IDLE BD10 ... 13 G
Cropredy Cl CUL/QBY BD13 ... 35 G
Crosby St KGHY BD21 ... 6 C
Croscombe Wk WBOW BD5 ... 31 F2
Crosley Vw BGLY BD16 ... 11 E
Crosley Wood Rd BGLY BD16 ... 11 E
Cross Banks SHPY BD18 ... 18 C
Crossdale Av WBSY BD6 ... 36 C
Cross Emily St KGHY BD21 ... 6 D3
Cross Hl HFAX HX1 ... 5 H
Cross La BGLY BD16 ... 10 C
BRIG HD6 ... 53 F
CUL/QBY BD13 ... 34 D
GTHN BD7 ... 30 B
HIPP HX3 ... 35 H
HIPP HX3 ... 43 E
WIL/AL BD15 ... 16 A
Cross Leeds St KGHY BD21 ... 6 C4
Crossley Hall Ms GIR BD8 ... 23 H5
Crossley Hall St GIR BD8 ... 23 G5
Crossley Hl HIPP HX3 ... 48 A
Crossley St BRIG HD6 ... 52 C
CUL/QBY BD13 ... 35 G
GTHN BD7 ... 30 C
HFAX HX1 ... 5 H
Crossley Ter North LUD/ILL HX2 ... 41 F
Crossley Ter South LUD/ILL HX2 ... 41 F
Cross River St KGHY BD21 ... 7 F2
Cross Rd GIR BD8 ... 24 C3
IDLE BD10 ... 20 B
LM/WK BD12 ... 38 C
Cross Rosse St SHPY BD18 ... 18 C1
Cross Rydal St KGHY BD21 ... 6 B5
Cross St BRIG HD6 ... 50 B
CLAY BD14 ... 29 F3
HFAX HX1 ... 5 J5
LM/WK BD12 ... 45 H
WBSY BD6 ... 37 E3
Cross St West LUD/ILL HX2 ... 40 D5
Cross Sun St BFD BD1 ... 2 E
Crossway BGLY BD16 ... 16 C2
Crowgill Rd SHPY BD18 ... 18 C
Crown Dr LM/WK BD12 ... 44 D
Crownest La BGLY BD16 ... 10 D
Crownest Rd BGLY BD16 ... 10 D
Crown Rd HIPP HX3 ... 41 G
Crown St BFD BD1 ... 24 D
BRIG HD6 ... 50 B
HFAX HX1 ... 5 G
LM/WK BD12 ... 44 D1
Crowther Av PDSY/CALV LS28 ... 21 E
Crowther St IDLE BD10 ... 20 C
LM/WK BD12 ... 44 D1
Crow Tree Cl BAIL BD17 ... 13 E3
Crow Tree La GIR BD8 ... 23 H
Crowtrees Ct YEA LS19 ... 15 G
Crowtrees Crs BRIG HD6 ... 52 A
Crowtrees La BRIG HD6 ... 52 A
Crowtrees Pk BRIG HD6 ... 52 A
Crow Trees Pk YEA LS19 ... 15 G
Crow Wood Pk LUD/ILL HX2 ... 46 C
Croydon Rd GTHN BD7 ... 30 A3
Crystal Ter BOW BD4 ... 32 B4
Culver St HFAX HX1 ... 5 G
Cumberland Cl LUD/ILL HX2 ... 40 D

Cumberland Rd *GTHN* BD7 .... 30 B2
Cunliffe La *BAIL* BD17 .... 14 A1
Cunliffe Rd *GIR* BD8 .... 24 D2
Cunliffe Ter *IDLE* BD8 .... 25 E1
Cure Hl *HWTH* BD22 .... 8 A3
Curlew La *WBOW* BD5 .... 30 D4 ⁷
Currer Av *BOW* BD4 .... 39 E1
Currer St *BFD* BD1 .... 2 E5
Curzon Rd *BFDE* BD3 .... 3 K4
Cuthberts Cl *CUL/QBY* BD13 .... 35 E2
Cutler Heights La *BOW* BD4 .... 32 D4
Cutler Pl *BOW* BD4 .... 32 C3
Cyprus Av *IDLE* BD10 .... 13 G5
Cyprus Dr *IDLE* BD10 .... 13 G5

D

Daffels Wood Cl *BOW* BD4 .... 39 E2 ⁴
Daffodil Ct *WIL/AL* BD15 .... 23 E4 ⁵
Dagenham Rd *BOW* BD4.......... 32 B4
Daisy Hl *LM/WK* BD12 .... 44 D2
Daisy Hill Back La *HTON* BD9 .... 23 H2 ⁴
Daisy Hill Gv *HTON* BD9.......... 23 H2
Daisy Hill La *HTON* BD9 .... 23 H2
Daisy Rd *BRIG* HD6 .... 52 C3
Daisy St *BRIG* HD6 .... 52 B1 ⁵
   GTHN BD7 .... 30 B4 ⁸
   HFAX HX1 .... 4 E5
Dalby Av *BFDE* BD3 .... 26 C3
Dalby St *BFDE* BD3 .... 26 B4 ⁷
Dalcross Gv *WBOW* BD5 .... 31 G3
Dalcross St *WBOW* BD5 .... 31 F3
Dale Croft Ri *WIL/AL* BD15 .... 22 D2
Dale Garth *BAIL* BD17 .... 12 C3
Dale Gv *SHPY* BD18 .... 13 F5 ⁵
Daleside Av *PDSY/CALV* LS28 .... 27 F4
Daleside Cl *PDSY/CALV* LS28 .... 27 E3 ⁶
Daleside Gv *LM/WK* BD12 .... 45 G1
   PDSY/CALV LS28.......... 27 F4
   BFDE BD3 .... 27 E3
   SHPY BD18 .... 13 F5
Daleside Wk *WBOW* BD5 .... 31 G5 ⁵
Daleson Cl *HIPP* HX3 .... 42 D2
Dale St *BFD* BD1 .... 2 D5
   KGHY BD21 .... 7 F2
   RPDN/SBR HX6 .... 46 A4
   SHPY BD18 .... 18 C2 ⁴
Dalesway *BGLY* BD16 .... 11 E1
Dales Way Link *BAIL* BD17 .... 11 H1
Dale View Cl *KGHY* BD21 .... 7 F5
Daleview Ct *BAIL* BD17 .... 12 B4
Dale View Gv *KGHY* BD21 .... 7 F5
Dallam Av *SHPY* BD18 .... 17 H1
Dallam Rd *SHPY* BD18 .... 17 H1
Dallam Wk *SHPY* BD18 .... 18 A1 ⁴
Dalton La *KGHY* BD21 .... 7 G4
Dalton Rd *KGHY* BD21 .... 7 G4
Dalton St *RPDN/SBR* HX6 .... 46 A3 ⁴
Dalton Ter *GIR* BD8 .... 24 C2 ²
Damask St *HFAX* HX1 .... 5 F2 ¹
Damems La *HWTH* BD22 .... 9 E4
Damems Rd *HWTH* BD22 .... 9 F4
Dames La *HWTH* BD22.......... 9 F4
Dam Head Rd *RPDN/SBR* HX6 .... 46 B3
Damside *KGHY* BD21 .... 6 C5
Danby Av *BOW* BD4 .... 39 E2 ⁸
Danebury Rd *BRIG* HD6.......... 52 C2
Danecourt La *BOW* BD4 .... 32 D4
Dane Hill Dr *BOW* BD4 .... 32 D4
Daniel Ct *BOW* BD4 .... 33 E5
Dan La *CUL/QBY* BD13 .... 29 F5
Danum Dr *BAIL* BD17 .... 12 D4
Darcey Hey La *LUD/ILL* HX2 .... 46 D3
Darfield St *GIR* BD8 .... 2 B3
Dark La *LUD/ILL* HX2 .... 46 A2
Darley St *BFD* BD1 .... 2 D5
   KGHY BD21 .... 6 C2
Darnes Av *LUD/ILL* HX2 .... 46 D3
Darren St *BOW* BD4 .... 32 D2 ⁵
Darryl Dr *LUD/ILL* HX2 .... 46 D3
Dartmouth Ter *GIR* BD8 .... 24 D2 ⁴
Darwin St *WBOW* BD5 .... 30 D4 ⁸
Dawnay Rd *WBOW* BD5 .... 30 D3
Dawson Av *WBSY* BD6 .... 37 H2
Dawson La *BOW* BD4 .... 39 F1
Dawson Mt *BOW* BD4 .... 39 F1
Dawson Pl *BOW* BD4 .... 39 F1
   KGHY BD21 .... 9 H1 ²
Dawson Rd *KGHY* BD21 .... 9 H1
Dawsons Meadow
   PDSY/CALV LS28 .... 27 H2
Dawson St *BOW* BD4 .... 32 B5 ⁵
   IDLE BD10 .... 14 A5 ⁷

Dawson Ter *BOW* BD4 .... 39 F1
Dawson Wy *KGHY* BD21 .... 9 H1
Dealburn Rd *LM/WK* BD12 .... 38 A5
Deal St *HFAX* HX1 .... 5 J5
   KGHY BD21 .... 7 F3
Dean Beck Av *WBSY* BD6 .... 38 B2
Dean Beck Ct *WBSY* BD6 .... 38 C2 ¹
Dean Cl *GIR* BD8 .... 23 G3
Dean Clough *HFAX* HX1 .... 5 G2
Deanery Gdns *IDLE* BD10 .... 20 B4 ²
Dean Rd *WBSY* BD6 .... 38 A2 ¹
Deanstones Crs *CUL/QBY* BD13 .... 35 F2
Deanstones La *CUL/QBY* BD13 .... 35 F2
Deanwood Av *WIL/AL* BD15 .... 22 D1 ¹
Deanwood Crs *WIL/AL* BD15 .... 22 D2
Deanwood Wk *WIL/AL* BD15 .... 22 D2 ¹
Dearden St *RPDN/SBR* HX6 .... 46 A3
Dee Ct *HWTH* BD22 .... 8 B4 ¹
Deepdale Cl *BAIL* BD17 .... 12 B4 ¹
Deep La *BRIG* HD6 .... 53 F1
   CLAY BD14 .... 29 F2
Defarge Ct *WBOW* BD5 .... 31 F4 ⁷
De Lacey Ms *BOW* BD4 .... 32 B5 ⁷
De Lacy Av *BOW* BD4 .... 39 E2 ⁸
Delamere St *WBOW* BD5.......... 31 E5
Delaware Ct *BOW* BD4 .... 39 E2
Delius Av *IDLE* BD10.......... 20 C4
Delph Crs *CLAY* BD14 .... 29 E3 ⁵
Delph Croft Vw *KGHY* BD21 .... 7 E5 ⁵
Delph Dr *CLAY* BD14.......... 28 D3
Delph Gv *CLAY* BD14 .... 29 E3
Delph Hl *BAIL* BD17 .... 12 D2 ⁵
Delph Hill Rd *LUD/ILL* HX2 .... 47 E4 ⁵
Delph St *HFAX* HX1 .... 5 F5
Delph Ter *CLAY* BD14 .... 29 E3 ⁷
Delph Wood Cl *BGLY* BD16 .... 11 F3
Delverne Gv *ECHL* BD2 .... 26 B1
Denbury Mt *BOW* BD4 .... 32 D5
Denby Ct *HWTH* BD22 .... 8 A4 ⁷
Denby Dr *BAIL* BD17 .... 12 C5
Denby Hill Rd *HWTH* BD22 .... 8 A4 ⁷
Denby La *WIL/AL* BD15 .... 23 E3
Denby Pl *RPDN/SBR* HX6 .... 46 A3
Denby Rd *KGHY* BD21 .... 6 C3 ⁷
Dence Gn *BOW* BD4 .... 32 D2 ⁷
Dene Crs *GTHN* BD7 .... 29 H3 ¹
Dene Hl *BAIL* BD17 .... 12 A3
Denehill *HTON* BD9 .... 23 G2
Dene Mt *WIL/AL* BD15 .... 23 F3 ⁵
Dene Pl *HFAX* HX1 .... 5 F2
Dene Rd *WBSY* BD6 .... 36 C1
Deneside Mt *WBOW* BD5 .... 37 H1
Deneside Ter *WBOW* BD5 .... 31 E5 ⁵
Deneway *PDSY/CALV* LS28 .... 27 H2
Denfield Av *HIPP* HX3 .... 40 D3
Denfield Crs *HIPP* HX3.......... 41 E3
Denfield Edge *HIPP* HX3 .... 41 E3 ⁵
Denfield Gdns *HIPP* HX3 .... 41 E3 ⁵
Denfield La *HIPP* HX3 .... 40 D3
Denfield Sq *HIPP* HX3 .... 41 E3
Denham St *BRIG* HD6 .... 52 B2 ¹
Denholme Gate Rd *HIPP* HX3 .... 43 F4
Dennison Fold *BOW* BD4 .... 32 D3 ¹
Denton Dr *BGLY* BD16 .... 11 F2
Derby Rd *BFDE* BD3.......... 26 D5
   YEA LS19 .... 15 G2
Derby St *CLAY* BD14 .... 29 E3 ⁶
   CUL/QBY BD13 .... 35 E1 ⁴
   GTHN BD7 .... 30 C3
   RPDN/SBR HX6 .... 46 B3
Derwent Rd *ECHL* BD2 .... 25 H1
Devonshire St *KGHY* BD21 .... 6 C4
Devonshire St West *KGHY* BD21 .... 6 B4
Devonshire Ter *GIR* BD8 .... 24 D2 ³
Devon St *HFAX* HX1 .... 4 A6
Devon Wy *BRIG* HD6 .... 50 C2
Dewhirst Cl *BAIL* BD17 .... 13 E4
Dewhirst Pl *BOW* BD4 .... 32 C1 ¹
Dewhirst Rd *BAIL* BD17 .... 13 E4
   BRIG HD6 .... 50 B4
Diamond St *BFD* BD1.......... 2 E6
   HFAX HX1 .... 4 C2
   HWTH BD22 .... 9 F2 ⁷
Diamond Ter *HFAX* HX1 .... 4 C1
Dicken's St *LUD/ILL* HX2 .... 46 D1
Dickens St *WBOW* BD5 .... 31 F4
Dick La *BFDE* BD3 .... 27 E4
   BOW BD4 .... 32 D2
Dirkhill Rd *GTHN* BD7 .... 30 C3
Dirkhill St *GTHN* BD7 .... 30 C2 ¹
Discovery Rd *HFAX* HX1 .... 5 J4
Dispensary Wk *HFAX* HX1 .... 5 J4
Dixon Av *GTHN* BD7 .... 30 A2
Dockfield Pl *BAIL* BD17 .... 12 D5
Dockfield Rd *BAIL* BD17 .... 18 D1
Dockfield Ter *BAIL* BD17 .... 12 D5
Dock La *BAIL* BD17 .... 18 D1 ⁷

Dockroyd La *HWTH* BD22 .... 8 B4
Doctor Hl *IDLE* BD10 .... 19 H3
   LUD/ILL HX2 .... 40 C4
Doctor La *IDLE* BD10 .... 14 A5
Dodgeholme Cl *LUD/ILL* HX2 .... 40 C1 ⁵
Dodge Holme Gdns *LUD/ILL* HX2.......... 40 C1
Dodge Holme Rd *LUD/ILL* HX2.......... 40 C1
Dog Kennel La *HIPP* HX3 .... 48 B3
Dole St *CUL/QBY* BD13 .... 28 B1
Dombey St *HFAX* HX1 .... 4 D4
Donald Av *WBSY* BD6 .... 37 H2
Doncaster St *HIPP* HX3 .... 48 A5 ⁵
Donisthorpe St *WBOW* BD5 .... 31 F4 ⁵
   WBOW BD5 .... 31 E4 ⁵
Don St *KGHY* BD21 .... 6 C3 ⁷
Dorchester Ct *BOW* BD4 .... 32 D4 ⁵
Dorchester Crs *BAIL* BD17 .... 13 G2
   BOW BD4 .... 32 D4
Dorchester Dr *LUD/ILL* HX2 .... 46 D3
Dorian Cl *IDLE* BD10 .... 20 C5 ¹
Dorothy St *KGHY* BD21 .... 9 F3
Dorset Cl *WBOW* BD5 .... 30 D4 ⁸
Dorset St *WBOW* BD5 .... 31 E4
Douglas Crs *SHPY* BD18 .... 19 E3
Douglas Dr *BOW* BD4 .... 32 B3 ⁸
Douglas Rd *BOW* BD4 .... 32 B3
Douglas St *HIPP* HX3 .... 41 G3 ⁵
Dovedale Cl *HIPP* HX3 .... 36 A4
Dover St *BFDE* BD3 .... 3 F1
Dovesdale Gv *WBOW* BD5 .... 30 D5
Dovesdale Rd *WBOW* BD5 .... 31 E5
Dove St *SHPY* BD18 .... 18 A1 ⁶
Dowker St *HFAX* HX1 .... 4 B4
Dowley Gap La *BGLY* BD16 .... 11 E5
Downham St *BFDE* BD3 .... 3 H6
Downing Cl *BFDE* BD3 .... 3 J4
Downside Crs *WIL/AL* BD15 .... 22 D3
Drake St *KGHY* BD21 .... 7 F3
Draughton Gv *WBOW* BD5 .... 38 A1 ¹
Draughton St *WBOW* BD5 .... 38 A1 ¹
Drewry Rd *KGHY* BD21 .... 6 C4
Drewton Rd *BFD* BD1 .... 2 B4
Drill Pde *GIR* BD8 .... 2 A1
Drill St *KGHY* BD21 .... 6 C5
The Drive *HIPP* HX3 .... 43 G5
   IDLE BD10 .... 20 C5 ³
Drovers Wy *ECHL* BD2 .... 25 F1
Druids St *CLAY* BD14 .... 29 E3
Drummond Rd *GIR* BD8 .... 24 D3
Dryclough Cl *HIPP* HX3 .... 47 H5
Dryclough La *HIPP* HX3.......... 47 H5
Dryden St *BFD* BD1 .... 3 F7
   BGLY BD16 .... 10 C3 ⁵
Dubb La *BGLY* BD16 .... 10 D3
Duchy Av *HTON* BD9 .... 23 H1
Duchy Crs *HTON* BD9 .... 23 H1
Duchy Dr *HTON* BD9 .... 23 H1
Duchy Gv *HTON* BD9 .... 23 H1
Duchy Vls *HTON* BD9 .... 23 H1 ¹
Duchywood *HTON* BD9 .... 23 H1 ¹
Ducie St *IDLE* BD10 .... 14 A5
Duckett Gv *PDSY/CALV* LS28.......... 27 E4
Duckworth Gv *HTON* BD9 .... 24 A2
Duckworth La *HTON* BD9 .... 23 H3
Duckworth Ter *HTON* BD9 .... 24 A2
Dudley Gv *BOW* BD4 .... 32 D2 ⁴
Dudley Hill Rd *ECHL* BD2 .... 26 A1
Dudley St *BOW* BD4 .... 32 B5
   BOW BD4 .... 32 D2
   BOW BD4 .... 32 B4 ⁸
Duich Rd *WBSY* BD6 .... 36 C1
Duinen St *WBOW* BD5 .... 31 G2 ³
Duke St *BFD* BD1 .... 2 D4
   KGHY BD21 .... 7 E5 ⁵
Dulverton Gv *BOW* BD4 .... 32 C4
Dunbar Cft *CUL/QBY* BD13 .... 35 G1 ⁸
Duncan St *WBOW* BD5 .... 31 F2 ⁵
Duncombe Rd *GIR* BD8 .... 24 A5
Duncombe St *GIR* BD8 .... 24 B5
Duncombe Wy *GTHN* BD7 .... 24 B5
Dundas St *HFAX* HX1 .... 4 B7
   KGHY BD21 .... 7 E5 ⁵
Dunkhill Cft *IDLE* BD10 .... 20 A2 ⁵
Dunkirk Crs *HFAX* HX1 .... 46 D2 ⁵
Dunkirk La *HFAX* HX1.......... 46 D3
Dunkirk Ri *AIRE* BD20 .... 7 F1
Dunkirk St *HFAX* HX1 .... 46 D2
Dunkirk Ter *HFAX* HX1 .... 4 A6
Dunlin Wy *GIR* BD8 .... 23 F5 ⁵
Dunnington Wk *LM/WK* BD12 .... 37 H4 ⁵
Dunsford Av *BOW* BD4 .... 39 E2
Durham Rd *GIR* BD8 .... 24 B3
Durham St *HFAX* HX1 .... 46 D1 ⁵
Durham Ter *GIR* BD8 .... 24 B3
Durley Av *HTON* BD9 .... 24 A1
Durling Dr *SHPY* BD18 .... 19 F2 ¹

Durliston Gv *LM/WK* BD12 .... 45 E1
Durliston Ter *LM/WK* BD12 .... 45 E1
Durrance St *HWTH* BD22 .... 6 A5 ²
Dyehouse La *BRIG* HD6.......... 52 D2
Dyehouse Rd *LM/WK* BD12 .... 38 C5
Dyer La *HIPP* HX3 .... 41 E4
Dyson Pl *HIPP* HX3 .... 48 A5 ⁵
Dyson Rd *HFAX* HX1.......... 5 F5
Dyson St *BFD* BD1 .... 2 A4
   BRIG HD6 .... 50 B5
   HTON BD9 .... 18 B5 ²

E

Eaglesfield Dr *WBSY* BD6 .... 37 E4
Eagle St *KGHY* BD21.......... 6 C4
Earl St *KGHY* BD21 .... 6 C3 ⁵
Earl Ter *HIPP* HX3 .... 41 F3 ⁵
Easby Rd *WBOW* BD5 .... 31 E2
East Av *KGHY* BD21 .... 6 D3
Eastbourne Rd *HTON* BD9 .... 18 C4 ¹⁰
Eastbury Av *WBSY* BD6.......... 36 C1
Eastfield Gdns *BOW* BD4 .... 32 D4 ⁴
Easthorpe Ct *ECHL* BD2 .... 20 C5
Eastleigh Gv *WBOW* BD5 .... 31 E4
East Mt *BRIG* HD6 .... 50 B5
East Pde *BAIL* BD17 .... 13 E2
   BFDE BD3 .... 3 F4
   KGHY BD21 .... 6 D4
   RPDN/SBR HX6 .... 46 C3
East Park Rd *HIPP* HX3 .... 41 F4 ⁵
East Rd *LM/WK* BD12 .... 38 A4
East Royd *HWTH* BD22 .... 8 C4 ²
East Squire La *GIR* BD8 .... 24 D2
East St *BRIG* HD6 .... 52 B2
   HIPP HX3 .... 50 B1
East Vw *CLECK* BD19 .... 51 H2
   WBSY BD6 .... 29 F5 ²
East View Ter *LM/WK* BD12 .... 45 E1
Eastwood St *BOW* BD4 .... 31 G2 ⁴
   BRIG HD6 .... 50 C5 ²
   HIPP HX3 .... 41 F3 ⁷
Eaton St *KGHY* BD21 .... 9 F2 ²
Ebenezer Pl *GTHN* BD7 .... 30 C3 ³
Ebenezer St *BFD* BD1 .... 2 E6
Eccles Ct *ECHL* BD2 .... 20 A5
Edale Gv *CUL/QBY* BD13 .... 34 C3
Edderthorpe St *BFDE* BD3 .... 3 H6
Eden Cl *LM/WK* BD12 .... 45 E2
Edensor Rd *KGHY* BD21 .... 6 B4
Ederoyd Av *PDSY/CALV* LS28 .... 27 G3
Ederoyd Crs *PDSY/CALV* LS28 .... 27 G3
Ederoyd Dr *PDSY/CALV* LS28 .... 27 G3
Ederoyd Gv *PDSY/CALV* LS28 .... 27 F3
Ederoyd Mt *PDSY/CALV* LS28 .... 27 F3
Ederoyd Ri *PDSY/CALV* LS28.......... 27 F3
Edgar St *CLAY* BD14 .... 29 G3
Edgebank Av *WBSY* BD6 .... 37 E4
Edge End Gdns *WBSY* BD6 .... 36 D3
Edge End Rd *WBSY* BD6 .... 36 D3
Edgehill Cl *CUL/QBY* BD13 .... 35 G1 ⁸
Edgeholme La *LUD/ILL* HX2 .... 46 A1
Edgemoor Cl *BOW* BD4 .... 39 H2
   HIPP HX3 .... 47 G4 ²
Edlington Cl *BOW* BD4 .... 32 D4 ⁷
Edmund St *GTHN* BD7 .... 2 B7
Edrich Cl *LM/WK* BD12 .... 38 B4
Edward Cl *HIPP* HX3 .... 48 C4 ⁵
Edwards Rd *LUD/ILL* HX2 .... 46 D3
Edward St *BOW* BD4 .... 2 E7
   BOW BD4 .... 39 F1
   BRIG HD6 .... 50 B5
   BRIG HD6 .... 52 B1
   RPDN/SBR HX6 .... 46 B3
   SHPY BD18 .... 12 A5 ²
Edward Turner Cl
   LM/WK BD12 .... 37 H4 ⁵
Eel Holme View St *KGHY* BD21 .... 6 C1 ⁸
Egerton Gv *WIL/AL* BD15 .... 22 C3
Egerton St *RPDN/SBR* HX6 .... 46 A4 ²
Eggleston Dr *BOW* BD4 .... 33 E5
Egremont Crs *WBSY* BD6 .... 37 E4
Elbow La *ECHL* BD2 .... 26 A2 ¹
Elder St *AIRE* BD20 .... 6 B1
   IDLE BD10 .... 20 D2
Elderwood Gdns *IDLE* BD10 .... 20 D4
Eldon Pl *BFD* BD1 .... 2 B3
Eldon St *HIPP* HX3 .... 5 H1
Eldroth Mt *HFAX* HX1 .... 47 F3 ⁵
Eldroth Rd *HFAX* HX1.......... 47 F3
Eleanor Dr *PDSY/CALV* LS28 .... 21 E2
Eleanor St *BRIG* HD6 .... 52 B2
Elia St *KGHY* BD21 .... 7 E3
Eli St *WBOW* BD5 .... 31 G4 ⁴
Elizabeth Av *LM/WK* BD12 .... 44 D1
Elizabeth Cl *LM/WK* BD12 .... 45 E1 ⁵

Elizabeth Crs *LM/WK* BD12...... 45 E1
Elizabeth Dr *LM/WK* BD12 ...... 45 E1
Elizabeth St *BGLY* BD16 ...... 10 D3
LM/WK BD12 ...... 45 E1
WBOW BD5 ...... 31 F2
Elland Rd *BRIG* HD6 ...... 52 B1
Ellar Carr Rd *IDLE* BD10...... 14 B4
Ellen Royd St *HIPP* HX3...... 1 F5
Ellen St *BGLY* BD16 ...... 10 D3
Ellenthorpe St *BOW* BD4 ...... 32 A2
Ellenthorpe St *BAIL* BD17 ...... 11 H4
Ellercroft Av *GTHN* BD7...... 30 B1
Ellercroft Rd *GTHN* BD7...... 30 B1
Ellercroft Ter *GTHN* BD7 ...... 30 B1
Ellerton St *BFDE* BD3...... 26 B5
Ellinthorpe St *BOW* BD4 ...... 32 A2
Elliott St *SHPY* BD18 ...... 18 B1
Ellis St *WBOW* BD5 ...... 31 G4
Ellton Gv *WBSY* BD6 ...... 37 F1
Elm Av *RPDN/SBR* HX6 ...... 46 A3
Elmfield *BAIL* BD17 ...... 13 E2
Elmfield Dr *WBSY* BD6...... 37 H2
Elmfield Ter *HFAX* HX1 ...... 47 G3
Elm Gv *HIPP* HX3 ...... 36 C4
HWTH BD22 ...... 9 F2
SHPY BD18 ...... 19 F2
Elm Pl *RPDN/SBR* HX6 ...... 46 A3
Elm Rd *SHPY* BD18 ...... 19 E2
Elmsall St *GIR* BD8 ...... 2 B2
Elm Tree Av *WBSY* BD6 ...... 37 H2
Elm Tree Cl *KGHY* BD21 ...... 7 E5
WBSY BD6 ...... 38 A2
Elm Tree Gdns *WBSY* BD6 ...... 37 H2
Elmwood Dr *BRIG* HD6...... 50 A5
HWTH BD22 ...... 9 E2
Elmwood Rd *HWTH* BD22...... 9 E3
Elm Wood St *BRIG* HD6 ...... 50 C4
Elmwood St *HFAX* HX1 ...... 47 F3
Elmwood Ter *HWTH* BD22 ...... 9 E2
Elsdon Gv *WBOW* BD5 ...... 31 F2
Elsie St *KGHY* BD21 ...... 6 C1
Elsworth Av *BFDE* BD3 ...... 26 C3
Eltham Gv *WBSY* BD6 ...... 37 F2
Elvey Cl *ECHL* BD2 ...... 20 C5
Elwell Cl *WBSY* BD6 ...... 36 C3
Elwyn Gv *WBOW* BD5 ...... 31 F4
Elwyn Rd *WBOW* BD5 ...... 31 G4
Emerald St *HWTH* BD22 ...... 9 F2
Emerson Av *HTON* BD9 ...... 23 G1
Emily St *KGHY* BD21 ...... 6 D3
Emmeline Cl *IDLE* BD10 ...... 20 A1
Emmfield Dr *HTON* BD9 ...... 18 B5
Emm La *HTON* BD9...... 24 B1
Emscote Av *HFAX* HX1 ...... 4 D7
Emscote Gdns *HFAX* HX1 ...... 4 D7
HFAX HX1 ...... 47 F3
Emscote Gv *HFAX* HX1...... 4 D7
Emscote Pl *HFAX* HX1 ...... 4 D7
Emscote St South *HFAX* HX1 ...... 4 D7
Emsley Cl *BOW* BD4 ...... 39 E2
Enderby Cl *HIPP* HX3 ...... 41 E2
Endsleigh Pl *CLAY* BD14...... 29 E3
Enfield Dr *GTHN* BD7 ...... 37 E1
WBSY BD6 ...... 37 F1
Enfield Pde *WBSY* BD6 ...... 37 F1
Enfield Rd *BAIL* BD17 ...... 12 D4
Enfield St *KGHY* BD21 ...... 6 C4
Enfield Wk *WBSY* BD6 ...... 37 F1
Englefield Cl *BOW* BD4 ...... 32 D5
Englefield Gv *BOW* BD4 ...... 32 D5
Ennerdale Dr *ECHL* BD2 ...... 26 A1
Ennerdale Rd *ECHL* BD2 ...... 25 H1
Enterprise Wy *IDLE* BD10 ...... 20 A3
Epworth Pl *HWTH* BD22 ...... 8 A3
Eric St *KGHY* BD21 ...... 6 D3
Escroft Cl *LM/WK* BD12...... 45 E4
Esholt La *BAIL* BD17 ...... 13 H2
Eshton Av *LM/WK* BD12 ...... 38 C5
Eskdale Av *HIPP* HX3 ...... 36 A5
Eskdale Ri *WIL/AL* BD15 ...... 23 C4
Eskine Pde *WBSY* BD6...... 37 E4
Esmond St *GTHN* BD7 ...... 30 A4
Essex St *BFDE* BD3...... 3 H7
BOW BD4 ...... 31 H2
HFAX HX1 ...... 4 A5
Estcourt Gv *GTHN* BD7 ...... 30 B2
Estcourt Rd *GTHN* BD7 ...... 30 B2
Ethel St *KGHY* BD21 ...... 6 C2
Etna St *GTHN* BD7 ...... 30 A4
Eton St *HFAX* HX1 ...... 4 B4
Evelyn Av *BFDE* BD3 ...... 26 D4
Evens Ter *WBOW* BD5 ...... 31 F5
Everest Av *SHPY* BD18...... 19 F2
Eversley Dr *BOW* BD4 ...... 32 D3
Eversley Pl *LUD/ILL* HX2 ...... 46 D2
Evesham Gv *IDLE* BD10 ...... 20 A2
Ewart Pl *GTHN* BD7 ...... 30 B4
Ewart St *CUL/QBY* BD13 ...... 35 F1

GTHN BD7 ...... 30 B4
Exe St *WBOW* BD5 ...... 30 D4
Exeter St *HIPP* HX3 ...... 48 A5
RPDN/SBR HX6 ...... 46 B4
Exhibition Rd *SHPY* BD18...... 18 A1
Exley Av *KGHY* BD21 ...... 9 F1
Exley Crs *KGHY* BD21 ...... 9 F1
Exley Dr *KGHY* BD21 ...... 9 F1
Exley Gv *KGHY* BD21 ...... 9 F2
Exley Mt *GTHN* BD7 ...... 30 A1
KGHY BD21 ...... 9 F1
Exley Rd *KGHY* BD21 ...... 9 F1
Exley St *KGHY* BD21 ...... 6 B5
Exley Wy *KGHY* BD21 ...... 9 F2
Exmoor St *HFAX* HX1 ...... 4 A6
Exmouth Pl *BFDE* BD3...... 25 G3

F

Factory La *BOW* BD4 ...... 32 A5
Factory St *BOW* BD4 ...... 32 A5
Fagley Crs *ECHL* BD2 ...... 26 B2
Fagley Cft *ECHL* BD2 ...... 26 C2
Fagley Dr *ECHL* BD2 ...... 26 B2
Fagley La *ECHL* BD2 ...... 26 C1
Fagley Pl *ECHL* BD2 ...... 26 C2
Fagley Rd *ECHL* BD2...... 26 D2
Fagley Ter *BFDE* BD3 ...... 26 B3
Fair Bank *SHPY* BD18...... 18 D3
Fairbank Rd *GIR* BD8...... 24 B3
Fairbank Ter *GIR* BD8 ...... 24 B3
Fairburn Gdns *ECHL* BD2 ...... 26 C1
Fairclough Gv *LUD/ILL* HX2 ...... 41 E2
Fairfax Av *BOW* BD4 ...... 39 F1
Fairfax Crs *BOW* BD4...... 39 F1
HIPP HX3 ...... 48 D3
Fairfax Rd *BGLY* BD16 ...... 10 C1
Fairfax St *BOW* BD4 ...... 31 G2
Fairfield Dr *BAIL* BD17 ...... 13 F2
Fairfield Rd *GIR* BD8 ...... 24 C3
LM/WK BD12 ...... 45 E2
Fairfield St *BOW* BD4...... 39 G1
Fairhaven Gn *IDLE* BD10 ...... 20 B2
Fairless Av *HIPP* HX3 ...... 50 B1
Fairmount *HTON* BD9 ...... 24 D2
Fairmount Pk *SHPY* BD18 ...... 17 H2
Fairmount Ter *KGHY* BD21 ...... 7 G5
Fair Rd *WBSY* BD6 ...... 37 F1
Fairview Ct *BAIL* BD17...... 12 C5
Fairview Ter *HIPP* HX3 ...... 41 F4
Fairway *IDLE* BD10 ...... 15 E5
SHPY BD18 ...... 18 A2
WBSY BD6 ...... 37 E1
Fairway Av *GTHN* BD7 ...... 37 E1
Fairway Cl *WBSY* BD6 ...... 37 E1
Fairway Dr *GTHN* BD7 ...... 30 A5
Fairway Gv *GTHN* BD7 ...... 30 A5
The Fairways *HIPP* HX3 ...... 17 H4
The Fairway *LUD/ILL* HX2 ...... 34 A3
PDSY/CALV LS28 ...... 27 G3
Fairway Wk *GTHN* BD7 ...... 30 A5
Fairweather Ms *GIR* BD8 ...... 23 H5
Fairy Dell *BGLY* BD16 ...... 16 D2
Falcon Ms *GIR* BD8 ...... 23 H4
Falcon Rd *BGLY* BD16 ...... 10 C1
Falcon St *GTHN* BD7 ...... 30 B2
HIPP HX3 ...... 48 A5
Falkland Rd *IDLE* BD10 ...... 20 D5
Fall Brow Cl *CLAY* BD14...... 28 C4
Fall La *HIPP* HX3 ...... 42 B1
RPDN/SBR HX6 ...... 46 C5
Fallowfield Cl *BOW* BD4 ...... 39 F2
Fallowfield Dr *BOW* BD4 ...... 39 F1
Fallowfield Gdns *BOW* BD4 ...... 39 F1
Falmouth Av *BFDE* BD3...... 3 F1
Falsgrave Av *ECHL* BD2 ...... 26 C2
Faltis *IDLE* BD10 ...... 20 B4
Fanny St *KGHY* BD21 ...... 6 C5
SHPY BD18 ...... 12 A5
Farcliffe Pl *GIR* BD8 ...... 24 C3
Farcliffe Rd *GIR* BD8 ...... 24 C3
Farcliffe Ter *GIR* BD8 ...... 24 C3
Farfield Av *PDSY/CALV* LS28 ...... 27 H2
WBSY BD6 ...... 36 D3
Farfield Crs *WBSY* BD6 ...... 37 E3
Farfield Dr *PDSY/CALV* LS28 ...... 27 H1
Farfield Gv *PDSY/CALV* LS28 ...... 27 H1
WBSY BD6 ...... 37 E3
Farfield Ri *PDSY/CALV* LS28 ...... 27 H1
Farfield Rd *BAIL* BD17 ...... 13 E4
SHPY BD18 ...... 18 B2
WBSY BD6 ...... 37 E3
Farfield St *HTON* BD9 ...... 24 B2
Farfield Ter *HTON* BD9 ...... 24 B2
Farlea Dr *ECHL* BD2 ...... 26 B1
Farleton Dr *ECHL* BD2 ...... 26 C2

Farley Crs *HWTH* BD22 ...... 8 A3
Farm Hill Rd *IDLE* BD10 ...... 20 A4
Farm Pond Dr *BRIG* HD6 ...... 49 H3
Farmstead Rd *BAIL* BD10 ...... 20 B3
Farndale Rd *BAIL* BD17 ...... 12 B4
Farnham Cl *BAIL* BD17 ...... 13 E2
Farnham Rd *GTHN* BD7...... 30 B2
Farrar Mill La *HIPP* HX3 ...... 48 A5
Farriers Cft *ECHL* BD2 ...... 19 G5
Farringdon Cl *BOW* BD4 ...... 32 D3
Farringdon Dr *BOW* BD4 ...... 32 D4
Farringdon Gv *WBSY* BD6...... 37 F3
Farside Gn *WBOW* BD5 ...... 30 D4
Farway *BOW* BD4...... 32 B3
Faversham Wk *BOW* BD4 ...... 32 D3
Fawcett Pl *BOW* BD4...... 39 F2
Faxfleet St *WBOW* BD5 ...... 38 A1
Faye Gdns *BOW* BD4 ...... 39 G1
Fearnsides St *GIR* BD8 ...... 24 C4
Fearnsides Ter *GIR* BD8 ...... 24 C4
Fearnville Dr *BOW* BD4 ...... 32 C2
Feather Rd *BFDE* BD3 ...... 3 J4
Federation St *WBOW* BD5 ...... 31 G5
Felbrigg Av *HWTH* BD22 ...... 6 A5
Felcourt Dr *BOW* BD4 ...... 32 D5
Felcourt Fold *BOW* BD4 ...... 32 D5
Fell Crs *HWTH* BD22 ...... 8 D1
Fell Gv *HWTH* BD22 ...... 6 A5
Fellside Cl *WBOW* BD5 ...... 31 G5
Fenby Av *BOW* BD4 ...... 32 A3
Fenby Cl *BOW* BD4 ...... 32 B4
Fenby Gdns *BOW* BD4 ...... 32 B4
Fenby Gv *BOW* BD4 ...... 32 B3
Fencote Crs *ECHL* BD2 ...... 26 C1
Fender Rd *WBSY* BD6 ...... 37 E1
Fennec Rd *BAIL* BD17 ...... 13 F2
Fenton Rd *HFAX* HX1 ...... 4 A7
Fenwick Dr *WBSY* BD6 ...... 37 E4
Fernbank Av *HWTH* BD22 ...... 9 E2
Fernbank Dr *BAIL* BD17...... 12 B5
BGLY BD16 ...... 10 D3
Fernbank Rd *BFDE* BD3 ...... 3 J1
Ferncliffe Dr *AIRE* BD20 ...... 6 A1
BAIL BD17 ...... 12 C3
Ferncliffe Rd *BGLY* BD16...... 10 D3
SHPY BD18 ...... 18 A1
Fern Ct *AIRE* BD20 ...... 6 B1
Ferndale Av *CLAY* BD14...... 28 C4
Ferndale Gv *HTON* BD9 ...... 18 D5
Ferndene *BGLY* BD16...... 11 E3
Ferndown Gn *WBOW* BD5 ...... 31 E4
Fernhill *BGLY* BD16 ...... 10 D1
Fern Hill Av *SHPY* BD18 ...... 18 A2
Fern Hill Gv *SHPY* BD18 ...... 18 A2
Fern Hill Mt *SHPY* BD18 ...... 18 A2
Fern Hill Rd *SHPY* BD18 ...... 18 A2
Fern Lea St *RPDN/SBR* HX6 ...... 46 A3
Fernley Gdns *LM/WK* BD12 ...... 44 D1
Fern St *BOW* BD4 ...... 32 C4
HIPP HX3 ...... 41 G3
KGHY BD21 ...... 6 D3
Ferrand Av *BOW* BD4 ...... 39 F1
Ferrand La *BGLY* BD16 ...... 10 C3
Ferrand St *BGLY* BD16 ...... 10 D3
Ferriby Cl *ECHL* BD2 ...... 26 C1
Festival Av *SHPY* BD18 ...... 19 E3
Fieldedge La *AIRE* BD20 ...... 7 H1
Fieldgate Rd *IDLE* BD10 ...... 20 C2
Fieldhead St *GTHN* BD7 ...... 24 D5
Fieldhouse Gv
PDSY/CALV LS28 ...... 27 H2
Field Hurst *CLECK* BD19 ...... 51 G1
Fieldhurst Ct *BOW* BD4 ...... 39 E2
Field La *BRIG* HD6...... 52 A3
Field Side *HFAX* HX1...... 4 A1
Fields Rd *LM/WK* BD12...... 38 B5
Field St *BFD* BD1 ...... 2 E5
Field Top Rd *BRIG* HD6 ...... 52 A3
Fieldway *CLAY* BD14 ...... 29 E3
Fifth Av *BFDE* BD3 ...... 26 B3
Filey St *BFD* BD1...... 3 F6
BFDE BD3 ...... 3 F6
Finchley St *WBOW* BD5 ...... 31 E4
Finch St *WBOW* BD5 ...... 31 E3
Findon Ter *IDLE* BD10 ...... 20 D5
Finkil St *BRIG* HD6 ...... 49 H3
Finsbury Dr *ECHL* BD2 ...... 19 G4
Firbank Gn *ECHL* BD2 ...... 26 C1
Firethorn Cl *GIR* BD8 ...... 24 B4
First Av *BFDE* BD3 ...... 26 B3
HIPP HX3 ...... 48 A5
KGHY BD21 ...... 6 C5
YEA LS19 ...... 15 H1
Fir St *KGHY* BD21 ...... 9 G2
First St *LM/WK* BD12 ...... 38 B4
Firth Av *BRIG* HD6 ...... 50 B5
Firth House La *BRIG* HD6 ...... 52 C4

Firth Rd *HTON* BD9 ...... 24 B1
Firth St *BRIG* HD6...... 52 E
CUL/QBY BD13...... 28 A
Fir Tree Gdns *IDLE* BD10 ...... 20 C3
Fitzgerald St *WBOW* BD5 ...... 31 F2
Fitzroy Rd *BFDE* BD3...... 3 K
Fitzwilliam St *BOW* BD4 ...... 31 C
Five Oaks *BAIL* BD17 ...... 12 E
Fixby Av *LUD/ILL* HX2 ...... 46 D
Flasby St *KGHY* BD21 ...... 6 D
Flat Nook *BGLY* BD16 ...... 11 E3
Flawith Dr *ECHL* BD2 ...... 26 C
Flaxen St *WBSY* BD6 ...... 38 A1
Flaxton Gn *ECHL* BD2 ...... 26 C
Flaxton Pl *GTHN* BD7...... 30 C
Fleece St *WBSY* BD6 ...... 37 E
Fleet La *CUL/QBY* BD13 ...... 35 E
Fletcher La *SHPY* BD18 ...... 19 E
Fletcher Rd *WBSY* BD6 ...... 37 G1
Fletton Ter *ECHL* BD2 ...... 26 A2
Flinton Gv *ECHL* BD2 ...... 26 C
Flockton Av *BOW* BD4 ...... 31 H3
Flockton Cl *BOW* BD4 ...... 31 H3
Flockton Crs *BOW* BD4 ...... 31 H
Flockton Dr *BOW* BD4 ...... 31 H
Flockton Gv *BOW* BD4 ...... 31 H
Flockton Rd *BOW* BD4 ...... 31 H
Florence St *BFDE* BD3 ...... 32 E
HFAX HX1 ...... 4 D
Florida Rd *WIL/AL* BD15 ...... 16 D
Florist St *KGHY* BD21 ...... 7 F
Flower Bank *ECHL* BD2 ...... 19 G5
Flower Cft *HWTH* BD22 ...... 9 E
Flower Garth *IDLE* BD10 ...... 20 C
Flower Hvn *HTON* BD9 ...... 17 G5
Flower Hl *HTON* BD9 ...... 18 A
Flowerlands *HIPP* HX3 ...... 43 H
Floyd St *WBOW* BD5 ...... 30 C
Foldings Av *CLECK* BD19 ...... 45 C
Foldings Cl *CLECK* BD19 ...... 45 C
Foldings Ct *CLECK* BD19 ...... 45 F5
Foldings Gv *CLECK* BD19 ...... 45 F
Foldings Pde *CLECK* BD19...... 45 F
Foldings Rd *CLECK* BD19 ...... 45 F
Folkestone St *BFDE* BD3 ...... 3 K4
Folkton Holme *ECHL* BD2 ...... 26 C
Folly Hall Av *WBSY* BD6...... 37 F
The Folly Hall Gdns *WBSY* BD6 .. 37 G2
Folly Hall Wk *WBSY* BD6 ...... 37 G2
Fontmell Cl *BOW* BD4 ...... 32 D5
Forber Gv *BOW* BD4 ...... 32 D2
Ford *CUL/QBY* BD13...... 34 D
Ford Hl *CUL/QBY* BD13 ...... 34 D
Ford St *KGHY* BD21 ...... 7 F
Forest Av *LUD/ILL* HX2 ...... 40 D
Forest Crs *LUD/ILL* HX2 ...... 40 D
Forest Gn *LUD/ILL* HX2 ...... 40 D
Forster Ct *BFDE* BD1 ...... 2 D
Forster Sq *BFD* BD1 ...... 2 E
Foster Av *CUL/QBY* BD13 ...... 28 C
Foster Rd *KGHY* BD21 ...... 9 G
Foster St *CUL/QBY* BD13 ...... 35 E
Foston Cl *ECHL* BD2 ...... 26 D
Foston La *ECHL* BD2 ...... 26 C
Foulds' Ter *BGLY* BD16 ...... 10 D2
Foundry Hl *BGLY* BD16 ...... 10 C3
Foundry La *BOW* BD4 ...... 32 A
Foundry St *BRIG* HD6 ...... 52 D
HFAX HX1 ...... 5 H
RPDN/SBR HX6 ...... 46 A3
Foundry St North *LUD/ILL* HX2 ...... 41 E
Fountain St *CUL/QBY* BD13 ...... 28 A1
CUL/QBY BD13 ...... 35 F1
HFAX HX1 ...... 5 G
LM/WK BD12 ...... 37 H4
Fountain Ter *LM/WK* BD12 ...... 45 E
Fountain Wy *SHPY* BD18 ...... 18 D2
Fourlands Ct *IDLE* BD10 ...... 20 B1
Fourlands Crs *IDLE* BD10 ...... 20 B1
Fourlands Dr *IDLE* BD10 ...... 20 B
Fourlands Gdns *IDLE* BD10 ...... 20 B1
Fourlands Gv *IDLE* BD10 ...... 20 B1
Fourlands Rd *IDLE* BD10 ...... 20 B
Fourth Av *BFDE* BD3 ...... 26 B
KGHY BD21 ...... 6 B5
Fourth St *LM/WK* BD12...... 38 B
Fowler St *BOW* BD4 ...... 32 A2
Foxcroft Cl *CUL/QBY* BD13 ...... 34 D3
Foxcroft Dr *BRIG* HD6 ...... 52 A
Foxhill *BAIL* BD17 ...... 12 B
Foxhill Av *CUL/QBY* BD13 ...... 35 E
Foxhill Cl *CUL/QBY* BD13 ...... 35 E
Foxhill Dr *CUL/QBY* BD13 ...... 35 E
Foxhill Gv *CUL/QBY* BD13 ...... 35 E
Foxhole La *PDSY/CALV* LS28 ...... 21 C
Foxholes Crs *PDSY/CALV* LS28 ...... 21 C
Foxstone Ri *BAIL* BD17 ...... 13 E
Fox St *BGLY* BD16 ...... 10 C3

WBOW BD5 .... 30 D4 10
Frances St BRIG HD6 .... 50 B5 8
KGHY BD21 .... 6 B3 8
Francis St BFDE BD3 .... 31 H2 9
HFAX HX1 .... 4 D5
Franklin St HFAX HX1 .... 4 B4
Frank Pl GTHN BD7 .... 30 C3
Frank St GTHN BD7 .... 30 C3 4
HFAX HX1 .... 4 C5
Fraser Rd PDSY/CALV LS28 .... 21 E3
Fraser St GIR BD8 .... 24 D4 8
Frederick Cl IDLE BD10 .... 13 C5 2
Frederick St BFD BD1 .... 3 F6
KGHY BD21 .... 7 E4
PDSY/CALV LS28 .... 27 H1 8
Fred's Pl BOW BD4 .... 32 B4
Fred St KGHY BD21 .... 6 C5 12
Freeman St HIPP HX3 .... 48 D3
Free School La HFAX HX1 .... 47 F3
Fremantle Gv BOW BD4 .... 32 D2 8
Frensham Dr GTHN BD7 .... 29 G4
Frensham Gv GTHN BD7 .... 29 G5
Frensham Wy GTHN BD7 .... 29 G4 8
Freshfield Gdns WIL/AL BD15 .... 23 E3
Friar Ct IDLE BD10 .... 20 B3 2
Friendly Fold Rd HIPP HX3 .... 41 F3
Friendly St CUL/QBY BD13 ... 28 A1 2
HIPP HX3 .... 41 F3 2
Frimley Dr WBOW BD5 .... 30 D5
Frizinghall Rd ECHL BD2 .... 18 D4
HTON BD9 .... 24 D1
Frizley Gdns HTON BD9 .... 18 D5 2
Frogmoor Av LM/WK BD12 .... 38 C5 2
Fruit St KGHY BD21 .... 7 F3
Fulford Wk ECHL BD2 .... 26 C2
Fullerton St BFDE BD3 .... 3 G6
Fulmar Ms GIR BD8 .... 23 F5 8
Fulton St BFD BD1 .... 2 B5
Furnace Gv LM/WK BD12 .... 38 C5 8
Furnace Inn St BOW BD4 .... 32 C2 8
Furnace Rd BOW BD4 .... 38 D4
LM/WK BD12 .... 38 C5
Furness Av LUD/ILL HX2 .... 40 D1 8
Furness Ct LUD/ILL HX2 .... 40 D1
Furness Gdns LUD/ILL HX2 .... 40 D1
Furness Gv LUD/ILL HX2 .... 40 D1
Furness Pl LUD/ILL HX2 .... 40 C1
Fyfe Crs BAIL BD17 .... 13 E4
Fyfe Gv BAIL BD17 .... 13 F4
Fyfe La BAIL BD17 .... 13 F4

G

The Gables BAIL BD17 .... 13 F3
Gainest LUD/ILL HX2 .... 47 E3
Gain La BFDE BD3 .... 26 D3
Gainsborough Cl BFDE BD3 .... 25 H2
Gaisby La ECHL BD2 .... 18 D5
SHPY BD18 .... 19 E4
Gaisby Mt SHPY BD18 .... 19 E4
Gaisby Pl SHPY BD18 .... 19 E4
Gaisby Ri SHPY BD18 .... 19 E3 8
Galefield Gn WBSY BD6 .... 37 E4 8
Gale St KGHY BD21 .... 6 D3
Galloway Ct PDSY/CALV LS28 .... 27 F4
Galloway La PDSY/CALV LS28 .... 27 F3
Galloway Rd IDLE BD10 .... 20 C2 8
Galsworthy Av HTON BD9 .... 23 G1 8
Gannerthorpe Cl LM/WK BD12 .. 44 D2 2
Ganny Rd BRIG HD6 .... 52 C1
Gaol La HFAX HX1 .... 5 H3
Garden Cl LM/WK BD12 .... 44 D1 10
Gardener's Sq HIPP HX3 .... 43 F3
Garden Fld LM/WK BD12 .... 44 D2
Garden Fold HIPP HX3 .... 43 F5
Garden La HTON BD9 .... 23 H1
Garden Rd BRIG HD6 .... 50 A4
Gardens St HTON BD9 .... 18 B5
The Gardens BGLY BD16 .... 11 G3 8
HFAX HX1 .... 47 H3
PDSY/CALV LS28 .... 27 H1
Garden St North HIPP HX3 .... 5 J2
Garden Ter HTON BD9 .... 24 B1 8
Garden Vw BGLY BD16 .... 11 F3
Gardiner Rw BOW BD4 .... 32 A5 8
Garfield Av GIR BD8 .... 24 C2
Garfield St HIPP HX3 .... 41 F4 10
WIL/AL BD15 .... 22 D3
Garforth Rd KGHY BD21 .... 6 D3
Garforth St WIL/AL BD15 .... 23 E3 4
Garibaldi St BFDE BD3 .... 26 D5
Garnett St BFDE BD3 .... 3 G5
Garsdale Av IDLE BD10 .... 20 B2 8
Garsdale Crs BAIL BD17 .... 13 F2
Garth Barn Cl HTON BD9 .... 24 B1 4
Garth Land Wy BOW BD4 .... 32 B4 6

Garth St KGHY BD21 .... 6 B4
Garthwaite Mt WIL/AL BD15 .... 23 E2
Garton Dr IDLE BD10 .... 20 B2
Garvey Vw WBOW BD5 .... 31 F3 5
Gas Works Rd KGHY BD21.......... 7 C4
RPDN/SBR HX6 .... 46 C4
Gatefield Mt LM/WK BD12 .... 37 G4 2
Gathorne St BRIG HD6.............. 50 C5
GTHN BD7 .... 30 C3
Gaukroger La HFAX HX1 .... 5 J7
Gavin Cl BFDE BD3 .... 26 D5
Gawthorpe Dr BGLY BD16 .... 10 C1
Gayle Cl LM/WK BD12 .... 44 D3 8
Gaynor St BFD BD1 .... 2 A4
Gaythorne Rd ECHL BD2 .... 26 B1 8
WBOW BD5 .... 31 F4
Gaythorne Ter CLAY BD14 .... 29 F3 8
Gaythorn Ter HIPP HX3.............. 43 F4
Geelong Cl ECHL BD2 .... 25 G1 8
George Sq HFAX HX1 .... 5 G4 2
George's Sq KGHY BD21 .... 6 C5 13
George's St LUD/ILL HX2 .... 41 E2
George St BAIL BD17 .... 12 D5 2
BFD BD1 .... 3 F6
BRIG HD6 .... 52 B2 7
CUL/QBY BD13 .... 28 A1
HFAX HX1 .... 5 G4
HIPP HX3 .... 49 G1
RPDN/SBR HX6 .... 46 A5
SHPY BD18 .... 18 A1 8
YEA LS19 .... 15 G2
Geraldton Av ECHL BD2 .... 25 F1
Gerrard St HFAX HX1 .... 4 E4
The Ghyll BGLY BD16 .... 16 D1
Ghyll Wood Dr BGLY BD16 .... 16 D1
Gibbet St HFAX HX1 .... 4 A4
Gibb La LUD/ILL HX2 .... 40 A2
Gibraltar Av HFAX HX1 .... 46 D3 8
Gibraltar Rd HFAX HX1 .... 46 D1
PDSY/CALV LS28 .... 27 G5
Gibson St BFDE BD3.................... 3 K6
Giles Hill La HIPP HX3 .... 35 H3
Giles St WBOW BD5 .... 31 E2 8
WBSY BD6 .... 37 F1
Gill Beck Cl BAIL BD17 .... 13 F2 8
Gillingham Gn BOW BD4 .... 32 D4 2
Gill La BAIL BD17 .... 14 D2
YEA LS19 .... 15 F1
Gillroyd Ri GTHN BD7 .... 24 C5
Gilmour St HIPP HX3 .... 41 F4 10
Gilpin St BFDE BD3.................... 3 K4
Gilstead Cl BGLY BD16 .... 11 F3 8
Gilstead Dr BGLY BD16 .... 11 F3
Gilstead La BAIL BD17 .... 11 H4 2
Gilynda Cl GIR BD8 .... 23 H5 2
Gipsy St BFDE BD3.................... 26 D4
Girlington Rd GIR BD8 .... 24 B4 6
Gisburn St KGHY BD21 .... 6 C5
The Glade PDSY/CALV LS28 .... 27 F2
Gladstone Crs YEA LS19 .... 15 G1 8
Gladstone St BFDE BD3.................... 3 G3
BGLY BD16 .... 10 C4 8
CUL/QBY BD13 .... 6 C5 14
KGHY BD21 .... 27 H1
PDSY/CALV LS28 .... 23 E3 8
WIL/AL BD15 .... 48 B5
Gladstone Vw HIPP HX3 .... 22 D1
Glaisdale Ct WIL/AL BD15 .... 49 G1 8
Glaisdale Gv WBSY BD6 .... 46 B4
Gleanings Av LUD/ILL HX2 .... 46 A1
Gleanings Dr LUD/ILL HX2 .... 47 F5
Gleddings Cl HIPP HX3.................... 3 K6
Gledhill Rd BFDE BD3 .... 13 F5
Glenaire SHPY BD18 .... 12 B5
Glenaire Dr BAIL BD17 .... 23 H5
Glenbrook Dr GTHN BD7 .... 16 C2 2
Glen Dl BGLY BD16 .... 37 F3
Glendale Cl WBSY BD6 .... 37 F3
Glendale Dr WBSY BD6 .... 30 A1
Glendare Av GTHN BD7 .... 30 A1 8
Glendare Rd GTHN BD7 .... 30 A1 8
Glendare Ter GTHN BD7 .... 16 C2 2
Glen Dene BGLY BD16 .... 39 E2
Gleneagles Cl BOW BD4 .... 13 F5
Glenfield SHPY BD18 .... 38 A2 8
Glenfield Av WBSY BD6 .... 13 F5
Glenholme SHPY BD18 .... 46 D1
Glenholme Heath HFAX HX1 .... 24 C3 2
Glenholme Rd GIR BD8 .... 27 H2
PDSY/CALV LS28 .... 12 D3
Glenholm Bdl BAIL BD17 .... 39 G1 8
Glenhurst BOW BD4 .... 17 H1
Glenhurst Rd SHPY BD18 .... 30 A1
Glenlee Rd GTHN BD7 .... 6 B2
Glenlyon Av KGHY BD21 .... 6 B2
Glenlyon Dr KGHY BD21 .... 26 B3 2
Glenmore Cl ECHL BD2 .... 16 C2 4
Glen Mt BGLY BD16 ....

Glen Mount Cl HIPP HX3 .... 40 D3 8
Glen Ri BAIL BD17 .... 12 B4
Glen Rd BAIL BD17 .... 11 G2
BGLY BD16 .... 11 F1
Glenrose Dr GTHN BD7 .... 29 H1
Glenroyd Av WBSY BD6 .... 38 A3
Glenroyd Cl PDSY/CALV LS28 .... 27 H5
Glenside Av SHPY BD18 .... 13 F5
Glenside Rd SHPY BD18 .... 13 G5 8
Glenstone Gv GIR BD8 .... 24 A5
Glen Ter HFAX HX1 .... 47 G3
Glenview Av HTON BD9 .... 23 H1
Glenview Cl SHPY BD18 .... 17 F2
Glenview Dr BGLY BD16 .... 17 F2
Glenview Gv SHPY BD18 .... 17 G2 8
Glen View Rd BGLY BD16 .... 11 F1
Glenview Rd SHPY BD18 .... 17 F2
Glenview Ter SHPY BD18 .... 18 A1 8
Glenwood Av BALD BD17 .... 11 H5
Globe Fold GIR BD8 .... 24 D4 8
Gloucester Av BFDE BD3 .... 26 C3
Gloucester Rd BGLY BD16 .... 11 E4
Glover Ct WBOW BD5 .... 31 F5 8
Glyndon Ct BRIG HD6 .... 52 C3
Glynn Ter HIPP HX3 .... 24 C4 8
Gobind Marg BFDE BD3 .... 3 G5
Godfrey St GIR BD8 .... 23 G5
Godley Branch Rd HIPP HX3 .... 42 B5
Godley La HIPP HX3 .... 42 B5
Godley Rd HIPP HX3 .... 5 K2
Godwin St BFD BD1 .... 2 C5
Goff Well La KGHY BD21 .... 9 H4
Goldcrest Av GIR BD8 .... 23 E5 8
Golden View Dr CLAY BD14 .... 29 H1
Golf Av LUD/ILL HX2 .... 46 B1
Golf Crs LUD/ILL HX2 .... 46 B1
Gondal Ct WBOW BD5 .... 30 C4
Gooder La BRIG HD6 .... 52 B2
Gooder St BRIG HD6 .... 52 B1
Goose Cote La HWTH BD22 .... 8 D4
Goose Cote Wy HWTH BD22 .... 8 D3
Gordon St CLAY BD14 .... 29 E3 10
HIPP HX3 .... 41 G3
KGHY BD21 .... 6 C4 10
SHPY BD18 .... 31 G2
Gordon Ter IDLE BD10 .... 14 A5 8
Gorse Av BAIL BD17 .... 11 H4
Gothic St CUL/QBY BD13 .... 35 F1
Gott's Ter AIRE BD20 .... 6 B1
Goulbourne St KGHY BD21 .... 6 C5
Gower St WBOW BD5 .... 31 F3
Gracechurch St GIR BD8 .... 2 A3
Grace St KGHY BD21 .... 7 E4 8
Gracey La WBSY BD6 .... 37 E1
Grafton Cl BAIL BD17 .... 13 E2
Grafton Pl HIPP HX3 .... 41 F2
Grafton Rd KGHY BD21 .... 9 F1
Grafton St KGHY BD21 .... 9 G1 14
WBOW BD5 .... 31 F2
Graham St HTON BD9 .... 24 B2 2
Grain St WBOW BD5 .... 30 C4
Grammar School St BFD BD1.......... 2 C3
Granary Ct ECHL BD2 .... 20 B4 8
Granby Dr AIRE BD20.................... 7 G2
Granby La AIRE BD20 .... 7 G2
Granby St BOW BD4 .... 31 G2 2
CUL/QBY BD13 .... 35 F1
Grandage Ter GIR BD8 .... 24 C4 8
Grandsmere Pl HIPP HX3 .... 47 G4 8
Grange Av BFDE BD3 .... 27 E4
LUD/ILL HX2 .... 34 A5
SHPY BD18 .... 17 H1
WIL/AL BD15 .... 23 F4
Grange Bank HIPP HX3 .... 36 B4
Grange Ct BGLY BD16 .... 17 E2 3
HIPP HX3 .... 48 D5 8
Grange Crs AIRE BD20 .... 7 F2
Grange Dr GIR BD8. .... 23 F4
Grange Gv AIRE BD20 .... 7 F2
BFDE BD3 .... 27 E4 8
Grange Hts HIPP HX3 .... 48 D5
Grange La BRIG HD6 .... 53 F1
Grange Pk BAIL BD17 .... 13 F3
HIPP HX3 .... 47 G5
Grange Park Dr BGLY BD16 .... 16 D1
Grange Park Rd BGLY BD16 .... 16 D1
Grange Rd AIRE BD20 .... 7 F2
BGLY BD16 .... 11 E2
WIL/AL BD15 .... 23 F4
Grange St HIPP HX3 .... 41 F4
KGHY BD21 .... 6 D3
Grange Ter SHPY BD18 .... 18 C3 8
WIL/AL BD15 .... 23 F4 8
Grange Vw BFDE BD3 .... 27 E4 2
Grangeway GIR BD8 .... 23 F4 8
Granny Hall Gv BRIG HD6 .... 50 A4 8
Granny Hall La BRIG HD6 .... 50 A4

Granny Hall Pk BRIG HD6 .... 50 A3
Grantham Pl GTHN BD7 .... 30 D2 8
HIPP HX3 .... 41 G3 8
Grantham Rd GTHN BD7 .... 30 D2
HIPP HX3 .... 41 G3
Grantham Ter GTHN BD7 .... 30 D2 8
Granton St BFDE BD3 .... 26 B5 2
Grant St BFDE BD3.................... 3 H4
HWTH BD22 .... 6 B4 10
Granville Pl WIL/AL BD15 .... 23 E3 8
Granville Rd HTON BD9 .... 18 C4
Granville St CLAY BD14 .... 29 F2 2
PDSY/CALV LS28 .... 27 H4
Granville Ter BGLY BD16 .... 10 D3
HTON BD9 .... 18 C4 12
Grape St HFAX HX1 .... 4 E4
KGHY BD21 .... 7 F3 8
WIL/AL BD15 .... 23 F3 2
Grasleigh Av WIL/AL BD15 .... 22 D2
Grasleigh Wy WIL/AL BD15 .... 22 D1
Grasmere Rd ECHL BD2 .... 25 H1
LM/WK BD12 .... 45 F4
Gratrix La RPDN/SBR HX6 .... 46 B4
Grattan Rd BFD BD1.................... 2 B5
Gray Av SHPY BD18 .... 19 E4
Grayshon Dr WBSY BD6 .... 37 H1
Grayswood Crs BOW BD4 .... 32 C4 8
Grayswood Dr BOW BD4 .... 32 C4 8
BOW BD4 .... 32 C3 8
Great Albion St HFAX HX1.......... 5 G3
Great Cross St BFDE BD3.......... 2 E6
Great Horton Rd GTHN BD7 .... 29 H5
Great Northern Rd KGHY BD21 .. 6 D5 2
Great Russell Ct GTHN BD7 .... 24 C5
Great Russell St GTHN BD7 .... 24 C5
Greaves St WBOW BD5 .... 31 E4
Greenacre Av LM/WK BD12 .... 45 E3
Greenacre Cl LM/WK BD12 .... 45 E3 8
Greenacre Dr LM/WK BD12 .... 45 E3
Greenacre Pk YEA LS19 .... 15 G1
Greenacre Park Av YEA LS19 .... 15 G1
Greenacre Park Ms YEA LS19 .... 15 H1
Greenacre Park Ri YEA LS19 .... 15 G1
Greenacres HIPP HX3 .... 36 C4
Greenacres Av HIPP HX3 .... 36 C4
Greenacres Dr HIPP HX3 .... 36 C4
KGHY BD21 .... 6 A2
Greenacres Gv HIPP HX3 .... 36 C4
Greenacre Wy LM/WK BD12 .... 45 E3
Greenaire Pl BFDT BD1 .... 2 B5 8
Greenbank Rd WIL/AL BD15 .... 23 F4
Greencliffe Av BAIL BD17 .... 12 C3
Green Cl GIR BD8 .... 23 H4
Green Ct CLECK BD19 .... 45 G5 8
GTHN BD7 .... 30 A3 8
Greencroft Av HIPP HX3 .... 43 E2
Green End BRIG HD6 .... 52 B2 8
CLAY BD14 .... 29 E3
Green End Rd WBSY BD6 .... 37 G2
Greenfell Cl HWTH BD22.......... 6 B5
Greenfield Av HIPP HX3 .... 50 B1
SHPY BD18 .... 18 D3
Greenfield Cl HIPP HX3 .... 42 D2
Greenfield Ct HWTH BD22 .... 6 B4 11
Greenfield Dr CLECK BD19 .... 45 G5
Greenfield La BOW BD4 .... 39 E4
GTHN BD7 .... 30 A3
IDLE BD10 .... 14 A5
Greenfield Pl HIPP HX3 .... 50 B1 8
Greengate Rd KGHY BD21 .... 6 D5
Greengates Av LM/WK BD12 .... 44 D4 8
Green Hall Pk HIPP HX3 .... 36 C5
Green Head Av AIRE BD20 .... 6 B1
Green Head Dr AIRE BD20.......... 6 B1
Green Head La AIRE BD20 .... 6 B1
Green Head Rd AIRE BD20 .... 6 C1
Green Hl LUD/ILL HX2 .... 46 A2
Greenhill La BFDE BD3 .... 26 B5
Greenhills YEA LS19 .... 15 H3
Greenhill St BFDE BD3 .... 26 B5
Greenholme Ct BOW BD4 .... 33 E5 8
Greenland Av CUL/QBY BD13 .. 35 E2 8
Greenland Vls CUL/QBY BD13 .. 35 F2 8
Green La BAIL BD17 .... 12 B2
BRIG HD6 .... 49 H3
BRIG HD6 .... 53 G1
CUL/QBY BD13 .... 28 B1 8
CUL/QBY BD13 .... 35 F3
ECHL BD2 .... 26 C1
GIR BD8. .... 24 D4
GTHN BD7 .... 30 B2 2
HIPP HX3 .... 35 F5
HIPP HX3 .... 36 D5
HIPP HX3 .... 48 B2 8
HWTH BD22 .... 8 C4 8
IDLE BD10 .... 19 H1
IDLE BD10 .... 20 B1 8

Street	Area / Postcode	Grid
	LM/WK BD12	44 D3
	LM/WK BD12	45 G1
	LUD/ILL HX2	46 D3
	YEA LS19	15 G1
Greenlea Cl	YEA LS19	15 E1
Greenlea Rd	YEA LS19	15 E1
Green Meadow	WIL/AL BD15	16 A5
Green Mt	BOW BD4	32 C4
Green Mount Rd	CUL/QBY BD13	28 B1
Green Park St	HIPP HX3	47 H5
Green Pl	ECHL BD2	26 A2
Green Rd	BAIL BD17	12 C4
Greenroyd Av	HWTH BD22	47 C5
Greenroyd La	LUD/ILL HX2	40 D4
Greenside	LM/WK BD12	45 H1
Greenside La	GIR BD8	24 A5
Green's Sq	LUD/ILL HX2	40 D5
Green St	BFD BD1	3 F5
Green Terrace Sq	HFAX HX1	47 F3
The Green	BGLY BD16	11 G3
Greenthwaite Cl	KGHY BD21	6 B2
Greenton Av	CLECK BD19	45 F4
Greenton Crs	CUL/QBY BD13	35 E2
Green Top St	GIR BD8	23 H5
Greenville	LM/WK BD12	38 B3
Greenway Dr	WIL/AL BD15	23 E5
Greenway Rd	WBOW BD5	31 F5
Greenwell Rw	CLAY BD14	29 E3
Greenwood Av	ECHL BD2	19 H4
Greenwood Dr	ECHL BD2	19 H5
Greenwood Mt	ECHL BD2	19 H5
Greenwood Rd	BAIL BD17	12 C5
Gregory Ct	CLAY BD14	29 F3
Gregory Crs	GTHN BD7	29 H5
Grenfell Dr	BFDE BD3	26 C4
Grenfell Rd	BFDE BD3	26 C4
Grenfell Ter	BFDE BD3	26 C4
Gresham Av	ECHL BD2	19 G5
Gresley Rd	KGHY BD21	6 C4
Greycourt Cl	ECHL BD2	19 H3
	HFAX HX1	4 C6
Greyfriar Wk	GTHN BD7	29 H4
Greystone Ct	BRIG HD6	52 B4
Greystone Crs	IDLE BD10	20 B3
Greystones Dr	HWTH BD22	9 E3
Greystones Mt	HWTH BD22	9 E4
Greystones Ri	HWTH BD22	9 E3
Griffe Dr	LM/WK BD12	44 D4
Griffe Gdns	HWTH BD22	8 A3
Griffe Head Crs	LM/WK BD12	44 D4
Griffe Head Rd	LM/WK BD12	44 D4
Griffe Rd	LM/WK BD12	44 D3
Grosvenor Av	SHPY BD18	18 A1
Grosvenor Rd	GIR BD8	2 A1
	SHPY BD18	18 A2
Grosvenor Ter	GIR BD8	2 A1
	HFAX HX1	4 D3
	HFAX HX1	4 D4
Grove Av	HIPP HX3	41 E3
	SHPY BD18	18 C4
Grove Cl	ECHL BD2	19 H5
Grove Cft	HIPP HX3	41 E5
Grove Cft	HIPP HX3	41 E5
Grove Edge	HIPP HX3	41 E3
Grove Gdns	HIPP HX3	41 F3
Grove House Crs	ECHL BD2	19 H5
Grove House Dr	ECHL BD2	25 H1
Grove House Rd	ECHL BD2	19 H5
Grovelands	ECHL BD2	25 H1
Grove Pk	HIPP HX3	41 F5
Grove Rd	SHPY BD18	18 C4
Grove Royd	HIPP HX3	41 F3
Grove Sq	HIPP HX3	41 E3
	HIPP HX3	41 E3
Grove St	BRIG HD6	52 C1
	RPDN/SBR HX6	46 C4
Grove St South	HFAX HX1	4 B4
The Grove	BAIL BD17	12 D2
	HIPP HX3	43 F5
	IDLE BD10	20 C2
	SHPY BD18	17 H2
	YEA LS19	15 F2
Groveville	HIPP HX3	43 F4
Groveway	ECHL BD2	19 H5
Guard House Av	HWTH BD22	6 B4
Guard House Dr	HWTH BD22	6 B4
Guard House Gv	HWTH BD22	6 A4
Guard House Rd	HWTH BD22	6 B4
Guild Wy	LUD/ILL HX2	46 A2
Gurbax Ct	BFDE BD3	26 D5
Gurney Cl	WBOW BD5	31 E4
Guy St	BOW BD4	2 E7
Gwynne Av	BFDE BD3	28 D3

H

Street	Area / Postcode	Grid
Hadassah St	HIPP HX3	48 A4
Haddon Av	HIPP HX3	47 H5
Hag La	HIPP HX3	41 H2
Haigh Beck Vw	IDLE BD10	20 B2
Haigh Cnr	IDLE BD10	20 C2
Haigh Fold	IDLE BD2	26 B1
Haigh Hall	IDLE BD10	20 C2
Haigh Hall Rd	IDLE BD10	20 C2
Haigh La	HIPP HX3	48 A4
Haigh St	BOW BD4	32 A4
	BRIG HD6	50 B5
	HFAX HX1	4 B2
Haincliffe Rd	KGHY BD21	9 G2
Hainsworth Moor Crs	CUL/QBY BD13	35 E2
Hainsworth Moor Dr	CUL/QBY BD13	35 E2
Hainsworth Moor Garth	CUL/QBY BD13	35 E2
Hainsworth Moor Gv	CUL/QBY BD13	35 E2
Hainsworth Moor Vw	CUL/QBY BD13	35 E2
Hainworth Crag Rd	KGHY BD21	9 F4
Hainworth La	KGHY BD21	9 G3
Hainworth Rd	KGHY BD21	9 H2
	KGHY BD21	9 G3
Hainworth Wood Rd	KGHY BD21	9 H1
Hainworth Wood Rd North	KGHY BD21	9 H1
Halcyon Wy	WBOW BD5	30 D4
Halesworth Crs	BOW BD4	32 D4
Haley Hl	HFAX HX1	5 G1
Half House La	BRIG HD6	49 G3
Half St	KGHY BD21	6 C2
Halifax Old Rd	HIPP HX3	43 E5
	CLECK BD19	51 F1
	CUL/QBY BD13	34 D4
	HIPP HX3	43 E5
	HIPP HX3	43 E5
	KGHY BD21	9 F5
	WBSY BD6	37 E5
Hall Av	IDLE BD10	20 C4
Hallbank Cl	WBOW BD5	38 A1
Hall Bank Dr	BGLY BD16	10 C2
Hallbank Dr	WBOW BD5	38 A1
Hallcliffe	BAIL BD17	13 E2
Hallfield Dr	BAIL BD17	12 D3
Hallfield Pl	BFD BD1	2 C2
Hallfield Rd	GIR BD8	2 B3
Hallfield St	BFDE BD1	2 C3
Hall Ings	BFD BD1	2 D6
Hall La	BOW BD4	31 G2
	HIPP HX3	42 C1
Hallows Rd	KGHY BD21	7 F2
The Hallows	KGHY BD21	6 B3
Hall Rd	IDLE BD10	20 C4
Hall Royd	SHPY BD18	18 C2
Hall Stone Ct	HIPP HX3	36 B5
Hall St	HFAX HX1	5 F3
	HWTH BD22	8 C4
	WBSY BD6	37 H1
Hallwood Gn	IDLE BD10	20 A1
Halstead Pl	GTHN BD7	30 B4
Halton Pl	GTHN BD7	30 C4
Hambleden Av	BOW BD4	39 E1
Hammerton St	BFDE BD3	3 G6
Hammond Pl	HTON BD9	24 B1
Hammond St	HFAX HX1	4 B5
Hamm Strasse	BFD BD1	2 B3
Hampden Pl	HFAX HX1	4 E4
	WBOW BD5	31 E3
Hampden St	WBOW BD5	31 E3
Hampton Pl	IDLE BD10	20 A1
Hampton St	HFAX HX1	4 A7
Hamworth Dr	HWTH BD22	8 C4
Handel St	GTHN BD7	24 D5
Hannah Ct	LM/WK BD12	44 D3
Hanover Cl	IDLE BD10	24 B3
Hanover Sq	BFD BD1	2 B2
Hanover St	HFAX HX1	5 F5
	KGHY BD21	6 D4
	RPDN/SBR HX6	46 C3
Hanson Cl	LM/WK BD12	44 C3
Hanson Fold	LM/WK BD12	44 D2
Hanson La	HFAX HX1	4 C3
Hanson Mt	LM/WK BD12	44 D3
Hanworth Rd	LM/WK BD12	37 H4

Street	Area / Postcode	Grid
Harbour Crs	WBSY BD6	37 F2
Harbour Pk	WBSY BD6	37 E3
Harbour Rd	WBSY BD6	37 F3
Harclo Rd	KGHY BD21	7 F3
Harcourt Av	CUL/QBY BD13	22 A5
Harcourt St	BOW BD4	32 A4
Hardaker La	BAIL BD17	12 B4
Hardaker St	GIR BD8	2 A3
Harden Gv	IDLE BD10	26 D1
Harden Rd	BGLY BD16	10 B4
Hard Ings Rd	KGHY BD21	6 D2
Hardknot Cl	GTHN BD7	29 H4
Hardwick Ct	KGHY BD21	6 B5
Hardy Av	WBSY BD6	37 H2
Hardy Pl	BRIG HD6	49 H3
Hardy St	BOW BD4	2 E7
	BRIG HD6	50 C5
Harehill Cl	IDLE BD10	14 A5
Harehill Rd	IDLE BD10	14 A5
Hare St	HFAX HX1	4 B4
Harewood Av	LUD/ILL HX2	40 C5
Harewood Crs	HWTH BD22	8 D3
Harewood Pl	LUD/ILL HX2	46 D2
Harewood Ri	HWTH BD22	9 E3
Harewood Rd	HWTH BD22	8 D3
Harewood St	BFDE BD3	3 J4
Harker Rd	WBSY BD6	37 H3
Harland Cl	ECHL BD2	25 F3
Harley St	BRIG HD6	52 B2
Harlow Rd	GTHN BD7	30 B2
Harmon Cl	BOW BD4	39 F2
Harold St	BGLY BD16	10 B3
Harper Av	IDLE BD10	14 A5
Harper Crs	IDLE BD10	14 B5
Harper Gv	IDLE BD10	14 A5
Harrier Cl	GIR BD8	23 E5
Harriet St	BRIG HD6	50 B4
	GIR BD8	24 C4
Harris Ct	GTHN BD7	30 B4
Harrison Rd	HFAX HX1	5 G5
Harrison St	BGLY BD16	10 D4
Harris St	BFD BD1	3 G5
	BGLY BD16	10 D4
Harrogate Av	BFDE BD3	25 H2
Harrogate Pl	BFDE BD3	25 H2
Harrogate Rd	ECHL BD2	26 B1
	IDLE BD10	20 C2
	YEA LS19	15 G2
Harrogate St	BFDE BD3	25 H2
Harrogate Ter	BFDE BD3	25 H2
Harrow St	HFAX HX1	4 B4
Harry La	CLAY BD14	29 E3
Harry St	BOW BD4	32 B4
Hartington St	KGHY BD21	6 D5
Hartington Ter	GTHN BD7	30 B2
Hartland Rd	BOW BD4	32 D4
Hartley St	BOW BD4	32 A2
	HFAX HX1	4 C2
Hartlington Ct	BAIL BD17	13 F2
Hartman Pl	HTON BD9	24 A2
Hart St	GTHN BD7	30 C5
Haslam Cl	BFDE BD3	3 H3
Haslam Gv	SHPY BD18	19 F3
Haslemere Cl	BOW BD4	32 C4
Haslingden Dr	HTON BD9	24 A2
Hastings Av	WBOW BD5	31 E5
Hastings Pl	WBOW BD5	31 E4
Hastings St	WBOW BD5	31 E5
Hastings Ter	WBOW BD5	31 E5
Hatchet La	WBOW BD12	45 H1
Hatfield Rd	ECHL BD2	26 A2
Hathaway Av	HTON BD9	23 G1
Hatton Cl	WBSY BD6	38 A2
Haugh Shaw Rd	HFAX HX1	4 C7
Haugh Shaw Rd West	HFAX HX1	47
Havelock Sq	CUL/QBY BD13	28 B1
Havelock St	CUL/QBY BD13	28 B1
	GTHN BD7	30 A3
The Haven	IDLE BD10	20 B3
Hawes Av	WBOW BD5	30 D5
Hawes Crs	WBOW BD5	30 D5
Hawes Dr	WBOW BD5	30 D5
Hawes Gv	WBOW BD5	30 D5
Hawes Mt	WBOW BD5	30 D5
Hawes Rd	WBOW BD5	30 D5
Hawes Ter	WBOW BD5	30 D5
Hawke Wy	LM/WK BD12	45 F1
Hawkshead Cl	WBOW BD5	31 F2
Hawkshead Dr	WBOW BD5	31 F2
Hawkstone Dr	KGHY BD21	6 B2
Hawkswood Av	HTON BD9	24 A1
Hawley Ter	IDLE BD10	20 D5
Haworth Gv	HTON BD9	23 H1
Haworth Rd	HTON BD9	23 H1
	WIL/AL BD15	17 E5
Hawthorn Av	BFDE BD3	26 D4
Hawthorn Cl	BRIG HD6	50 D5
Hawthorn Dr	IDLE BD10	20 B2

Street	Area / Postcode	Grid
Hawthorne Av	SHPY BD18	19
Hawthorn St	BFDE BD3	26 D4
	HFAX HX1	4 C7
	HIPP HX3	43 G5
Hawthorn Vw	BAIL BD17	13
Haycliffe Av	GTHN BD7	30
Haycliffe Dr	GTHN BD7	30 A5
Haycliffe Gv	GTHN BD7	30 B5
Haycliffe Hill Rd	GTHN BD7	30 C4
Haycliffe La	WBSY BD6	30
Haycliffe Rd	GTHN BD7	30
Haycliffe Ter	GTHN BD7	30
Hayclose Md	WBSY BD6	37
Hayden St	BFDE BD3	3
Haynes St	KGHY BD21	7 E5
Hazel Beck	BGLY BD16	16 D1
Hazelcroft	IDLE BD10	20
Hazel Cft	SHPY BD18	19
Hazeldene	CUL/QBY BD13	35 E2
Hazel Gv	HIPP HX3	50
Hazelheads	BAIL BD17	12
Hazelhurst Av	BGLY BD16	16 D1
Hazelhurst Brow	HTON BD9	23
Hazelhurst Ct	BFDE BD3	26 B5
Hazel Hurst Gv	CUL/QBY BD13	35
Hazel Hurst Rd	CUL/QBY BD13	35
Hazelhurst Rd	HTON BD9	23
Hazelhurst Ter	HTON BD9	23
Hazelmere Av	BGLY BD16	16
Hazel Mt	SHPY BD18	18
Hazel Wk	HTON BD9	23
Hazelwood Av	AIRE BD20	7 G2
Hazelwood Rd	HTON BD9	23
Headland Gv	WBSY BD6	37 E1
Headley La	CUL/QBY BD13	28
Healey Av	BGLY BD16	10
Healey La	BGLY BD16	10
Healey Wood Crs	BRIG HD6	52
Healey Wood Gdns	BRIG HD6	52
Healey Wood Gv	BRIG HD6	52
Healey Wood Rd	BRIG HD6	52
Heap La	BFDE BD3	3
Heap St	BFDE BD3	3
	HIPP HX3	41
Heath Av	HIPP HX3	47
Heatherbank Av	HWTH BD22	9
Heather Gv	HTON BD9	23
	KGHY BD21	6 A3
Heather Rd	BAIL BD17	13 E2
Heather Side	BAIL BD17	12
Heatherstones	HIPP HX3	47 G4
Heather Vw	BGLY BD16	11
Heathfield Cl	BGLY BD16	10
Heathfield Gv	GTHN BD7	29
Heath Gdns	HIPP HX3	47
Heath Gv	PDSY/CALV LS28	27
Heath Hall	HFAX HX1	47
Heath Hall Av	BOW BD4	39
Heath La	HIPP HX3	47
Heath Lea	HFAX HX1	5
Heathmoor Cl	IDLE BD10	19
Heath Mount Rd	BRIG HD6	52
Heath Park Av	HFAX HX1	47 H3
Heath Rd	BFDE BD3	3
	HFAX HX1	47
Heath Royd	HIPP HX3	47
Heath St	BFDE BD3	26
	BGLY BD16	10 D3
	HIPP HX3	47
Heath Ter	BFDE BD3	3
Heath View St	HFAX HX1	5
Heathy Av	LUD/ILL HX2	34
Heathy La	LUD/ILL HX2	34
Heaton Cl	BGLY BD16	11
Heaton Crs	BGLY BD16	11 E2
Heaton Dr	BAIL BD17	12
	BGLY BD16	11
Heaton Gv	HTON BD9	18 C5
	SHPY BD18	18
Heaton Hl	WBSY BD6	37 E3
Heaton Park Dr	HTON BD9	24
Heaton Park Rd	HTON BD9	24
Heaton Rd	HTON BD9	24
Heaton Royds La	SHPY BD18	18
Heaton St	BFDE BD3	31 H2
	BRIG HD6	52
Hebble Brook Cl	LUD/ILL HX2	40 B1
Hebble La	HFAX HX1	41
Hebble Vale Dr	LUD/ILL HX2	40
Hebb Vw	WBSY BD6	29
Heber St	KGHY BD21	6
Hector Cl	WBSY BD6	37
Heddon Cl	WBOW BD5	31 F2
Heddon Gv	WBOW BD5	31 F2
Hedge Cl	GIR BD8	23
Hedge Side	GIR BD8	23
Hedge Top La	HIPP HX3	42
Hedge Wy	GIR BD8	23

Heidelberg Rd *HTON* BD9 .... 24 B2 ⑤
Height Gn *RPDN/SBR* HX6 .... 46 A4
Heights La *HTON* BD9 .... 23 C1
Helena Wy *BOW* BD4 .... 39 F2
Helen Rose Ct *SHPY* BD18 .... 13 F5 ②
Helen St *SHPY* BD18 .... 18 A1 ⑤
Hellewell St *WBSY* BD6 .... 37 E3 ⑦
Helmsley St *BOW* BD4 .... 31 H3
Hemingway Rd *IDLE* BD10 .... 20 C1
Hemsby St *KGHY* BD21 .... 9 F2 ⑩
Henacrewood Ct *CUL/QBY* BD13 .. 35 F3
Henderson Pl *WBSY* BD6 .... 37 H1 ⑧
Hendford Dr *BFDE* BD3 .... 3 H4
Henley Av *BOW* BD5 .... 31 F5
Henley Ct *WBOW* BD5 .... 31 G5 ⑧
Henley Dr *YEA* LS19 .... 15 H3
Henley Gv *WBOW* BD5 .... 31 F5
Henley Hl *YEA* LS19 .... 15 H3 ①
Henley Rd *WBOW* BD5 .... 31 F5
Henry St *BRIG* HD6 .... 50 B4
CLAY BD14 .... 29 F3 ⑦
CUL/QBY BD13 .... 28 A1 ⑩
HFAX HX1 .... 5 F5
KGHY BD21 .... 6 D4 ⑥
Herbert Pl *BFDE* BD3 .... 26 D4 ④
Herbert St *BGLY* BD16 .... 10 D3
CLAY BD14 .... 29 F4 ①
HFAX HX1 .... 4 A5
SHPY BD18 .... 12 A5 ④
WBOW BD5 .... 31 E3 ⑧
Heritage Wy *HWTH* BD22 .... 8 B4 ②
Hermit St *HWTH* BD22 .... 9 F4
Hermon Av *HFAX* HX1 .... 4 C5
Hermon Gv *HFAX* HX1 .... 4 C5
Herschel Rd *GIR* BD8 .... 23 F5
Heshbon St *BOW* BD4 .... 32 B4 ⑦
Hetton Dr *BFDE* BD3 .... 32 C1 ③
Hew Clews *GTHN* BD7 .... 29 H4
Heybeck Wk *BOW* BD4 .... 33 E5 ⑦
Heyford Ct *ECHL* BD2 .... 25 E1
Heygate Cl *BAIL* BD17 .... 13 E2
Heygate La *BAIL* BD17 .... 13 E2
Heys Av *CUL/QBY* BD13 .... 28 C1
Heys Crs *CUL/QBY* BD13 .... 28 C1
Heysham Dr *BOW* BD4 .... 33 E4
Hey St *BRIG* HD6 .... 50 C4
GTHN BD7 .... 2 A5
Heywood Cl *HIPP* HX3 .... 42 D3
Heywood Pl *HFAX* HX1 .... 4 D3
Heywood St *HIPP* HX3 .... 42 D3
Hick St *BFD* BD1 .... 3 F5 ②
Higgin La *HIPP* HX3 .... 48 B3
High Ash *SHPY* BD18 .... 19 F2
High Ash Pk *WIL/AL* BD15 .... 22 C3
High Bank La *SHPY* BD18 .... 17 G3
High Banks Cl *AIRE* BD20 .... 7 G1 ⑩
Highbridge Ter *WBOW* BD5 .... 38 C1
High Bury Cl *CUL/QBY* BD13 .. 34 D2 ③
High Busy La *IDLE* BD10 .... 19 G1
SHPY BD18 .... 19 F1
Highcliffe Dr *LUD/ILL* HX2 .... 46 C1 ③
High Cl *YEA* LS19 .... 15 C3
High Cft *CUL/QBY* BD13 .... 35 F1 ⑧
HIPP HX3 .... 41 E3
Highcroft Cl *PDSY/CALV* LS28 ... 27 H4 ①
Highcroft Gdns *KGHY* BD21 .... 7 G5 ②
High Cross La *HIPP* HX3 .... 35 H3
Highdale Cft *IDLE* BD10 .... 20 C1 ④
Higher Coach Rd *BAIL* BD17 .... 11 H4
BGLY BD16 .... 11 F4
Higher Downs *GIR* BD8 .... 23 G4
Higher Intake Rd *ECHL* BD2 .... 26 B3
Higher School St *SHPY* BD18 .. 18 A1 ⑧
Higherwood Cl *KGHY* BD21 .... 7 F4
Highfell Ri *HWTH* BD22 .... 8 D3 ②
High Fernley Ct
LM/WK BD12 .... 44 D1 ⑪
High Fernley Rd *LM/WK* BD12 .. 44 B2
Highfield *BOW* BD4 .... 39 G1
HIPP HX3 .... 36 B5 ③
Highfield Av *BRIG* HD6 .... 44 C5
HIPP HX3 .... 36 C3
IDLE BD10 .... 19 H2
Highfield Ct *HWTH* BD22 .... 8 B4 ②
Highfield Crs *BAIL* BD17 .... 12 D2
HTON BD9 .... 17 G5
Highfield Dr *HTON* BD9 .... 17 G5
YEA LS19 .... 15 H3 ②
Highfield Gdns *HTON* BD9 .. 17 G5 ②
Highfield Gv *IDLE* BD10 .... 19 H3
High Field La *HWTH* BD22 .... 8 B3
Highfield La *KGHY* BD21 .... 6 B3
Highfield Ms *BAIL* BD17 .... 12 D2 ④
Highfield Pl *HFAX* HX1 .... 4 B6
Highfield Rd *HTON* BD9 .... 18 D4
IDLE BD10 .... 19 H3
KGHY BD21 .... 6 B3
PDSY/CALV LS28 .... 27 H4

High Flds *LUD/ILL* HX2 .... 46 D4
Highfield St *KGHY* BD21 .... 6 C4 ⑪
PDSY/CALV LS28 .... 27 H4
Highfield Ter *PDSY/CALV* LS28 .. 27 H4 ②
SHPY BD18 .... 17 H1 ①
High Fold *HWTH* BD22 .... 9 E1
Highfold *YEA* LS19 .... 15 F1
High Fold La *AIRE* BD20 .... 6 B1
Highgate *HTON* BD9 .... 18 A5
Highgate Cl *CUL/QBY* BD13 .... 29 F5
Highgate Gv *CLAY* BD14 .... 29 F5
Highgate Rd *CUL/QBY* BD13 .... 29 E5
High Grove La *HIPP* HX3 .... 48 B3
High Holly Garth *KGHY* BD21 .... 7 E5
High House Av *ECHL* BD2 .... 19 H5
High House Rd *ECHL* BD2 .... 19 H5
Highlands Cl *GTHN* BD7 .... 29 H4 ③
Highlands Gv *GTHN* BD7 .... 29 H4
Highlands La *LUD/ILL* HX2 .... 34 A4
Highland Ville *HIPP* HX3 .... 43 C5
High La *LUD/ILL* HX2 .... 40 A5
Highlea Cl *YEA* LS19 .... 15 E1
High Level Wy *HFAX* HX1 .... 4 B1
Highley Hall Cft *BRIG* HD6 .... 53 F1
Highley Pk *BRIG* HD6 .... 53 F1
High Meadow *KGHY* BD21 .... 6 B2 ②
Highmoor *BAIL* BD17 .... 12 B3
Highmoor Crs *BRIG* HD6 .... 51 E5
Highmoor La *BRIG* HD6 .... 51 E5
CLECK BD19 .... 51 H3
Highmoor Wk *BAIL* BD17 .... 12 B4 ①
Highoak Garth *HWTH* BD22 .... 8 B4
High Park Crs *HTON* BD9 .... 23 H1
High Park Dr *HTON* BD9 .... 23 G1
High Park Rd *HTON* BD9 .... 23 H1
High Poplars *ECHL* BD2 .... 19 G5 ⑧
Highroad Well La *LUD/ILL* HX2 .. 46 B1
High Spring Gardens La
KGHY BD21 .... 6 B2
High Spring Rd *KGHY* BD21 .... 7 C5
High St *BRIG* HD6 .... 50 C5
CUL/QBY BD13 .... 28 A1 ④
CUL/QBY BD13 .... 35 F1
HFAX HX1 .... 5 F5
IDLE BD10 .... 20 A1
KGHY BD21 .... 6 C4 ⑫
WBSY BD6 .... 37 H1
High Sunderland La *HIPP* HX3 .. 41 H4
Hilda St *HTON* BD9 .... 18 B5 ③
Hillam Rd *ECHL* BD2 .... 25 E1
Hillam St *WBOW* BD5 .... 30 C4
Hillary Rd *SHPY* BD18 .... 19 F2
Hill Brow *WIL/AL* BD15 .... 22 D3
Hill Cl *BAIL* BD17 .... 12 C4
Hillcote Dr *WBOW* BD5 .... 31 F3 ⑧
Hill Crs *HIPP* HX3 .... 48 B3
YEA LS19 .... 15 H1
Hillcrest Av *CUL/QBY* BD13 .... 35 G2
Hillcrest Dr *CUL/QBY* BD13 .... 35 G2
Hillcrest Mt *CLECK* BD19 .... 51 G1
Hill Crest Rd *CUL/QBY* BD13 .. 35 A5
Hillcrest Rd *CUL/QBY* BD13 .... 35 G2
Hill Cft *CUL/QBY* BD13 .... 22 B5
Hill End Cl *HIPP* HX3 .... 44 D1
Hill End Gv *GTHN* BD7 .... 29 H4
Hill End La *CUL/QBY* BD13 .... 35 E2
Hill Foot *SHPY* BD18 .... 17 G2
Hillfoot Av *PDSY/CALV* LS28 .... 27 G4
Hillfoot Crs *PDSY/CALV* LS28 .... 27 G4
Hillfoot Dr *PDSY/CALV* LS28 .... 27 G4
Hillfoot Ri *PDSY/CALV* LS28 .... 27 G4
Hill Lands *LM/WK* BD12 .... 44 C1
Hill Park Av *HIPP* HX3 .... 41 E4
Hillside Av *HWTH* BD22 .... 8 A4
Hillside Gv *HWTH* BD22 .... 8 A4 ②
Hill Side Rd *BFDE* BD3 .... 3 G4
BGLY BD16 .... 10 C3
Hillside Rd *SHPY* BD18 .... 18 D3
Hillside Ter *BAIL* BD17 .... 12 D3 ③
Hill St *BOW* BD4 .... 32 A2
HFAX HX1 .... 5 F6
WBSY BD6 .... 37 F1
Hill Top Cottages *HTON* BD9 .. 23 H2 ③
Hill Top Gv *WIL/AL* BD15 .... 22 D3
Hill Top La *WIL/AL* BD15 .... 22 D3
Hill Top Rd *HWTH* BD22 .... 8 A4
KGHY BD21 .... 9 F5
HWTH BD22 .... 6 A4
Hill Top Wy *HWTH* BD22 .... 6 A4 ②
Hill Vw *LUD/ILL* HX2 .... 34 A3
Hillview Gdns *HIPP* HX3 .... 42 D4
Hilton Av *SHPY* BD18 .... 18 C4
Hilton Crs *BAIL* BD17 .... 12 D4 ①
Hilton Dr *SHPY* BD18 .... 18 C4
Hilton Gv *GTHN* BD7 .... 30 B1
SHPY BD18 .... 18 C4 ⑬
Hilton Rd *GTHN* BD7 .... 30 B1

SHPY BD18 .... 18 C4
Hinchliffe St *BFDE* BD3 .... 3 J2
Hinchliffe Av *BAIL* BD17 .... 13 E4
Hindley Wk *GTHN* BD7 .... 29 G5
Hind St *GIR* BD8 .... 24 D4 ②
LM/WK BD12 .... 44 D3
Hions Cl *BRIG* HD6 .... 52 B3
Hipswell St *BFDE* BD3 .... 26 B4
Hird Av *WBSY* BD6 .... 37 H2
Hird Rd *LM/WK* BD12 .... 38 A4
Hird St *BAIL* BD17 .... 13 E2
KGHY BD21 .... 9 G1 ⑩
Hirst La *SHPY* BD18 .... 17 H1
Hirst Lodge Ct *ECHL* BD2 .... 19 G4 ⑧
Hirst Mill Crs *SHPY* BD18 .... 11 H5
Hirst Wood Crs *SHPY* BD18 .... 17 H1
Hirst Wood Rd *SHPY* BD18 .... 17 G1
Hive St *HWTH* BD22 .... 6 B5 ⑩
Hockney Rd *GIR* BD8 .... 24 C4
Hodgson Av *BFDE* BD3 .... 26 C4
Holborn Ct *WBSY* BD6 .... 37 H4
Holden La *BAIL* BD17 .... 13 E2
Holdsworth Rd *LUD/ILL* HX2 .. 34 B3
Holdsworth St *BFD* BD1 .... 2 E3
SHPY BD18 .... 18 D3
Holker St *GIR* BD8 .... 24 C4 ②
KGHY BD21 .... 6 D3
Hollin Close La *ECHL* BD2 .... 25 F1
Hollin Greaves La *HIPP* HX3 .. 41 H4
Hollings Rd *GIR* BD8 .... 24 C4
Hollings Sq *GIR* BD8 .... 24 C4 ⑧
Hollings St *BGLY* BD16 .... 17 E2
GIR BD8 .... 24 C4 ③
Hollings Ter *GIR* BD8 .... 24 C4
Hollingwood Av *GTHN* BD7 .. 30 A3 ②
Hollingwood Dr *GTHN* BD7 .... 29 H4
Hollingwood La *GTHN* BD7 .... 29 H4
Hollingwood Mt *GTHN* BD7 .... 29 H4
Hollin Hall Rd *SHPY* BD18 .... 17 H3
Hollin Head *BAIL* BD17 .... 13 G2
Hollin La *SHPY* BD18 .... 19 E3
Hollin Park Ct *PDSY/CALV* LS28 .. 21 F3
Hollin Park Dr *PDSY/CALV* LS28 .. 21 F3
Hollin Park Rd *PDSY/CALV* LS28 .. 21 F3
Hollin Ri *SHPY* BD18 .... 18 D3 ⑧
Hollin Rd *SHPY* BD18 .... 18 D3
Hollins Bank *RPDN/SBR* HX6 .. 46 A4 ③
Hollins Cl *AIRE* BD20 .... 6 A1
Hollins La *RPDN/SBR* HX6 .... 46 A3
Hollin Ter *SHPY* BD18 .... 18 D3 ③
Hollin Wood Cl *SHPY* BD18 .. 17 H2 ⑧
Hollowfield Cft *LM/WK* BD12 .. 39 E5 ①
Holly Bank *HIPP* HX3 .... 43 G5
Hollybank Gdns *GTHN* BD7 .... 29 H4
Holly Bank Gv *GTHN* BD7 .... 29 H4
Holly Bank Pk *BRIG* HD6 .... 52 A3
Hollybank Rd *GTHN* BD7 .... 29 H4
Holly Gv *HFAX* HX1 .... 4 C5
Holly Hall La *LM/WK* BD12 .... 44 D1
Holly Park Dr *GTHN* BD7 .... 29 H3
Holly Park Gv *GTHN* BD7 .... 29 H3
Holly St *WBSY* BD6 .... 29 G5 ⑧
Holme Dr *LUD/ILL* HX2 .... 45 H1
Holme Farm *WBSY* BD6 .... 36 C1 ⑧
Holme House La *HWTH* BD22 .. 8 A1
Holme La *BOW* BD4 .... 33 E4
BOW BD4 .... 39 H1
Holme Mill La *HWTH* BD22 .... 6 A5
Holme Rd *LUD/ILL* HX2 .... 46 A2
Holmes Rd *RPDN/SBR* HX6 .... 46 B5
Holmes St *GIR* BD8 .... 24 C3
Holme St *BRIG* HD6 .... 50 B1 ⑧
WBOW BD5 .... 31 E3
Holme Top La *WBOW* BD5 .... 31 E3 ⑧
Holme Top St *WBOW* BD5 .... 31 E3 ⑩
Holme Wood Rd *BOW* BD4 .... 32 C4 ⑦
HWTH BD22 .... 6 A5 ⑧
Holroyd Hl *WBSY* BD6 .... 37 H1
Holsworthy Rd *BOW* BD4 .... 32 D4 ⑧
Holtby Gv *BRIG* HD6 .... 50 B1
Holt Gdns *IDLE* BD10 .... 19 G1
Holts La *CLAY* BD14 .... 29 E2
Holts Ter *HIPP* HX3 .... 48 A4
The Holt *SHPY* BD18 .... 18 D2
Holybrook Av *IDLE* BD10 .... 20 C5
Holycroft St *KGHY* BD21 .... 6 C5 ⑮
Holyoake Av *BGLY* BD16 .... 10 C5
Holywell Ash La *GIR* BD8 .... 2 B1
Home View Ter *GIR* BD8 .... 24 C3
The Hoods *BRIG* HD6 .... 52 A4
Hopbine Av *WBOW* BD5 .... 31 F5
Hopbine Rd *WBOW* BD5 .... 31 F5
Hope Av *SHPY* BD18 .... 19 E1
WBOW BD5 .... 30 D5
Hopefield Wy *BOW* BD4 .... 39 E1 ④
Hope Hall St *HFAX* HX1 .... 5 H6
Hope Hall Ter *HFAX* HX1 .... 5 H6
Hope Hill Vw *BGLY* BD16 .... 16 D2

Hope La *BAIL* BD17 .... 12 C3
Hope Pl *KGHY* BD21 .... 9 G1 ⑩
Hope St *HFAX* HX1 .... 4 E3
RPDN/SBR HX6 .... 46 B5
Hope Vw *SHPY* BD18 .... 18 D2
Hopkinson Dr *BOW* BD4 .... 39 F2 ⑦
Hopkinson St *LUD/ILL* HX2 .. 41 E1 ⑦
Hopkin St *BOW* BD4 .... 39 H1 ①
Hopton Av *BOW* BD4 .... 39 E1
Hopwood La *HIPP* HX3 .... 42 B4
Horley Green La *HIPP* HX3 .... 42 D3
Hornbeam Cl *WIL/AL* BD15 .... 16 C5
Hornby St *HFAX* HX1 .... 4 B7 ⑥
Horne St *HFAX* HX1 .... 4 E3
Horsfall St *HFAX* HX1 .... 47 F3
Horsham Ct *HWTH* BD22 .... 8 D1
Horsley St *WBSY* BD6 .... 37 H1 ⑩
Horsman St *BOW* BD4 .... 39 H1 ③
Horton Grange Rd *GTHN* BD7 .. 30 C1
Horton Hall Cl *WBOW* BD5 .... 31 E3
Horton Park Av *GTHN* BD7 .... 30 C2
Horton St *HFAX* HX1 .... 5 H5
Hospital Rd *AIRE* BD20 .... 7 H2
Hough *HIPP* HX3 .... 42 D3
Houghton Pl *BFD* BD1 .... 2 B3
Houghton St *BRIG* HD6 .... 50 C5
Howard St *HFAX* HX1 .... 4 C2
WBOW BD5 .... 2 B7 ①
Howarth Av *ECHL* BD2 .... 19 H4
Howarth Crs *ECHL* BD2 .... 19 H4 ①
Howbeck Dr *AIRE* BD20 .... 7 H2
Howbeck Dr *AIRE* BD20 .... 7 H3
Howcans La *HIPP* HX3 .... 41 F1
Howden Av *AIRE* BD20 .... 6 B1 ⑦
Howdenbrook *HIPP* HX3 .... 36 C3
Howden Cl *BOW* BD4 .... 33 E5
Howes La *HIPP* HX3 .... 42 C2
Howgate *IDLE* BD10 .... 20 B1
Howgill Gn *WBSY* BD6 .... 37 F4
Hoxton St *GIR* BD8 .... 24 B4 ⑧
Hoyle Court Av *BAIL* BD17 .... 13 F3
Hoyle Court Dr *BAIL* BD17 .... 13 F3
Hoyle Court Rd *BAIL* BD17 .... 13 F3
Hoyle Fold *HWTH* BD22 .... 9 E1 ⑩
Hoyle Ing Rd *CUL/QBY* BD13 .. 28 C1
Hubert St *BFDE* BD3 .... 3 K7
LUD/ILL HX2 .... 46 C1 ③
Huddersfield Rd *BRIG* HD6 .... 52 C1
HFAX HX1 .... 47 H3
HIPP HX3 .... 47 H4
LM/WK BD12 .... 44 D2
LM/WK BD12 .... 44 D1
LM/WK BD12 .... 44 D1
Hud Hl *HIPP* HX3 .... 43 E1
Hudson Av *GTHN* BD7 .... 30 C3
Hudson Cl *GTHN* BD7 .... 30 C4 ⑧
Hudson Crs *GTHN* BD7 .... 30 C4
Hudson Gdns *GTHN* BD7 .... 30 C3 ⑧
Hudson St *BFDE* BD3 .... 26 C5 ⑧
The Hudson *LM/WK* BD12 .... 44 D2
Hughendon Dr *CUL/QBY* BD13 .. 28 D1
Hughendon Wk *CUL/QBY* BD13.. 28 D1
Hugill St *CUL/QBY* BD13 .... 28 A1 ⑪
Hulbert St *BGLY* BD16 .... 10 D4
Humboldt St *BFD* BD1 .... 3 G5
Hunger Hl *HFAX* HX1 .... 5 G6
Hunsworth La *BIRK/DRI* BD11 .. 39 H4
Hunters Ct *HTON* BD9 .... 17 F5 ⑧
Hunters Park Av *CLAY* BD14 .. 29 G2
Huntingdon Rd *BRIG* HD6 .... 52 D2
Huntock Pl *BRIG* HD6 .... 50 A3
Huntsmans Cl *BGLY* BD16 .... 11 F1
KGHY BD21 .... 6 B3 ⑧
Hustlergate *BFD* BD1 .... 2 D5
Hustler St *BFDE* BD3 .... 3 H1
Hutson St *WBOW* BD5 .... 31 E3
Hutton Rd *WBOW* BD5 .... 30 D5
Hutton Ter *IDLE* BD10 .... 20 C4
Hydale Ct *LM/WK* BD12 .... 37 H4
Hyde Pk *HFAX* HX1 .... 4 D6
Hyde Park Rd *HFAX* HX1 .... 4 C7
Hyde Park St *HFAX* HX1 .... 4 D6
Hyde St *IDLE* BD10 .... 14 A5 ⑪
Hyne Av *BOW* BD4 .... 39 F1

I

Ida St *WBOW* BD5 .... 30 D4 ⑪
Iddesleigh St *BOW* BD4 .... 32 B1
Idlecroft Rd *IDLE* BD10 .... 20 A1
Idle Rd *ECHL* BD2 .... 19 H4
Idlethorp Wy *IDLE* BD10 .... 20 B2
Ilbert Av *BOW* BD4 .... 39 F1
Ilkley Rd *AIRE* BD20 .... 7 G1
Illingworth Cl *YEA* LS19 .... 15 H1 ①

Illingworth Rd *LM/WK* BD12 ...... 45 G1 🔳
The Incline *HIPP* HX3 ...... 5 K2
Independent St *WBOW* BD5 ...... 30 D4
Industrial Rd *RPDN/SBR* HX6 ...... 46 A4
Industrial St *BGLY* BD16 ...... 10 C3 🔳
  BRIG HD6 ...... 50 C5 🔳
  CLECK BD19 ...... 45 G5 🔳
  HWTH BD22 ...... 8 D3
Industrial Ter *HFAX* HX1 ...... 47 G3 🔳
Infirmary St *BFD* BD1 ...... 2 B4
Ingham Cl *LUD/ILL* HX2 ...... 34 A2
Ingham La *LUD/ILL* HX2 ...... 34 A1
Ingham's Av *PDSY/CALV* LS28 ...... 27 C4
Inghams Ct *HIPP* HX3 ...... 41 F4 🔳
Inghams Ter *PDSY/CALV* LS28 ...... 27 C4 🔳
Ingham's Vw *PDSY/CALV* LS28 ...... 27 C4 🔳
Inghead Gdns *HIPP* HX3 ...... 43 E1 🔳
Ingleborough Cl *BOW* BD4 ...... 32 D4 🔳
Ingleby Pl *GTHN* BD7 ...... 30 B1 🔳
Ingleby Rd *GIR* BD8 ...... 24 B5
Ingleby St *GIR* BD8 ...... 24 B5
Ingram St *HFAX* HX1 ...... 47 F3 🔳
  KGHY BD21 ...... 9 G3
Ingrow La *HWTH* BD22 ...... 9 E2
The Ings *BRIG* HD6 ...... 50 B2
Ing St *BFDE* BD3 ...... 32 C1 🔳
Ings Wy *GIR* BD8 ...... 23 H4
Inkerman St *BOW* BD4 ...... 32 C3 🔳
  ECHL BD2 ...... 20 C5 🔳
Inkersley Rd *CUL/QBY* BD13 ...... 1 C2
The Innings *IDLE* BD10 ...... 19 H1
Institute Rd *ECHL* BD2 ...... 20 B4
Intake Gv *ECHL* BD2 ...... 26 B2 🔳
Intake Rd *ECHL* BD2 ...... 26 B2
Intake Ter *ECHL* BD2 ...... 26 B2 🔳
Invertrees Av *YEA* LS19 ...... 15 H2
Iona Pl *HIPP* HX3 ...... 41 H3 🔳
Iona St *HIPP* HX3 ...... 41 H3
Iqbal Ct *BOW* BD4 ...... 32 C1 🔳
Ireland St *BGLY* BD16 ...... 10 B3
Ireland Ter *BGLY* BD16 ...... 10 B3 🔳
Ireton St *GTHN* BD7 ...... 30 C1 🔳
Irving St *HFAX* HX1 ...... 4 A7
Irving Ter *CLAY* BD14 ...... 29 F4 🔳
Irwell St *BOW* BD4 ...... 31 H2
Isaac St *GIR* BD8 ...... 24 C4
Isles St *GIR* BD8 ...... 24 A4 🔳
Ivanhoe Rd *GTHN* BD7 ...... 30 C2
Ivegate *BFD* BD1 ...... 2 D5
Iver Wy *SHPY* BD18 ...... 18 B2 🔳
Ives St *BAIL* BD17 ...... 18 C1
Ivy Crs *HIPP* HX3 ...... 49 H1
Ivy Gv *SHPY* BD18 ...... 17 H2
Ivy House Rd *WBOW* BD5 ...... 31 F5 🔳
Ivy La *WIL/AL* BD15 ...... 22 D3
  SHPY BD18 ...... 17 H2
Ivy St *BRIG* HD6 ...... 50 A5 🔳
  HFAX HX1 ...... 47 F3 🔳
  HIPP HX3 ...... 6 C3
Ivy Ter *BRIG* HD6 ...... 50 A5 🔳
  HIPP HX3 ...... 49 H1
  KGHY BD21 ...... 7 G5

J

Jackie Smart Rd *WBOW* BD5 ...... 31 F3 🔳
Jackson Hill La *CUL/QBY* BD13 ...... 35 G3
Jackson St *BFDE* BD3 ...... 3 H7
Jacob St *WBOW* BD5 ...... 31 E3 🔳
James Ga *BFD* BD1 ...... 2 C5
James St *BFD* BD1 ...... 2 C5
  BRIG HD6 ...... 50 B4
  CUL/QBY BD13 ...... 22 A5
  HWTH BD22 ...... 8 A4
  WIL/AL BD15 ...... 23 F3 🔳
  YEA LS19 ...... 15 C2
Jamie Ct *IDLE* BD10 ...... 20 C3
Jane St *SHPY* BD18 ...... 18 A1 🔳
Jardine Rd *BGLY* BD16 ...... 10 D3 🔳
Jarratt St *GIR* BD8 ...... 24 C3 🔳
Jarratt St (East) *GIR* BD8 ...... 24 C3 🔳
Jarrom Cl *BOW* BD4 ...... 32 C3 🔳
Jasmin Ter *GIR* BD8 ...... 24 D4 🔳
Jasper St *HFAX* HX1 ...... 4 B4
  IDLE BD10 ...... 20 A1 🔳
Javelin Cl *IDLE* BD10 ...... 20 A3
Jay House La *BRIG* HD6 ...... 51 E3
Jennings Pl *GTHN* BD7 ...... 30 B3 🔳
Jennings St *GTHN* BD7 ...... 30 B3 🔳
Jenny La *BAIL* BD17 ...... 13 E2
Jer Gv *WBSY* BD6 ...... 29 H5
Jer La *WBSY* BD6 ...... 29 H5
Jermyn St *BFDE* BD3 ...... 2 E4
Jervaulx Crs *GIR* BD8 ...... 24 D4
Jerwood Hill Cl *HIPP* HX3 ...... 42 A4
Jerwood Hill Rd *HIPP* HX3 ...... 42 A4
Jesmond Av *HTON* BD9 ...... 24 A2
Jesmond Gv *HTON* BD9 ...... 24 A2 🔳
Jesse St *GIR* BD8 ...... 23 C5
  WBOW BD5 ...... 31 F3 🔳
Joba Av *BFDE* BD3 ...... 3 K5
John Escritt Rd *BGLY* BD16 ...... 10 B4
Johnson St *BFDE* BD3 ...... 26 C5 🔳
  BGLY BD16 ...... 10 D3 🔳
John St *BAIL* BD17 ...... 12 D5
  BFD BD1 ...... 2 C4
  BOW BD4 ...... 39 H1
  BRIG HD6 ...... 50 B5
  CLAY BD14 ...... 29 F3
  CUL/QBY BD13 ...... 28 A1
  HFAX HX1 ...... 5 G4
  HWTH BD22 ...... 8 D1
  SHPY BD18 ...... 18 B1
  YEA LS19 ...... 15 G2
John St West *RPDN/SBR* HX6 ...... 46 A4
Joseph Av *HIPP* HX3 ...... 42 D3
Joseph St *BFD* BD1 ...... 3 C5
  BOW BD4 ...... 39 H1 🔳
Jowett Park Crs *IDLE* BD10 ...... 13 H4
Jowett St *BFD* BD1 ...... 24 D5
Jubilee Ct *KGHY* BD21 ...... 9 F1
Jubilee Rd *HIPP* HX3 ...... 48 B5
Jubilee St *HIPP* HX3 ...... 5 K6
Jubilee St North *HIPP* HX3 ...... 41 F1
Jubilee Wy *SHPY* BD18 ...... 17 H2
Julian Dr *CUL/QBY* BD13 ...... 29 F5
Jumble Dyke *BRIG* HD6 ...... 52 A3 🔳
Jumples *LUD/ILL* HX2 ...... 40 C1
Jumples Cl *LUD/ILL* HX2 ...... 40 C1 🔳
Junction Rd *BAIL* BD17 ...... 18 D1 🔳
June St *KGHY* BD21 ...... 6 D3 🔳
Juniper St *GIR* BD8 ...... 24 D4 🔳

K

Katherine St *SHPY* BD18 ...... 18 A1 🔳
Kaycell St *BOW* BD4 ...... 32 A5
Kay St *HTON* BD9 ...... 18 C4
Keeldar Cl *GTHN* BD7 ...... 30 C4 🔳
Keelham La *AIRE* BD20 ...... 6 B1
Keighley Dr *LUD/ILL* HX2 ...... 40 D1
Keighley Rd *BGLY* BD16 ...... 10 B1
  HTON BD9 ...... 24 D1
  HWTH BD22 ...... 8 D3
Kelburn Gv *HWTH* BD22 ...... 8 A3
Kell La *HIPP* HX3 ...... 42 C3
Kell St *BGLY* BD16 ...... 10 D3 🔳
Kelmore Gv *WBSY* BD6 ...... 36 D4
Kelsey St *HFAX* HX1 ...... 4 B2
Kelvin Av *LUD/ILL* HX2 ...... 46 C1
Kelvin Crs *LUD/ILL* HX2 ...... 46 C2
Kelvin Wy *ECHL* BD2 ...... 26 B2
Kendall Av *SHPY* BD18 ...... 17 H1
Kendal Mellor Ct *KGHY* BD21 ...... 6 C4 🔳
Kendal St *KGHY* BD21 ...... 7 E5
Kenilworth Dr *BRIG* HD6 ...... 50 B2 🔳
Kenilworth St *BOW* BD4 ...... 32 A3 🔳
Kenley Av *WBSY* BD6 ...... 37 F1
Kenley Mt *WBSY* BD6 ...... 30 B5 🔳
Kenley Pde *GTHN* BD7 ...... 30 A5
Kenmore Crs *WBSY* BD6 ...... 30 B5
Kenmore Dr *WBSY* BD6 ...... 30 B5
Kenmore Gv *WBSY* BD6 ...... 30 B5 🔳
Kenmore Rd *WBSY* BD6 ...... 30 B5
Kenmore Wk *WBSY* BD6 ...... 30 B5 🔳
Kennion St *WBOW* BD5 ...... 31 E2 🔳
Kensington Cl *HIPP* HX3 ...... 47 F4
Kensington Rd *HFAX* HX1 ...... 47 F4
Kensington St *GIR* BD8 ...... 24 B3
  KGHY BD21 ...... 6 C5
Kenstone Crs *IDLE* BD10 ...... 19 H2
Kentmere Av *LM/WK* BD12 ...... 45 F4
Kent Ms *BGLY* BD16 ...... 11 E4
Kenton Wy *BOW* BD4 ...... 32 D4 🔳
Kent Rd *BGLY* BD16 ...... 11 E4
Kent St *HFAX* HX1 ...... 5 F5
Kenya Mt *HWTH* BD22 ...... 6 A3
Kenyon La *LUD/ILL* HX2 ...... 46 C1
Kershaw St *BFDE* BD3 ...... 26 C5
Kesteven Cl *BOW* BD4 ...... 33 E5 🔳
Kesteven Rd *BOW* BD4 ...... 33 D5
Kestrel Dr *ECHL* BD2 ...... 19 H5
Kestrel Mt *ECHL* BD2 ...... 19 H5
Keswick Cl *HIPP* HX3 ...... 48 B4
Keswick St *BOW* BD4 ...... 32 C2
Kettlewell Dr *WBOW* BD5 ...... 30 C4 🔳
Khaliq St *BFDE* BD3 ...... 3 K3
Khus Wk *KGHY* BD21 ...... 9 H2 🔳
Kildare Crs *WIL/AL* BD15 ...... 22 D3
Killinghall Av *ECHL* BD2 ...... 26 A3 🔳
Killinghall Dr *ECHL* BD2 ...... 26 A3
Killinghall Gv *ECHL* BD2 ...... 26 A3 🔳
Killinghall Rd *BFDE* BD3 ...... 26 B3
Kilner Rd *WBSY* BD6 ...... 37 F1 🔳
Kilnsea Mt *BOW* BD4 ...... 32 D4
Kilnsey Ms *BAIL* BD17 ...... 12 C3
Kimberley Pl *HIPP* HX3 ...... 41 F1 🔳
Kimberley St *BFDE* BD3 ...... 32 B1 🔳
  BRIG HD6 ...... 50 C5
  HIPP HX3 ...... 41 F1
King Edward Rd
  CUL/QBY BD13 ...... 28 A1 🔳
King Edward St *HFAX* HX1 ...... 5 H4 🔳
Kingfisher Gv *GIR* BD8 ...... 23 F5
Kingsbury Pl *HFAX* HX1 ...... 4 B4 🔳
Kingsdale Av *ECHL* BD2 ...... 25 H1
Kingsdale Crs *ECHL* BD2 ...... 25 H1
Kingsdale Dr *ECHL* BD2 ...... 25 H1
  ECHL BD2 ...... 25 G1 🔳
King's Dr *ECHL* BD2 ...... 19 G3
Kings Gv *BGLY* BD16 ...... 10 D2
Kingsley Av *BAIL* BD17 ...... 25 F1
Kingsley Crs *BAIL* BD17 ...... 12 D4 🔳
Kingsley Pl *HFAX* HX1 ...... 4 B6
  ECHL BD2 ...... 19 G3
  ECHL BD2 ...... 25 F1
Kingston Cl *HFAX* HX1 ...... 4 B5
  HFAX HX1 ...... 4 B5 🔳
Kingston Ct *HFAX* HX1 ...... 4 A5
Kingston Dr *HFAX* HX1 ...... 4 A5
Kingston Gv *IDLE* BD10 ...... 14 A5
Kingston Rd *IDLE* BD10 ...... 14 A5
Kingston St *HFAX* HX1 ...... 4 B5
King St *BRIG* HD6 ...... 52 C1
  HFAX HX1 ...... 5 J3
  IDLE BD10 ...... 20 B4
  KGHY BD21 ...... 6 C5
  YEA LS19 ...... 15 F2
Kings Vw *HIPP* HX3 ...... 48 D4 🔳
Kingsway *AIRE* BD20 ...... 7 G2
  BGLY BD16 ...... 10 D4
  ECHL BD2 ...... 19 G3
Kingswood Pl *GTHN* BD7 ...... 30 B3 🔳
Kingswood St *GTHN* BD7 ...... 30 B3 🔳
Kingswood Ter *GTHN* BD7 ...... 30 B3 🔳
Kipling Ct *IDLE* BD10 ...... 20 C2
Kipping La *CUL/QBY* BD13 ...... 28 A1 🔳
Kipping Pl *CUL/QBY* BD13 ...... 28 A1 🔳
Kirby St *KGHY* BD21 ...... 7 E3 🔳
Kirkbourne Gv *BAIL* BD17 ...... 13 F4
Kirkburn Pl *GTHN* BD7 ...... 30 C1 🔳
Kirkby Leas *HFAX* HX1 ...... 5 G6
Kirk Dr *BAIL* BD17 ...... 13 E2
Kirkfields *BAIL* BD17 ...... 13 F2
Kirkgate *BFD* BD1 ...... 2 C5
  SHPY BD18 ...... 18 B2
Kirkham Rd *GTHN* BD7 ...... 30 C2 🔳
Kirklands Av *BAIL* BD17 ...... 13 F3
Kirklands Cl *BAIL* BD17 ...... 13 F4 🔳
Kirklands Gdns *BAIL* BD17 ...... 13 F3 🔳
Kirklands La *BAIL* BD17 ...... 13 F3
Kirklands Rd *BAIL* BD17 ...... 13 E3
Kirklees Rd *WIL/AL* BD15 ...... 23 E5 🔳
Kirklees Wy *CLECK* BD19 ...... 45 H2
  HUDN HD2 ...... 53 E5
Kirkley Av *LM/WK* BD12 ...... 44 D4 🔳
Kirkstall Gr *GIR* BD8 ...... 23 C5
Kirkstone Dr *LUD/ILL* HX2 ...... 40 D1
Kirkwall Dr *BOW* BD4 ...... 32 D4
Kismet Gdns *BFDE* BD3 ...... 26 B4
Kitchener St *LM/WK* BD12 ...... 38 D5
Kite Ms *GIR* BD8 ...... 23 F5 🔳
Kitson St *SHPY* BD18 ...... 18 D2 🔳
Kliffen Pl *HIPP* HX3 ...... 48 A4
Knightsbridge Wk *BOW* BD4 ...... 39 E2
Knight's Fold *GTHN* BD7 ...... 30 B3
Knight St *HFAX* HX1 ...... 4 B7 🔳
Knoll Park Dr *BAIL* BD17 ...... 12 C5
Knowle Av *LM/WK* BD12 ...... 45 E3
Knowles Av *BOW* BD4 ...... 32 C5
Knowles La *BOW* BD4 ...... 32 C5
Knowle Spring Rd *KGHY* BD21 ...... 9 G1 🔳
Knowles Rd *BRIG* HD6 ...... 52 C5
Knowles St *BOW* BD4 ...... 39 F1
Knowles Vw *BOW* BD4 ...... 32 C5
Knowle Top Dr *HIPP* HX3 ...... 43 H5
Knowle Top Rd *HIPP* HX3 ...... 43 H5
Knowsley St *BFDE* BD3 ...... 3 H6
Knutsford Gv *BOW* BD4 ...... 32 D5 🔳
Knutsford Ms *BOW* BD4 ...... 32 D5 🔳
Kyffin Pl *BOW* BD4 ...... 32 D4

L

Laburnum Dr *BAIL* BD17 ...... 13 E
Laburnum Gv *BRIG* HD6 ...... 50 B2 🔳
Laburnum Pl *GIR* BD8 ...... 24 D3 🔳
  IDLE BD10 ....
Laburnum Rd *SHPY* BD18 ...... 19 E4 🔳
Laburnum St *GIR* BD8 ...... 24 D
  PDSY/CALV LS28 ...... 27 H
Ladbroke Gv *BOW* BD4 ...... 39 H1 🔳
Ladderbanks La *BAIL* BD17 ...... 13 E
Ladyroyd Dr *BIRK/DRI* BD11 ...... 39 H
Ladysmith Rd *CUL/QBY* BD13 ...... 34 D
Ladywell St *WBOW* BD5 ...... 31 F4 🔳
Ladywood Ter *HFAX* HX1 ...... 4 C
Laisterdyke *BFDE* BD3 ...... 32 C
Laisteridge La *WBOW* BD5 ...... 30 D
Laithe Gv *WBSY* BD6 ...... 36 D
Laithe Rd *WBSY* BD6 ...... 37 G1 🔳
Lake Rw *BOW* BD4 ...... 32 A
Lakeside Cha *YEA* LS19 ...... 15 H2 🔳
Lakeside Gdns *YEA* LS19 ...... 15 H
Lakeside Ter *YEA* LS19 ...... 15 H2 🔳
Lakeside Vw *YEA* LS19 ...... 15 H
Lake St *BOW* BD4 ...... 32 A
  KGHY BD21 ...... 7 F
Lake Vw *HFAX* HX1 ...... 5 F
Lamb Cote Rd *HUDN* HD2 ...... 53 E
Lambourne Av *IDLE* BD10 ...... 20 D4
Lampards Cl *WIL/AL* BD15 ...... 22 D
Landor St *BFDE* BD3 ...... 7 E3 🔳
Landscove Av *BOW* BD4 ...... 32 D
Lands Head La *HIPP* HX3 ...... 42 C
Landsholme Ct *BOW* BD4 ...... 33 E5 🔳
Lands La *IDLE* BD10 ...... 20 B4 🔳
Landsmoor Gv *BGLY* BD16 ...... 11 E
Lane End *CUL/QBY* BD13 ...... 28 A1 🔳
Lane Ends *LUD/ILL* HX2 ...... 40 D
Lane Ends Cl *GIR* BD8 ...... 23 H
Lane Ends Gn *HIPP* HX3 ...... 43 E
Lane Side *CUL/QBY* BD13 ...... 28 A
Lane Side Cl *LM/WK* BD12 ...... 44 D1 🔳
Langbar Av *HTON* BD9 ...... 23 C
Langdale Av *GIR* BD8 ...... 23 H
  LM/WK BD12 ...... 45 F
Langdale Ct *BGLY* BD16 ...... 10 D1 🔳
Langdale Crs *LUD/ILL* HX2 ...... 40 D4 🔳
Langdale Dr *CUL/QBY* BD13 ...... 35 E1 🔳
Langdale Rd *IDLE* BD10 ...... 20 D
Langlands Rd *BGLY* BD16 ...... 16 D
Lang La *ECHL* BD2 ...... 19 E5 🔳
Langley Av *BGLY* BD16 ...... 10 D
  BOW BD4 ...... 39 F
Langley Crs *BAIL* BD17 ...... 13 F
Langley Gv *BGLY* BD16 ...... 10 D2 🔳
Langley La *BAIL* BD17 ...... 13 F
Langley Rd *BGLY* BD16 ...... 10 D
Langport Cl *CUL/QBY* BD13 ...... 35 G1 🔳
Langton Av *BOW* BD4 ...... 39 E
Langton St *RPDN/SBR* HX6 ...... 46 A
Lansdale Ct *BOW* BD4 ...... 33 E5 🔳
Lansdowne Cl *BAIL* BD17 ...... 13 G
Lapage St *BFDE* BD3 ...... 26 B
Lapage Ter *BFDE* BD3 ...... 32 B1 🔳
Lapwing Cl *GIR* BD8 ...... 23 E
Larch Cl *HWTH* BD22 ...... 8 C4 🔳
Larch Dr *WBSY* BD6 ...... 37 H
Larch Gv *BGLY* BD16 ...... 10 C
Larch Hl *WBSY* BD6 ...... 38 A
Larch Hill Crs *WBSY* BD6 ...... 38 A
Larchmont *CLAY* BD14 ...... 29 F3 🔳
Larch St *KGHY* BD21 ...... 9 G
Larkfield Av *YEA* LS19 ...... 15 H
Larkfield Crs *YEA* LS19 ...... 15 H
Larkfield Dr *YEA* LS19 ...... 15 H
Larkfield Mt *YEA* LS19 ...... 15 H
Larkfield Rd *YEA* LS19 ...... 15 H
Lark St *BGLY* BD16 ...... 10 C3 🔳
  HWTH BD22 ...... 8 C4 🔳
  KGHY BD21 ...... 6 C4 🔳
Larwood Av *IDLE* BD10 ...... 20 D5 🔳
Lastingham Gn *WBSY* BD6 ...... 36 D1 🔳
Latimer St *BFDE* BD3 ...... 32 C1 🔳
Launceston Dr *BOW* BD4 ...... 32 D5 🔳
Launton Wy *WBOW* BD5 ...... 31 E5 🔳
Laura St *BRIG* HD6 ...... 52 B2 🔳
  HIPP HX3 ...... 41 H4 🔳
Laurel Bank Cl *LUD/ILL* HX2 ...... 34 B4 🔳
Laurel Cl *HIPP* HX3 ...... 36 B3 🔳
Laurel Gv *BGLY* BD16 ...... 10 B
Laurel Mt *HFAX* HX1 ...... 4 D7 🔳
Laurel St *BFDE* BD3 ...... 32 B
  HFAX HX1 ....
Lavender Hl *IDLE* BD10 ...... 20 B4 🔳
Laverock Crs *BRIG* HD6 ...... 50 A
Laverock La *BRIG* HD6 ...... 50 A

Laverton Rd *BOW* BD4 .... 32 A3
Lavinia Ter *CLAY* BD14 .... 29 G3
Lawkholme Crs *KGHY* BD21 .... 6 D4 🔢
Lawkholme La *KGHY* BD21 .... 6 D4 🔢
Law La *HIPP* HX3 .... 48 D3
Lawnswood Rd *KGHY* BD21 .... 9 F1
Lawrence Dr *GTHN* BD7 .... 29 H5
Lawrence Rd *HIPP* HX3 .... 47 G5
Lawrence St *HIPP* HX3 .... 41 F4 🔢
Lawson Rd *HIPP* HD6 .... 52 C1
Lawson St *BFDE* BD3 .... 32 B5
Law St *BOW* BD4 .... 32 B5
Lea Av *HIPP* HX3 .... 47 H5
Leach Crs *AIRE* BD20 .... 7 F1 🔢
Leach Ri *AIRE* BD20 .... 7 F1
Leach Ri *AIRE* BD20 .... 7 F1
Leach Ri *AIRE* BD20 .... 7 F1
Lea Cl *BRIG* HD6 .... 50 D4
Lea Ct *GTHN* BD7 .... 29 H5 🔢
Leadenhall St *HFAX* HX1 .... 4 B7 🔢
Leafield Av *ECHL* BD2 .... 26 B1
Leafield Crs *ECHL* BD2 .... 26 A1
Leafield Dr *ECHL* BD2 .... 20 B5
Leafield Gv *ECHL* BD2 .... 26 B1
Leafield Ter *ECHL* BD2 .... 26 B1
Leafield Wy *ECHL* BD2 .... 26 B1
Leafland St *HFAX* HX1 .... 4 C4
Leafsway *WBSY* BD6 .... 37 E4 🔢
Leamington Dr *IDLE* BD10 .... 20 B1
Leamington St *HTON* BD9 .... 24 C2
Leamside Wk *BOW* BD4 .... 32 D5 🔢
Leaside Dr *CUL/QBY* BD13 .... 22 A3
The Leavens *IDLE* BD10 .... 20 C1
Leaventhorpe Av *GIR* BD8 .... 23 F5 🔢
Leaventhorpe Cl *GIR* BD8 .... 23 G5 🔢
Leaventhorpe Gv
   CUL/QBY BD13 .... 29 F1
Leaventhorpe La *CUL/QBY* BD13 .. 29 F1
Leaventhorpe Wy *GIR* BD8 .... 23 G5
Leavington Cl *LM/WK* BD12 .... 37 G4 🔢
Lee Bank *HIPP* HX3 .... 41 G4
Lee Br *HFAX* HX1 .... 5 F1
Lee Ct *KGHY* BD21 .... 7 G5
Leeds Country Wy
   PDSY/CALV LS28 .... 15 F5
   PDSY/CALV LS28 .... 27 F1
Leeds Old Rd *BFDE* BD3 .... 26 C4
Leeds Rd *BFD* BD1 .... 3 F5
   BFDE BD3 .... 3 K6
   BFDE BD3 .... 26 A1
   ECHL BD2 .... 26 A1
   HIPP HX3 .... 42 D4
   SHPY BD18 .... 19 E1
   YEA LS19 .... 15 H3
Leeds St *KGHY* BD21 .... 6 C4
Lee La *BGLY* BD16 .... 16 D4
   HIPP HX3 .... 42 A2
Leeming St *BFD* BD1 ....
Legrams Dr *GTHN* BD7 .... 30 A2
Legrams La *GTHN* BD7 .... 30 B1
Legrams Mill La *GTHN* BD7 .... 30 B1
Legrams St *GTHN* BD7 .... 24 C5
Legrams Ter *GTHN* BD7 .... 24 D5 🔢
Leicester Gn *BOW* BD4 .... 31 H3
Leicester Ter *HIPP* HX3 .... 47 G4 🔢
Leigh St *RPDN/SBR* HX6 .... 46 B3
Leith St *KGHY* BD21 .... 6 C3
Lemington Av *HFAX* HX1 .... 4 D6
Lemon St *HFAX* HX1 ....
   WBOW BD5 .... 30 D5 🔢
Lennie St *KGHY* BD21 .... 6 C5
Lennon Dr *GIR* BD8 .... 24 C3
Lens Dr *BAIL* BD17 .... 12 D2
Lentilfield St *HIPP* HX3 .... 41 F3 🔢
Lentilfield Ter *HIPP* HX3 .... 41 F3 🔢
Lenton Vls *IDLE* BD10 .... 14 A5 🔢
Leonard's Pl *BGLY* BD16 .... 10 D4 🔢
Leonard St *BGLY* BD16 .... 10 D4
   LM/WK BD12 .... 45 E2
Lesmere Gv *GTHN* BD7 .... 30 A5 🔢
Lever St *WBSY* BD6 .... 37 F1 🔢
Levita Gv *BOW* BD4 .... 32 C3 🔢
Levita Pl *BOW* BD4 .... 32 D2 🔢
Lewis Cl *CUL/QBY* BD13 .... 35 E1
Lewis St *HFAX* HX1 .... 5 F3
Lexington Cl *BOW* BD4 .... 39 E2 🔢
Leyburn Av *HIPP* HX3 .... 43 G5
Leyburn Gv *BGLY* BD16 .... 10 D4
   SHPY BD18 .... 18 B2
Leyden Ri *WIL/AL* BD15 .... 23 E4 🔢
Leyfield *BAIL* BD17 .... 12 B3

Ley Fleaks Rd *IDLE* BD10 .... 20 A2
Leyland Cft *HUDN* HD2 .... 53 F5
Leylands Av *HTON* BD9 .... 24 A1
Leylands Gv *HTON* BD9 .... 24 A1
Leylands La *HTON* BD9 .... 24 A1
   KGHY BD21 .... 7 E5
Leylands Ter *HTON* BD9 .... 24 A1
Leys Cl *IDLE* BD10 .... 13 H5
Leyside Dr *WIL/AL* BD15 .... 23 E2
Leyton Crs *IDLE* BD10 .... 20 A2 🔢
Leyton Dr *IDLE* BD10 .... 20 A2
Leyton Gv *IDLE* BD10 .... 20 A2 🔢
Leyton Ter *IDLE* BD10 .... 20 A2 🔢
Ley Top La *WIL/AL* BD15 .... 23 F4
Lichen Cl *GTHN* BD7 .... 30 B4
Lichfield Mt *BFDE* BD2 .... 19 F5
Lidget Av *GTHN* BD7 .... 30 A2 🔢
Lidget Pl *GTHN* BD7 .... 30 A2
Lidget Ter *CLAY* BD14 .... 29 G3 🔢
   GTHN BD7 .... 30 A2
Lightcliffe Rd *BRIG* HD6 .... 50 B3
Lightowler Cl *HFAX* HX1 .... 4 D3
Lightowler Rd *HFAX* HX1 .... 4 D3
Lightowler St *WBSY* BD6 .... 37 H1 🔢
Lilac Cl *BRIG* HD6 .... 50 D5
   SHPY BD18 .... 19 E4
Lilac St *HIPP* HX3 .... 41 F4
Lilian St *BOW* BD4 .... 32 B4 🔢
Lilands Av *BRIG* HD6 .... 52 A1
Lilands La *BRIG* HD6 .... 52 A1
Lilands Ter *BRIG* HD6 .... 52 A1 🔢
Lilly La *HIPP* HX3 .... 5 J5
Lilly St *RPDN/SBR* HX6 .... 46 A5
Lily Cft *GIR* BD8 .... 24 C2
Lilycroft Rd *GIR* BD8 .... 24 C2
Lilycroft Wk *HTON* BD9 .... 24 C2
Lily St *GIR* BD8 .... 24 C2
Lilythorne Av *IDLE* BD10 .... 20 B1
Lime Cl *KGHY* BD21 .... 6 B2
Lime Gv *YEA* LS19 .... 15 F1 🔢
Limes Av *HIPP* HX3 .... 47 H4
Lime St *BGLY* BD16 .... 10 C3
   GTHN BD7 .... 30 B3 🔢
   KGHY BD21 .... 6 B4 🔢
Lime Tree Sq *SHPY* BD18 .... 17 G1
Lincoln Cl *GIR* BD8 .... 24 D3
Lincoln Rd *GIR* BD8 .... 24 D3
Lincoln Wy *HIPP* HX3 .... 41 G4
Linden Av *BFDE* BD3 .... 26 D4
Linden Cl *BRIG* HD6 .... 50 D5
Linden Rd *HIPP* HX3 .... 47 H4
Lindisfarne Rd *SHPY* BD18 .... 18 A2
Lindley Dr *GTHN* BD7 .... 30 A5
Lindley Rd *WBOW* BD5 .... 31 E4
Lindrick Gv *LUD/ILL* HX2 .... 34 A3 🔢
Lindrick Wk *LUD/ILL* HX2 .... 34 A3
Lindrick Wy *LUD/ILL* HX2 .... 34 A3
Ling Bob *LUD/ILL* HX2 .... 40 C5
Ling Bob Cft *LUD/ILL* HX2 .... 40 C4 🔢
Lingdale Rd *LM/WK* BD12 .... 37 F4
Lingfield Crs *CLAY* BD14 .... 29 F5 🔢
Lingfield Dr *HWTH* BD22 .... 9 F5
Lingfield Gv *WIL/AL* BD15 .... 16 A4
Lingfield Ter *WBSY* BD6 .... 29 F5
Ling Royd Av *LUD/ILL* HX2 .... 40 C5
Lingwood Av *GIR* BD8 .... 24 A3
Lingwood Rd *GIR* BD8 .... 24 A4
Lingwood Ter *GIR* BD8 .... 24 A4 🔢
Linkway *BGLY* BD16 .... 16 D2 🔢
Linnet Cl *GIR* BD8 .... 23 F4 🔢
Linnet St *KGHY* BD21 .... 7 E3 🔢
Linnhe Av *WBSY* BD6 .... 37 E4 🔢
Linton St *BOW* BD4 .... 31 G3
Lismore Rd *KGHY* BD21 .... 6 C3
Lister Av *BOW* BD4 .... 32 A4
Listerhills Rd *GTHN* BD7 .... 30 D1
Lister La *ECHL* BD2 .... 25 G2
   HFAX HX1 .... 4 D4
Lister's Rd *HIPP* HX3 .... 42 B5
Lister St *BOW* BD4 .... 32 B5
   BOW BD4 .... 39 H1 🔢
   BRIG HD6 .... 50 B5
   HFAX HX1 .... 5 H3
   KGHY BD21 .... 6 C5
Lister Vw *GIR* BD8 .... 24 D3
Little Baines St *HFAX* HX1 .... 4 C3
Littlebeck Dr *BGLY* BD16 .... 11 F3 🔢
Little Cote *IDLE* BD10 .... 13 H5
Little Cross St *WBOW* BD5 .... 31 F5 🔢
Littlefield Wk *WBOW* BD5 .... 37 G2
Little Horton Gn *WBOW* BD5 ..... 30 D2
Little Horton La *WBOW* BD5 ...... 2 F7
   WBOW BD5 .... 30 D4
Littlelands *BGLY* BD16 .... 16 D2
Little La *HTON* BD9 .... 24 A2
Little Pk *IDLE* BD10 .... 14 D5
Littlewood Cl *WBSY* BD6 .... 37 H3

Little Woodhouse *BRIG* HD6 ...... 52 B1
Littondale Cl *BAIL* BD17 .... 13 F2 🔢
Litton Rd *HWTH* BD22 .... 6 B5
Livingstone Cl *ECHL* BD2 .... 19 G3 🔢
Livingstone Rd *ECHL* BD2 .... 19 G4
   SHPY BD18 .... 19 E5
Livingstone St *HIPP* HX3 .... 41 F4 🔢
Livingstone St North
   LUD/ILL HX2 .... 34 B5 🔢
Lloyds Dr *LM/WK* BD12 .... 38 B4
Locarno Av *HTON* BD9 .... 23 H2
Locherbie Gn *WIL/AL* BD15 ...... 23 E3 🔢
Lochy Rd *WBSY* BD6 .... 37 E4 🔢
Locksley Rd *BRIG* HD6 .... 53 G2
The Locks *BGLY* BD16 .... 10 C3
Lock St *HIPP* HX3 .... 5 K6 🔢
Lockwood St *LM/WK* BD12 .... 38 B5
   SHPY BD18 .... 18 A1 🔢
   WBSY BD6 .... 37 H1 🔢
Lode Pit La *BGLY* BD16 .... 11 G2
Lodge Hl *BAIL* BD17 .... 12 A3
Lodore Pl *ECHL* BD2 .... 26 A1
Lodore Rd *ECHL* BD2 .... 25 H1
Loft St *GIR* BD8 .... 24 A4 🔢
Lombard St *HFAX* HX1 .... 4 B7
   YEA LS19 .... 15 F2
London La *YEA* LS19 .... 15 F2
London Rd *RPDN/SBR* HX6 .... 46 C5
London St *YEA* LS19 .... 15 F2 🔢
Longbottom Ter *HIPP* HX3 .... 48 A4 🔢
Long Cl *LM/WK* BD12 .... 44 C1
Longcroft *KGHY* BD21 .... 6 D5
Longcroft Pl *BFD* BD1 .... 2 B5
Long Fallas Crs *BRIG* HD6 .... 52 C4
Longfield Av *HIPP* HX3 .... 42 D4 🔢
Longfield Dr *BOW* BD4 .... 32 B4
Longford Ter *GTHN* BD7 .... 30 A2 🔢
Long La *CUL/QBY* BD13 .... 35 E3
   HIPP HX3 .... 40 D3
   HIPP HX3 .... 48 B1
   HTON BD9 .... 17 G4
   WIL/AL BD15 .... 22 A3
Long Mdw *ECHL* BD2 .... 19 F5
Long Preston Cha *IDLE* BD10 ..... 20 D2 🔢
Long Rdg *BRIG* HD6 .... 52 B4
Long Rw *LM/WK* BD12 .... 44 B5
Longroyd *SHPY* BD18 .... 19 G1 🔢
Long Royd Dr *BAIL* BD17 .... 13 F2
Longroyde Cl *BRIG* HD6 .... 52 A5
Longroyde Gv *BRIG* HD6 .... 52 A5 🔢
Longroyde Rd *BRIG* HD6 .... 52 A4
Longside La *GTHN* BD7 .... 30 D1
Long St *BOW* BD4 .... 32 A2
Longwood Av *BGLY* BD16 .... 10 B1
Longwood Vw *BGLY* BD16 .... 10 B1
Lonsdale St *BFDE* BD3 .... 3 J3
Lordsfield Pl *BOW* BD4 .... 39 G1
Lord's La *BRIG* HD6 .... 52 C2
Lord St *HFAX* HX1 .... 5 F4
   KGHY BD21 .... 6 D4 🔢
   RPDN/SBR HX6 .... 46 B3
Loris St *BOW* BD4 .... 39 G1
Lorne St *BOW* BD4 .... 32 A4 🔢
   KGHY BD21 .... 7 F3
Loughrigg St *WBOW* BD5 .... 31 F4 🔢
Louisa St *IDLE* BD10 .... 20 A1 🔢
Louis Av *WBOW* BD5 .... 30 D3
Love La *HFAX* HX1 .... 5 F5
Low Ash Av *SHPY* BD18 .... 19 E2
Low Ash Crs *SHPY* BD18 .... 19 F2 🔢
Low Ash Dr *SHPY* BD18 .... 19 E2
Low Ash Gv *SHPY* BD18 .... 19 E2
Low Ash Rd *SHPY* BD18 .... 19 F2
Low Bank *HWTH* BD22 .... 8 A3
Low Bank La *HWTH* BD22 .... 8 A3
Low Bank St *PDSY/CALV* LS28 ... 27 H1
Low Cl *BGLY* BD16 .... 11 E4 🔢
Lowell Av *HFAX* HX1 .... 30 A2 🔢
Lower Ashgrove *WBOW* BD5 ...... 2 B7
Lower Clifton St
   RPDN/SBR HX6 .... 46 B4 🔢
Lower Clyde St
   RPDN/SBR HX6 .... 46 A5 🔢
Lower Cross St *HFAX* HX1 .... 5 J1
Lower Crow Nest Dr *BRIG* HD6 ... 50 C1
Lower Finkil St *BRIG* HD6 .... 49 H3
Lower Fold *BRIG* HD6 .... 52 B1
Lower George St *WBSY* BD6 ...... 37 G1 🔢
Lower Globe St *BFD* BD8 .... 24 D4
Lower Gra *HUDN* HD2 .... 53 F5
Lower Grattan Rd *BFD* BD1 .... 2 A5
Lower Green Av *CLECK* BD19 .... 45 G5 🔢
Lower Holme *BAIL* BD17 .... 12 D5
Lower House Cl *SHPY* BD18 ...... 19 G1
Lower Kipping La
   CUL/QBY BD13 .... 28 A1 🔢
Lower Kirkgate *HFAX* HX1 .... 5 K4
Lower La *BIRK/DRI* BD11 .... 39 G5

   BOW BD4 .... 32 B3
Lower Newlands *BRIG* HD6 .... 52 C2 🔢
Lower Quarry Rd *HUDN* HD2 ..... 53 H4
Lower Rushton Rd *BFDE* BD3 .... 26 D5
Lower School St *LM/WK* BD12 .... 37 H4
   SHPY BD18 .... 18 A1 🔢
Lower Westfield Rd *GIR* BD8 ...... 24 B3 🔢
Lower Wyke Gn *LM/WK* BD12 .... 44 C5
Lower Wyke La *LM/WK* BD12 .... 44 D5
Loweswater Av *WBSY* BD6 .... 37 E4
Lowfield Cl *LM/WK* BD12 .... 38 B5
Low Fold *CLECK* BD19 .... 45 G5 🔢
Low Gn *GTHN* BD7 .... 30 B4 🔢
   YEA LS19 .... 15 H3
Low Green Ter *GTHN* BD7 .... 30 C4 🔢
Low La *BRIG* HD6 .... 50 D2
   CLAY BD14 .... 28 D2
Low Mill La *KGHY* BD21 .... 7 E4
Low Moor St *LM/WK* BD12 .... 38 A4 🔢
Low Moor Ter *LUD/ILL* HX2 .... 46 C1 🔢
Lowry Vw *KGHY* BD21 .... 6 D5
Low Spring Rd *KGHY* BD21 .... 7 F5
Low St *KGHY* BD21 .... 6 D4
Lowther St *ECHL* BD2 .... 26 A3
Low Well Rd *WBOW* BD5 .... 31 E4 🔢
Low Wd *WIL/AL* BD15 .... 16 A5
Lucy Hall Dr *BAIL* BD17 .... 11 H4
Lucy St *HIPP* HX3 .... 5 K1
Ludlam St *WBOW* BD5 .... 31 F2
Luke Rd *WBOW* BD5 .... 30 D3
Lulworth Gv *BOW* BD4 .... 32 C5 🔢
Lumb La *GIR* BD8 .... 24 D3
   HIPP HX3 .... 41 G3
Lumbrook Cl *HIPP* HX3 .... 43 F2 🔢
Lumby St *IDLE* BD10 .... 20 A1 🔢
Lund St *BGLY* BD16 .... 10 D3 🔢
   GIR BD8 .... 23 H5 🔢
   KGHY BD21 .... 6 D3
Lupton St *GIR* BD8 .... 2 B1
Lustre St *KGHY* BD21 .... 6 B4
Luther Wy *ECHL* BD2 .... 25 G1 🔢
Luton St *HFAX* HX1 .... 4 B3
   KGHY BD21 .... 6 C4
Lydgate *HIPP* HX3 .... 42 D2
Lydgate Pk *HIPP* HX3 .... 49 H1
Lydgate Pl *PDSY/CALV* LS28 ..... 21 F2
Lydgate Pl *PDSY/CALV* LS28 ..... 21 F2
Lydget Ct *AIRE* BD20 .... 6 B1 🔢
Lymington Dr *BOW* BD4 .... 32 D3
Lynch Av *GTHN* BD7 .... 30 A4 🔢
Lyncroft *ECHL* BD2 .... 19 G5
Lyndale Dr *SHPY* BD18 .... 19 G2 🔢
Lyndale Rd *BGLY* BD16 .... 11 F1
Lyndean Gdns *IDLE* BD10 .... 19 H2
Lynden Av *SHPY* BD18 .... 19 F1
Lynden Ct *WBSY* BD6 .... 37 F3
Lyndhurst Av *BRIG* HD6 .... 52 B4
Lyndhurst Gv *WIL/AL* BD15 ...... 23 F3
Lyndhurst Grove Rd *BRIG* HD6 ... 52 B3
Lyndhurst Rd *BRIG* HD6 .... 52 B3
Lyndon Ter *BGLY* BD16 .... 10 D3 🔢
Lynfield Dr *HTON* BD9 .... 23 F1
Lynfield Mt *SHPY* BD18 .... 19 F1 🔢
Lynmoor Ct *IDLE* BD10 .... 19 H2
Lynwood Gdns
   PDSY/CALV LS28 .... 33 H1
Lynsey Gdns *BOW* BD4 .... 39 E3
Lynthorne Rd *HTON* BD9 .... 18 C5
Lynton Av *HTON* BD9 .... 24 A1
Lynton Dr *AIRE* BD20 .... 7 G2
   HTON BD9 .... 23 H2
   SHPY BD18 .... 18 B2
Lynton Gv *LUD/ILL* HX2 .... 34 A1
Lynton Vls *HTON* BD9 .... 24 A2
Lynwood Av *SHPY* BD18 .... 19 F1 🔢
Lynwood Ct *HWTH* BD22 .... 4 A7
Lynwood Crs *HFAX* HX1 .... 4 A7
Lynwood Ms *BOW* BD4 .... 33 E5 🔢
Lyon St *CUL/QBY* BD13 .... 22 A5 🔢
   CUL/QBY BD13 .... 35 G1 🔢
Lytham Dr *CUL/QBY* BD13 .... 29 E5
Lytton Rd *GIR* BD8 .... 24 A4

M

Mabel Royd *GTHN* BD7 .... 30 A2
Mackingstone Dr *HWTH* BD22 ..... 8 A3
Mackingstone La *HWTH* BD22 .... 8 A3
Macturk Gv *GIR* BD8 .... 24 C3 🔢
Maddocks St *SHPY* BD18 .... 18 B1 🔢
Madison Av *BOW* BD4 .... 39 H1
Madni Cl *HFAX* HX1 .... 4 E4
Maidstone St *BFDE* BD3 .... 26 B5
Maidwell Wy *WBSY* BD6 .... 37 F4
Main St *BAIL* BD17 .... 14 B1
   BGLY BD16 .... 10 C3

BGLY BD16 .... 17 E3
LM/WK BD12 .... 38 B4
LM/WK BD12 .... 44 D1
Maister Pl *HWTH* BD22 .... 8 A3 ⑧
Maitland Cl *WIL/AL* BD15.... 23 E5
Maize St *HWTH* BD22 .... 9 F2
Malham Av *HTON* BD9.......... 23 F1
Mallard Cl *IDLE* BD10 .... 20 B4
Mallard Ct *GIR* BD8 .... 23 F5 ⑥
Mallory Cl *HTON* BD7 .... 30 A1 ⑧
Malmesbury Cl *BOW* BD4 ..... 39 H1 ⑧
Malsis Crs *KGHY* BD21 .... 6 B5 ⑪
Malsis Rd *KGHY* BD21............ 6 B5
Maltings Rd *LUD/ILL* HX2 ...... 40 C3
Malton St *HIPP* HX3............ 41 H3
RPDN/SBR HX6 .... 46 A3
Malt St *HWTH* BD22 .... 9 F2 ⑫
Malvern Brow *HTON* BD9....... 23 G2
Malvern Gv *HTON* BD9......... 23 G3
Malvern Rd *HTON* BD9.......... 23 G3
Manchester Rd *WBOW* BD5 ... 31 E4
WBOW BD5....................... 38 A1
WBSY BD6 .... 38 A2 ⑧
Mandale Gv *WBSY* BD6 .... 36 C2
Mandale Rd *WBSY* BD6 .... 36 C1
Mandeville Crs *WBSY* BD6 ..... 37 E2
Manley St *BRIG* HD6............ 50 B5
Mannheim Rd *HTON* BD9 ...... 24 B2 ⑧
Manningham La *GIR* BD8 ...... 24 D2
Mannville Gv *HWTH* BD22 ...... 6 B5
Mannville Pl *HWTH* BD22 .... 6 B5
Mannville Rd *KGHY* BD21 ...... 9 F1
Mannville St *HWTH* BD22 ...... 6 B5 ⑫
Mannville Ter *GTHN* BD7........ 2 B7
Mannville Wy *HWTH* BD22 ..... 6 B5 ⑬
Manor Cl *GIR* BD8.............. 23 G4
HIPP HX3 .... 47 G4
Manor Dr *BGLY* BD16........... 16 D2
HIPP HX3 .... 47 G4
Manor Farm Cl *BGLY* BD16 .... 17 E3
Manor Fold *BGLY* BD16......... 17 E3
Manor Gv *AIRE* BD20 .... 7 H3
Manor Heath Rd *HIPP* HX3..... 47 G4
Manor La *HIPP* BD18 .... 18 C2 ⑧
Manorley La *HIPP* HX3 .... 36 D4
Manor Pk *GIR* BD8 .... 23 G4
HWTH BD22 .... 8 B4 ⑧
Manor Rd *AIRE* BD20............ 6 B1
BGLY BD16 .... 17 E2
Manor Rw *BFD* BD1............. 2 C3
WBSY BD6........................ 37 H3
Manor St *CLECK* BD19.......... 51 G2
ECHL BD2 .... 26 A1 ⑧
Manor Ter *ECHL* BD2 .... 26 A1
Manscombe Rd *WIL/AL* BD15.... 23 F3
Mansel Ms *BOW* BD4 .... 39 H1
Manse St *BFDE* BD3 .... 26 B5 ⑧
Mansfield Av *BGLY* BD16........ 11 F1
Mansfield Rd *GIR* BD8 .... 24 D2
Mansion La *HIPP* HX3 .... 47 H4
Maple Av *BFDE* BD3............ 26 D4
HWTH BD22 .... 8 C4
Maple Gv *KGHY* BD21.......... 6 B2
Maple St *HFAX* HX1 .... 4 B7
Marbridge Ct *WBSY* BD6 ...... 30 C5 ⑧
Marchbank Rd *BFDE* BD3 ..... 26 B4
March Cote La *BGLY* BD16 .... 16 D3
Marchwood Gv *CLAY* BD14 .... 29 G3 ⑧
Margaret St *HFAX* HX1 .... 4 E4
KGHY BD21 .... 6 B3
Margate Rd *BOW* BD4 .... 31 H3 ⑩
Marion Dr *SHPY* BD18 .... 18 D2
Marion St *BGLY* BD16.......... 10 D3 ⑪
BRIG HD6 .... 50 B4
GTHN BD7 .... 24 D5 ⑧
Mark Cl *IDLE* BD10 .... 20 B1
Market Cl *CUL/QBY* BD13 ..... 28 B1 ⑧
Market Pl *KGHY* BD21 .... 6 D4 ⑧
Market Sq *SHPY* BD18 .... 18 C1
Market St *BFD* BD1............. 2 D5
BGLY BD16 .... 10 C3 ⑩
BRIG HD6 .... 52 C1
CUL/QBY BD13 .... 28 A1 ⑰
HFAX HX1 .... 5 H4
KGHY BD21 .... 6 D5
SHPY BD18 .... 18 C2 ⑧
WBSY BD6 .... 37 H1 ⑬
Markfield Av *LM/WK* BD12 ..... 37 H5
Markfield Cl *LM/WK* BD12 ..... 37 H5
Markfield Crs *LM/WK* BD12 .... 37 H5
Markfield Dr *LM/WK* BD12 ..... 37 H5
Markham Av *YEA* LS19......... 15 H1
Markham Crs *YEA* LS19 .... 15 H1
Markham Cft *YEA* LS19 .... 15 H1
Mark St *WBOW* BD5 .... 31 F4 ⑪
Marland Rd *KGHY* BD21 .... 7 F3
Marlborough Av *HIPP* HX3 .... 47 G4 ⑧
Marlborough Rd *GIR* BD8 ...... 24 D3

SHPY BD18 .... 18 B2 ⑧
Marlborough St *KGHY* BD21 ... 7 E3 ⑫
Marldon Rd *HIPP* HX3 .... 42 D4
Marley Cl *GIR* BD8 .... 23 H4
Marley La *CUL/QBY* BD13 ..... 28 B4
Marley Rd *KGHY* BD21.......... 7 G3
Marley St *BFDE* BD3............ 3 G5
KGHY BD21 .... 6 C5
Marlott Rd *SHPY* BD18 .... 19 E1 ⑧
Marlow St *KGHY* BD21 .... 7 F3 ⑧
Marmion Av *GIR* BD8 .... 23 F5
Marne Av *CLAY* BD14 .... 29 F4
Marne Crs *IDLE* BD10 .... 20 A2
Marquis Av *LM/WK* BD12 ...... 39 E5
Marriner Rd *KGHY* BD21 .... 6 D5
Marriner's Dr *HTON* BD9 ...... 18 C5
Marriner's Wk *KGHY* BD21 ..... 9 H1
Marsh *PDSY/CALV* LS28........ 27 H5
Marshall St *KGHY* BD21 .... 6 C2 ⑧
Marsh Ct *PDSY/CALV* LS28..... 27 H5
Marsh Delves La *HIPP* HX3 .... 48 C1
Marshfield Pl *WBOW* BD5 ..... 31 E4 ⑩
Marshfield St *WBOW* BD5...... 31 E4
Marsh Gv *WBOW* BD5 .... 30 D4 ⑫
Marsh La *HIPP* HX3 .... 48 C2
Marsh St *WBOW* BD5 .... 31 E4
Marsh Ter *PDSY/CALV* LS28.... 27 H5
Marshway *HFAX* HX1 .... 4 D2
Marsland Pl *BFDE* BD3 .... 26 C5
Marston Cl *CUL/QBY* BD13 .... 35 G1 ⑧
Marten Rd *WBOW* BD5 .... 30 D4 ⑬
Martin St *BRIG* HD6 .... 50 C5 ⑧
Martlett Dr *WBOW* BD5........ 31 G5
Marton Ct *BFDE* BD3 .... 26 C5 ⑧
Mary St *BOW* BD4.............. 32 B2
BRIG HD6 .... 50 B4
CUL/QBY BD13 .... 28 A1 ⑱
LM/WK BD12 .... 44 D1 ⑬
SHPY BD18 .... 18 A1 ⑰
Maryville Av *BRIG* HD6 .... 50 A3
Masefield Av *HTON* BD9 .... 23 F1
Masham Pl *HTON* BD9 .... 24 A2 ⑧
Masonic St *HFAX* HX1 .... 46 D2
Master La *LUD/ILL* HX2 .... 47 E4
Matlock St *HIPP* HX3 .... 41 F4
Matthew Cl *AIRE* BD20 .... 7 F2 ⑦
Maude Av *BAIL* BD17 .... 12 D4
Maude St *HIPP* HX3 .... 41 F1 ⑧
Maudsley St *BFDE* BD3 .... 3 H5
Maud St *BFDE* BD3 .... 3 J6
Maurice Av *BRIG* HD6 .... 50 A4
Mavis St *BFDE* BD3 .... 3 J4
Mawcroft Cl *YEA* LS19 .... 15 F1
Mawcroft Grange Dr *YEA* LS19 .. 15 F1
Mawson St *SHPY* BD18 .... 18 A1 ⑪
Maw St *BOW* BD4.............. 31 G2
Maxwell Rd *WBSY* BD6 .... 37 E2
May Av *CUL/QBY* BD13 .... 28 B1
Mayfair *WBOW* BD5 .... 31 E3 ⑫
Mayfair Wy *BOW* BD4 .... 32 C2 ⑧
Mayfield Av *BRIG* HD6 .... 44 C5
HFAX HX1 .... 4 C6
LM/WK BD12 .... 44 D2
Mayfield Dr *HFAX* HX1 .... 4 C6
Mayfield Gdns *HFAX* HX1 ...... 4 C6
Mayfield Gv *BAIL* BD17 .... 13 E3
BRIG HD6 .... 44 C5
HFAX HX1 .... 4 C6
Mayfield Mt *HFAX* HX1......... 4 C6 ⑧
Mayfield Pl *LM/WK* BD12 ...... 44 D2
Mayfield Ri *LM/WK* BD12 ...... 45 E2
Mayfield Rd *KGHY* BD21 .... 6 C3
Mayfield St *HFAX* HX1 .... 4 D6
Mayfield Ter *CLAY* BD14 .... 29 F3
LM/WK BD12 .... 45 E2 ⑧
Mayfield Vw *LM/WK* BD12 ..... 45 E2
Mayo Av *WBOW* BD5 .... 31 E5
Mayo Crs *WBOW* BD5 .... 38 B1
Mayo Dr *WBOW* BD5 .... 38 B1
Mayo Gv *WBOW* BD5 .... 38 B1
Mayo Rd *WBOW* BD5 .... 38 B1
May St *KGHY* BD21 .... 6 D3 ⑧
Maythorne Crs *CLAY* BD14 .... 29 G3
Maythorne Dr *CLAY* BD14 ..... 29 H3 ⑧
May Tree Cl *CLAY* BD14 .... 29 G2
Mcmahon Dr *CUL/QBY* BD13 .. 29 F5
Meadowbank Av *WIL/AL* BD15 .. 23 E3
Meadow Cl *HIPP* HX3.......... 36 C4
Meadow Ct *BRIG* HD6 .... 53 F1 ⑪
WIL/AL BD15 .... 16 D5
Meadow Crest *HIPP* HX3 ..... 40 D3 ②
Meadow Croft Cl *IDLE* BD10.... 19 G1
Meadowcroft Rd *BOW* BD4.... 39 F2
Meadow Dr *HIPP* HX3 .... 40 D3
Meadowlands *CLECK* BD19..... 45 F4
Meadow La *HIPP* HX3 .... 40 D3
Meadow Park Crs
PDSY/CALV LS28 .... 27 G2

Meadow Park Dr
PDSY/CALV LS28 .... 27 G2
Meadow Rd *IDLE* BD10 .... 20 D1
The Meadows *HIPP* BD6 .... 37 H1
Meadow Vw *HWTH* BD22 ...... 8 C4 ⑧
LM/WK BD12 .... 44 D2
Mead Vw *BOW* BD4 .... 32 C4 ⑧
Meadway *WBSY* BD6 .... 36 D4 ②
Mearclough Rd *RPDN/SBR* HX6 ... 46 C4
Medeway *PDSY/CALV* LS28..... 27 H2
Medley La *HIPP* HX3 .... 42 C1
Medway *CUL/QBY* BD13 .... 35 G2
Meggison Gv *WBOW* BD5 ..... 30 D3
Megnaway *WBOW* BD5 .... 31 F5 ⑩
Melba Rd *GTHN* BD7 .... 30 C4
Melbourne Gv *BFDE* BD3 ..... 26 D4 ⑧
Melbourne Pl *WBOW* BD5..... 31 E2
Melbourne St *HIPP* HX3 ...... 41 F4
SHPY BD18 .... 18 B1 ⑧
Melbourne Ter *WBOW* BD5 ... 31 F2 ⑬
Melcombe Wk *BOW* BD4...... 32 D3 ⑧
Melford St *BOW* BD4 .... 32 B5
Mellor St *BRIG* HD6 .... 52 C1 ⑪
HFAX HX1 .... 47 F3
Melrose St *GTHN* BD7 .... 30 B5 ⑬
HIPP HX3 .... 41 F4 ⑭
Melton Ter *IDLE* BD10 .... 20 D4
Melville St *GTHN* BD7 .... 24 D5
Mendip Wy *LM/WK* BD12 ..... 37 G4
Menin Dr *BAIL* BD17 .... 12 C1
Menstone St *GIR* BD8 .... 24 D4 ⑧
Merchants Ct *BOW* BD4 ...... 31 H2 ④
Merlin Gv *GIR* BD8 .... 23 F5
Merrivale Rd *WIL/AL* BD15 ..... 22 D4
Merrydale Rd *BOW* BD4 ...... 38 D4
Merton Dr *PDSY/CALV* LS28.... 27 H2
Merton Fold *WBOW* BD5 ..... 31 F3 ⑪
Merton Gdns *PDSY/CALV* LS28 ... 27 H2
Merton Rd *GTHN* BD7 .... 30 C2
Merville Av *BAIL* BD17 .... 12 D1
Metcalfe St *BOW* BD4 .... 32 A3 ⑧
Methuen Ov *LM/WK* BD12 .... 44 D4 ⑬
Mexborough Rd *SHPY* BD18 ... 19 E4 ②
Miall St *HFAX* HX1 .... 4 C2
Mickledore Cl *GTHN* BD7 ..... 29 H4 ⑬
Mickledore Rdg *GTHN* BD7 .... 29 H4 ⑧
Micklefield Ct *YEA* LS19 .... 15 G2 ②
Micklefield La *YEA* LS19 .... 15 F2
Micklefield Rd *YEA* LS19 ...... 15 G2
Micklethwaite Dr
CUL/QBY BD13 .... 35 F2
CLECK BD19 .... 51 F
Middlebrook Cl *GIR* BD8 ...... 23 H5 ⑦
Middlebrook Crs *GIR* BD8...... 29 C1
Middlebrook Dr *GIR* BD8 ...... 23 G5 ⑧
Middlebrook Hi *GIR* BD8....... 23 G5 ⑧
Middlebrook Ri *GIR* BD8 ...... 23 G5 ⑦
Middlebrook Vw *GIR* BD8...... 23 H5
Middlebrook Wk *GIR* BD8...... 23 H5
Middlebrook Wy *GIR* BD8 ..... 29 G1
Middlegate Ct *BOW* BD4 ...... 39 E2 ⑧
Middleham Ct *BOW* BD4 ..... 32 D4 ⑪
Middle La *CLAY* BD14......... 29 F2
Middleton St *GIR* BD8 .... 24 C3 ⑪
Middle Wy *KGHY* BD21 .... 7 F3
Midgeley Rd *BAIL* BD17........ 12 B5
Midland Hl *BGLY* BD16 .... 10 C3
Midland Rd *BAIL* BD17 .... 13 E4
GIR BD8.......................... 25 E2
HTON BD9........................ 18 D4
Midland Ter *HTON* BD9 .... 18 D4
Midway Av *BGLY* BD16 .... 16 D2 ②
Mile Cross Gdns *HFAX* HX1 ... 46 D2
Mile Cross Pl *HFAX* HX1 ...... 46 D2
Mile Cross Rd *HFAX* HX1 ..... 46 D2
Mile Cross Ter *HFAX* HX1 ..... 46 D2
Miles Hill Crs *BOW* BD4 ...... 39 F1
Miles Hill Dr *BOW* BD4 .... 39 F1
Mile Thorn St *HFAX* HX1 ...... 4 B4
Milford Pl *HTON* BD9 .... 24 B1 ⑧
Millbeck Cl *GIR* BD8 .... 29 F1 ⑪
Mill Carr Hill Rd *BOW* BD4.... 39 E4
Millersdale Cl *BOW* BD4 ...... 38 D3
Mill Gv *BRIG* HD6 .... 50 A4
Mill Hill La *BRIG* HD6 .... 50 A4
BRIG HD6 .... 53 G2
Mill House Ri *BOW* BD4 ...... 39 E1 ⑧
Milligan Av *ECHL* BD2 .... 19 H4 ②
Mill La *BRIG* HD6 .... 52 C1
HIPP HX3 .... 36 D4
HIPP HX3 .... 41 G3
HWTH BD22 .... 8 A4
WBOW BD5....................... 31 F2
Millmoor Cl *HTON* BD9........ 23 G2
Mill Royd St *BRIG* HD6 .... 52 C1
Mill St *BFD* BD1............... 2 E3
WBSY BD6 .... 37 H1 ⑧
Milner Ing *LM/WK* BD12 ...... 44 D1
Milner Rd *BAIL* BD17 .... 12 C5

Milner St *HFAX* HX1 .... 4 E
Milne St *GTHN* BD7 .... 24 D5
Milton Av *RPDN/SBR* HX6 ..... 46 B
Milton Pl *HFAX* HX1 .... 4 E
Milton St *GTHN* BD7 .... 24 D5
RPDN/SBR HX6 .... 46 A
Minnie St *KGHY* BD21 .... 6 C5 ⑧
Mint St *ECHL* BD2 .... 26 A
Mirfield Av *ECHL* BD2 .... 19 H4 ⑧
Mission St *BRIG* HD6 .... 52 D
Mistral Cl *LM/WK* BD12 .... 44 D
Mitcham Dr *HTON* BD9 .... 24 B2 ⑧
Mitchell Cl *IDLE* BD10 .... 14 B5
Mitchell La *IDLE* BD10 .... 14 B
Mitchell Sq *WBOW* BD5 ...... 31 F5 ⑧
Mitchell St *BRIG* HD6.......... 50 B
KGHY BD21 .... 7 E3 ⑪
RPDN/SBR HX6 .... 46 B
Mitchell Ter *BGLY* BD16 ...... 10 C
Mitre Ct *BOW* BD4 .... 32 C4
Mitton St *WBOW* BD5 .... 30 D4 ⑧
Moffat Cl *WBSY* BD6 .... 37 E2
Mond Av *BFDE* BD3 .... 26 C
Monk Barn Cl *BGLY* BD16 .... 10 D2
Monk St *GTHN* BD7 .... 24 D5
Monson Av *PDSY/CALV* LS28... 21 C
Montague St *WBOW* BD5 ..... 30 D
Montrose St *ECHL* BD2 .... 19 E
Moody St *BOW* BD4 .... 31 C
Moor Bottom La *BGLY* BD16... 10 D
KGHY BD21 .... 9 C
Moor Bottom Rd *LUD/ILL* HX2 ... 34 A
Moor Close Av *CUL/QBY* BD13 .. 34 D2
Moor Close Farm Ms
CUL/QBY BD13 .... 34 D2
Moor Close La *CUL/QBY* BD13 .. 34 D
Moor Close Pde *CUL/QBY* BD13 .. 34 D
Moor Close Rd *CUL/QBY* BD13 .. 34 D
Moor Cft *BGLY* BD16 .... 11 E
Moor Dr *HWTH* BD22 .... 8 B
Moore Av *GTHN* BD7 .... 30 A
Moor End Av *LUD/ILL* HX2 ... 40 A
Moor End Gdns *LUD/ILL* HX2 ... 40 C
Moor End Rd *LUD/ILL* HX2.... 40 A
Moore St *KGHY* BD21 .... 6 D5
Moore Vw *GTHN* BD7.......... 30 A
Moorfield Av *BFDE* BD3 ...... 26 C
CLECK BD19 .... 51 F
Moorfield Dr *BAIL* BD17 ...... 12 D
HWTH BD22 .... 8 C
Moorfield Gdns *PDSY/CALV* LS28... 33 H
Moorfield Gv *PDSY/CALV* LS28 ... 33 H1
Moorfield Pl *IDLE* BD10 .... 20 A1
Moorfield Rd *BGLY* BD16 ..... 16 D2
Moorfield St *HFAX* HX1 .... 4 C
Moorfield Wy *CLECK* BD19.... 51 F1
Moorgarth Av *BFDE* BD3 ..... 26 C3
Moorgate *BAIL* BD17 .... 12 C
Moorgate Av *BFDE* BD3 ...... 26 B3
Moorgate St *HFAX* HX1 .... 4 B7
Moor Gv *HIPP* HX3 .... 36 E
Moorhead Crs *SHPY* BD18 ... 17 H3
Moorhead La *SHPY* BD18 ..... 17 H
Moorhead Ter *SHPY* BD18 .... 17 H
Moorhouse Av *ECHL* BD2 .... 19 H
The Moorings *IDLE* BD10 ..... 20 C
Moorland Av *BAIL* BD17 ...... 13 E
Moorland Cl *LUD/ILL* HX2 .... 40 D
Moorland Crs *BAIL* BD17 ..... 13 E
Moorland Dr *PDSY/CALV* LS28 .. 27 H
Moorland Gv *PDSY/CALV* LS28 ... 27 H
Moorland Pl *LM/WK* BD12 .... 38 B
Moorland Rd *PDSY/CALV* LS28 ... 27 H
Moorlands Av *BFDE* BD3 ..... 26 C3
HWTH BD22 .... 9 E
LUD/ILL HX2 .... 40 D
Moorlands Dr *LUD/ILL* HX2... 40 D3
Moorlands Pl *HFAX* HX1 ...... 47 E
Moorlands Vw *HFAX* HX1 ..... 47 E
Moorland Ter *KGHY* BD21 ..... 7 F
Moorland Vw *LM/WK* BD12 ... 38 E
Moor La *LUD/ILL* HX2 .... 40 C
Moorlea Dr *BAIL* BD17 .... 13 E3
Moor Park Dr *BFDE* BD3 ..... 26 B
Moor Park Rd *BFDE* BD3 ..... 26 B4
Moor Royd *HFAX* HX3........... 47 E
Moorside *BAIL* BD17 .... 13 E
CLECK BD19 .... 51 H
HTON BD9........................ 23 E
Moorside Av *ECHL* BD2 ...... 26 C2
Moorside Cl *ECHL* BD2 .... 26 B1
Moorside Gdns *ECHL* BD2 .... 26 B
LUD/ILL HX2 .... 41 E
Moorside La *BFDE* BD3 .... 26 C5
Moorside Pl *BFDE* BD3 .... 26 C5

Moorside Rd *BFDE* BD3 .... 26 C5 ⑤
  ECHL BD2 .... 20 B1
  ECHL BD2 .... 26 B1
Moorside St *LM/WK* BD12 .... 37 G4
Moorside Ter *ECHL* BD2 .... 26 C2 ②
Moor Stone Pl *HIPP* HX3 .... 36 B5 ③
Moor St *CUL/QBY* BD13 .... 35 F1 ⑨
  HWTH BD22 .... 8 C3
Moorthorpe Av *BFDE* BD3 .... 26 C3 ④
Moor Top Rd *LM/WK* BD12 .... 37 G2
  LUD/ILL HX2 .... 40 A5
Moor View Av *SHPY* BD18 .... 18 B1
Moorview Dr *SHPY* BD18 .... 19 G2 ②
Moorville Av *BFDE* BD3 .... 26 C3
Moor Wy *HWTH* BD22 .... 8 B3
Moorwell Pl *ECHL* BD2 .... 20 A5
Moravian Pl *WBOW* BD5 .... 31 E3 ⑬
Moresby Rd *WBSY* BD6 .... 36 D4
Morley Av *ECHL* BD2 .... 20 A4
Morley Carr Rd *LM/WK* BD12 .... 38 A5
Morley St *BFD* BD1 .... 2 B7
Morningside *GIR* BD8 .... 24 C3
Morning St *KGHY* BD21 .... 9 G2 ⑧
Mornington Rd *BGLY* BD16 .... 10 D3
Mornington St *KGHY* BD21 .... 6 C3
Mornington Vls *GIR* BD8 .... 25 E3 ④
Morpeth St *CUL/QBY* BD13 ...... 35 F1 ①
  GTHN BD7 .... 24 D5 ②
Mortimer Av *ECHL* BD2 .... 26 C3
Mortimer Rw *BFDE* BD3 .... 32 C1 ②
Mortimer St *GIR* BD8 .... 24 A4
Morton Rd *BOW* BD4 .... 32 C2 ②
Mortons Cl *HIPP* HX3 .... 48 B5
Moser Av *ECHL* BD2 .... 19 H4
Moser Crs *ECHL* BD2 .... 19 H4 ②
Mossdale Av *HTON* BD9 .... 23 F1 ①
Moss Side *HTON* BD9 .... 23 H2 ④
Mossy Bank Cl *CUL/QBY* BD13 .. 28 B5
Mostyn Gv *WBSY* BD6 .... 37 F2 ②
Mostyn Mt *HIPP* HX3 .... 41 F2 ②
Moulson St *WBOW* BD5 .... 31 F4 ②
Mountain Vw *LUD/ILL* HX2 .... 34 B4
  SHPY BD18 .... 19 E3
Mount Av *ECHL* BD2 .... 20 A4
  LUD/ILL HX2 .... 46 B1
Mount Crs *LUD/ILL* HX2 .... 46 A1
Mountfields *HIPP* HX3 .... 43 H5
Mount Gv *ECHL* BD2 .... 20 A4
Mountleigh Cl *BOW* BD4 .... 32 D5 ②
Mount Pellon Rd *LUD/ILL* HX2 .. 40 D5
Mount Pl *SHPY* BD18 .... 18 C1 ④
Mount Pleasant *WBSY* BD6 ...... 36 D3
Mount Pleasant Av *HFAX* HX1 ..... 4 C2
Mount Rd *ECHL* BD2 .... 20 A4
  WBSY BD6 .... 37 F1
Mount Royd *GIR* BD8 .... 24 D2
Mount St *BFDE* BD3 .... 3 H6
  BOW BD4 .... 3 K7
  ECHL BD2 .... 20 A4
  HFAX HX1 .... 5 F4
  HWTH BD22 .... 6 B4
  RPDN/SBR HX6 .... 46 A4
Mount St West *LUD/ILL* HX2 ..... 40 D5 ⑦
Mount Tabor St
  PDSY/CALV LS28 .... 27 H5 ①
Mount Vernon Rd *YEA* LS19 ..... 15 H2 ⑥
Mount Vw *HWTH* BD22 .... 8 A4
Mozley Dr *LUD/ILL* HX2 .... 34 A4
Muff St *BOW* BD4 .... 32 A2
Muirhead Ct *BOW* BD4 .... 32 D5 ⑩
Muirhead Dr *BOW* BD4 .... 32 D5
Muirhead Fold *BOW* BD4 .... 32 D5 ⑪
Mulberry La *KGHY* BD21 .... 7 E3 ⑯
Mulcture Hall Rd *HFAX* HX1 ...... 5 J3
Mulgrave St *BFDE* BD3 .... 3 J7
  BFDE BD3 .... 3 J6
Mumford St *WBOW* BD5 .... 31 F4 ⑬
Munby St *GIR* BD8 .... 23 H5
Munster St *BOW* BD4 .... 32 A4 ③
Munton Cl *WBSY* BD6 .... 36 D4 ③
Murdoch St *KGHY* BD21 .... 7 G3
Murgatroyd St *SHPY* BD18 .... 18 C1 ③
  WBOW BD5 .... 31 F4 ⑭
  WBOW BD5 .... 31 F5 ②
Murray St *WBOW* BD5 .... 30 D4 ⑮
Museum Ct *ECHL* BD2 .... 26 B2 ⑦
Musgrave Dr *ECHL* BD2 .... 26 B2
Musgrave Gv *ECHL* BD2 .... 26 B2 ⑧
Musgrave Mt *ECHL* BD2 .... 26 B2 ⑨
Musgrave Rd *ECHL* BD2 .... 26 B2
Musselburgh St *GTHN* BD7 ..... 24 D5 ⑥
Mutton La *WIL/AL* BD15 .... 22 A2
Myers Av *ECHL* BD2 .... 19 H5
Myers La *ECHL* BD2 .... 19 H5
Myrtle Av *BGLY* BD16 .... 10 C4 ②
  LUD/ILL HX2 .... 40 D1
Myrtle Ct *BGLY* BD16 .... 10 C4

Myrtle Dr *HWTH* BD22 .... 9 E5
  LUD/ILL HX2 .... 40 D1
Myrtle Gdns *LUD/ILL* HX2 .... 40 D1 ①
Myrtle Gv *BGLY* BD16 .... 10 C4
  LUD/ILL HX2 .... 40 D1
Myrtle Pl *BGLY* BD16 .... 10 C3
  LUD/ILL HX2 .... 40 D1
Myrtle St *BFD* BD3 .... 32 B1
  BGLY BD16 .... 10 C3 ⑫
Mytholmes La *HWTH* BD22 .... 8 C5

N

Nab La *SHPY* BD18 .... 17 G2
Nab Wood Bank *SHPY* BD18 ..... 17 G2
Nab Wood Cl *SHPY* BD18 .... 17 H2 ⑦
Nab Wood Crs *SHPY* BD18 ...... 17 G2
Nab Wood Dr *BGLY* BD16 .... 17 G3
Nab Wood Gdns *SHPY* BD18 .... 17 H2 ②
Nab Wood Gv *SHPY* BD18 .... 17 G2
Nab Wood Mt *SHPY* BD18 .... 17 G2 ④
Nab Wood Pl *SHPY* BD18 .... 17 G2 ③
Nab Wood Ri *SHPY* BD18 .... 17 G2 ⑤
Nab Wood Rd *SHPY* BD18 .... 17 G3
Nab Wood Ter *SHPY* BD18 ...... 17 G2 ⑥
Napier Rd *BFDE* BD3 .... 26 C5
Napier St *BFDE* BD3 .... 26 C5 ③
  CUL/QBY BD13 .... 35 G1 ⑩
Napier Ter *BFDE* BD3 .... 26 C5 ⑩
Naples St *GIR* BD8 .... 24 C3
Nares St *KGHY* BD21 .... 6 C4
Nares Street Upper
  KGHY BD21 .... 6 C4 ⑮
Naseby Ri *CUL/QBY* BD13 .... 35 G1 ⑪
Nashville Av *HWTH* BD22 .... 6 B5 ⑭
Nashville St *HWTH* BD22 .... 6 B5 ⑮
Nature Wy *WBSY* BD6 .... 36 D3 ②
Navigation Rd *HIPP* HX3 .... 5 K5
Naylor St *HFAX* HX1 .... 4 A3
Neal St *WBOW* BD5 .... 2 C7
Nearcliffe Rd *HTON* BD9 .... 24 B2
Near Crook *SHPY* BD18 .... 13 C5 ④
Necropolis Rd *GTHN* BD7 .... 30 A2
Ned La *BOW* BD4 .... 33 E3
Nelson Pl *CUL/QBY* BD13 .... 35 F1 ⑪
Nelson St *BFD* BD1 .... 2 D7
  CUL/QBY BD13 .... 35 F1
  RPDN/SBR HX6 .... 46 A4
  WBOW BD5 .... 2 D7
  WIL/AL BD15 .... 23 F3
Nene St *WBOW* BD5 .... 30 D3
Nesfield St *BFD* BD1 .... 2 B2
Nessfield Dr *HWTH* BD22 .... 9 E1
Nessfield Gv *HWTH* BD22 .... 9 E1 ②
Nessfield Rd *HWTH* BD22 .... 9 E1
Netherby St *BFDE* BD3 .... 3 K5
Netherhall Rd *BAIL* BD17 .... 13 E3
Netherlands Av *WBSY* BD6 ...... 37 H3
Netherlands Sq *WBSY* BD6 ...... 38 A3
Nether Moor Vw *BGLY* BD16 .... 10 D3 ⑬
Nettle Gv *HIPP* HX3 .... 42 C4
Neville Av *BOW* BD4 .... 39 E1
Neville Rd *BOW* BD4 .... 32 A3
Neville St *KGHY* BD21 .... 7 E3 ⑮
Nevill Gv *HTON* BD9 .... 23 C1
Newall St *WBOW* BD5 .... 31 E3
Newark Rd *BGLY* BD16 .... 10 C3
Newark St *BOW* BD4 .... 32 A4 ③
New Augustus St *BFD* BD1 .... 3 F7
New Bank *HIPP* HX3 .... 5 J1
New Bank Ri *BOW* BD4 .... 32 C4 ⑩
New Brighton *BGLY* BD16 .... 17 F3
New Bond St *HFAX* HX1 .... 5 F5
New Brunswick St *HFAX* HX1 .... 5 F5
Newburn Rd *GTHN* BD7 .... 30 C2 ⑨
Newbury Rd *BRIG* HD6 .... 52 A4
Newby St *WBOW* BD5 .... 31 F3
New Cl *SHPY* BD18 .... 17 G2 ⑦
New Close Rd *SHPY* BD18 .... 17 G2 ⑤
New Cross St *LM/WK* BD12 ..... 39 E5 ②
  WBOW BD5 .... 31 F4
New England Rd *KGHY* BD21 ... 9 G2
New Fold *WBSY* BD6 .... 36 D3
Newforth Gv *WBOW* BD5 .... 30 D5 ⑤
Newhall Dr *WBSY* BD6 .... 38 C2 ②
Newhall Mt *WBSY* BD6 .... 38 C2 ②
Newhall Rd *BOW* BD4 .... 39 E1 ⑤
New Hey Rd *BOW* BD4 .... 31 H3
New House La *CUL/QBY* BD13 .. 36 A1
Newill Cl *WBOW* BD5 .... 31 E5
New Kirkgate *SHPY* BD18 .... 18 C1 ⑥
New Laithe Rd *WBSY* BD6 .... 37 F1 ⑦
Newlands Av *BFDE* BD3 .... 26 C3
  HIPP HX3 .... 42 D1
Newlands Cl *BRIG* HD6 .... 52 C2 ④
Newlands Dr *BGLY* BD16 .... 10 B1

  HIPP HX3 .... 42 D2
Newlands Gv *HIPP* HX3 .... 42 D2
Newlands Pl *BFDE* BD3 .... 3 H2
Newlands Rd *CUL/QBY* BD13 ... 35 E1
New La *BOW* BD4 .... 32 C1
  BOW BD4 .... 33 C5
  CLECK BD19 .... 51 H2
  HIPP HX3 .... 48 A4
Newlay Cl *IDLE* BD10 .... 20 D2 ③
New Line *IDLE* BD10 .... 20 D2
Newlyn Rd *AIRE* BD20 .... 7 H2
Newman St *BOW* BD4 .... 32 A5 ⑧
New Occupation La
  PDSY/CALV LS28 .... 33 H1
New Otley Rd *BFDE* BD3 .... 3 G3
New Park Rd *CUL/QBY* BD13 ... 35 E1
New Popplewell La *CLECK* BD19 . 45 C5
Newport Pl *GIR* BD8 .... 24 D3 ⑩
Newport St *GIR* BD8 .... 24 D3 ⑪
New Rd *HFAX* HX1 .... 5 H5
New Rd East *CLECK* BD19 ...... 45 F5
New Road Side *YEA* LS19 .... 15 C1
Newroyd Rd *WBOW* BD5 .... 31 F5
Newstead Av *HFAX* HX1 .... 46 D1
Newstead Gdns *HFAX* HX1 ...... 46 D1
Newstead Gv *HFAX* HX1 .... 46 D1
Newstead Heath *HFAX* HX1 ..... 46 D1 ②
Newstead Pl *HFAX* HX1 .... 46 D1
Newstead Ter *HFAX* HX1 .... 46 D1
Newstead Wk *WBOW* BD5 .... 31 E3 ⑬
New St *BOW* BD4 .... 39 E2
  BRIG HD6 .... 50 C1 ⑧
  BRIG HD6 .... 53 E1
  HIPP HX3 .... 48 D4
  IDLE BD10 .... 20 A1
  LM/WK BD12 .... 39 E5
  LUD/ILL HX2 .... 40 D5 ⑤
Newton Pk *BRIG* HD6 .... 50 A2
Newton Pl *WBOW* BD5 .... 31 F3 ⑬
Newton St *RPDN/SBR* HX6 ...... 46 A4 ⑩
  WBOW BD5 .... 31 F4
  WBOW BD5 .... 31 F3
Newton Wy *BAIL* BD17 .... 12 D2
New Works Rd *LM/WK* BD12 .... 37 H5
Nicholas Cl *GTHN* BD7 .... 24 A5 ③
Nidderdale Wk *BAIL* BD17 .... 13 F2 ②
Nighthorne Av *BFDE* BD3 .... 26 B3 ②
Nile Crs *HWTH* BD22 .... 6 A5
Nile St *HWTH* BD22 .... 6 A5 ④
Nina Rd *GTHN* BD7 .... 30 A4 ⑧
Noble St *GTHN* BD7 .... 30 C2 ②
Nog La *HTON* BD9 .... 18 B5
The Nook *RPDN/SBR* HX6 .... 46 A5
Norbury Rd *IDLE* BD10 .... 20 D4
Norcliffe La *HIPP* HX3 .... 48 D2 ②
Norcroft Brow *GTHN* BD7 .... 2 A6
Norcroft St *BFD* BD1 .... 24 D5
Norfolk Gdns *BFD* BD1 .... 2 D6
Norfolk Pl *HFAX* HX1 .... 4 A7
Norfolk St *BGLY* BD16 .... 10 D3 ⑭
Norham Gv *LM/WK* BD12 .... 45 E3
Norland Rd *RPDN/SBR* HX6 ..... 46 A1
Norland St *BFDE* BD3 .... 3 H1
Norland St *GTHN* BD7 .... 30 A4
Norland Vw *RPDN/SBR* HX6 .... 46 A1
Norman Av *ECHL* BD2 .... 20 A4
Norman Crs *ECHL* BD2 .... 20 A4
Norman Gv *ECHL* BD2 .... 20 A4
Norman La *ECHL* BD2 .... 20 A4
Norman Mt *ECHL* BD2 .... 20 A4 ②
Norman St *BGLY* BD16 .... 10 D3 ⑱
  HFAX HX1 .... 4 A7
  SHPY BD18 .... 18 E2
Norman Ter *ECHL* BD2 .... 20 A4 ⑧
Northallerton Rd *BFDE* BD3 ...... 3 F1
North Av *HTON* BD9 .... 25 E1
North Bank Rd *BGLY* BD16 ...... 16 D4
North Br *HFAX* HX1 .... 5 H2
North Bridge St *HFAX* HX1 ...... 5 H2
North Brook St *BFD* BD1 .... 2 D2
North Cliffe Av *CUL/QBY* BD13 . 28 C1
North Cliffe Cl *CUL/QBY* BD13 .. 28 B1 ②
North Cliffe Dr *CUL/QBY* BD13 . 28 B1
North Cliffe Gv *CUL/QBY* BD13 . 22 B5
North Cliffe La *CUL/QBY* BD13 . 22 C5
Northcliffe Rd *SHPY* BD18 .... 18 B3 ⑭
North Cote Rd *ECHL* BD2 .... 26 A4
Northcroft Ri *HTON* BD9 .... 23 H3
Northdale Av *WBOW* BD5 .... 30 D5 ⑤
Northdale Crs *WBOW* BD5 .... 30 D5
Northdale Mt *WBOW* BD5 .... 30 D5 ⑥
Northdale Rd *HTON* BD9 .... 18 D4 ⑪
North Dean Rd *HWTH* BD22 ..... 6 A4
Northedge La *HIPP* HX3 .... 43 C4 ⑦
Northedge Meadow *IDLE* BD10 . 20 A3 ④
Northedge Pk *HIPP* HX3 .... 43 C4
Northern Cl *GTHN* BD7 .... 30 A5 ⑪
Northfield Crs *BGLY* BD16 .... 16 D2
Northfield Gdns *WBSY* BD6 ..... 37 H1

Northfield Gv *WBSY* BD6 .... 37 H1
Northfield Pl *GIR* BD8 .... 24 D3
Northfield Rd *WBSY* BD6 .... 37 G1
Northfield Ter *CUL/QBY* BD13 .. 35 H1 ⑪
Northgate *BAIL* BD17 .... 12 D2
  BFD BD1 .... 2 C4
  HFAX HX1 .... 5 H2
North Hall Av *IDLE* BD10 .... 13 H4
North Holme St *BFD* BD1 .... 2 D2
Northlea Av *IDLE* BD10 .... 13 H5
Northowram Gn *HIPP* HX3 .... 42 D1
North Pde *BFD* BD1 .... 2 C4
  HFAX HX1 .... 5 C3
  WIL/AL BD15 .... 22 D2
North Park Rd *HTON* BD9 .... 24 C1
North Park Ter *HTON* BD9 .... 24 D2 ②
North Pollard St *HFAX* HX1 .... 5 H2
North Queen St *KGHY* BD21 ..... 6 D4
North Rd *WBSY* BD6 .... 37 G1 ③
Northrop Cl *GIR* BD8 .... 24 B5 ③
Northside Av *GTHN* BD7 .... 30 B1
Northside Rd *GTHN* BD7 .... 30 B1
Northside Ter *GTHN* BD7 .... 30 A1
North St *BFD* BD1 .... 3 F4
  IDLE BD10 .... 14 A4
  KGHY BD21 .... 6 D4
  LM/WK BD12 .... 45 H1 ③
  YEA LS19 .... 15 C2
North Vw *WIL/AL* BD15 .... 22 D3
North View Rd *BFDE* BD3 .... 25 C2
North Vw St *KGHY* BD21 .... 6 D2 ③
North Wing *BFDE* BD3 .... 3 F3
Northwood Crs *IDLE* BD10 .... 20 B2
Norton Cl *LUD/ILL* HX2 .... 46 A1
Norton Dr *LUD/ILL* HX2 .... 46 A1
Norwood Av *SHPY* BD18 .... 18 C3
Norwood Green Hl *HIPP* HX3 ... 44 A3
Norwood Pl *SHPY* BD18 .... 18 C3
Norwood Rd *SHPY* BD18 .... 18 C3 ⑥
Norwood St *SHPY* BD18 .... 18 C3 ④
  WBOW BD5 .... 31 E5 ⑦
Norwood Ter *SHPY* BD18 .... 18 C3
Nostell Cl *GIR* BD8 .... 2 A2
Nottingham St *BFDE* BD3 .... 26 D5 ②
Nunburnholme Wk *IDLE* BD10 .. 20 B3 ⑤
Nunlea Royd *BRIG* HD6 .... 50 B2
Nurser La *WBOW* BD5 .... 30 D3
Nurser Pl *WBOW* BD5 .... 30 D3 ①
Nursery Av *LUD/ILL* HX2 .... 41 E2
Nursery Cl *BAIL* BD17 .... 11 H4 ②
Nursery Gv *LUD/ILL* HX2 .... 41 E2
Nursery La *HIPP* HX3 .... 41 E2
Nursery Rd *GTHN* BD7 .... 30 A5
Nuttall Rd *BFDE* BD3 .... 3 H2
Nutwood Wk *WBSY* BD6 .... 37 E4 ⑧

O

Oak Av *BGLY* BD16 .... 10 C5
  GIR BD8 .... 24 D2
  RPDN/SBR HX6 .... 46 A3
Oak Bank *BGLY* BD16 .... 10 C5
  SHPY BD18 .... 19 E4
Oakbank Av *HWTH* BD22 .... 9 E1
Oakbank Broadway *HWTH* BD22 . 9 E1
Oakbank Ct *HWTH* BD22 .... 9 E2 ①
Oakbank Crs *HWTH* BD22 .... 9 E1
Oakbank Dr *HWTH* BD22 .... 9 E1 ④
Oakbank Gv *HWTH* BD22 .... 9 E1 ⑤
Oakbank La *HWTH* BD22 .... 9 E2 ②
Oakbank Mt *HWTH* BD22 .... 9 E2 ③
Oakdale *BGLY* BD16 .... 10 D1
Oakdale Av *SHPY* BD18 .... 19 E3
  WBSY BD6 .... 37 G1
Oakdale Cl *HIPP* HX3 .... 41 F3
  IDLE BD10 .... 26 D1 ②
Oakdale Crs *WBSY* BD6 .... 37 G1
Oakdale Dr *IDLE* BD10 .... 26 D1 ①
  SHPY BD18 .... 19 F3
Oakdale Gv *SHPY* BD18 .... 19 F3
Oakdale Rd *SHPY* BD18 .... 19 F3
Oakdale Ter *SHPY* BD18 .... 37 G1 ⑦
Oakenshaw Ct *LM/WK* BD12 ... 44 D3
Oakenshaw La *CLECK* BD19 ... 45 H2
Oakfield Av *BGLY* BD16 .... 11 F4
Oakfield Dr *BAIL* BD17 .... 13 E4
Oakfield Gv *HTON* BD9 .... 24 D2
Oakfield Rd *HWTH* BD22 .... 9 F2
Oakfield Ter *SHPY* BD18 .... 19 E2 ③
Oak Gv *HWTH* BD22 .... 9 F3
Oakhall Pk *CUL/QBY* BD13 ..... 22 A5 ②
Oak Hill Rd *BRIG* HD6 .... 50 C5
Oaklands *BRIG* HD6 .... 52 A2
  IDLE BD10 .... 19 H1
  SHPY BD18 .... 17 G2

Oaklands Av *HIPP* HX3 .... 42 D2
Oak La *GIR* BD8 .... 24 D2 ▣
　HFAX HX1 .... 4 C3 ▣
Oakleigh Av *CLAY* BD14 .... 29 E4
　HIPP HX3 .... 47 H5
Oakleigh Cl *CLAY* BD14 .... 29 E3 ▣
Oakleigh Gdns *CLAY* BD14 .... 29 E4 ▣
Oakleigh Gv *CLAY* BD14 .... 29 E4
Oakleigh Rd *CLAY* BD14 .... 29 E4
Oakleigh Ter *CLAY* BD14 .... 29 E3 ▣
Oakleigh Vw *BAIL* BD17 .... 12 C5
Oak Mt *GIR* BD8 .... 25 E2
Oak Pl *HFAX* HX1 .... 4 C4 ▣
　RPDN/SBR HX6 .... 46 A3 ▣
Oakridge Ct *BGLY* BD16 .... 10 D2
Oakroyd Av *WBSY* BD6 .... 37 H1 ▣
Oakroyd Cl *BRIG* HD6 .... 50 C3 ▣
Oakroyd Dr *BRIG* HD6 .... 50 C3
Oakroyd Rd *WBSY* BD6 .... 37 H2
Oakroyd Ter *BAIL* BD17 .... 13 E4 ▣
Oaks Dr *GIR* BD8 .... 23 F4
Oaks Fold *WBOW* BD5 .... 31 F4 ▣
Oaks Green Mt *BRIG* HD6 .... 52 A4
Oaks La *GIR* BD8 .... 23 F4
Oak St *CLAY* BD14 .... 29 E3
　PDSY/CALV LS28 .... 27 H4
　RPDN/SBR HX6 .... 46 A3
Oak Vls *GIR* BD8 .... 25 E2
Oakwell Cl *GTHN* BD7 .... 30 C4 ▣
Oakwood Av *ECHL* BD2 .... 19 E5
Oakwood Ct *GIR* BD8 .... 24 D4
Oakwood Dr *BGLY* BD16 .... 10 C1
Oakwood Gv *GIR* BD8 .... 24 B3
Oakworth Hall *HWTH* BD22 .... 8 B4
Oakworth Rd *HWTH* BD22 .... 9 E2 ▣
　KGHY BD21 .... 9 F1
Oasby Cft *BOW* BD4 .... 39 H1
Oastler Pl *LM/WK* BD12 .... 38 A4 ▣
Oastler Rd *PDSY/CALV* LS28 .... 21 G3
　SHPY BD18 .... 18 A1
Occupation La *HWTH* BD22 .... 8 C2
　PDSY/CALV LS28 .... 33 H1
Octagon Ter *LUD/ILL* HX2 .... 46 D4
Oddfellows' Ct *BFD* BD7 .... 2 C5
Oddfellows St *BRIG* HD6 .... 50 C4 ▣
　CLECK BD19 .... 44 D5
Oddy Pl *WBSY* BD6 .... 37 G1 ▣
Oddy St *BOW* BD4 .... 39 H1
Odsal Pl *WBSY* BD6 .... 38 A2 ▣
Odsal Rd *WBSY* BD6 .... 37 H1
Ogden La *BRIG* HD6 .... 52 A3
Old Bank *HIPP* HX3 .... 5 K3
Old Canal Rd *BFD* BD1 .... 2 D1
Old Cawsey *RPDN/SBR* HX6 .... 46 B4
Old Cock Yd *HFAX* HX1 .... 5 H4 ▣
Old Corn Mill La *GTHN* BD7 .... 30 B3 ▣
Old Dalton La *KGHY* BD21 .... 7 F4
Oldfield St *HIPP* HX3 .... 41 F1 ▣
Old Godley La *HIPP* HX3 .... 42 B5
Old La *BRIG* HD6 .... 50 C5
　HIPP HX3 .... 41 F3
Old Langley La *BAIL* BD17 .... 13 E2
Old Lee Bank *HIPP* HX3 .... 41 F4
Old Main St *BGLY* BD16 .... 10 C3 ▣
Old Market *HFAX* HX1 .... 5 H4
Old Mill Rd *BAIL* BD17 .... 18 B1 ▣
Old Park Rd *IDLE* BD10 .... 20 B2
Old Popplewell La *CLECK* BD19 .... 45 F5
Old Rd *CUL/QBY* BD13 .... 28 C1
　GTHN BD7 .... 29 H5
Old Schools Gdns *HIPP* HX3 .... 41 H4 ▣
Olive Gv *GIR* BD8 .... 23 H4
Oliver St *BOW* BD4 .... 31 H2 ▣
Ollerdale Av *WIL/AL* BD15 .... 22 D1
Ollerdale Cl *WIL/AL* BD15 .... 22 D2 ▣
Olympic Pk *LM/WK* BD12 .... 38 C5
Onslow Crs *BOW* BD4 .... 32 A5
Opal St *HWTH* BD22 .... 9 F2 ▣
Orange St *BFDE* BD3 .... 32 B1 ▣
　HFAX HX1 .... 5 G3
Orchard Cl *LUD/ILL* HX2 .... 46 C2
Orchard Gv *IDLE* BD10 .... 20 C2
The Orchards *BGLY* BD16 .... 10 D1
The Orchard *KGHY* BD21 .... 7 G4 ▣
Orchard Wy *BRIG* HD6 .... 50 B5
Orleans St *WBSY* BD6 .... 37 E3
Ormonde Dr *WIL/AL* BD15 .... 22 D4
Ormond Rd *WBSY* BD6 .... 37 H2 ▣
Ormondroyd Av *WBSY* BD6 .... 37 H2 ▣
Ormond St *GTHN* BD7 .... 30 B3 ▣
Osborne St *HFAX* HX1 .... 4 B2
　WBOW BD5 .... 31 E2 ▣
Osbourne Dr *CUL/QBY* BD13 .... 35 F1 ▣
Osprey Cl *GIR* BD8 .... 23 F5 ▣
Osterley Gv *IDLE* BD10 .... 20 D4
Oswald St *SHPY* BD18 .... 19 E2
Oswaldthorpe Av *BFDE* BD3 .... 26 C3

Otley Rd *BAIL* BD17 .... 13 G3
　BAIL BD17 .... 18 D1
　BFDE BD3 .... 3 F4
　SHPY BD18 .... 18 C3
Otley St *HFAX* HX1 .... 4 A3
　KGHY BD21 .... 6 C5
Otterburn Cl *HIPP* HX3 .... 42 B5
Otterburn St *KGHY* BD21 .... 6 D2 ▣
Oulton Ter *GTHN* BD7 .... 30 D2
Outlands Ri *IDLE* BD10 .... 20 C1
The Oval *BGLY* BD16 .... 11 E4
　GIR BD8 .... 23 H4
Ovenden Av *HIPP* HX3 .... 41 F4
Ovenden Cl *HIPP* HX3 .... 41 F4 ▣
Ovenden Crs *HIPP* HX3 .... 41 F3
Ovenden Gn *HIPP* HX3 .... 41 F3
Ovenden Rd *HIPP* HX3 .... 41 F2
Ovenden Ter *HIPP* HX3 .... 41 F3 ▣
Ovenden Wy *HIPP* HX3 .... 41 F3
Ovenden Wood Rd *LUD/ILL* HX2 .... 40 B3
Overdale Dr *SHPY* BD18 .... 13 G5
Overdale Mt *LUD/ILL* HX2 .... 46 C5
Overland Crs *IDLE* BD10 .... 20 C1
Over La *YEA* LS19 .... 15 H3
Overton Dr *WBSY* BD6 .... 29 G5
Ovington Dr *BOW* BD4 .... 32 D5
Owlcotes Dr *PDSY/CALV* LS28 .... 27 H4
Owlcotes Gdns *PDSY/CALV* LS28 .... 27 H4
Owlcotes Garth *PDSY/CALV* LS28 .... 27 G4
Owlcotes La *PDSY/CALV* LS28 .... 27 G4
　PDSY/CALV LS28 .... 27 G3
Owlcotes Rd *PDSY/CALV* LS28 .... 27 G4
Owlcotes Ter *PDSY/CALV* LS28 .... 27 H4
Owler Ings Rd *BRIG* HD6 .... 52 B1
Owlet Rd *SHPY* BD18 .... 18 D2
Oxford Cl *CUL/QBY* BD13 .... 34 D3
Oxford Crs *CLAY* BD14 .... 29 E3
　HIPP HX3 .... 48 A4
Oxford La *HIPP* HX3 .... 48 A4
Oxford Pl *BAIL* BD17 .... 13 F4 ▣
　BFDE BD3 .... 3 F2
Oxford Rd *CUL/QBY* BD13 .... 34 D2 ▣
　ECHL BD2 .... 25 H2
　HFAX HX1 .... 5 G6
Oxford St *CLAY* BD14 .... 29 E3
　KGHY BD21 .... 6 B5 ▣
　RPDN/SBR HX6 .... 46 C3
Ox Heys Mdw *CUL/QBY* BD13 .... 28 D1 ▣
Oxley Gdns *WBSY* BD6 .... 37 H3
Oxley St *GIR* BD8 .... 24 D4 ▣

P

Padan St *HIPP* HX3 .... 48 A4
Paddock *HIPP* BD9 .... 18 D5 ▣
Paddock Cl *LM/WK* BD12 .... 44 D4
Paddock La *LUD/ILL* HX2 .... 40 B5
Paddock Rd *HIPP* HX3 .... 35 F5
Paddocks Church *BRIG* HD6 .... 53 F1
The Paddock *BAIL* BD17 .... 13 G2
　CLECK BD19 .... 45 G5 ▣
Padgum *BAIL* BD17 .... 12 D2 ▣
Page Hl *LUD/ILL* HX2 .... 40 D3
Paget St *KGHY* BD21 .... 6 B4 ▣
Pagewood Ct *IDLE* BD10 .... 13 H5
Pakington St *WBOW* BD5 .... 31 E3 ▣
Paley Rd *BOW* BD4 .... 31 H3
Paley Ter *BOW* BD4 .... 31 H3
Palm Cl *BFDE* BD3 .... 26 C3
Palm Cl *WBSY* BD6 .... 37 G2
Palm St *HIPP* HX3 .... 41 G3
Palmerston St *ECHL* BD2 .... 26 A4 ▣
Palm St *HIPP* HX3 .... 41 G3
Panelagh Av *IDLE* BD10 .... 20 D4
Pannal St *GTHN* BD7 .... 30 B4
The Parade *BGLY* BD16 .... 16 D2 ▣
Paradise La *LUD/ILL* HX2 .... 46 A2
Paradise Rd *HTON* BD9 .... 18 A5 ▣
Paradise St *BFD* BD1 .... 2 A4
　HFAX HX1 .... 5 F5
Park Av *BGLY* BD16 .... 10 C4
　HWTH BD22 .... 8 C4
　IDLE BD10 .... 14 A4
　KGHY BD21 .... 6 C5
　SHPY BD18 .... 18 B1 ▣
Park Cliffe Rd *ECHL* BD2 .... 25 H2
Park Cl *BGLY* BD16 .... 10 D2
　CUL/QBY BD13 .... 35 G1
　HIPP HX3 .... 49 H1
　IDLE BD10 .... 20 B4
　KGHY BD21 .... 9 H1 ▣
　LUD/ILL HX2 .... 40 A4
Park Crs *BFDE* BD3 .... 25 H2
　HIPP HX3 .... 41 H2
Park Dr *BGLY* BD16 .... 11 E1

Park Drive Rd *KGHY* BD21 .... 9 H1
Parkfield Dr *CUL/QBY* BD13 .... 35 E1 ▣
Parkfield La *RPDN/SBR* HX6 .... 46 C5
Parkfield Rd *GIR* BD8 .... 25 E2
　SHPY BD18 .... 17 H1 ▣
Park Flds *LUD/ILL* HX2 .... 40 A3
Park Gdns *LUD/ILL* HX2 .... 46 C3
Park Ga *BFDE* BD3 .... 3 F4
Park Gv *CUL/QBY* BD13 .... 35 E1
　HTON BD9 .... 18 D5
　SHPY BD18 .... 18 A1 ▣
Park Hl *HUDN* HD2 .... 53 C5
Park Hill Cl *GIR* BD8 .... 23 G3
Park Hill Dr *GIR* BD8 .... 23 G3
Park House Cl *LM/WK* BD12 .... 38 B3 ▣
Park House Crs *LM/WK* BD12 .... 38 B5
Park House Gv *LM/WK* BD12 .... 38 B3 ▣
Park House Rd *LM/WK* BD12 .... 38 A4
Park House Wk *LM/WK* BD12 .... 38 B5
Parkin La *IDLE* BD10 .... 21 E1
Parkinson St *WBOW* BD5 .... 31 E5 ▣
Parkland Dr *IDLE* BD10 .... 20 B2
Park La *BAIL* BD17 .... 13 G2
　CLAY BD14 .... 29 E3
　CUL/QBY BD13 .... 35 G1
　KGHY BD21 .... 6 D5
　WBOW BD5 .... 31 E3
Park Lea *HUDN* HD2 .... 53 C5
Park Md *IDLE* BD10 .... 14 A4
Parkmere Cl *BOW* BD4 .... 39 E3 ▣
Park Mount Av *BAIL* BD17 .... 13 F3
Park Pl *IDLE* BD10 .... 14 A4
Park Pl East *HIPP* HX3 .... 49 H1
Park Pl West *HIPP* HX3 .... 49 H1
Park Rd *BGLY* BD16 .... 10 C3
　HFAX HX1 .... 4 E5
　IDLE BD10 .... 14 A4
　IDLE BD10 .... 20 B4
　RPDN/SBR HX6 .... 46 B4
　SHPY BD18 .... 18 D2
　WBOW BD5 .... 31 E2
　WBSY BD6 .... 37 H3
　YEA LS19 .... 15 G2
Park Rw *BRIG* HD6 .... 52 C1 ▣
Parkside *BGLY* BD16 .... 10 D2
Parkside Av *CUL/QBY* BD13 .... 35 E1
Parkside Gv *HTON* BD9 .... 24 B1
Parkside Rd *WBOW* BD5 .... 31 E4 ▣
Park Sq *WBSY* BD6 .... 37 E2
Parkstone *HUDN* HD2 .... 53 C5
Parkstone Dr *IDLE* BD10 .... 20 B4
Park Stone Hl *HIPP* HX3 .... 36 A4
Park St *BRIG* HD6 .... 52 C1
　RPDN/SBR HX6 .... 46 B4
　SHPY BD18 .... 18 B1
Park Ter *KGHY* BD21 .... 7 E4
　SHPY BD18 .... 18 B1 ▣
The Park *Towngate HIPP* HX3 .... 48 D5
Park Vw *HIPP* HX3 .... 49 H1 ▣
Park View Av *HIPP* HX3 .... 42 D4
Park View Rd *HTON* BD9 .... 24 C2
Park View Ter *HTON* BD9 .... 24 C1
　YEA LS19 .... 15 G2
Park Wy *BAIL* BD17 .... 12 D5
Parkway *CUL/QBY* BD13 .... 35 E1
　KGHY BD21 .... 9 H1 ▣
　WBOW BD5 .... 38 C1
Park Willow *HIPP* HX3 .... 36 C4
Parkwood Gdns
　PDSY/CALV LS28 .... 21 G3
Parkwood Ri *KGHY* BD21 .... 9 H1
Parkwood Rd *PDSY/CALV* LS28 .... 21 F3
　SHPY BD18 .... 18 A2
Parkwood St *KGHY* BD21 .... 7 E5
Parma St *WBOW* BD5 .... 31 F2
Parratt Rw *BFDE* BD3 .... 26 C5
Parrott St *BOW* BD4 .... 39 G1
Parry La *BOW* BD4 .... 32 B2
Parsonage La *BRIG* HD6 .... 52 B1 ▣
Parsonage Rd *BOW* BD4 .... 32 B2
　WBOW BD5 .... 31 F4 ▣
Parsonage St *HIPP* HX3 .... 42 A4 ▣
Parsons Rd *HTON* BD9 .... 18 B5
Parson St *KGHY* BD21 .... 6 D3
Pasture Av *HWTH* BD22 .... 8 B5
Pasture Cl *CLAY* BD14 .... 29 G3
Pasture La *CLAY* BD14 .... 29 G3
Pasture Ri *CLAY* BD14 .... 29 G3
Pasture Rd *BAIL* BD17 .... 13 E4
Pasture Side Ter (East)
　CLAY BD14 .... 29 G3 ▣
Pasture Side Ter (West)
　CLAY BD14 .... 29 F3 ▣
Pasture Wk *CLAY* BD14 .... 29 F3
Patent St *HTON* BD9 .... 24 C2
Paternoster La *GTHN* BD7 .... 30 B3 ▣
Pattie St *KGHY* BD21 .... 6 C2 ▣

Paw La *CUL/QBY* BD13 .... 35 G5
Pawson St *BOW* BD4 .... 32 C
Peabody St *HIPP* HX3 .... 41 F1 ▣
Peace St *BOW* BD4 .... 32 B2
Pearl St *HWTH* BD22 .... 9 F2 ▣
Pearson La *GIR* BD8 .... 23 G3 ▣
　HTON BD9 .... 23 G3
Pearson Rd *WBSY* BD6 .... 38 A2
Pearson Rw *LM/WK* BD12 .... 45 E2 ▣
Pearson St *BFDE* BD3 .... 32 B1 ▣
　PDSY/CALV LS28 .... 21 G2
Pear St *HFAX* HX1 .... 4 A5
　HWTH BD22 .... 9 F3 ▣
Peasehill Cl *YEA* LS19 .... 15 H2
Peasehill Pk *YEA* LS19 .... 15 H2 ▣
Peckover Dr *PDSY/CALV* LS28 .... 27 E3
Peckover St *BFD* BD1 .... 3 F5
Peel Cl *BOW* BD4 .... 32 D2
Peel Park Dr *ECHL* BD2 .... 26 A2
Peel Park Ter *ECHL* BD2 .... 25 H1
Peel Park Vw *BFDE* BD3 .... 25 H3
Peel Rw *GTHN* BD7 .... 30 B5 ▣
Peel St *BGLY* BD16 .... 11 E5
　CUL/QBY BD13 .... 28 A1 ▣
　CUL/QBY BD13 .... 35 G1
　RPDN/SBR HX6 .... 46 A4 ▣
Pelham Ct *ECHL* BD2 .... 26 A1 ▣
Pelham Rd *ECHL* BD2 .... 26 A1 ▣
Pellon La *HFAX* HX1 .... 4 A1
Pellon New Rd *LUD/ILL* HX2 .... 40 D5
Pellon Ter *IDLE* BD10 .... 14 A5
Pellon Wk *IDLE* BD10 .... 14 A5
Pemberton Dr *GTHN* BD7 .... 2 A7
Pembroke St *WBOW* BD5 .... 31 F3
Pendle Rd *BGLY* BD16 .... 11 E3
Pendragon *ECHL* BD2 .... 25 H3
Pendragon La *ECHL* BD2 .... 26 A1 ▣
Penfield Gv *CLAY* BD14 .... 29 F3
Pengarth *BGLY* BD16 .... 11 E1
Penn Cl *ECHL* BD2 .... 20 A5
Pennine Cl *CUL/QBY* BD13 .... 35 E3
Pennington Ter *WBOW* BD5 .... 30 D3 ▣
Pennithorne Av *BAIL* BD17 .... 12 D2
Penn St *HFAX* HX1 .... 4 C2
Penny Hill Dr *CLAY* BD14 .... 29 G3
Penrose Dr *GTHN* BD7 .... 30 A4 ▣
Pentland Av *CLAY* BD14 .... 29 G3
Pentland Cl *HWTH* BD22 .... 6 B5 ▣
Percival St *BFDE* BD3 .... 3 H5
Percy St *BGLY* BD16 .... 10 D5
　KGHY BD21 .... 6 D2
Perry Cl *HWTH* BD22 .... 9 F3
Perseverance La *GTHN* BD7 .... 30 B4 ▣
Perseverance St *BAIL* BD17 .... 13 E2 ▣
　LM/WK BD12 .... 44 D1 ▣
　PDSY/CALV LS28 .... 27 H5
　RPDN/SBR HX6 .... 46 A4
Perseverance Ter *HFAX* HX1 .... 47 F5 ▣
Perth Av *ECHL* BD2 .... 25 F1
Peterborough Pl *ECHL* BD2 .... 26 A1 ▣
Peterborough Rd *ECHL* BD2 .... 26 A2 ▣
Peterborough Ter *ECHL* BD2 .... 26 A1 ▣
Petergate *BFD* BD1 .... 2 E5
Peter La *LUD/ILL* HX2 .... 46 A1
Petrie Gv *BFDE* BD3 .... 26 D5
Petrie Rd *BFDE* BD3 .... 26 D5
Peverell Cl *BOW* BD4 .... 32 D4 ▣
Peverill Mt *ECHL* BD2 .... 26 B2
Pheasant St *KGHY* BD21 .... 7 E3 ▣
Phoebe La *HIPP* HX3 .... 48 A4
Phoenix St *BRIG* HD6 .... 52 C1
Phoenix Wy *BOW* BD4 .... 32 D1
Piccadilly *BFD* BD1 .... 2 C4
The Pickerings *CUL/QBY* BD13 .... 35 F2
Pickles La *GTHN* BD7 .... 30 A4
Pickles St *KGHY* BD21 .... 9 G1 ▣
Picton St *GIR* BD8 .... 2 A1
Piggott St *BRIG* HD6 .... 50 B5
Pine Cft *KGHY* BD21 .... 6 B2
Pinedale *BGLY* BD16 .... 10 C1
Pine St *BFD* BD1 .... 3 F4
　HFAX HX1 .... 5 G5
Pinnar La *HIPP* HX3 .... 48 C3
Pipercroft *WBSY* BD6 .... 36 D4 ▣
Pirie Cl *ECHL* BD2 .... 25 G1
Pitcliffe Wy *BOW* BD4 .... 31 G2
　WBOW BD5 .... 31 F3
Pits La *CLECK* BD19 .... 51 F2
Pitts St *BOW* BD4 .... 32 C3
Pitt St *KGHY* BD21 .... 7 E4
Plane Tree Nest La *LUD/ILL* HX2 .... 46 D2
Plane Tree Rd
　RPDN/SBR HX6 .... 46 A3 ▣
Planetrees Rd *BFDE* BD3 .... 32 B1
Planetrees St *WIL/AL* BD15 .... 22 D2 ▣
Plantation Pl *BOW* BD4 .... 32 B3
Plantation Wy *BAIL* BD17 .... 13 E3
Pleasant St *GTHN* BD7 .... 30 B5

►levna Ter BGLY BD16 ...... 10 C2
►limsoll St BOW BD4 ...... 31 H3 [11]
►loughcroft La HIPP HX3 ...... 41 G3
►loughmans Cft ECHL BD2 ...... 19 F5 [2]
►lover St KGHY BD21 ...... 6 D3 [7]
  WBOW BD5 ...... 30 D4
►lumpton Av ECHL BD2 ...... 19 G3
►lumpton Cl ECHL BD2 ...... 19 H4
►lumpton Dr ECHL BD2 ...... 19 H3
►lumpton End ECHL BD2 ...... 19 H3
►lumpton Gdns ECHL BD2 ...... 19 G3
►lumpton Lea ECHL BD2 ...... 19 G3
►lumpton Md ECHL BD2 ...... 19 G3
►lumpton St GIR BD8 ...... 24 B4
►lumpton Wk ECHL BD2 ...... 19 G3
►lum St HFAX HX1 ...... 4 B6
  HWTH BD22 ...... 9 F3 [9]
►ohlman St HFAX HX1 ...... 4 B7 [8]
►ollard Av BGLY BD16 ...... 11 E1
►ollard La BFDE BD3 ...... 26 A3
►ollard St BOW BD4 ...... 31 G2 [9]
►ond St KGHY BD21 ...... 6 D3 [9]
►ool Ct BFDE BD3 ...... 3 H3
►ool St KGHY BD21 ...... 7 F2 [9]
►ope St KGHY BD21 ...... 7 E3
►oplar Av GTHN BD7 ...... 30 A5
  RPDN/SBR HX6 ...... 46 A3
  SHPY BD18 ...... 18 D4 [7]
►oplar Crs LUD/ILL HX2 ...... 34 A3 [2]
  SHPY BD18 ...... 18 D4
►oplar Dr SHPY BD18 ...... 18 D4 [3]
►oplar Gv GTHN BD7 ...... 30 A5
  SHPY BD18 ...... 18 D4 [4]
►oplar Rd GTHN BD7 ...... 30 B5
  SHPY BD18 ...... 18 D4
►oplars Park Rd ECHL BD2 ...... 19 H6
►oplar St HIPP HX3 ...... 5 G1
►oplar Vw BRIG HD6 ...... 50 B2
  GTHN BD7 ...... 29 H5
►oplarwood Gdns IDLE BD10 ...... 20 D4 [2]
►opples Dr LUD/ILL HX2 ...... 34 A3
►oppy Cl WBSY BD6 ...... 37 E4 [8]
►ortland Pl BGLY BD16 ...... 10 D4 [8]
  HFAX HX1 ...... 5 H6
►ortland Rd HIPP HX3 ...... 5 H1
►ortland St HFAX HX1 ...... 5 H3
  WBOW BD5 ...... 2 D7
►ortman St PDSY/CALV LS28 ...... 21 G3
►ortsmouth Av BFDE BD3 ...... 3 F1
►ortwood St HTON BD9 ...... 23 G2 [1]
►ost Office Rd IDLE BD10 ...... 20 B4
►othouse Rd WBSY BD6 ...... 37 G2
►owell Av WBOW BD5 ...... 30 D3
►owell Rd BGLY BD16 ...... 10 D3
►owell St HFAX HX1 ...... 19 E4
►ratt La SHPY BD18 ...... 18 D4
►rescott St HFAX HX1 ...... 5 G4
►rescott Ter WIL/AL BD15 ...... 23 E3 [2]
►reston La LUD/ILL HX2 ...... 40 B3
►reston Pl HFAX HX1 ...... 5 G4
►reston St BFDE BD3 ...... 24 D4 [11]
  GIR BD8 ...... 24 D5
►riesthorpe Av PDSY/CALV LS28 ...... 27 G2
►riesthorpe La PDSY/CALV LS28 ...... 27 G1
►riesthorpe Rd PDSY/CALV LS28 ...... 21 G1
►riestley Av WBSY BD6 ...... 37 G2
►riestley St CUL/QBY BD13 ...... 28 A1 [20]
►riestley Ter WBSY BD6 ...... 37 H1 [15]
►riestman Cl GIR BD8 ...... 24 D3 [12]
►riestman St GIR BD8 ...... 24 D3 [13]
►riestthorpe Cl BGLY BD16 ...... 10 D2
►riestthorpe La BGLY BD16 ...... 10 D2
►riestthorpe Rd BGLY BD16 ...... 10 D2
►rimrose Bank BGLY BD16 ...... 11 E4
►rimrose Dr BGLY BD16 ...... 11 F4
►rimrose Gv KGHY BD21 ...... 7 F4
►rimrose La BGLY BD16 ...... 11 E4
  ECHL BD2 ...... 19 E5
►rimrose St GIR BD8 ...... 24 D4 [12]
  KGHY BD21 ...... 7 F4
►rimrose Wy HIPP HX3 ...... 36 C3 [1]
►rinceroyd Wy GTHN BD7 ...... 24 B5
►rince's Crs ECHL BD2 ...... 25 F1
►rince's Ga HIPP HX3 ...... 47 G4
►rincess St BRIG HD6 ...... 52 C1
  HFAX HX1 ...... 5 H3
  RPDN/SBR HX6 ...... 46 B4
  YEA LS19 ...... 15 F2
►rince's St WBSY BD6 ...... 36 D3 [1]
  WBSY BD6 ...... 37 G2 [3]
►rince St BOW BD4 ...... 39 F1
►rince's Wy WBOW BD5 ...... 2 C6
►rinceville Rd GTHN BD7 ...... 24 B5
►rinceville St GTHN BD7 ...... 24 C5
►rior St KGHY BD21 ...... 7 F3
►riory Cl BGLY BD16 ...... 10 D2 [7]
►riory Ct GIR BD8 ...... 2 A2 [1]

Priory Gv BGLY BD16 ...... 10 D2
Priory Rd BRIG HD6 ...... 52 D2
Proctor St BOW BD4 ...... 39 G1
Prod La BAIL BD17 ...... 11 H4
Prospect Av LUD/ILL HX2 ...... 46 D4
  SHPY BD18 ...... 18 D2
Prospect Cl LUD/ILL HX2 ...... 46 D4
  SHPY BD18 ...... 18 D2 [3]
Prospect Ct LUD/ILL HX2 ...... 40 A5
Prospect Crs HWTH BD22 ...... 8 D1
Prospect Dr HWTH BD22 ...... 8 D1 [4]
Prospect Gv SHPY BD18 ...... 18 D2
Prospect Mt HWTH BD22 ...... 8 D1 [3]
  SHPY BD18 ...... 18 D2
Prospect Pl BRIG HD6 ...... 52 B1
  ECHL BD2 ...... 26 B2
  HTON BD9 ...... 24 A3
  LUD/ILL HX2 ...... 41 E2
Prospect Rd BFDE BD3 ...... 3 F2
  BGLY BD16 ...... 11 F1
Prospect St BOW BD4 ...... 39 H3
  CUL/QBY BD13 ...... 28 B1 [10]
  HIPP HX3 ...... 5 J1
  HWTH BD22 ...... 6 A5 [8]
  IDLE BD10 ...... 20 B4
  PDSY/CALV LS28 ...... 27 H4 [3]
  SHPY BD18 ...... 18 D2 [2]
  WBSY BD6 ...... 37 E3 [8]
  YEA LS19 ...... 15 H3 [3]
Prospect Ter WIL/AL BD15 ...... 23 F3 [2]
Prospect Wk SHPY BD18 ...... 18 D2 [2]
Providence Av BAIL BD17 ...... 12 D2 [7]
Providence Crs HWTH BD22 ...... 8 B4
Providence La HWTH BD22 ...... 8 B4
Providence Pl BRIG HD6 ...... 52 D2 [1]
Providence Rw BAIL BD17 ...... 12 D2
  LUD/ILL HX2 ...... 41 E2
Providence St BFD BD1 ...... 5 G1
  CLECK BD19 ...... 45 F4 [1]
Providence Ter CUL/QBY BD13 ...... 28 A1 [21]
Prune Park La WIL/AL BD15 ...... 22 B1
Pule Green La HIPP HX3 ...... 41 G2
Pullan Av ECHL BD2 ...... 20 B5
Pullan Dr ECHL BD2 ...... 20 B5 [1]
Pullan Gv ECHL BD2 ...... 20 B5
Pullan La BAIL BD17 ...... 14 B1
Pullan St WBOW BD5 ...... 31 E2
Purbeck Ct BOW BD4 ...... 32 D5 [12]
Purley Wk WBOW BD5 ...... 37 G2 [2]
Pye Nest Av LUD/ILL HX2 ...... 46 C3
Pye Nest Dr LUD/ILL HX2 ...... 46 D4
Pye Nest Gdns LUD/ILL HX2 ...... 46 D4
Pye Nest Gv LUD/ILL HX2 ...... 46 D4
Pye Nest Ri LUD/ILL HX2 ...... 46 D4
Pye Nest Rd RPDN/SBR HX6 ...... 46 C4
Pyrah Rd LM/WK BD12 ...... 38 A3
Pyrah St LM/WK BD12 ...... 45 E1

Q

Quail St KGHY BD21 ...... 7 E3 [17]
Quaker La WBOW BD5 ...... 30 C4
Quakers La YEA LS19 ...... 15 G1
Quarry Pl ECHL BD2 ...... 26 A2
Quarry Rd HIPP HX3 ...... 40 D3
Quarry St HTON BD9 ...... 18 B5
  KGHY BD21 ...... 6 D2 [3]
Quayside BAIL BD17 ...... 18 C1 [7]
Quebec St KGHY BD21 ...... 6 C5 [17]
Queen's Av ECHL BD2 ...... 25 G1
Queensbury Rd HIPP HX3 ...... 34 C5
Queensbury Sq
  CUL/QBY BD13 ...... 35 F1 [3]
Queens Cl BGLY BD16 ...... 11 E4 [2]
Queens Dr HIPP HX3 ...... 48 D4 [1]
Queen's Ga HIPP HX3 ...... 47 G4
Queens Gv KGHY BD21 ...... 9 G1 [19]
Queens Md HIPP HX3 ...... 42 D2 [1]
Queens Pl SHPY BD18 ...... 18 A1 [30]
Queen's Ri ECHL BD2 ...... 25 G1
Queen's Rd ECHL BD2 ...... 25 G2 [1]
  HFAX HX1 ...... 4 B2
  HIPP HX3 ...... 44 A3
  KGHY BD21 ...... 9 F2
  SHPY BD18 ...... 18 A1
Queen St BAIL BD17 ...... 12 D5 [3]
  BGLY BD16 ...... 10 C3 [3]
  IDLE BD10 ...... 20 B4
  WBSY BD6 ...... 36 D3 [4]
  YEA LS19 ...... 15 G2
Queensway BGLY BD16 ...... 11 E4
  HFAX HX1 ...... 4 A2
Queen Victoria Crs HIPP HX3 ...... 43 E2
Quincy Cl ECHL BD2 ...... 20 B5 [2]
Qunsworth St BOW BD4 ...... 32 A3

R

Race Moor La HWTH BD22 ...... 8 A3
Radcliffe Av ECHL BD2 ...... 19 H4
Radfield Dr WBSY BD6 ...... 38 B1
Radnor St BFDE BD3 ...... 26 B5
Radwell Dr WBOW BD5 ...... 31 F2 [6]
Raeburn Dr WBSY BD6 ...... 37 F3
Rae Rd SHPY BD18 ...... 18 B3
Raglan Av HWTH BD22 ...... 6 A5
Raglan Ct BFDE BD3 ...... 26 C5 [1]
  CUL/QBY BD13 ...... 35 F1 [4]
  HFAX HX1 ...... 4 D3
Raglan St HWTH BD22 ...... 6 A5
Raikes La BOW BD4 ...... 33 F5
  BOW BD4 ...... 39 H3
Raikes Wood Dr BOW BD4 ...... 39 H3
Railway Rd IDLE BD10 ...... 20 A1
Railway St BOW BD4 ...... 32 B5 [3]
  BRIG HD6 ...... 52 C2 [3]
  KGHY BD21 ...... 6 D2 [2]
Rainbow Ms WBSY BD6 ...... 37 E4 [7]
Raistrick Wy SHPY BD18 ...... 19 E1
Raleigh St HFAX HX1 ...... 4 B7 [9]
Ramsden Av HWTH BD22 ...... 29 H2 [1]
Ramsden Ct GTHN BD7 ...... 30 B3 [3]
Ramsden Pl CLAY BD14 ...... 29 E2
Ramsden St HIPP HX3 ...... 40 D3
Ramsey St WBOW BD5 ...... 31 E4 [2]
Ramsgate St HFAX HX1 ...... 4 A3
Randall Pl HTON BD9 ...... 24 B1
Randall Well St BFD BD1 ...... 2 B6
Randolph St BFDE BD3 ...... 26 D4 [8]
  HIPP HX3 ...... 5 G1
Random Cl HWTH BD22 ...... 9 E1
Rand Pl GTHN BD7 ...... 30 D2 [3]
Rand St GTHN BD7 ...... 30 D2 [1]
Ranelagh Av IDLE BD10 ...... 20 D4 [3]
Range Bank HIPP HX3 ...... 41 H4
Range Gdns HIPP HX3 ...... 41 H4 [3]
Range La HIPP HX3 ...... 5 H1
Range St HIPP HX3 ...... 41 H4
Ransdale Dr WBOW BD5 ...... 31 E4 [2]
Ransdale Gv WBOW BD5 ...... 31 E4 [13]
Ransdale Rd WBOW BD5 ...... 31 E4
Rastrick Common BRIG HD6 ...... 52 B3
Rathmell St WBOW BD5 ...... 38 A1
Ravenscliffe Av IDLE BD10 ...... 20 D4
Ravenscliffe Rd
  PDSY/CALV LS28 ...... 20 D3
Raven St BGLY BD16 ...... 10 D3 [16]
  HFAX HX1 ...... 4 B3
  KGHY BD21 ...... 6 C4 [16]
Raven Ter GIR BD8 ...... 23 F5
Rawdon Dr YEA LS19 ...... 15 G3
Rawdon Hall Dr YEA LS19 ...... 15 G3
Rawdon St HWTH BD22 ...... 6 B5 [13]
Raw Hl BRIG HD6 ...... 52 A3 [4]
Rawling St WBOW BD5 ...... 31 H3
Raw Nook LM/WK BD12 ...... 38 C5 [4]
Rawson Av BFDE BD3 ...... 26 C4
  HIPP HX3 ...... 47 G5
Rawson Pl BFD BD1 ...... 2 C4
Rawson Rd BFD BD1 ...... 2 B4
Rawson Sq BFD BD1 ...... 2 C4
  IDLE BD10 ...... 20 A1 [10]
Rawson St HFAX HX1 ...... 5 G4
  LM/WK BD12 ...... 45 E1
Rawson St North HIPP HX3 ...... 41 G4
Rayleigh St BOW BD4 ...... 31 H3
Raymond Dr WBOW BD5 ...... 31 F5
Raymond St WBOW BD5 ...... 31 F5
Raynbron Cresent WBOW BD5 ...... 31 C5 [8]
Rayner Av GIR BD8 ...... 24 A3
Rayner Dr BRIG HD6 ...... 50 B4
Rayner Mt WIL/AL BD15 ...... 23 E4
Rayner Rd BRIG HD6 ...... 50 B4
Rebecca St GIR BD8 ...... 2 A3
Recreation Rd RPDN/SBR HX6 ...... 46 A4
Rectory Rw KGHY BD21 ...... 6 C4 [17]
Red Beck Rd HIPP HX3 ...... 42 C4
Red Beck V SHPY BD18 ...... 18 C4
Redburn Av SHPY BD18 ...... 18 B4
Redburn Dr SHPY BD18 ...... 18 B4
Redburn Rd SHPY BD18 ...... 18 B4
Redcar St IDLE BD10 ...... 20 D2
Redcar St HFAX HX1 ...... 4 A3
Redcliffe Av KGHY BD21 ...... 6 B4
Redcliffe Gv KGHY BD21 ...... 6 B4 [14]
Redcliffe St KGHY BD21 ...... 6 C4 [15]
Red La PDSY/CALV LS28 ...... 27 H1
Redmire St BFDE BD3 ...... 26 D5 [8]
Rees Wy BFDE BD3 ...... 3 F2
Reevy Av WBSY BD6 ...... 37 E1
Reevy Crs WBSY BD6 ...... 36 D3
Reevy Dr WBSY BD6 ...... 37 F2

Reevylands Dr WBSY BD6 ...... 37 F2
Reevy Rd WBSY BD6 ...... 37 E2
Reevy Rd West WBSY BD6 ...... 36 D2
Reevy St WBSY BD6 ...... 37 F1
Regency Ct GIR BD8 ...... 24 B4
Regency Vw ECHL BD2 ...... 25 H2 [3]
Regent Pl IDLE BD10 ...... 13 H5 [4]
  RPDN/SBR HX6 ...... 46 A4
Regent St CUL/QBY BD13 ...... 35 G1 [11]
  HFAX HX1 ...... 5 F5
  IDLE BD10 ...... 13 H5 [3]
  IDLE BD10 ...... 20 C2 [7]
Reginald St WBOW BD5 ...... 31 E4
Reighton Cft IDLE BD10 ...... 20 D3
Reins Av BAIL BD17 ...... 12 C5
Renee Cl BOW BD4 ...... 39 F2
Renshaw St IDLE BD10 ...... 14 A5 [13]
Reservoir Rd LUD/ILL HX2 ...... 40 D5
Retford Pl GTHN BD7 ...... 30 D2 [3]
Reva Cl BGLY BD16 ...... 11 E2 [2]
Reva Syke Rd CLAY BD14 ...... 29 E3
Reydon Wk WBSY BD6 ...... 37 E1 [3]
Reyhill Gv WBOW BD5 ...... 31 F2
Reyner House Ms
  WBOW BD5 ...... 31 F2 [17]
Reynolds Av GTHN BD7 ...... 29 H2 [3]
Rhine St BOW BD4 ...... 31 H3 [13]
Rhodesia Av HIPP HX3 ...... 47 H5
  WIL/AL BD15 ...... 23 F4
Rhodes Pl BAIL BD17 ...... 18 C1 [3]
Rhodes St HFAX HX1 ...... 4 E4
  SHPY BD18 ...... 18 B1
Rhodesway GIR BD8 ...... 23 G5
Rhodes Wy GIR BD8 ...... 23 G3
Rhondda Pl HFAX HX1 ...... 46 D1
Rhum Cl WBSY BD6 ...... 37 E4
Rhylstone Mt GTHN BD7 ...... 30 A1 [3]
Ribble St KGHY BD21 ...... 7 F3 [7]
Ribbleton Gv BFDE BD3 ...... 3 G3
Riccall Nook IDLE BD10 ...... 20 C5 [3]
Richardson Av WBSY BD6 ...... 37 H2 [3]
Richardson St LM/WK BD12 ...... 45 H1 [3]
Richard St BRIG HD6 ...... 50 B4
Richmond Cl HFAX HX1 ...... 5 F2
Richmond Ms SHPY BD18 ...... 18 A1 [34]
Richmond Pl SHPY BD18 ...... 18 A1 [22]
Richmond Rd GTHN BD7 ...... 30 D1
  HFAX HX1 ...... 5 F2
  PDSY/CALV LS28 ...... 27 H2
  SHPY BD18 ...... 18 A1 [23]
Richmond St HFAX HX1 ...... 5 F2
  KGHY BD21 ...... 6 C3 [4]
Riddlesden St AIRE BD20 ...... 7 G2 [2]
Ridge Lea BRIG HD6 ...... 52 A2
Ridgemount Rd AIRE BD20 ...... 7 F1
Ridge View Gdns IDLE BD10 ...... 20 B2
Ridge View Rd BRIG HD6 ...... 52 B2 [13]
Ridgeway CUL/QBY BD13 ...... 35 G2
  SHPY BD18 ...... 19 F3
Ridgeway Gdns BRIG HD6 ...... 49 H3
Ridgeway Mt HWTH BD22 ...... 9 E1
Ridgewood Cl BAIL BD17 ...... 13 F3
Riding Hl HIPP HX3 ...... 36 D4
Riding La LUD/ILL HX2 ...... 40 B2
Ridings Wy WBSY BD6 ...... 36 D1
Rievaulx Av GIR BD8 ...... 24 D4 [13]
Rigton St WBOW BD5 ...... 31 E4 [6]
Riley La LUD/ILL HX2 ...... 34 A2
Rillington Md IDLE BD10 ...... 20 C3
Rilston St GTHN BD7 ...... 30 C1 [3]
Rimswell Holt IDLE BD10 ...... 20 D3
Ringby La HIPP HX3 ...... 41 G1
Ring Road Farsley
  PDSY/CALV LS28 ...... 27 H1
Ringwood Rd WBOW BD5 ...... 30 C4
Ripley Rd BOW BD4 ...... 31 G3
Ripley St AIRE BD20 ...... 7 G2 [3]
  BOW BD4 ...... 31 G3
  HIPP HX3 ...... 50 B1
  WBOW BD5 ...... 31 F3
  WIL/AL BD15 ...... 22 D2 [4]
Ripon St HFAX HX1 ...... 46 D1
Ripon Ter HIPP HX3 ...... 41 G4
The Rise HIPP HX3 ...... 42 D3
Rishworth St HWTH BD22 ...... 6 A5
Riverside KGHY BD21 ...... 7 F4
Riverside Est BAIL BD17 ...... 18 B1
River St BRIG HD6 ...... 52 D2
  KGHY BD21 ...... 7 F2
River Wk BGLY BD16 ...... 10 C3
Roans Brae IDLE BD10 ...... 20 D3
Robertson Av BRIG HD6 ...... 52 B3 [2]
Roberts Pl BFD BD1 ...... 2 B4
Robert St BFDE BD3 ...... 3 C6
  HIPP HX3 ...... 41 F3 [2]
Robert St North HIPP HX3 ...... 41 H3 [3]
Robin Cl ECHL BD2 ...... 20 B5
Robin Dr ECHL BD2 ...... 20 B5

Robin Hood Wy *BRIG* HD6 .... 53 F1
Robinson Ct *GTHN* BD7 .... 30 A1
Robin St *WBOW* BD5 .... 30 D3
Robin Wk *SHPY* BD18 .... 19 E3
Rochdale Rd *LUD/ILL* HX2....... 46 C3
Rochester St *BFDE* BD3 .... 26 B5
  SHPY BD18 .... 18 D3
Rockcliffe Av *BAIL* BD17 ...... 12 D5
Rockhill La *BOW* BD4 .... 38 D3
Rockland Crs *GTHN* BD7 .... 30 F1
Rocklands Av *BAIL* BD17 .... 12 D2
Rocklands Pl *BAIL* BD17 .... 12 D2
Rocks Rd *HIPP* HX3 .... 47 F5
Rock St *BGLY* BD16 .... 50 B5
Rock Ter *CUL/QBY* BD13 .... 28 A1
Rockville Ter *HFAX* HX1 .... 47 F3
Rockwell La *IDLE* BD10 .... 20 B3
Rockwood Cl *HUDN* HD2 .... 53 F5
Rockwood Crs *PDSY/CALV* LS28... 27 F1
Rockwood Gv *PDSY/CALV* LS28 ... 27 G1
Rockwood Rd *PDSY/CALV* LS28 ... 27 F2
Rodin Av *GIR* BD8 .... 23 G5
Rodley La *PDSY/CALV* LS28 ..... 21 H3
Roger Ct *ECHL* BD2 .... 26 A3
Rogerson Sq *BRIG* HD6 .... 50 B5
Roils Head Rd *LUD/ILL* HX2..... 46 A1
Rokeby Gdns *IDLE* BD10 .... 20 D3
Romanby Shaw *IDLE* BD10....... 20 C3
Rombalds Dr *BGLY* BD16........ 11 E3
Romsey Gdns *BOW* BD4 .... 32 C4
Romsey Ms *BOW* BD4 .... 32 C4
Ronald Dr *GTHN* BD7 .... 24 B5
Rookery La *HIPP* HX3 .... 48 A5
Rookes Av *WBSY* BD6 .... 37 H2
Rookes La *HIPP* HX3 .... 44 B4
Rook La *BOW* BD4 .... 32 A5
Rooks Cl *LM/WK* BD12.......... 45 E4
Rook St *BGLY* BD16 .... 10 C3
Rookwith Pde *IDLE* BD10 ...... 20 C3
Rooley Av *WBSY* BD6 .... 38 A2
Rooley Cl *WBOW* BD5 .... 38 B1
Rooley Crs *WBSY* BD6 .... 38 B1
Rooley La *BOW* BD4 .... 32 A5
  WBOW BD5 .... 38 A1
Roper Gn *LUD/ILL* HX2......... 40 C1
Roper La *CUL/QBY* BD13 .... 34 D2
  LUD/ILL HX2 .... 34 A2
Roper St *KGHY* BD21 .... 6 C4
Rose Bank Pl *IDLE* BD10 ...... 23 H5
Rosebery Av *HIPP* HX3 .... 48 A4
  SHPY BD18 .... 18 D2
Rosebery Mt *SHPY* BD18........ 18 D2
Rosebery Rd *GIR* BD8 .... 24 D2
Rosebery St *PDSY/CALV* LS28 .. 27 H4
Rosebery Ter *HFAX* HX1 .... 4 C1
Rosechapel Cl *WBSY* BD6 ...... 37 E4
Rosedale Av *WIL/AL* BD15 ..... 22 C2
Rosedale Cl *BAIL* BD17 .... 12 B4
Rosehill Crs *LM/WK* BD12 ..... 44 D1
Roselee Cl *HIPP* HX3 .... 48 B5
Rosemary La *BRIG* HD6 .... 52 B3
  HIPP HX3 .... 48 B5
Rose Mdw *HWTH* BD22 .... 8 D1
Rosemont La *BAIL* BD17 .... 13 E4
Rose Mt *ECHL* BD2 .... 25 H1
Rose St *GIR* BD8 .... 24 C3
  HFAX HX1 .... 4 B4
  KGHY BD21 .... 7 G4
Rosewood Av *KGHY* BD21 .... 7 G2
Rosewood Gv *BOW* BD4 .... 32 C2
Rosley Mt *WBSY* BD6........... 37 H4
Roslyn Pl *GTHN* BD7 .... 30 C1
Rossefield Pk *HTON* BD9....... 18 C5
Rossefield Rd *HTON* BD9 ...... 18 B5
Rossendale Pl *SHPY* BD18 ..... 18 B2
Rosse St *GIR* BD8 .... 24 B5
  SHPY BD18 .... 18 C1
Rossmore Dr *WIL/AL* BD15 ..... 23 F3
Rothesay Ter *GTHN* BD7 .... 30 D2
Rothwell Mt *HFAX* HX1 .... 4 E7
Rothwell Rd *HFAX* HX1 .... 4 E7
  HFAX HX1 .... 4 E7
Roundell Av *BOW* BD4.......... 39 E2
Roundhead Fold *IDLE* BD10 .... 20 D1
Round Hl *LUD/ILL* HX2......... 34 A4
Roundhill Av *BGLY* BD16 ...... 17 E2
Roundhill Cl *CUL/QBY* BD13 ... 29 E5
Roundhill Mt *BGLY* BD16 ...... 17 E2
Roundhill Pl *BFD* BD1 .... 2 B4
Roundhill St *WBOW* BD5 .... 31 E3
Round St *WBOW* BD5 .... 31 F4
Round Thorn Pl *GIR* BD8 ...... 24 B4
Roundwood *SHPY* BD18 .... 17 H2
Roundwood Av *BAIL* BD17 ...... 13 G5
  IDLE BD10 .... 20 D4
Roundwood Gln *IDLE* BD10 ..... 20 D3
Roundwood Rd *BAIL* BD17 ...... 13 F2

Roundwood Vw *IDLE* BD10 ...... 20 D3
Rouse Fold *BOW* BD4 .... 31 G2
Rowan Av *BFDE* BD3 .... 26 D5
Rowanberry Cl *ECHL* BD2 ...... 20 A5
Rowan Ct *ECHL* BD2 .... 26 B3
  YEA LS19 .... 15 G1
Rowan Dr *BRIG* HD6 .... 50 D5
The Rowans *BAIL* BD17 .... 12 A3
Rowan St *AIRE* BD20 .... 6 B1
Rowantree Av *BAIL* BD17 ...... 12 A2
Rowantree Dr *IDLE* BD10 ...... 20 B3
Rowanwood Gdns *IDLE* BD10 .. 20 D4
Rowlestone Ri *IDLE* BD10...... 20 B3
Rowsley St *KGHY* BD21 .... 7 E4
Rowton Thorpe *IDLE* BD10...... 20 D3
Roxburgh Gv *WIL/AL* BD15..... 23 E4
Roxby St *WBOW* BD5............ 31 E4
Royd Av *BGLY* BD16 .... 11 E3
Royd Ings Av *KGHY* BD21 ...... 7 E2
Roydlands St *HIPP* HX3 .... 49 G1
Royd La *HIPP* HX3 .... 41 F2
  KGHY BD21 .... 6 D2
Royd Mt *HIPP* HX3 .... 41 H3
Roydon Gv *HTON* BD9.......... 24 B2
Royd Pl *HIPP* HX3 .... 41 H3
Royds Av *BRIG* HD6 .... 44 C5
Roydscliffe Dr *HTON* BD9 ..... 18 A5
Roydscliffe Rd *HTON* BD9...... 23 H1
Royds Crs *BRIG* HD6 .... 50 C1
Roydsdale Wy *BOW* BD4......... 38 D4
Royds Hall Av *WBSY* BD6 ...... 37 H2
Royds Hall La *LM/WK* BD12..... 37 F5
  LM/WK BD12 .... 44 B2
  WBSY BD6 .... 37 F4
Royds Park Crs *LM/WK* BD12.... 45 E1
Roydstone Ter *BFDE* BD3 ...... 26 C4
Roydstone Ter *BFDE* BD3 ...... 26 C4
Royd St *AIRE* BD20 .... 6 C1
  KGHY BD21 .... 6 C1
Royd Wy *KGHY* BD21 .... 6 D2
Roy Rd *WBSY* BD6 .... 36 C1
Ruby St *HWTH* BD22 .... 9 F2
Rudding Av *WIL/AL* BD15 ...... 22 D3
Rudding Crs *WIL/AL* BD15...... 22 D2
Rudd St *GTHN* BD7 .... 30 B4
Ruffield Side *LM/WK* BD12 .... 37 H5
Rufford Pl *HFAX* HX1 .... 47 G4
Rufford Rd *HFAX* HX1 .... 47 G4
Rufford St *BFDE* BD3.......... 26 B5
Rufford Vls *HIPP* HX3......... 47 G4
Rufus St *KGHY* BD21 .... 6 D3
  WBOW BD5 .... 30 C4
Rugby Av *HIPP* HX3 .... 41 E2
Rugby Dr *HIPP* HX3 .... 41 E2
Rugby Gdns *HIPP* HX3 .... 41 E2
Rugby Mt *HIPP* HX3 .... 41 E2
Rugby Pl *GTHN* BD7 .... 30 C1
Rugby Ter *HIPP* HX3 .... 41 E2
Runswick Av *WBOW* BD5 .... 38 A1
Runswick St *WBOW* BD5......... 38 A1
Runswick Ter *WBOW* BD5........ 38 A1
Rushdene Ct *LM/WK* BD12 ...... 44 D4
Rushmoor Rd *BOW* BD4 .... 32 C2
Rusholme Dr *PDSY/CALV* LS28 .. 27 H1
Rushton Av *BFDE* BD3.......... 26 D4
Rushton Hill Cl *LUD/ILL* HX2.. 40 B4
Rushton Rd *BFDE* BD3 .... 26 D4
Rushton St *HFAX* HX1 .... 4 B2
  PDSY/CALV LS28 .... 21 G3
Rushton Ter *BFDE* BD3......... 26 D5
Rushworth St *HIPP* HX3 .... 41 H4
Ruskin Av *HTON* BD9 .... 23 G1
Ruskin St *PDSY/CALV* LS28 .... 27 H3
Ruskin Ter *HIPP* HX3 .... 41 H4
Russell Av *CUL/QBY* BD13...... 35 E2
Russell Hall La *CUL/QBY* BD13. 35 F2
Russell Rd *CUL/QBY* BD13...... 35 E2
Russell St *CUL/QBY* BD13 ..... 35 F1
  HFAX HX1 .... 5 H4
  HTON BD9 .... 18 D4
  KGHY BD21 .... 6 C4
  WBOW BD5 .... 31 E2
Rustic Av *HIPP* HX3 .... 48 D4
Ruswarp Crs *IDLE* BD10 .... 20 C3
Rutland St *BOW* BD4 .... 31 H3
  KGHY BD21 .... 6 B5
Ryan St *WBOW* BD5 .... 31 E4
Ryburn St *RPDN/SBR* HX6 ...... 46 A5
Ryburn Ter *HFAX* HX1 .... 4 B3
Rycroft Av *BGLY* BD16 .... 16 D3
Rycroft St *SHPY* BD18 .... 19 E3
Rydal Av *HTON* BD9 .... 18 D5
Rydal St *KGHY* BD21 .... 6 B5
Rydings Av *BRIG* HD6 .... 50 B5
Rydings Cl *BRIG* HD6 .... 50 B5
Rydings Dr *BRIG* HD6 .... 50 A5
Rye Cft *LUD/ILL* HX2 .... 34 A4

Ryecroft Crs *LUD/ILL* HX2..... 40 C4
Ryecroft La *BRIG* HD6 .... 52 D3
  LUD/ILL HX2 .... 40 C5
Ryecroft Ter *LUD/ILL* HX2 .... 40 C4
Ryedale Wy *WIL/AL* BD15 ...... 22 D2
Ryefield Av *CLAY* BD14 .... 29 E2
Ryelands Gv *HTON* BD9 .... 17 G5
Rye La *LUD/ILL* HX2 .... 40 B4
Rye St *HWTH* BD22............. 9 C2
Rylands Av *BGLY* BD16 .... 11 E3
Rylstone Gdns *BFDE* BD3 ...... 25 H3
Rylstone Rd *BAIL* BD17 .... 12 A4
Rylstone St *KGHY* BD21 .... 7 E3
Ryton Dl *IDLE* BD10 .... 20 D3

S

Sable Crest *ECHL* BD2 .... 19 G5
Sackville St *BFD* BD1 .... 2 C5
Saddler St *LM/WK* BD12 .... 44 D1
Saffron Dr *WIL/AL* BD15 ...... 22 D3
Sage St *WBOW* BD5 .... 30 D3
Sahara Ct *GIR* BD8 .... 25 E2
St Abbs Cl *WBSY* BD6.......... 37 H3
St Abbs Dr *WBSY* BD6 .... 37 H3
St Abbs Fold *WBSY* BD6 .... 37 H3
St Abbs Ga *WBSY* BD6 .... 37 H3
St Abbs Wk *WBSY* BD6 .... 37 H3
St Abbs Wy *WBSY* BD6 .... 37 H3
St Aidan's Rd *BAIL* BD17 ..... 13 E4
St Alban's Av *HIPP* HX3 ...... 47 H5
St Albans Cft *HIPP* HX3 ...... 48 A4
St Alban's Rd *HIPP* HX3 ...... 47 H5
St Andrew's Cl *LM/WK* BD12 ... 45 H1
St Andrew's Dr *BRIG* HD6 ..... 50 B4
St Andrew's Pl *GTHN* BD7 ..... 30 D1
St Andrew's Vls *GTHN* BD7 .... 24 D5
St Anns Sq *RPDN/SBR* HX6 ..... 46 B4
St Anuil *GIR* BD8 .... 24 C3
St Augustine's Ter *BFDE* BD3.. 3 G1
St Bevan's Rd *HIPP* HX3 ...... 47 H5
St Blaise Ct *WBOW* BD5 .... 31 F2
St Blaise Wy *BFD* BD1 .... 2 D4
St Chad's Av *BRIG* HD6 .... 49 H3
St Chad's Rd *HIPP* HX3 .... 24 C3
St Clare's Av *ECHL* BD2 ...... 26 C2
St Eloi Av *BAIL* BD17 .... 12 D2
St Enoch's Rd *WBSY* BD6 ...... 37 G1
St George's Crs *HFAX* HX1 .... 4 D1
St George's Pl *WBOW* BD5 ..... 31 F2
St George's Rd *HIPP* HX3 ..... 41 F4
St Giles Cl *BRIG* HD6 .... 49 H3
St Giles Rd *HIPP* HX3......... 49 H2
St Helena *WBSY* BD6 .... 37 G1
St Helier Gv *BAIL* BD17 ...... 13 E2
St Hilda's Ter *BFDE* BD3 ..... 26 D4
St Ive's Gdns *HIPP* HX3 ...... 47 H5
St Ive's Rd *HIPP* HX3......... 47 G5
St James Crs *PDSY/CALV* LS28 . 27 G5
St James Rd *HFAX* HX1 .... 5 G3
St James's Sq *WBOW* BD5 ...... 31 F2
St James St *HFAX* HX1 .... 5 F3
St John's Ct *BAIL* BD17 ...... 13 F4
St John's Crs *GIR* BD8 .... 23 H4
St John's La *HFAX* HX1........ 5 G6
St John's Pl *HFAX* HX1........ 5 G6
St John's Rd *AIRE* BD20 ...... 6 B1
St John St *BRIG* HD6 .... 52 B2
St Johns Wy *HWTH* BD22 .... 6 A5
St Jude's St *BFD* BD1 .... 2 A2
  HFAX HX1 .... 47 G5
St Laurence's Cl *SHPY* BD18 .. 19 F4
St Leonard's Gv *GIR* BD8...... 24 A3
St Leonard's Rd *GIR* BD8...... 24 A3
St Margaret's Av *BOW* BD4..... 32 C5
St Margaret's Pl *GTHN* BD7 ... 30 C2
St Margaret's Rd *GTHN* BD7 ... 30 C2
St Margaret's Ter *GTHN* BD7 .. 30 C2
St Mark's Av *LM/WK* BD12 ..... 37 H5
St Mark's Ter *LM/WK* BD12 .... 37 H5
St Martins Av *HTON* BD9 ...... 24 D5
St Martin's Vw *BRIG* HD6 ..... 50 B5
St Mary's Av *LM/WK* BD12 ..... 44 D3
St Mary's Cl *LM/WK* BD12 ..... 44 C4
St Mary's Crs *LM/WK* BD12 .... 44 C4
St Mary's Dr *LM/WK* BD12 ..... 44 C4
St Mary's Gdns *LM/WK* BD12 ... 44 D3
St Mary's Mt *LM/WK* BD12 ..... 44 C3
St Mary's Rd *AIRE* BD20 ...... 7 G1
  BOW BD4 .... 32 C2
  GIR BD8 .... 24 D2
  HTON BD9 .... 24 D2
St Mary's Sq *LM/WK* BD12 ..... 44 C3
St Mary St *HFAX* HX1 .... 24 E5
St Matthew's Dr *HIPP* HX3 .... 42 D2
St Matthew's Rd *WBSY* BD6 .... 38 A1

St Merrien Crs *HIPP* HX3 ..... 48 B
St Michael's Rd *GIR* BD8 ..... 24 D
St Paul's Av *WBSY* BD6 .... 37 G
St Pauls Gv *WBSY* BD6......... 37 G
St Paul's Rd *GIR* BD8 .... 24 D
  HFAX HX1 .... 4 E
  KGHY BD21 .... 7 E5
  SHPY BD18 .... 18 B2
  WBSY BD6 .... 37 G
St Stephen's Rd
  PDSY/CALV LS28 .... 21 F
  WBOW BD5 .... 30 B
St Stephen's Ter *WBOW* BD5 ... 31 F4
Saint St *GTHN* BD7 .... 30 B
St Thomas Gdns *HUDN* HD2 ..... 53 G
St Wilfrid's Cl *GTHN* BD7 .... 30 A2
St Wilfrid's Crs *GTHN* BD7 ... 30 A2
St Wilfrid's Rd *GTHN* BD7..... 30 A2
Salcombe Pl *BOW* BD4 .... 32 D5
Salem St *BFD* BD1 .... 2 D
  CUL/QBY BD13 .... 35 E1
Salisbury Av *BAIL* BD17 ...... 12 D
Salisbury Pl *HIPP* HX3 .... 41 G
  PDSY/CALV LS28 .... 21 F
Salisbury Rd *CLECK* BD19...... 45 G
  HTON BD9 .... 18 D
  HWTH BD22 .... 6 B
  LM/WK BD12 .... 37 H4
Salisbury St *PDSY/CALV* LS28 . 21 G
  YEA LS19 .... 15 G
Sal Nook Cl *LM/WK* BD12 ...... 38 A
Sal Royd Rd *LM/WK* BD12....... 38 B
Saltaire Rd *BGLY* BD16........ 11 G
  SHPY BD18 .... 18 B
Saltburn Pl *HTON* BD9 .... 24 A2
Saltburn St *HFAX* HX1......... 4 A
Salt Horn Cl *LM/WK* BD12 ..... 38 C
Salts Mill Rd *BAIL* BD17 ..... 18 B
  BAIL BD17 .... 18 C1
  BAIL BD17 .... 18 C1
Salt St *GIR* BD8 .... 24 D
  HFAX HX1 .... 4 C
Samuel St *KGHY* BD21 .... 6 D4
Sandale Wk *WBSY* BD6 .... 37 E3
Sandall Magna *WBSY* BD6 ...... 36 D
Sandals Rd *BAIL* BD17 .... 12 D
Sand Beds *CUL/QBY* BD13 ...... 35 F
Sandbeds Crs *LUD/ILL* HX2 .... 40 D4
Sandbeds Rd *LUD/ILL* HX2 ..... 40 D
Sandbeds Ter *LUD/ILL* HX2 .... 40 D
Sanderling Ct *GIR* BD8........ 23 F5
Sanderson Av *WBSY* BD6 .... 37 H
Sandfield Rd *IDLE* BD10 ...... 20 A
Sandford Rd *BFDE* BD3......... 26 B
Sandforth Av *HIPP* HX3........ 41 H
Sandhall Av *LUD/ILL* HX2 ..... 46 C
Sandhall Dr *LUD/ILL* HX2 ..... 46 C
Sandhall Gn *LUD/ILL* HX2 ..... 40 C5
Sandhall La *LUD/ILL* HX2 ..... 46 C
Sandhill Mt *IDLE* BD10 .... 20 B
Sandholme Crs *HIPP* HX3 ...... 49 G
Sandholme Dr *IDLE* BD10 ...... 20 B
Sandmead Cl *BOW* BD4 .... 32 D4
Sandmoor Cl *CUL/QBY* BD13 .... 28 B1
Sandmoor Gdns *HIPP* HX3 ...... 43 E
Sandmoor Garth *IDLE* BD10 ... 14 A5
Sandown Av *LUD/ILL* HX2 ...... 40 D1
Sandown Rd *LUD/ILL* HX2 ...... 40 D1
Sandpiper Ms *GIR* BD8 .... 23 F5
Sandringham Cl *CLAY* BD14 .... 29 G2
Sandringham Ct *CLAY* BD14 .... 29 G2
Sandringham Rd *CLAY* BD14 .... 29 G2
Sandsend Cl *HTON* BD9........ 23 G
Sandside Cl *WBOW* BD5 .... 31 G5
Sand St *KGHY* BD21 .... 6 D4
Sandy Beck *WIL/AL* BD15 ...... 22 D1
Sandy Ga *KGHY* BD21.......... 6 B
Sandygate Ter *BOW* BD4 .... 32 C
Sandymoor *WIL/AL* BD15 .... 16 D
Sandywood St *KGHY* BD21 ...... 6 D3
Sangster Wy *WBOW* BD5 .... 38 D
Santa Monica Crs *IDLE* BD10 .. 19 H2
Santa Monica Gv *IDLE* BD10 .. 19 H2
Santa Monica Rd *IDLE* BD10.... 19 H
Sapgate La *CUL/QBY* BD13 ..... 28 B1
Saplin St *GIR* BD8 .... 20 B
Savile Av *IDLE* BD10 .... 20 B
Savile Cl *BRIG* HD6........... 51 E
Savile Crs *HFAX* HX1.......... 5 F
Savile Dr *HFAX* HX1 .... 5 F
Savile Gln *HFAX* HX1.......... 5 F
Savile Gv *HFAX* HX1 .... 5 G
Savile La *BRIG* HD6........... 51 E
Savile Lea *HFAX* HX1 .... 5 F
Savile Pde *HFAX* HX1 .... 47 G3
Savile Pk *HFAX* HX1 .... 47 F
  HFAX HX1 .... 47 F
  HFAX HX1 .... 47 F3

HIPP HX3 ..... 47 G4
vile Park Gdns HFAX HX1 ..... 47 G3 [7]
vile Park Rd HFAX HX1 ..... 5 F6
vile Park St HFAX HX1 ..... 47 F5
vile Rd HFAX HX1 ..... 5 F6
vile Royd HFAX HX1 ..... 4 E7
wley St KGHY BD21 ..... 6 C5 [18]
wrey Pl WBOW BD5 ..... 2 E7
axon St GIR BD8 ..... 24 D4
..... 4 A3
axton Av WBSY BD6 ..... 37 E1
ayle Av BOW BD4 ..... 39 E2
caley St BFDE BD3 ..... 26 C5 [3]
carborough Gv SHPY BD18 ..... 18 B2
carborough Rd SHPY BD18 ..... 18 B2
carlet Hts CUL/QBY BD13 ..... 35 G1
carr Bottom Rd LUD/ILL HX2 ..... 4 E4
carwood Cl BGLY BD16 ..... 10 D2 [8]
cholars Wk ECHL BD2 ..... 26 A1
cholebrook La BOW BD4 ..... 33 H4
cholemoor Av GTHN BD7 ..... 29 H2
cholemoor La GTHN BD7 ..... 29 H2
cholemoor Rd GTHN BD7 ..... 30 A2
choles St CLECK BD19 ..... 51 G1 [1]
choles St WBOW BD5 ..... 31 E5 [8]
choley Av BRIG HD6 ..... 52 B3
choley Rd BRIG HD6 ..... 52 B3
chool Cl LUD/ILL HX2 ..... 34 A3
chool Cote Brow LUD/ILL HX2 ..... 34 C4
chool Gn BRIG HD6 ..... 52 B3
CUL/QBY BD13 ..... 28 D1 [2]
chool Green Av
CUL/QBY BD13 ..... 28 C1 [2]
chool La HIPP HX3 ..... 48 D5
LUD/ILL HX2 ..... 34 A2
chool Pl LM/WK BD12 ..... 44 D1 [15]
chool Rd HWTH BD22 ..... 6 A4 [4]
chool Sq BFDE BD3 ..... 26 C5 [3]
chool St AIRE BD20 ..... 6 B1 [8]
BGLY BD16 ..... 17 E2 [3]
BOW BD4 ..... 32 B4
BOW BD4 ..... 39 E2 [7]
CLAY BD14 ..... 29 E3
HFAX HX1 ..... 5 J5
LM/WK BD12 ..... 37 H4
LM/WK BD12 ..... 45 H1 [3]
chool Wk HWTH BD22 ..... 6 A4
chool Yard Vw HIPP HX3 ..... 41 H4 [3]
core Hl HIPP HX3 ..... 42 D1
coresby St BFD BD1 ..... 3 F5
cotchman Rd HTON BD9 ..... 24 A2
cott La AIRE BD20 ..... 7 F1
cott La West AIRE BD20 ..... 7 E1
cott St KGHY BD21 ..... 6 C4
cotty Bank BRIG HD6 ..... 52 B1 [2]
cotty Croft La BRIG HD6 ..... 52 B2 [12]
eaton St BFDE BD3 ..... 3 J4
econd Av BFDE BD3 ..... 26 B3
HIPP HX3 ..... 47 G4
KGHY BD21 ..... 6 C5 [19]
YEA LS19 ..... 15 H1
econd St LM/WK BD12 ..... 38 B4
edan St HFAX HX1 ..... 5 G5 [1]
edburgh Rd HIPP HX3 ..... 5 J7
edgwick Cl GIR BD8 ..... 2 A3
eed St LM/WK BD12 ..... 38 A4
efton Av BRIG HD6 ..... 50 A3
efton Crs BRIG HD6 ..... 50 A3
efton Dr BRIG HD6 ..... 50 A3
efton Gv ECHL BD2 ..... 26 A1
efton Pl KGHY BD21 ..... 6 D3 [10]
efton St HFAX HX1 ..... 4 D2
KGHY BD21 ..... 6 D3 [11]
efton Ter HFAX HX1 ..... 4 D2
elborne Gv HTON BD9 ..... 24 C1
elborne Mt HTON BD9 ..... 24 D2 [10]
elborne Ter HTON BD9 ..... 24 C2
SHPY BD18 ..... 18 C3 [5]
elborne Vls CLAY BD14 ..... 29 F4 [8]
eldon St WBOW BD5 ..... 30 C4
ellars Fold GTHN BD7 ..... 30 B3 [15]
ellerdale Av LM/WK BD12 ..... 45 E3
ellerdale Dr LM/WK BD12 ..... 45 E3
ellerdale Ri LM/WK BD12 ..... 45 E3
ellerdale Rd LM/WK BD12 ..... 45 E3
ellerdale Wy LM/WK BD12 ..... 45 E4 [1]
emon Av ECHL BD2 ..... 19 G4 [3]
enior Vw WBOW BD5 ..... 2 C7
evenoaks Md WIL/AL BD15 ..... 23 E3 [3]
evern Rd ECHL BD2 ..... 25 H1 [1]
ewell Rd BFDE BD3 ..... 3 K6
eymour St BFDE BD3 ..... 3 H6
haftesbury Av BRIG HD6 ..... 52 C4
HTON BD9 ..... 23 G2
SHPY BD18 ..... 18 D2
hakespeare St HFAX HX1 ..... 5 H5 [1]

Shalimar St HFAX HX1 ..... 4 A3
Shann Av KGHY BD21 ..... 6 A3
Shann Crs KGHY BD21 ..... 6 A3
Shann La KGHY BD21 ..... 6 A3
Shann St SHPY BD18 ..... 19 E5
Shapla Cl HWTH BD22 ..... 6 B5
Sharp Av WBSY BD6 ..... 37 H2
Sharpe St WBOW BD5 ..... 2 C7
Sharp St WBSY BD6 ..... 37 H1 [16]
Shaw Hl HFAX HX1 ..... 47 H3 [3]
Shaw Hill La HIPP HX3 ..... 5 J7
Shaw La HIPP HX3 ..... 35 G4
HIPP HX3 ..... 48 A4
Shaw St LM/WK BD12 ..... 37 G4 [4]
Shay Cl HTON BD9 ..... 17 H5
Shay Crs HTON BD9 ..... 17 H5
Shay Dr HTON BD9 ..... 17 H5
Shay Fold HTON BD9 ..... 17 H5
Shay Gra HTON BD9 ..... 17 H4
Shay Gv HTON BD9 ..... 18 A5
Shay La HIPP HX3 ..... 41 F1
HTON BD9 ..... 17 H4
LUD/ILL HX2 ..... 41 F1
WIL/AL BD15 ..... 16 B5
Shay Syke HFAX HX1 ..... 5 J6
Shearbridge Rd GTHN BD7 ..... 30 D1
Shearbridge Ter GTHN BD7 ..... 30 D1 [8]
Shed St KGHY BD21 ..... 6 D4 [17]
Sheep Hill La CUL/QBY BD13 ..... 29 E5
Sheldon Rdg BOW BD4 ..... 39 E3
Sheldrake Av GIR BD8 ..... 23 F5
Shelf Hall La HIPP HX3 ..... 36 A5
Shelf Moor HIPP HX3 ..... 36 B3
Shelf Moor Rd HIPP HX3 ..... 36 B3
Shelley Gv GIR BD8 ..... 23 H4 [8]
Shell La PDSY/CALV LS28 ..... 21 G5
Shepherds Thorn La HUDN HD2 ..... 52 D5
Sherborne Dr HWTH BD22 ..... 8 D1
Sherborne Rd IDLE BD10 ..... 14 A5 [13]
Sheridan St BOW BD4 ..... 31 H3
Sheriff La BGLY BD16 ..... 11 F1
Sherwell Av WIL/AL BD15 ..... 23 F3 [2]
Sherwell Ri WIL/AL BD15 ..... 23 F3
Sherwood Cl BGLY BD16 ..... 11 F1
Sherwood Gv SHPY BD18 ..... 17 H1 [4]
Sherwood Pl ECHL BD2 ..... 26 A2 [7]
Sherwood Rd BRIG HD6 ..... 52 B5
Shetcliffe La BOW BD4 ..... 39 F2
Shetcliffe Rd BOW BD4 ..... 39 E2
Shetland Cl ECHL BD2 ..... 19 G5 [7]
Shibden Garth HIPP HX3 ..... 42 D5
Shibden Grange Dr HIPP HX3 ..... 42 C4
Shibden Hall Cft HIPP HX3 ..... 42 C5
Shibden Hall Rd HIPP HX3 ..... 42 C5
Shibden Head La CUL/QBY BD13 ..... 34 D3
Shibden Vw CUL/QBY BD13 ..... 35 E3 [6]
Shipley Airedale Rd BFDE BD3 ..... 2 E2
Shipley Fields Rd SHPY BD18 ..... 18 C4
Ship St HIPP HX3 ..... 52 C1 [3]
Shire Cl WBSY BD6 ..... 37 E3
Shirley Av LM/WK BD12 ..... 44 C4
Shirley Crs LM/WK BD12 ..... 44 C4
Shirley Gv WBSY BD6 ..... 50 B1
Shirley Pl LM/WK BD12 ..... 44 C4
Shirley Rd BOW BD4 ..... 30 C1 [3]
GTHN BD7 ..... 30 C1 [1]
Shirley St SHPY BD18 ..... 18 A1 [2]
Short Cl LM/WK BD12 ..... 37 G5
Shortway CUL/QBY BD13 ..... 28 D1 [3]
PDSY/CALV LS28 ..... 27 F3 [1]
Shroggs Rd HFAX HX1 ..... 4 D1
Shroggs St HFAX HX1 ..... 4 D2
Shroggs Vue Ter HFAX HX1 ..... 4 D1
Shuttleworth La GIR BD8 ..... 23 H4 [2]
Shutts La HIPP HX3 ..... 43 H5
Siddal Gv HIPP HX3 ..... 48 A4
Siddal La HIPP HX3 ..... 48 A5
Siddal New Rd HIPP HX3 ..... 48 A5
Siddal St HIPP HX3 ..... 48 B5 [1]
Siddal Top La HIPP HX3 ..... 48 A4
The Sidings SHPY BD18 ..... 18 D1 [1]
Silk St HTON BD9 ..... 24 B2
Silson La BAIL BD17 ..... 13 F2
Silver Birch Av LM/WK BD12 ..... 45 E3
Silver Birch Cl LM/WK BD12 ..... 45 E3
Silver Birch Dr LM/WK BD12 ..... 45 E3
Silver Birch Gv LM/WK BD12 ..... 45 E3 [8]
Silverdale Av AIRE BD20 ..... 7 F2
Silverdale Rd WBOW BD5 ..... 31 F5
Silverhill Dr BFDE BD3 ..... 26 A4
Silverhill Rd BFDE BD3 ..... 26 A4
Silver St GIR BD8 ..... 24 C3 [14]
HFAX HX1 ..... 5 G4
Silverwood Av LUD/ILL HX2 ..... 40 B4
Silwood Dr ECHL BD2 ..... 26 B1
Simes St BFD BD1 ..... 2 C4
Simm Carr La HIPP HX3 ..... 42 A1
Simmonds La HFAX HX1 ..... 5 J7

Simms Dene WIL/AL BD15 ..... 16 D5
Simon Cl BOW BD4 ..... 33 E5 [12]
Simpson Gv IDLE BD10 ..... 14 B5 [3]
Simpson St HIPP HX3 ..... 41 G3 [6]
KGHY BD21 ..... 6 B4 [15]
Sinclair Rd ECHL BD2 ..... 19 G4 [4]
Sinden Ms IDLE BD10 ..... 14 A4 [2]
Singleton St BFD BD1 ..... 2 D2
Sion Hl HIPP HX3 ..... 48 B5
Sir Isaac Holden Pl GTHN BD7 ..... 24 C5 [1]
Sir Wilfred Pl IDLE BD10 ..... 20 A1 [11]
Sixth Av BFDE BD3 ..... 26 B3
Sizers Ct YEA LS19 ..... 15 F1
Skelton Wk IDLE BD10 ..... 20 C2 [8]
Skinner La GIR BD8 ..... 24 D2
Skipton Rd KGHY BD21 ..... 6 D3
Skircoat Moor Cl LUD/ILL HX2 ..... 47 F4 [1]
Skircoat Moor Rd LUD/ILL HX2 ..... 47 F4
Skircoat Rd HFAX HX1 ..... 5 H7
Skirrow St BGLY BD16 ..... 17 E3 [1]
Skye Rd HTON BD9 ..... 24 B1 [8]
Slack Bottom Rd WBSY BD6 ..... 37 F2
Slack La HWTH BD22 ..... 8 A3
Sladdin Rw CUL/QBY BD13 ..... 34 D2 [6]
Slade La AIRE BD20 ..... 7 F1
BRIG HD6 ..... 52 A5
Sladen St KGHY BD21 ..... 6 B4 [18]
Slaymaker La HWTH BD22 ..... 8 B3
Slead Av BRIG HD6 ..... 50 A4
Slead Ct BRIG HD6 ..... 50 A4
Slead Crs BRIG HD6 ..... 50 A4
Slead Gv BRIG HD6 ..... 50 A4
Slead Royd BRIG HD6 ..... 50 A4
Sleningford Gv SHPY BD18 ..... 17 H1
Sleningford Ri BGLY BD16 ..... 10 C1 [1]
Sleningford Rd BGLY BD16 ..... 10 C1
SHPY BD18 ..... 17 H1 [2]
Slingsby Cl IDLE BD10 ..... 20 C1 [4]
Sloan Sq GIR BD8 ..... 24 C4 [10]
Smalewell Dr PDSY/CALV LS28 ..... 33 H1 [2]
Smalewell Gdns
PDSY/CALV LS28 ..... 33 H1
Smalewell Rd PDSY/CALV LS28 ..... 33 G1
Small Page Fold
CUL/QBY BD13 ..... 35 F1 [15]
Smiddles La WBOW BD5 ..... 30 D5 [7]
Smith Av WBSY BD6 ..... 37 H1
Smitherds St KGHY BD21 ..... 6 D5 [5]
Smithfield Av HIPP HX3 ..... 43 G5 [3]
Smith House Av BRIG HD6 ..... 50 B2
Smith House Crs BRIG HD6 ..... 50 B2
Smith House Dr BRIG HD6 ..... 50 B2
Smith House Gv BRIG HD6 ..... 50 B3
Smith House La BRIG HD6 ..... 50 B3
Smith La HTON BD9 ..... 23 H2
Smith Rd GTHN BD7 ..... 30 C4 [10]
Smith's Ter HIPP HX3 ..... 41 F2 [3]
Smith St BGLY BD16 ..... 17 E3 [2]
BOW BD4 ..... 39 E2
GTHN BD7 ..... 2 A5
KGHY BD21 ..... 6 C5
Smithville AIRE BD20 ..... 7 G2
Smithy Carr La BRIG HD6 ..... 50 B4
Smithy Hl WBSY BD6 ..... 37 H1 [17]
Smithy St HFAX HX1 ..... 5 J3
Snaith Wood Dr YEA LS19 ..... 15 H5
Snaith Wood Ms YEA LS19 ..... 15 H5
Snape Dr GTHN BD7 ..... 29 G5
Snowden Rd SHPY BD18 ..... 19 E2 [3]
Snowden St BFD BD1 ..... 2 C3
Snowdens Wk CLAY BD14 ..... 29 G3 [6]
Snowdrop Ms WIL/AL BD15 ..... 23 E4 [3]
Soaper House La HIPP HX3 ..... 43 F3
Soaper La WBSY BD6 ..... 36 C3
Sod House Gn HIPP HX3 ..... 41 F2
Soho St HFAX HX1 ..... 4 B4
Somerset Av BAIL BD17 ..... 12 C2
BRIG HD6 ..... 50 C3
Somerton Dr BOW BD4 ..... 32 C5
Somerville Av WBSY BD6 ..... 37 G3 [3]
Somerville Pk WBSY BD6 ..... 37 G3
Sonning Rd WIL/AL BD15 ..... 23 E4 [2]
Sorrin Cl IDLE BD10 ..... 19 H2
Southampton St BFDE BD3 ..... 3 F1
South Bank CUL/QBY BD13 ..... 35 G1 [12]
South Cliffe CUL/QBY BD13 ..... 28 A1
Southcliffe Dr BAIL BD17 ..... 12 C5
Southcliffe Wy BAIL BD17 ..... 12 D5
Southcote Pl IDLE BD10 ..... 20 A1 [12]
Southdown Cl HTON BD9 ..... 23 H2
Southdown Rd BAIL BD17 ..... 12 C5
South Edge KGHY BD21 ..... 6 B3
SHPY BD18 ..... 17 G2 [10]
Southedge Cl HIPP HX3 ..... 49 F1
Southfield Av AIRE BD20 ..... 7 G1
WBSY BD6 ..... 37 H1
Southfield Dr AIRE BD20 ..... 7 H1
Southfield La GTHN BD7 ..... 30 B4

WBOW BD5 ..... 30 C4
Southfield Mt AIRE BD20 ..... 7 H1 [2]
Southfield Rd BGLY BD16 ..... 10 D5
WBOW BD5 ..... 30 C4
Southfield Sq GIR BD8 ..... 24 D3 [14]
Southfield Ter HIPP HX3 ..... 43 F4
Southfield Wy AIRE BD20 ..... 7 H1 [3]
Southgate BFD BD1 ..... 2 C6
HFAX HX1 ..... 5 H4
South Gv WBSY BD6 ..... 49 G3 [3]
SHPY BD18 ..... 17 G2 [9]
South Hill Dr BGLY BD16 ..... 11 E3
Southlands BAIL BD17 ..... 12 C5
LUD/ILL HX2 ..... 34 A1
Southlands Av AIRE BD20 ..... 7 H2 [1]
BGLY BD16 ..... 10 D5
CUL/QBY BD13 ..... 29 F1
Southlands Dr AIRE BD20 ..... 7 H2 [2]
BGLY BD16 ..... 10 C5
CUL/QBY BD13 ..... 29 E1
Southlands Gv West AIRE BD20 ..... 7 H1 [3]
BGLY BD16 ..... 10 C5
CUL/QBY BD13 ..... 29 E1
Southlands Mt AIRE BD20 ..... 7 H2
Southlands Rd AIRE BD20 ..... 7 H1
South La HIPP HX3 ..... 36 A3
Southlea Av HWTH BD22 ..... 8 D4
Southlea Cl LM/WK BD12 ..... 38 D5
Southmere Av GTHN BD7 ..... 30 B4
Southmere Crs GTHN BD7 ..... 30 B4 [3]
Southmere Dr GTHN BD7 ..... 30 A4
Southmere Gv GTHN BD7 ..... 30 B4 [10]
Southmere Ov GTHN BD7 ..... 30 A5 [7]
Southmere Rd GTHN BD7 ..... 30 B4
Southmere Ter GTHN BD7 ..... 30 B4 [15]
Southowram Bank HIPP HX3 ..... 48 B2
South Pde HFAX HX1 ..... 5 J6
South Rd HTON BD9 ..... 18 D5 [2]
South Royde Av HIPP HX3 ..... 47 H5
South Sq CUL/QBY BD13 ..... 28 A1 [23]
South St BRIG HD6 ..... 50 B5
CUL/QBY BD13 ..... 22 A5 [3]
HFAX HX1 ..... 5 F5
KGHY BD21 ..... 6 C5
KGHY BD21 ..... 9 G2
LM/WK BD12 ..... 45 H1
WBOW BD5 ..... 30 D4 [16]
South Vw HX3 ..... 48 B3
HTON BD9 ..... 18 D5 [3]
IDLE BD10 ..... 20 C2
PDSY/CALV LS28 ..... 27 H3
South View Cl BOW BD4 ..... 39 H3
South View Ct HIPP HX3 ..... 49 G2 [3]
South View Ter BAIL BD17 ..... 12 D3 [1]
Southway BGLY BD16 ..... 11 F1 [1]
South Wy BOW BD4 ..... 39 H3
SHPY BD18 ..... 17 G2 [10]
Sovereign St HFAX HX1 ..... 5 H4 [8]
Sowden Buildings ECHL BD2 ..... 26 A2 [3]
Sowden Gra CUL/QBY BD13 ..... 28 A1 [23]
Sowden Rd HTON BD9 ..... 23 G1
Sowden St GTHN BD7 ..... 30 C4 [11]
Sowerby Croft La
RPDN/SBR HX6 ..... 46 A5
Sowerby St RPDN/SBR HX6 ..... 46 A5
Spa La BGLY BD16 ..... 10 D5
Spark House La RPDN/SBR HX6 ..... 46 B5
Spartan Rd LM/WK BD12 ..... 38 A5
Spearhead Wy KGHY BD21 ..... 6 D3
Speeton Av WBSY BD6 ..... 29 H5
Speeton Gv GTHN BD7 ..... 29 G5 [1]
Spencer Av GTHN BD7 ..... 30 B2
Spencer Rd GTHN BD7 ..... 30 B2
Spencer St KGHY BD21 ..... 6 B4 [17]
Spen Cl BOW BD4 ..... 39 E3
Spen Valley Heritage Trail
BIRK/DRI BD11 ..... 39 H4
Spen View La BOW BD4 ..... 39 H3
Spicer St WBOW BD5 ..... 30 D4 [17]
Spindle St LUD/ILL HX2 ..... 34 C4
Spinners Wy CLECK BD19 ..... 45 G5 [2]
The Spinney BRIG HD6 ..... 50 B3
IDLE BD10 ..... 15 F4
Spinning Mill Ct SHPY BD18 ..... 17 H1 [3]
Spout House La BRIG HD6 ..... 49 H2
Spring Av KGHY BD21 ..... 7 F5
Spring Bank Pl GIR BD8 ..... 25 E3
Spring Bank Ri KGHY BD21 ..... 9 H2 [3]
Springcliffe GIR BD8 ..... 24 C3
Springcliffe St GIR BD8 ..... 24 C3
Spring Cl BGLY BD16 ..... 11 E4 [3]
KGHY BD21 ..... 7 F5
Spring Ct WIL/AL BD15 ..... 22 D1 [3]
Springdale Crs IDLE BD10 ..... 20 B1
Spring Dr KGHY BD21 ..... 7 F5
Spring Edge North HFAX HX1 ..... 4 F7
Spring Edge South HFAX HX1 ..... 47 F3
Spring Edge West HFAX HX1 ..... 47 E3

Springfield Av GTHN BD7 .... 30 A2
Springfield Ct KGHY BD21 .... 6 B3 ⑤
Springfield Gdns KGHY BD21 .... 6 B3
Springfield Gv BGLY BD16 .... 10 C2 ⑧
  BRIG HD6 .... 50 B4
Springfield Pl GIR BD8 .... 2 B2
Springfield Rd BAIL BD17 .... 12 C2
  KGHY BD21 .... 6 B3
Springfield St CUL/QBY BD13 .. 28 B1 ⑬
  GIR BD8 .... 24 D4
Springfield Ter CLECK BD19 .... 45 C4 ②
Spring Gdns GIR BD8 .... 2 B2
Spring Gardens La KGHY BD21 .... 6 B2
Spring Gardens Mt KGHY BD21 .... 6 C2
Spring Garden Rd HTON BD9 .. 24 B1 ⑦
Spring Garden St
  CUL/QBY BD13 .... 35 F1 ⑩
Spring Gv HFAX HX1 .... 46 D1 ⑨
Spring Hall Cl HIPP HX3 .... 36 A5
Spring Hall Ct HFAX HX1 .... 40 D5 ⑨
Spring Hall Dr HFAX HX1 .... 46 D1
Spring Hall Gdns HFAX HX1 .... 46 D1
Spring Hall La HFAX HX1 .... 46 D1
Spring Hall Pl HFAX HX1 .... 46 D1
Spring Head Rd CUL/QBY BD13 .. 28 B1
Spring Hl BAIL BD17 .... 12 A3
  SHPY BD18 .... 19 F2
Springhurst Rd SHPY BD18 .... 18 B2
Springlodge Pl GIR BD8 .... 2 B1 ②
Spring Mill St WBOW BD5 .... 31 F2
Spring Pl GTHN BD7 .... 30 D2
Spring Ri KGHY BD21 .... 7 F5
Spring Rw KGHY BD21 .... 6 C5 ⑳
Springroyd Ter GIR BD8 .... 24 A4
Springs Rd BAIL BD17 .... 14 D1
Spring St BRIG HD6 .... 52 B1 ⑦
  IDLE BD10 .... 20 A3
  KGHY BD21 .... 6 D3
Springwood Av SHPY BD18 ...... 18 B2 ③
Springwood Rd SHPY BD18 ... 18 B2 ⑩
Springwood Rd SHPY BD18 .. 18 B2 ⑪
Spring Ter HIPP HX3 .... 5 J2
Spring Wy KGHY BD21 .... 7 F5 ③
Springwell Dr WBOW BD5 ...... 31 F3 ⑭
Springwood Av WBOW BD5 .... 31 G4
Spring Wood Gdns
  WBOW BD5 .... 31 G5 ⑧
Springwood Rd YEA LS19 .... 15 F3
Sprinkwell Cl BFDE BD3 .... 2 E1
Spruce St KGHY BD21 .... 7 E3 ⑩
Square Rd HFAX HX1 .... 5 J4
Square St BOW BD4 .... 31 H2
The Square GIR BD8 .... 23 F5 ②
Squire Gn GIR BD8 .... 24 A3 ①
Squire La HTON BD9 .... 24 A3
Stable Fold LM/WK BD12 .... 45 E3 ③
Stable La HIPP HX3 .... 41 G4
Stackgarth BRIG HD6 .... 52 B3
Stadium Rd WBSY BD6 .... 38 A2
Stafford Av HIPP HX3 .... 47 H4
Stafford Pde HIPP HX3 .... 47 H5 ⑧
Stafford Rd HIPP HX3 .... 47 H5
Stafford Sq HIPP HX3 .... 48 A5
Stafford St BOW BD4 .... 32 A3
Stainbeck Gdns WBSY BD6 ..... 36 C2 ①
Stainton Cl WBSY BD6 .... 36 D2 ③
Staithgate La WBSY BD6 .... 38 C1
Stallabrass St GIR BD8 .... 24 D4 ⑮
Stamford St BOW BD4 .... 32 A2
Stanacre Pl BFDE BD3 .... 3 F1
Stanage La HIPP HX3 .... 36 B3
Stanley Rd ECHL BD2 .... 19 E5
  HFAX HX1 .... 4 A6
  HWTH BD22 .... 9 F2
Stanley St BGLY BD16 .... 10 D3
  BRIG HD6 .... 50 C5 ⑤
  HTON BD9 .... 18 D4 ⑧
  IDLE BD10 .... 20 A1 ⑬
  KGHY BD21 .... 6 C3 ⑧
  RPDN/SBR HX6 .... 46 B4 ⑧
Stanmore Pl GTHN BD7 .... 30 B2 ③
Stannary Pl HFAX HX1 .... 5 F2
Stanningley By-pass
  PDSY/CALV LS28 .... 27 H3
Stansfield Cl HFAX HX1 .... 4 D3
Stansfield Ct RPDN/SBR HX6 .. 46 A5 ④
Starkie St KGHY BD21 .... 6 C5 ㉑
Star St WBOW BD5 .... 30 D4
Station Rd BAIL BD17 .... 13 E3
  BRIG HD6 .... 52 D1
  CLAY BD14 .... 29 F3
  CUL/QBY BD13 .... 35 F1
  HIPP HX3 .... 44 B3
  HIPP HX3 .... 49 F1
  HWTH BD22 .... 8 C4
  LM/WK BD12 .... 38 B5
  RPDN/SBR HX6 .... 46 B5

  SHPY BD18 .... 18 C1
Staups La HIPP HX3 .... 42 C4
Staveley Dr SHPY BD18 .... 17 G2 ⑬
Staveley Gv HWTH BD22 .... 9 F3
Staveley Rd BGLY BD16 .... 10 C2
  GTHN BD7 .... 30 C1 ③
  HWTH BD22 .... 9 F3
  SHPY BD18 .... 17 G1
Staveley Wy HWTH BD22 .... 9 F2
Stavely Ms BGLY BD16 .... 10 D2 ②
Staverton St LUD/ILL HX2 .... 46 D1 ③
Staybrite Av BGLY BD16 .... 16 D2
Staygate Gn WBSY BD6 .... 38 B1 ①
Stead Hill Wy IDLE BD10 .... 13 G5
Steadman St BFDE BD3 .... 3 K6
Steadman Ter BFDE BD3 .... 3 K6
Stead Rd BOW BD4 .... 39 H2
Stead St BAIL BD17 .... 18 C1
  HFAX HX1 .... 5 F4 ④
Steeplands HUDN HD2 .... 53 G5
Stell Hl HWTH BD22 .... 8 C1
Stephen Cl HIPP HX3 .... 42 D4
Stephen Crs ECHL BD2 .... 25 F1
Stephen Rd WBSY BD6 .... 30 A5
Stephenson Rd WIL/AL BD15 ...... 22 A2
Stephenson St GTHN BD7 .... 30 C4 ③
Steps La RPDN/SBR HX6 .... 46 B3
Sterne Hl LUD/ILL HX2 .... 47 E4
Stewart Cl ECHL BD2 .... 20 B4
Sticker La BOW BD4 .... 32 B3
Stirling Crs BOW BD4 .... 32 D4
Stirling St HFAX HX1 .... 4 E5
Stirrup Gv ECHL BD2 .... 19 G5 ⑤
Stirton St WBOW BD5 .... 31 E4 ⑬
Stockhill Fold IDLE BD10 .... 20 C1
Stockhill Rd IDLE BD10 .... 20 C2
Stock La CUL/QBY BD13 .... 36 A1
Stocks La CUL/QBY BD13 .... 36 A1
Stonecroft ECHL BD2 .... 20 B4 ⑤
Stonefield Cl IDLE BD10 .... 20 A4 ④
Stonefield St CLECK BD19 .... 51 H2
Stonegate BGLY BD16 .... 10 D1
Stonegate Rd IDLE BD10 .... 20 B3
Stone Hall Rd ECHL BD2 .... 20 A5
Stone Hl BRIG HD6 .... 11 E2
Stonehouse Dr CUL/QBY BD13 ... 34 D2
Stoneleigh CUL/QBY BD13 ..... 35 G1 ⑱
Stone St BAIL BD17 .... 13 F4
  BFD BD1 .... 2 D4
  WIL/AL BD15 .... 22 D1
Stoney Battery HFAX HX1 .... 5 H1
Stoneycroft La AIRE BD20 .... 6 C1 ③
Stoney Hl BRIG HD6 .... 52 B1
Stoneyhurst Sq BOW BD4 ...... 32 D4 ⑪
Stoney La HIPP HX3 .... 41 B1
  HIPP HX3 .... 50 B1
Stoney Ridge Av WIL/AL BD15 .... 17 E5
Stoney Ridge Rd BGLY BD16 ...... 17 F4
Stoney St AIRE BD20 .... 6 C1 ③
Stony La ECHL BD2 .... 20 B4 ⑦
  HIPP HX3 .... 49 F4
  WIL/AL BD15 .... 22 C2
Stony Royd PDSY/CALV LS28 ..... 27 H1
Stoodley Ter LUD/ILL HX2 .... 46 D2
Storr Hl LM/WK BD12 .... 44 D1
Stott Ter ECHL BD2 .... 20 C5
Stowell Mill St WBOW BD5 .... 31 E3 ⑰
Strafford Wy IDLE BD10 .... 20 D1
Straightacres La IDLE BD10 .... 20 C4 ③
Straits BAIL BD17 .... 12 D2
Strangford Ct IDLE BD10 .... 20 C1 ⑧
Stratford Rd GTHN BD7 .... 30 C2
Strathallan Dr BAIL BD17 .... 13 E3
Strathmore Dr BAIL BD17 .... 12 C2
Stratton Cl BRIG HD6 .... 52 C2 ③
Stratton Pk BRIG HD6 .... 52 C2
Stratton Rd BRIG HD6 .... 52 C2
Stratton Vw BOW BD4 .... 32 D3 ⑦
Strawberry Flds KGHY BD21 .... 6 D3 ⑬
Strawberry St KGHY BD21 .... 6 D3
Strensall Gn WBSY BD6 .... 36 D2 ④
Stretchgate La LUD/ILL HX2 .... 40 D5
Strong Close Gv KGHY BD21 ..... 7 F4 ③
Strong Close Rd KGHY BD21 ..... 7 F4 ⑧
Stubbings Rd BAIL BD17 .... 12 A4
Stubbing Wy SHPY BD18 .... 18 D3 ④
Studley Av WBSY BD6 .... 37 G3
Studley Crs BGLY BD16 .... 11 E3
Studley Rd ECHL BD2 .... 25 G2
Sturges Gv ECHL BD2 .... 26 A2 ⑩
Suffolk Pl ECHL BD2 .... 19 G5
Sugden Cl BRIG HD6 .... 52 B3
Sugden St BFD BD1 .... 24 D5
  LM/WK BD12 .... 45 G1
Sulby Gv IDLE BD10 .... 20 D3
Summerbridge Crs IDLE BD10 ... 20 C4
Summerbridge Dr IDLE BD10 .. 20 C4 ③
Summerfield Av BRIG HD6 .... 50 C2

Summerfield Cl BAIL BD17 .... 12 B3
Summerfield Dr BAIL BD17 ..... 12 C3 ③
Summerfield Gn BAIL BD17 .... 12 C3 ②
Summerfield Gv BAIL BD17 .... 12 B3
Summerfield Pk BAIL BD17 .... 12 B3
Summerfield Rd IDLE BD10 .... 20 B3
Summergate Pl HFAX HX1 .... 4 A6
Summergate St HFAX HX1 .... 5 F4 ④
Summer Hall Ing LM/WK BD12 .... 44 C1
Summer Hill St GTHN BD7 .... 30 B2 ④
Summerlands Gv WBOW BD5 ..... 31 H5
Summer Lea IDLE BD10 .... 19 H1
Summerscale St HFAX HX1 .... 4 C2 ⑤
Summerseat Pl GTHN BD7 ...... 30 D2 ③
Summer St HFAX HX1 .... 4 B7
  PDSY/CALV LS28 .... 27 H2
Summerville Rd GTHN BD7....... 30 D1
Summit St KGHY BD21 .... 6 C3 ⑥
Sunbridge Rd BFD BD1 .... 2 C5
  GIR BD8 .... 24 D4
Sunderland Ct BRIG HD6 .... 50 B5 ⑦
Sunderland Rd HTON BD9 .... 24 C2
Sunderland St HFAX HX1 .... 5 F4 ⑬
  KGHY BD21 .... 6 C5
Sundown Av BOW BD7 .... 29 H3
Sun Fold HFAX HX1 .... 5 J6
Sun Hill Dr BAIL BD17 .... 11 H3
Sunhurst Cl HWTH BD22 .... 8 B4 ⑧
Sunhurst Dr HWTH BD22 .... 8 B4
Sunningdale GIR BD8 .... 23 G4
Sunny Bank SHPY BD18 .... 18 C2 ③
Sunny Bank Av WBOW BD5 .... 38 A1 ⑩
Sunny Bank Cl CLECK BD19 ...... 51 G2
Sunny Bank Dr RPDN/SBR HX6 ... 46 B4
Sunnybank La BFDE BD3 .... 27 E3
Sunny Bank La HIPP HX3 .... 49 E2
Sunny Bank Rd BRIG HD6 .... 50 A5
  WBOW BD5 .... 38 A1
Sunny Bank St RPDN/SBR HX6 ... 46 B4
Sunny Bank Ter HIPP HX3 ...... 41 H4 ⑩
Sunnybrae Crs BGLY BD16 .... 11 E4 ⑥
Sunny Brow La HTON BD9 .... 23 G2
Sunnydale Av BRIG HD6 .... 52 B3 ⑬
Sunnydale Gv KGHY BD21........ 7 G5 ⑤
Sunny Hill Av HWTH BD22......... 9 E1
Sunny Hill Gv HWTH BD22 .... 9 E1
Sunny Mt KGHY BD21 .... 6 C3
Sunnyridge Av PDSY/CALV LS28 .. 27 G5
Sunnyside BRIG HD6 .... 53 E5
Sunnyside La BFDE BD3 .... 25 G3
Sunny Side St HIPP HX3 .... 41 H4 ⑪
Sunny View Ter
  CUL/QBY BD13 .... 34 D2 ⑨
Sunshine Ct WBSY BD6 .... 37 E4 ⑧
Sun St BFDE BD3 .... 3 F3
  KGHY BD21 .... 6 D5 ⑧
Sun Wy HIPP HX3 .... 48 C3
Sun Wood Av HIPP HX3 .... 43 E1
Suresnes Rd KGHY BD21 .... 6 C4
Surrey Gv WBOW BD5 .... 31 F3 ⑬
Surrey St HFAX HX1 .... 46 D2
  KGHY BD21 .... 7 F3
Sussex St KGHY BD21 .... 7 F5 ③
Sutcliffe St LUD/ILL HX2 .... 40 D5
Sutcliffe Wood La HIPP HX3 ...... 49 F2
Sutherland Rd HIPP HX3 .... 43 H5
Sutton Av ECHL BD2 .... 19 G4
Sutton Crs BOW BD4 .... 32 D3
Sutton Gv BOW BD4 .... 32 D2 ③
Sutton Rd BOW BD4 .... 32 D2
Swain House Crs ECHL BD2 ...... 19 H4
Swain House Rd ECHL BD2 .... 19 H4
Swain Mt ECHL BD2 .... 19 H4
Swales Moor Rd HIPP HX3 .... 34 B5
Swallow Fold GIR BD8 .... 23 F5 ⑩
Swallow St KGHY BD21 .... 7 E3 ⑩
Swan Bank La HIPP HX3 .... 5 K7
Swarland Gv WBOW BD5 .... 31 F3
Swinton Pl GTHN BD7 .... 30 C2 ③
Swinton Ter HFAX HX1 .... 4 A6
Swires Rd ECHL BD2 .... 26 A5
  HFAX HX1 .... 4 E6 ①
Swires Ter HFAX HX1 .... 5 F6
Sycamore Av BGLY BD16 .... 10 C4
  GTHN BD7 .... 24 A5
Sycamore Cl BFDE BD3 .... 3 G2
Sycamore Dr BRIG HD6 .... 50 B2
Sycamore Vw HWTH BD22 .... 6 A5 ⑧
Sydenham Pl BFDE BD3 .... 26 C2
Sydney St BGLY BD16 .... 10 D3 ⑰
Syke La CUL/QBY BD13 .... 35 F3
  HIPP HX3 .... 43 H4
Syke Side AIRE BD20 .... 6 C1 ⑦
Sykes La HWTH BD22 .... 8 C3
  LM/WK BD12 .... 45 H1
Sylhet Cl BFD BD1 .... 2 B3

Sylvan Av CUL/QBY BD13 35
Syringa Av WIL/AL BD15 16

T

Tabbs Ct CLECK BD19 45
Tabbs La CLECK BD19 45
Tagore Ct BOW BD4 .... 32 C1 ③
Talbot St GTHN BD7 24
  KGHY BD21 .... 6 B4 ③
Tamar St WBOW BD5 .... 30 ①
Tamworth St BOW BD4 .... 32 D1
Tanglewood Ct WBSY BD6 ...... 37 F1
Tanhouse Hl HIPP HX3 49
Tan House La HIPP HX3 .... 42 ①
Tanhouse Pk HIPP HX3 49
Tan La BOW BD4 39
Tannerbrook Cl CLAY BD14 ..... 29 G3
Tanner Hill Rd GTHN BD7 .... 29 ①
Tannery Ct IDLE BD10 .... 20 C1
Tanton Crs CLAY BD14 29
Tanton Wk CLAY BD14 .... 29 ①
Tarn Ct HWTH BD22 .... 6 A3
Tarnhill Ms WBOW BD5 .... 31 F3 ③
Taunton St SHPY BD18 .... 18 ①
Tawny Cl BOW BD4 .... 39 H1 ③
Taylor Rd WBSY BD6 .... 38 A2
Teasdale St BOW BD4 .... 32 ①
Teasel Cl LM/WK BD12 .... 45 H
Tees St WBOW BD5 .... 30 D4 ①
Telscombe Dr BOW BD4 .... 32 ①
Temperance Flds CLECK BD19 ... 45 ①
Templar's Wy GIR BD8 .... 23 H
Temple Rhydding Dr BAIL BD17 .. 12 ①
Temple St HTON BD9 .... 24 ①
Tenbury Fold BOW BD4 .... 32 ①
Tennis Av BOW BD4 .... 39 H
Tennis Wy BAIL BD17 .... 12 ①
Tennyson Pl BFDE BD3 .... 3 ①
Tennyson Rd WBSY BD6 .... 37 ①
Tennyson St HIPP HX3 .... 41 F
  KGHY BD21 .... 9 G1 ②
Tenterfield Ri HIPP HX3 .... 42 ①
Tenterfields IDLE BD10 .... 20 ①
Tenter Hl CLAY BD14 .... 29 E3 ①
Ternhill Gv WBOW BD5 .... 31 F
Tern St WBOW BD5 .... 30 ①
Terrace Gdns HIPP HX3 .... 41 ①
Terrington Crest CLAY BD14...... 29 ①
Terry Rd LM/WK BD12 .... 38 ①
Tetley La HIPP HX3 .... 42 ①
Tetley Pl ECHL BD2 .... 25 G1
Tetley St BFD BD1 .... 2 ①
Teville Ct BOW BD4 .... 31 H3 ①
Tewit Cl LUD/ILL HX2 .... 34 A
Tewit Gn LUD/ILL HX2 .... 34 A
Tewit Hall Gdns LUD/ILL HX2 .. 34 A4 ①
Tewit Hall Rd BFDE BD3 .... 26 B
Tewit La LUD/ILL HX2 .... 34 A
Thackeray Rd IDLE BD10 .... 20 C
Thackley Av IDLE BD10 .... 13 H4 ①
Thackley Ct SHPY BD18 .... 18 D1 ①
Thackley Old Rd SHPY BD18 ..... 19 E
Thackley Rd IDLE BD10 .... 13 H4 ①
Thackley Vw IDLE BD10 .... 13 H
Thackray St LUD/ILL HX2 .... 46 C
Theakston Md CLAY BD14........... 29 F
Thearne Gn CLAY BD14 .... 29 G
Third Av BFDE BD3..................... 26 B
  HIPP HX3 .... 47 G
  KGHY BD21 .... 6 C5 ②
Third St LM/WK BD12 .... 38 B
Thirkleby Royd CLAY BD14 .... 29 F
Thirlmere Av LM/WK BD12......... 45 F
Thirlmere Gdns ECHL BD2 ...... 26 A2 ①
Thirsk Gra CLAY BD14 .... 29 F
Thomas Ct WBSY BD6 .... 37 H1 ①
Thomas St BRIG HD6 .... 52 B
  HFAX HX1 .... 5 H
Thomas St South HFAX HX1........ 4 B
Thomas St West HFAX HX1 ...... 47 F5 ①
Thompson Av ECHL BD2 .... 19 G
Thompson Gn BAIL BD17 .... 12 B
Thompson La BAIL BD17 .... 12 B5 ①
Thompson St HFAX HX1 .... 5 F
  SHPY BD18 .... 18 B1 ①
Thoresby Gv GTHN BD7 .... 29 H4 ⑧
Thornaby Dr CLAY BD14 .... 29 G2 ⑧
Thornacre Crs SHPY BD18 .... 19 F3
Thornacre Rd SHPY BD18 .... 19 F2 ①
Thorn Av HTON BD9 .... 17 F
Thornbridge Ms ECHL BD2 ...... 20 A5 ①
Thornbury Av BFDE BD3 .... 26 C
Thornbury Crs BFDE BD3 .... 26 C
Thornbury Dr BFDE BD3 .... 26 C
Thornbury Gv BFDE BD3............. 26 C

hornbury Rd *BFDE* BD3 .... 26 C5
horncliffe St *BFDE* BD3 .... 26 C5
horncliffe Rd *GIR* BD8 .... 25 E3
  HWTH BD22 .... 6 A5
horn Cl *SHPY* BD18 .... 19 F3
horncroft Rd *WBSY* BD6 .... 37 F1
horndale Ri *ECHL* BD2 .... 19 F5
horn Dr *CUL/QBY* BD13 .... 34 D3
  HTON BD9 .... 17 G5
horne Cl *PDSY/CALV* LS28 .... 27 G4
hornes Pk *BRIG* HD6 .... 52 B2
  SHPY BD18 .... 19 E4
hornfield *BGLY* BD16 .... 10 B2
hornfield Av *PDSY/CALV* LS28 ..... 27 H1
  WBSY BD6 .... 38 A2
hornfield Pl *ECHL* BD2 .... 26 B1
horn Garth *KGHY* BD21 .... 6 B2
horn Gv *HTON* BD9 .... 17 G5
hornhill Av *HWTH* BD22 .... 8 D3
  SHPY BD18 .... 19 E4
hornhill Bridge La *BRIG* HD6 ...... 50 B5
hornhill Cl *PDSY/CALV* LS28 .... 21 G3
hornhill Dr *PDSY/CALV* LS28 ...... 21 E1
  SHPY BD18 .... 19 E4
hornhill Gv *PDSY/CALV* LS28 ...... 21 G2
  SHPY BD18 .... 19 E4
hornhill Pl *BFDE* BD3 .... 26 D4
hornhill Rd *BRIG* HD6 .... 52 A3
hornhills Beck La *BRIC* HD6 .... 50 C4
hornhills La *BRIG* HD6 .... 50 D4
hornhill St *PDSY/CALV* LS28 ...... 21 G3
horn La *HTON* BD9 .... 17 F5
hornlea Cl *YEA* LS19 .... 15 E1
hornmead Rd *BAIL* BD17 .... 13 E4
horn Royd Dr *BOW* BD4 .... 33 E5
hornsgill Av *BOW* BD4 .... 32 B4
horn St *GIR* BD8 .... 24 A3
hornton La *WBOW* BD5 .... 30 D4
hornton Old Rd *GIR* BD8 .... 23 G5
hornton *CUL/QBY* BD13 .... 28 C1
  GIR BD8 .... 23 G5
  GIR BD8 .... 24 B4
hornton St *BFD* BD1 .... 24 D5
  CLECK BD19 .... 51 H2
  HFAX HX1 .... 4 A7
hornton Ter *HFAX* HX1 .... 4 B7
hornton View Rd *CLAY* BD14 ...... 29 F3
horn Tree St *HFAX* HX1 .... 4 B7
horpe Cv *CUL/QBY* BD13 .... 28 C1
horpe Gv *CUL/QBY* BD13 .... 29 E1
horpe Rd *CUL/QBY* BD13 .... 28 C1
horpe St *HIPP* HX3 .... 41 G3
  KGHY BD21 .... 6 D3
horp Garth *IDLE* BD10 .... 20 A1
horverton Dr *BOW* BD4 .... 39 H2
horverton Gv *BOW* BD4 .... 39 H2
hrift Wy *BGLY* BD16 .... 10 C4
hroxenby Wy *CLAY* BD14 .... 29 F3
hrum Hall Dr *HFAX* HX1 .... 4 A3
hrum Hall La *HFAX* HX1 .... 4 A3
hrush St *KGHY* BD21 .... 7 E3
hryberg St *BFDE* BD3 .... 3 H6
hurley Dr *BOW* BD4 .... 32 A5
hurley Rd *BOW* BD4 .... 32 A5
hurnscoe Rd *BFD* BD1 .... 2 E2
hursby St *BFDE* BD3 .... 3 J5
hurston Gdns *WIL/AL* BD15 ...... 23 E4
hwaites Br *KGHY* BD21 .... 7 F4
hwaites Brow Rd *KGHY* BD21 .... 7 G4
hwaites La *KGHY* BD21 .... 7 F4
chborne Rd *WBOW* BD5 .... 31 F4
chborne Rd West
  WBOW BD5 .... 31 F4
ckhill St *BFDE* BD3 .... 3 J6
le St *GIR* BD8 .... 24 C3
ley Sq *WBOW* BD5 .... 31 F3
ll Carr La *HIPP* HX3 .... 50 B1
mber St *KGHY* BD21 .... 7 F3
mble Dr *BGLY* BD16 .... 11 E2
m La *HWTH* BD22 .... 8 A5
nkler Stile *SHPY* BD18 .... 19 G1
ntern Av *GIR* BD8 .... 23 G5
sma Dr *BOW* BD4 .... 39 F2
the House Wy *HUDN* HD2 .... 53 F5
tus St *SHPY* BD18 .... 18 A1
voli Pl *WBOW* BD5 .... 30 D4
oby La *GTHN* BD7 .... 30 B2
odd Ter *GTHN* BD7 .... 30 B2
odwell La *WBOW* BD5 .... 30 D4
ofts Av *LM/WK* BD12 .... 44 D3
ofts Gv *BRIG* HD6 .... 52 A4
ofts Grove Gdns *BRIG* HD6 ..... 52 A4
oftshaw Fold *BOW* BD4 .... 39 G2
oftshaw La *BOW* BD4 .... 39 F1
oftshaw New Rd *BOW* BD4 ..... 39 G2
oller Dr *HTON* BD9 .... 23 H1
oller Gv *HTON* BD9 .... 24 A1

Toller La *GIR* BD8 .... 24 B3
  HTON BD9 .... 24 A1
Toller Pk *HTON* BD9 .... 24 A1
Tolworth Fold *WIL/AL* BD15 ..... 23 E4
Tonbridge Cl *WBSY* BD6 .... 37 E2
Tong St *BOW* BD4 .... 39 G1
Toothill Av *BRIG* HD6 .... 52 B4
Toothill Bank *BRIG* HD6 .... 52 B4
Toothill La *BRIG* HD6 .... 52 B5
Tor Av *LM/WK* BD12 .... 44 D4
Tordoff Av *GTHN* BD7 .... 29 H2
Tordoff Gn *WBSY* BD6 .... 37 G2
Tordoff Rd *LM/WK* BD12 ...... 38 B4
Torre Crs *WBSY* BD6 .... 36 C1
Torre Gv *WBSY* BD6 .... 36 C1
Torre Rd *WBSY* BD6 .... 36 C1
Torridon Crs *WBSY* BD6 .... 36 C1
Tower Gdns *LUD/ILL* HX2 ...... 47 E4
Tower Hl *RPDN/SBR* HX6 ...... 46 A4
Tower Rd *SHPY* BD18 .... 17 H1
Tower St *ECHL* BD2 .... 19 H5
Town End *GTHN* BD7 .... 30 B3
Town End Rd *BGLY* BD14 ...... 29 E2
Towngate *BRIG* HD6 .... 51 E5
  BRIG HD6 .... 53 F1
Town Ga *CLECK* BD19 .... 45 G5
  HIPP HX3 .... 42 D2
Towngate *HIPP* HX3 .... 43 F5
  HIPP HX3 .... 48 D4
  KGHY BD21 .... 6 D4
  LM/WK BD12 ...... 44 D3
Town Ga *PDSY/CALV* LS28 ..... 21 G2
Towngate *SHPY* BD18 .... 19 E2
Towngate Av *BRIG* HD6 .... 51 E5
Town Hall St *KGHY* BD21 ...... 6 D4
  RPDN/SBR HX6 ..... 46 A4
Town Hall St East *HFAX* HX1 ... 5 H3
Town Hill St *BGLY* BD16 .... 17 E3
Town La *IDLE* BD10 .... 14 A5
  IDLE BD10 .... 20 A1
Townley Av *HIPP* HX3 .... 48 D4
Town Wells Dr *PDSY/CALV* LS28 . 21 G3
Trafalgar Sq *HFAX* HX1 .... 4 C7
Trafalgar St *BFD* BD1 .... 2 C5
  HFAX HX1 .... 4 C7
Tramways *LM/WK* BD12 .... 38 C5
Transperience Wy *LM/WK* BD12 . 38 C4
Tranter Gv *BOW* BD4 .... 32 D2
Trees St *BOW* BD4 .... 24 D3
Trenam Park Dr *IDLE* BD10 .... 13 H4
Trenance Dr *WBSY* BD6 .... 38 A2
Trenholme Av *LM/WK* BD12 ... 37 G4
Trenton Dr *GIR* BD8 .... 24 D3
Trevelyan St *BRIG* HD6 .... 50 B3
Trimmingham La *LUD/ILL* HX2 .. 46 C2
Trimmingham Rd *LUD/ILL* HX2 .. 46 C2
Trinity Cl *LUD/ILL* HX2 .... 34 B4
Trinity Pl *BGLY* BD16 .... 10 D4
  HFAX HX1 .... 5 G5
Trinity Rd *HFAX* HX1 .... 5 G5
  WBOW BD5 .... 31 E2
Trinity St *HFAX* HX1 .... 5 G5
Trinity Vw *HIPP* HX3 .... 5 K6
  LM/WK BD12 ...... 38 B3
Trinity Wk *LM/WK* BD12 ...... 38 B3
Tristram Av *WBOW* BD5 ...... 31 H5
Trooper La *HIPP* HX3 .... 5 K6
Trooper Ter *HIPP* HX3 .... 5 K6
Trueman Ct *LM/WK* BD12 ..... 38 B4
Truncliffe *WBSY* BD6 .... 38 A1
Tudor Barn Ct *SHPY* BD18 ..... 19 E2
Tudor Cl *PDSY/CALV* LS28 ..... 27 H2
Tudor St *WBOW* BD5 .... 31 E3
Tuel La *RPDN/SBR* HX6 .... 46 A4
Tumbling Hill St *GTHN* BD7 .... 2 A6
Tunstall Gn *BOW* BD4 .... 32 D4
Tunwell La *ECHL* BD2 .... 20 B5
Tunwell St *ECHL* BD2 .... 20 B5
Turner Av *GTHN* BD7 .... 30 A2
Turner Av (South) *LUD/ILL* HX2 . 40 A1
Turner La *HIPP* HX3 .... 42 A4
Turner Pl *GTHN* BD7 .... 30 C2
  LUD/ILL HX2 ...... 40 D1
Turner's Ct *HIPP* HX3 .... 41 G3
Turney St *HIPP* HX3 .... 41 F3
Twickenham Ct *GIR* BD8 ..... 25 E3
Tyersal Av *BOW* BD4 .... 27 E5
Tyersal Cl *BOW* BD4 .... 27 E5
Tyersal Ct *BOW* BD4 .... 33 E1
Tyersal Cr *BOW* BD4 .... 33 E1
Tyersal Crs *BOW* BD4 .... 33 E1
Tyersal Dr *BOW* BD4 .... 33 E1
Tyersal Garth *BOW* BD4 ..... 33 E1
Tyersal Gn *BOW* BD4 .... 33 E1
Tyersal Gv *BOW* BD4 .... 27 E5
Tyersal La *BOW* BD4 .... 33 E1
  PDSY/CALV LS28 .. 33 H1
Tyersal Pk *BOW* BD4 .... 33 E1
Tyersal Rd *BOW* BD4 .... 33 E1

Tyersal Ter *BOW* BD4 .... 32 D1
Tyersal Vw *BOW* BD4 .... 32 D1
Tyersal Wk *BOW* BD4 .... 33 E1
Tyne St *BFDE* BD3 .... 3 H5
  KGHY BD21 ...... 7 E4
Tyrrel St *BFD* BD1 .... 2 D5
Tyson St *HFAX* HX1 .... 46 D2

U

Ullswater Dr *WBSY* BD6 ..... 37 E4
Undercliffe La *BFDE* BD3 .... 3 G1
Undercliffe Rd *ECHL* BD2 .... 26 A1
Undercliffe St *BFDE* BD3 .... 3 J1
Underwood Dr *YEA* LS19 .... 15 G5
Union House La *CLAY* BD14 .. 29 F5
Union Rd *GTHN* BD7 .... 30 C2
  WBSY BD6 ...... 37 H3
Union St *BAIL* BD17 .... 13 F4
  CUL/QBY BD13 .. 35 F1
  HFAX HX1 ...... 5 H5
  RPDN/SBR HX6 .. 46 B3
Union Yd *IDLE* BD10 ...... 20 B1
Unwin Pl *HTON* BD9 ...... 23 H2
Unity St *AIRE* BD20 .... 7 G1
Unity St North *BGLY* BD16 .. 10 C4
Unity St South *BGLY* BD16 .. 10 C4
Unity Ter *HFAX* HX1 ...... 46 D2
Uplands *KGHY* BD21 ...... 6 B2
Uplands Av *CUL/QBY* BD13 . 29 E5
Uplands Cl *CUL/QBY* BD13 . 29 E5
Uplands Crs *CUL/QBY* BD13 . 29 E5
Uplands Gv *CUL/QBY* BD13 . 29 E5
Upper Ada St *SHPY* BD18 ... 18 A1
Upper Addison St *BOW* BD4 . 31 G2
Upper Allerton La *WIL/AL* BD15 . 22 B4
Upper Ashley La *SHPY* BD18 . 18 C1
Upper Bell Hall *HFAX* HX1 .. 47 F3
Upper Bolton Brow
  RPDN/SBR HX6 .. 46 C3
Upper Bonegate *BRIG* HD6 .. 50 C5
Upper Calton St *KGHY* BD21 . 9 G1
Upper Carr La *PDSY/CALV* LS28 . 21 F3
Upper Castle St *WBOW* BD5 . 31 F2
Upper Chelsea St *KGHY* BD21 . 9 G1
Upper Ferndown Gn
  WIL/AL BD15 .... 22 D3
Upper Forge *HFAX* HX1 .... 5 H4
Upper Fountain St
  RPDN/SBR HX6 .. 46 A4
Upper Fyfe La *BAIL* BD17 .. 13 F3
Upper George St *WBSY* BD6 . 37 G1
Upper Grange Av *WIL/AL* BD15 . 23 E4
Upper Green Av *CLECK* BD19 . 45 G5
Upper Green La *BRIG* HD6 .. 49 H3
Upper Hall Vw *HIPP* HX3 ... 42 D2
Upper Haugh Shaw *HFAX* HX1 . 4 D7
Upper Hird St *KGHY* BD21 .. 9 F1
Upper House St *BOW* BD4 .. 32 A2
Upper Kirkgate *HFAX* HX1 .. 5 J4
Upper La *HIPP* HX3 .... 42 C1
Upper Lombard St *YEA* LS19 . 15 F2
Upper Mary St *SHPY* BD18 .. 18 A1
Upper Mdw *CUL/QBY* BD13 . 35 F2
Uppermoor *PDSY/CALV* LS28 . 27 H5
Upper Mosscar St *BFDE* BD3 . 3 H5
Upper Nidd St *BFDE* BD3 ... 3 K6
Upper Quarry Rd *HUDN* HD2 . 53 H5
Upper Rushton Rd *BFDE* BD3 . 26 C3
Upper Seymour St *BFDE* BD3 . 3 J6
Upper Sutherland Rd *HIPP* HX3 . 43 H5
Upper Washer La *LUD/ILL* HX2 . 46 D1
Upper Willow Hall *LUD/ILL* HX2 . 46 C2
Upper Woodlands Rd *GIR* BD8 . 24 B3
Usher St *BOW* BD4 .... 31 H2
Uttley St *HIPP* HX3 ...... 41 G3

V

Vale Gv *CUL/QBY* BD13 .... 35 G1
Vale Mill La *HWTH* BD22 ... 8 C5
Valentine Ct *CUL/QBY* BD13 . 22 B5
Vale St *BRIG* HD6 .... 50 D5
  KGHY BD21 ..... 7 F2
Valley Av *HIPP* HX3 ...... 44 A5
Valley Cl *BFDE* BD3 ...... 25 F3
Valley Fold *CUL/QBY* BD13 . 35 F2
Valley Gv *LUD/ILL* HX2 .... 34 A3
Valley Pde *GIR* BD8 ...... 2 B1
Valley Pl *BFD* BD1 .... 2 D1
Valley Rd *BFD* BD1 ...... 2 D1
  KGHY BD21 .... 7 F4
  SHPY BD18 .... 18 C3
Valley Vw *BAIL* BD17 .... 12 C5

  LUD/ILL HX2 ... 34 A3
Valley View Cl *HWTH* BD22 . 8 D3
Valley View Gv *ECHL* BD2 .. 25 H2
Valley Wy *LUD/ILL* HX2 ... 34 A3
Vaughan St *BFD* BD1 .... 2 A4
  HFAX HX1 .... 4 A7
Ventnor St *BFDE* BD3 .... 3 H5
Ventnor Ter *HIPP* HX3 ... 47 G4
Vento Cl *WBSY* BD6 ..... 37 G2
Verdun Rd *WBSY* BD6 ... 37 G2
Vere Sq *WBOW* BD5 .... 31 F3
Vernon Ct *KGHY* BD21 ... 6 C3
Vernon Pl *ECHL* BD2 .... 26 A2
Vestry St *BOW* BD4 .... 32 A4
Vicarage Cl *LM/WK* BD12 . 44 D3
Vicarage Gdns *BRIG* HD6 . 52 A3
Vicarage Rd *SHPY* BD18 .. 19 F1
Vicar La *BFD* BD1 ...... 2 E6
Vicar Park Dr *LUD/ILL* HX2 . 40 A5
Vickerman St *HFAX* HX1 .. 4 B5
Victoria Av *BRIG* HD6 .... 50 D5
  ECHL BD2 .... 20 C5
  HFAX HX1 .... 4 A6
  KGHY BD21 ... 6 D3
  RPDN/SBR HX6 . 46 B3
  SHPY BD18 ... 18 A1
Victoria Ct *KGHY* BD21 .. 6 C3
Victoria Crs *PDSY/CALV* LS28 . 27 H5
Victoria Dr *ECHL* BD2 ... 20 C5
  HIPP HX3 ... 43 F2
Victoria Gdns *PDSY/CALV* LS28 . 27 H5
Victoria Pk *SHPY* BD18 .. 18 A2
Victoria Park St *KGHY* BD21 . 7 E3
Victoria Park Vw *KGHY* BD21 . 7 E3
Victoria Pl *BRIG* HD6 .... 52 C2
Victoria Ri *PDSY/CALV* LS28 . 27 H5
Victoria Rd *BRIG* HD6 ... 50 C1
  ECHL BD2 ... 20 B5
  HFAX HX1 ... 4 C3
  HIPP HX3 ... 43 F2
  HWTH BD22 .. 8 C4
  KGHY BD21 .. 6 C5
  PDSY/CALV LS28 . 27 H5
  RPDN/SBR HX6 . 46 A5
  SHPY BD18 .. 18 A1
  WBSY BD6 .. 37 F2
Victoria St *BAIL* BD17 ... 12 D5
  BAIL BD17 .. 18 C1
  BFD BD1 .... 2 B2
  BRIG HD6 ... 50 D5
  BRIG HD6 ... 52 C2
  CLAY BD14 .. 29 E3
  CUL/QBY BD13 . 35 G1
  ECHL BD2 ... 26 B2
  HFAX HX1 ... 5 G3
  IDLE BD10 .. 14 A5
  PDSY/CALV LS28 . 21 F3
  RPDN/SBR HX6 . 46 A5
  WIL/AL BD15 . 22 D1
Victor Rd *HTON* BD9 .... 24 C2
Victor St *BFDE* BD3 ..... 26 D5
  HTON BD9 .. 24 C2
Victor Ter *HFAX* HX1 .... 4 C1
  HTON BD9 .. 24 C2
View Croft Rd *BAIL* BD17 . 18 C1
View Rd *KGHY* BD21 .... 6 B3
Vignola Ter *CLAY* BD14 .. 29 F2
Village St *HIPP* HX3 ..... 44 A3
Villa Gv *BGLY* BD16 .... 10 D2
Villa Mt *LM/WK* BD12 .. 44 D4
Villa Rd *BGLY* BD16 .... 10 D2
Villa St *RPDN/SBR* HX6 .. 46 B4
Villier Ct *WIL/AL* BD15 .. 23 E3
Vincent St *HFAX* HX1 ... 4 B5
Vine Cl *BRIG* HD6 ..... 53 E1
Vine Ct *BRIG* HD6 ..... 53 E1
Vine Garth *BRIG* HD6 .. 53 E1
Vine Gv *BRIG* HD6 .... 53 E1
Vine St *GTHN* BD7 .... 30 C2
Vine Ter *CUL/QBY* BD13 . 28 A1
  HFAX HX1 .. 5 F6
Vine Ter (East) *GIR* BD8 .. 23 H4
Vine Ter (West) *GIR* BD8 .. 23 H4
Violet St *HFAX* HX1 .... 4 C5
Violet St North *HFAX* HX1 . 4 C2
Virginia St *CLAY* BD14 .. 29 F4
Vivian Pl *GTHN* BD7 ... 30 B4
Vivien Rd *GIR* BD8 .... 23 F4
Vulcan St *BOW* BD4 ... 39 G1
  BRIG HD6 ... 52 D2

W

Waddington St *KGHY* BD21 . 6 D5
Wade House Av *HIPP* HX3 .. 36 B4
Wade House Rd *HIPP* HX3 .. 36 B5

Wade St *HFAX* HX1 .... **5** H3
Wadlands Cl *PDSY/CALV* LS28 ...... **21** H5
Wadlands Dr *PDSY/CALV* LS28 ...... **27** H1
Wadlands Gv *PDSY/CALV* LS28 ...... **21** H5
Wadlands Ri *PDSY/CALV* LS28 ...... **27** H1
Wadsworth St *HFAX* HX1 .... **4** B2
Wagon La *BGLY* BD16 .... **10** D5
Wainhouse Rd *HFAX* HX1 .... **4** A7
Wainman St *BAIL* BD17 .... **13** E2 🟦
　BAIL BD17 .... **18** C1 🟦
　HFAX HX1 .... **4** B3
Wakefield Ga *LUD/ILL* HX2 .... **47** E4
Wakefield Rd *BFD* BD1 .... **2** E7
　BOW BD4 .... **32** A3
　BRIG HD6 .... **53** E2
　HIPP HX3 .... **50** A1
　RPDN/SBR HX6 .... **46** D4
Walden Dr *HTON* BD9 .... **23** F1
Walker Av *GTHN* BD7 .... **29** H2
Walker Dr *GIR* BD8 .... **24** B4
Walker La *RPDN/SBR* HX6.............. **46** C4
Walker Pl *SHPY* BD18 .... **19** E1
Walker Rd *LM/WK* BD12 .... **45** C1
Walker St *BOW* BD4 .... **39** E2
　CLECK BD19 .... **45** G3 🟦
Walker Ter *BOW* BD4 .... **32** A3 🟩
Walker Wd *BAIL* BD17 .... **12** A4
The Walk *KGHY* BD21 .... **6** D5 🟦
　PDSY/CALV LS28 .... **27** H2
Wallace St *HFAX* HX1 .... **4** A5
Wallbank Dr *SHPY* BD18 .... **18** D3
Wallingford Mt *WIL/AL* BD15 .... **23** E5
Wallis St *GIR* BD8 .... **24** A5
　RPDN/SBR HX6 .... **46** A4
Wall St *HWTH* BD22 .... **6** A5 🟦
Walmer Vls *GIR* BD8 .... **25** E3
Walnut St *BFDE* BD3 .... **32** B1 🟨
　HFAX HX1 .... **4** C4
　KGHY BD21 .... **9** G2 🟨
Walshaw St *GTHN* BD7 .... **30** B3 🟦
Walsh La *HIPP* HX3 .... **41** G4 🟦
Walsh St *HFAX* HX1 .... **4** B3
Walter Clough La *HIPP* HX3 .... **49** E3
Walter St *ECHL* BD2 .... **19** E5
　IDLE BD10 .... **20** A1 🟦
Walton La *BRIG* HD6 .... **51** F3
Walton St *BOW* BD4 .... **31** G2 🟩
　RPDN/SBR HX6 .... **46** A4
Wansford Cl *BOW* BD4 .... **32** D5 🟦
Wanstead Crs *WIL/AL* BD15 .... **23** E4
Wapping Rd *BFDE* BD3 .... **2** E2
Wardle Crs *KGHY* BD21 .... **6** A3
Wardman St *KGHY* BD21 .... **7** F2
Ward's End *HFAX* HX1 .... **5** H5
Ward St *GTHN* BD7 .... **30** B4
　KGHY BD21 .... **6** C5 🟦
Wareham Cnr *BOW* BD4 .... **32** D5 🟦
Warley Av *BFDE* BD3 .... **26** C4
Warley Dene *LUD/ILL* HX2 .... **46** A2
Warley Dr *BFDE* BD3 .... **26** C5
Warley Edge La *LUD/ILL* HX2 ...... **46** A1
Warley Gv *BFDE* BD3 .... **26** C4 🟦
　LUD/ILL HX2 .... **46** C1
Warley Rd *LUD/ILL* HX2 .... **46** C2
Warley St *HFAX* HX1 .... **4** C5
Warley Vw *LUD/ILL* HX2 .... **46** C1
Warm La *YEA* LS19 .... **15** F1
Warmliegh Pk *CUL/QBY* BD13 ...... **34** C1
Warren Av *BGLY* BD16 .... **11** E3
Warren Dr *BGLY* BD16 .... **11** E2
Warren La *BGLY* BD16 .... **11** E3
Warren Pk *BRIG* HD6 .... **49** H2
Warren Park Cl *BRIG* HD6 .... **49** H2 🟩
Warrenton Pl *GTHN* BD7 .... **30** B2 🟦
Warton Av *BOW* BD4 .... **39** E1
Warwick Cl *BOW* BD4 .... **32** A3
Warwick Dr *BOW* BD4 .... **32** A3
Warwick Rd *BOW* BD4 .... **32** A3
Washer La *LUD/ILL* HX2 .... **47** E4
Washington St *GIR* BD8 .... **24** A3
　HIPP HX3 .... **41** F4 🟦
Wastwater Dr *WBSY* BD6 .... **37** E4 🟦
Watercock St *BOW* BD4 .... **31** H2
Watergate *HIPP* HX3 .... **49** F1 🟩
Waterhouse St *HFAX* HX1 .... **5** G4
　KGHY BD21 .... **6** C4
Water La *BFD* BD1 .... **24** D5 🟦
　HFAX HX1 .... **5** J6
　KGHY BD21 .... **6** C5 🟨
Waterloo Crs *IDLE* BD10 .... **21** E3 🟩
Waterloo Fold *LM/WK* BD12 ...... **45** E4 🟦
Waterloo Gv *PDSY/CALV* LS28 ...... **27** G5
Waterloo Mt *PDSY/CALV* LS28 ...... **27** G4
Waterloo Rd *BGLY* BD16 .... **10** D5 🟨
　BRIG HD6 .... **50** B5
　PDSY/CALV LS28 .... **27** G4
Waterloo Ter *LUD/ILL* HX2 .... **46** B2

Waterside *BGLY* BD16 .... **10** A1
　HIPP HX3 .... **5** J6
Water St *BRIG* HD6 .... **50** C5 🟨
　RPDN/SBR HX6 .... **46** A5
Watford Av *HIPP* HX3 .... **44** A2
Watkin Av *CUL/QBY* BD13 .... **28** C1
Watkinson Av *LUD/ILL* HX2 .... **41** E1
Watkinson Dr *LUD/ILL* HX2 .... **41** E1 🟦
Watkinson Rd *LUD/ILL* HX2 .... **41** E1
Watmough St *BFD* BD1 .... **30** B4 🟦
Watson Mill La *RPDN/SBR* HX6 .... **46** A5
Watts St *CLAY* BD14 .... **29** E3
Watt St *BOW* BD4 .... **32** C2 🟨
Watty Hall Av *WBSY* BD6 .... **30** B5
Watty Hall La *WBSY* BD6 .... **30** C5
Watty Hall Rd *WBSY* BD6 .... **30** B5
Wauds Gates *BAIL* BD17 .... **12** D5 🟩
Waverley Av *GTHN* BD7.................. **30** C2
Waverley Crs *HIPP* HX3 .... **49** F1 🟦
Waverley Pl *GTHN* BD7 .... **30** C2 🟨
Waverley Rd *GTHN* BD7 .... **30** C2
Waverley Ter *GTHN* BD7 .... **30** C2 🟨
Waverton Gn *WBSY* BD6 .... **36** D3 🟨
Wavertree Park Gdns
　LM/WK BD12 .... **44** D1 🟦
Wayside Crs *IDLE* BD10 .... **20** A4 🟨
Weardale Cl *BOW* BD4 .... **39** F1
Weatherhouse Ter *LUD/ILL* HX2 .. **40** C4
Weavers Cft *IDLE* BD10 .... **14** A4 🟨
Weaverthorpe Rd *BOW* BD4 .... **39** H2
Webb Dr *ECHL* BD2 .... **25** H2 🟨
Webb's Ter *HFAX* HX1 .... **5** K1
Webster St *BFDE* BD3 .... **3** J3
Wedgemoor Cl *LM/WK* BD12 .... **44** D1 🟨
Weetwood Rd *GIR* BD8 .... **29** H3
Welbeck Dr *GTHN* BD7 .... **29** H3
Welbeck Ri *GTHN* BD7 .... **29** G3
Welburn Av *HIPP* HX3 .... **49** G1
Welburn Mt *WBSY* BD6 .... **36** D2
Welbury Dr *GIR* BD8 .... **24** D2
Weldon Ct *BOW* BD4 .... **32** D3 🟨
Welham Wk *BFDE* BD3 .... **3** G2
Wellands La *CLECK* BD19 .... **45** G5
Wellands Ter *BFDE* BD3 .... **26** B5 🟨
Well Cl *YEA* LS19 .... **15** H3
Well Close St *BRIG* HD6 .... **50** C5 🟨
Well Cft *SHPY* BD18 .... **18** C2
Wellgarth *HFAX* HX1 .... **5** H7
Well Green La *BRIG* HD6 .... **50** A3
Well Gv *BRIG* HD6 .... **50** A3
Well Head Dr *HFAX* HX1 .... **5** G6
Well Head La *HFAX* HX1.................. **5** G6
Wellholme *BRIG* HD6 .... **50** B5
Wellington Crs *SHPY* BD18 ...... **18** B2 🟨
Wellington Gv *ECHL* BD2 .... **26** A2 🟨
　PDSY/CALV LS28 .... **27** H5
Wellington Rd *ECHL* BD2 .... **26** A2
　KGHY BD21 .... **6** D5 🟨
Wellington St *BFD* BD1 .... **2** E4
　BGLY BD16 .... **10** C3
　BOW BD4 .... **32** C1
　CUL/QBY BD13 .... **35** G1 🟨
　ECHL BD2 .... **26** A1 🟨
　IDLE BD10 .... **20** A2 🟨
　WIL/AL BD15 .... **23** F3
Wellington St South *HFAX* HX1 ...... **5** J5
Wellington St West *HFAX* HX1 .... **4** E6
Well La *BRIG* HD6 .... **53** F1
　HFAX HX1 .... **5** J3
　YEA LS19 .... **15** H3
Well Road Cl *LUD/ILL* HX2 .... **46** C1
Well Royd Av *LUD/ILL* HX2 .... **46** B1
The Wells *LUD/ILL* HX2 .... **46** B1
Well St *BFD* BD1 .... **2** E5
　KGHY BD21 .... **6** C4
Welwyn Av *SHPY* BD18 .... **19** G2
Welwyn Dr *BAIL* BD17 .... **12** D4
　SHPY BD18 .... **19** G2 🟨
Wembly Av *CUL/QBY* BD13 .... **28** C1
Wenborough La *BOW* BD4 .... **33** E5 🟨
　BOW BD4 .... **33** E4 🟨
Wendron Wy *IDLE* BD10 .... **20** A2
Wenlock St *BFDE* BD3 .... **3** G6
Wenning St *KGHY* BD21 .... **7** F5
Wensley Av *SHPY* BD18 .... **18** B2 🟨
Wensleydale Ri *BAIL* BD17 .... **13** F2
Wensleydale Rd *BFDE* BD3 .... **26** D5
Wentworth Cft *BRIG* HD6 .... **52** A4
Wentworth Dr *LUD/ILL* HX2 .... **34** A3
Wentworth Gv *LUD/ILL* HX2 .... **34** A3
Wesleyan Ter *BOW* BD4 .... **32** B4 🟦
Wesley Av *LM/WK* BD12 .... **38** A3
Wesley Av South *LM/WK* BD12 .... **38** B4
Wesley Ct *HFAX* HX1 .... **5** H3 🟨
Wesley Dr *LM/WK* BD12 .... **38** B3
Wesley Gv *IDLE* BD10 .... **14** B5
Wesley Pl *KGHY* BD21 .... **9** G3
Wesley Rd *PDSY/CALV* LS28 .... **27** H3

West Av *BAIL* BD17 .... **12** D2
　HIPP HX3 .... **47** G4
　HIPP HX3 .... **50** B1
West Bank *BAIL* BD17 .... **40** C1
West Bank Cl *HWTH* BD22 .... **6** A3
West Bank Av *AIRE* BD20 .... **7** F1 🟨
West Bank Ri *HWTH* BD22 .... **6** A3
West Bank Rd *AIRE* BD20 .... **7** E1
Westborough Dr *LUD/ILL* HX2 .... **46** C1
Westbourne Gv *HIPP* HX3 ...... **48** A5 🟨
Westbourne Rd *GIR* BD8 .... **24** C2 🟨
Westbourne Ter *HIPP* HX3 ...... **48** A5 🟨
Westburn Av *HWTH* BD22 .... **9** E1
Westburn Crs *HWTH* BD22 .... **9** E1
Westburn Gv *HWTH* BD22 .... **9** E1 🟨
Westburn Wy *HWTH* BD22 .... **9** E1 🟨
Westbury Cl *BOW* BD4 .... **32** C2
Westbury Pl *HFAX* HX1 .... **46** D2
Westbury Rd *WBSY* BD6 .... **36** C1
Westbury St *BOW* BD4 .... **32** C2
Westbury Ter *HFAX* HX1 .... **46** D2
Westcliffe Av *BAIL* BD17 .... **12** C2
Westcliffe Dr *LUD/ILL* HX2 .... **46** D2
Westcliffe Rd *SHPY* BD18 ...... **18** B2 🟨
Westcombe Ct *LM/WK* BD12 .. **44** D1 🟨
West Cft *LM/WK* BD12.................. **44** D2
Westcroft Av *HIPP* HX3.................. **43** E1
Westcroft Rd *GTHN* BD7 .... **30** B3
West End *CUL/QBY* BD13 .... **35** E2
West End Av *HFAX* HX1 .... **46** D2
　PDSY/CALV LS28 .... **21** G3
Westend St *BFD* BD1 .... **2** B4
West End Ter *ECHL* BD2 .... **20** A4 🟨
　SHPY BD18 .... **18** B1 🟨
Westercroft La *HIPP* HX3 .... **43** E2
Westercroft Vw *HIPP* HX3 .... **43** E2
Western Pl *CUL/QBY* BD13 .... **36** A1
Western Wy *WBSY* BD6 .... **37** F3
Westerton Ct *LM/WK* BD12 .... **39** E5
Westfell Cl *HWTH* BD22 .... **6** A5 🟨
Westfell Rd *HWTH* BD22 .... **6** A5
Westfell Wy *HWTH* BD22 .... **6** A5
Westfield *CUL/QBY* BD13 .... **28** D1
Westfield Av *HIPP* HX3 .... **49** G1
Westfield Crs *AIRE* BD20 .... **7** G1 🟨
　SHPY BD18 .... **19** F3 🟨
Westfield Dr *AIRE* BD20 .... **7** G2 🟨
　HIPP HX3 .... **49** G1
Westfield Gdns *HIPP* HX3 .... **49** G1 🟨
Westfield Gv *IDLE* BD10 .... **19** H1
　SHPY BD18 .... **19** F3 🟨
Westfield La *ECHL* BD2 .... **19** G2
　IDLE BD10 .... **19** G2 🟨
　LM/WK BD12 .... **45** E4
Westfield Pl *CLECK* BD19 .... **45** F4
　HFAX HX1 .... **4** C6
Westfield Rd *AIRE* BD20 .... **7** G2 🟨
　CLAY BD14 .... **29** E3
　HTON BD9 .... **24** B2
Westfield St *HFAX* HX1 .... **4** E5
Westfield Ter *BAIL* BD17 .... **12** D2
　CLAY BD14 .... **29** E3 🟨
　ECHL BD2 .... **26** A3 🟨
　HFAX HX1 .... **4** C1
Westgate *BAIL* BD17 .... **12** D2
　BFD BD1 .... **2** B4
　BRIG HD6 .... **53** F1
　ECHL BD2 .... **20** B5
　GIR BD8 .... **2** B3
　HFAX HX1 .... **5** H4
　SHPY BD18 .... **18** C1
West Gv *BAIL* BD17 .... **12** D2 🟨
West Grove Ter *HFAX* HX1 .... **4** D1
West Hill St *HFAX* HX1 .... **4** A4
Westholme Rd *HFAX* HX1 .... **4** A4
Westholme St *BFD* BD1 .... **2** B6
Westlands Dr *WIL/AL* BD15 .... **23** E3
Westlands Gv *WIL/AL* BD15 ...... **23** F7 🟨
West La *BAIL* BD17 .... **12** B3
　CUL/QBY BD13.......................... **22** A5
　CUL/QBY BD13 .... **28** A1
　HIPP HX3 .... **48** C5
　HWTH BD22 .... **6** A4
Westlea Av *KGHY* BD21 .... **7** G2
West Leeds St *HWTH* BD22 ...... **6** B4 🟨
Westleigh *BGLY* BD16 .... **10** D3
Westleigh Cl *BAIL* BD17 .... **12** B4 🟨
Westleigh Dr *BAIL* BD17 .... **12** B3
Westleigh Rd *BAIL* BD17 .... **12** B3
Westleigh Wy *BAIL* BD17 .... **12** A4
Westminster Av *CLAY* BD14 .... **28** D3
Westminster Crs *CLAY* BD14 .... **28** D3
Westminster Dr *CLAY* BD14 .... **28** D3
Westminster Gdns *CLAY* BD14 .. **28** D3 🟨
Westminster Pl *BFDE* BD3 .... **3** F1
Westminster Rd *BFDE* BD3 .... **3** F1
Westminster Ter *BFDE* BD3 .... **3** F1
Westmoor Av *BAIL* BD17................ **12** C2

Westmoor Cl *BAIL* BD17 .... **12** C2
Weston Av *CUL/QBY* BD13 .... **35** H
Weston St *HWTH* BD22 .... **9** H
Weston Vale Rd *CUL/QBY* BD13... **34** D1
Westover Gdns *PDSY/CALV* LS28... **27** H
West Pde *HFAX* HX1 .... **4** H
　RPDN/SBR HX6 .... **46** C
West Park Rd *GIR* BD8 .... **24** H
West Park St *BRIG* HD6 .... **52** C1
West Park Ter *GIR* BD8 .... **24** A4
Westroyd *PDSY/CALV* LS28 .... **33** H
West Royd Av *ECHL* BD2 .... **20** A5
　HFAX HX1 .... **4** H
Westroyd Av *PDSY/CALV* LS28 ...... **33** H
West Royd Av *SHPY* BD18 .... **19** H
West Royd Cl *HFAX* HX1 .... **4** H
　SHPY BD18 .... **19** H
Westroyd Crs *PDSY/CALV* LS28 .... **33** H
West Royd Crs *SHPY* BD18 .... **19** H
West Royd Dr *SHPY* BD18 .... **19** H
Westroyd Gdns *PDSY/CALV* LS28... **33** H
West Royd Gv *SHPY* BD18 .... **19** F1
West Royd Mt *SHPY* BD18 .... **19** F1
West Royd Rd *SHPY* BD18 .... **19** H
West Royd Ter *SHPY* BD18 .... **19** H
West Royd Wk *SHPY* BD18 .... **19** H
West St *BAIL* BD17 .... **12** D2
　BFD BD1 .... **2** H
　BRIG HD6 .... **50** H
　BRIG HD6 .... **50** H
　ECHL BD2 .... **26** A1
　HFAX HX1 .... **4** H
　HIPP HX3 .... **43** H
　RPDN/SBR HX6 .... **46** H
West Vw *BOW* BD4 .... **31** H3
　HIPP HX3 .... **41** H
West View Av *HFAX* HX1 .... **46** H
Westview Av *KGHY* BD21 .... **6** H
West View Av *SHPY* BD18 .... **6** H
West View Cl *SHPY* BD18 .... **19** F2
Westview Ct *KGHY* BD21 .... **6** F3
West View Crs *HFAX* HX1 .... **46** H
West View Dr *LUD/ILL* HX2 .... **46** H
Westview Gv *KGHY* BD21 .... **6** H
West View Rd *HIPP* HX3 .... **41** G3
West View Ter *LUD/ILL* HX2 .... **40** D5
Westview Wy *KGHY* BD21 .... **6** H
Westville Wy *CUL/QBY* BD13 .... **6** H
Westward Ho *HIPP* HX3 .... **41** F1
Westway *HTON* BD9 .... **23** H
　KGHY BD21 .... **6** H
　PDSY/CALV LS28 .... **23** H
West Wy *SHPY* BD18 .... **17** H
Westwood Av *ECHL* BD2 .... **20** H
Westwood Crs *BGLY* BD16 .... **16** H
Westwood Gv *ECHL* BD2 .... **20** A4
Westwood St *HUDN* HD2 .... **53** H5
Wetton Ct *BFDE* BD3 .... **26** C5
Weyhill Dr *WIL/AL* BD15 .... **23** H
Weymouth Av *WIL/AL* BD15 .... **22** C
Wharfedale Gdns *BAIL* BD17 ...... **13** F2
Wharfedale Mt *HIPP* HX3 .... **36** H
Wharfedale Ri *HTON* BD9 .... **23** H
Wharfedale Rd *BOW* BD4 .... **38** H
Wharf St *BAIL* BD17 .... **18** C
　BFDE BD3 .... **2** H
　BRIG HD6 .... **53** H
　RPDN/SBR HX6 .... **46** H
Wharncliffe Crs *ECHL* BD2 .... **20** C5
Wharncliffe Dr *ECHL* BD2 .... **20** C
Wharncliffe Gv *ECHL* BD2 .... **20** C
　SHPY BD18 .... **18** C3
Wharncliffe Rd *SHPY* BD18 .... **18** C
Wheater Rd *GTHN* BD7 .... **30** B2
Wheat Head Crs *HWTH* BD22 .... **8** D
Wheat Head Dr *HWTH* BD22 .... **9** H
Wheat Head La *HWTH* BD22 .... **8** D
Wheatlands *PDSY/CALV* LS28 ...... **27** H
Wheatlands Av *HTON* BD9 .... **23** H2
Wheatlands Crs *HTON* BD9 .... **23** H2
Wheatlands Dr *HTON* BD9 .... **23** H
Wheatlands Gv *HTON* BD9 .... **23** H
Wheatlands Sq *HTON* BD9 .... **23** H
Wheatley La *HIPP* HX3 .... **41** H
Wheatley Rd *HIPP* HX3 .... **41** H
Wheat St *HWTH* BD22 .... **9** F2
Whernside Mt *GTHN* BD7 .... **29** H5
Wherwell Rd *BRIG* HD6 .... **52** C
Whetley Cl *GIR* BD8 .... **24** D4
Whetley Gv *GIR* BD8 .... **24** H
Whetley Hl *GIR* BD8 .... **24** H
Whetley La *GIR* BD8 .... **24** H
Whetley Ter *GIR* BD8 .... **24** H
Whimbrel Cl *GIR* BD8 .... **23** F5
Whinfield Cl *HWTH* BD22 .... **9** H
Whin Knoll Av *KGHY* BD21 .... **6** H
Whinney Hill Pk *BRIG* HD6 .... **50** H
Whinney Royd La *HIPP* HX3........... **41** H

Whin St HWTH BD22 .... 6 B4
Whiskers La HIPP HX3 .... 42 B2
Whitaker Av ECHL BD2 .... 26 B1
Whitaker Cl ECHL BD2 .... 26 B1 [2]
Whitby Rd GIR BD8 .... 24 B3 [4]
Whitby Ter GIR BD8 .... 24 B3
White Abbey Rd GIR BD8 .... 24 D4
Whitechapel Gv CLECK BD19 .... 45 H4
Whitechapel Rd CLECK BD19 .... 45 H5
Whitefield Pl GIR BD8 .... 24 B4 [2]
Whitegate HIPP HX3 .... 48 A4
Whitegate Dr HIPP HX3 .... 48 A4
Whitegate Rd HIPP HX3 .... 48 A3
Whitegate Ter HIPP HX3 .... 48 A4 [6]
Whitegate Top HIPP HX3 .... 48 A4
Whitehall Av LM/WK BD12 .... 44 D4
Whitehall Rd CLECK BD19 .... 45 G4
  LM/WK BD12 .... 45 F4
Whitehall St HIPP HX3 .... 43 G5
Whitehaven Cl WBSY BD6 .... 37 E3 [10]
Whitehead Gv ECHL BD2 .... 26 B3
Whitehead Pl ECHL BD2 .... 26 B2
Whitehead's Ter HFAX HX1 .... 4 B5
Whitehill Gn LUD/ILL HX2 .... 34 A4 [7]
Whitehill St BFDE BD3 .... 3 K6
Whitehall St HIPP HX3 .... 43 G5
Whitelands Crs BAIL BD17 .... 13 E3
Whitelands Rd BAIL BD17 .... 13 E3
White La WBSY BD6 .... 38 A1
Whiteley St HFAX HX1 .... 5 F5
White's Ter GIR BD8 .... 24 C3 [3]
White's Vw GIR BD8 .... 24 C4 [11]
Whiteways ECHL BD2 .... 25 F1
Whitlam St SHPY BD18 .... 18 A1 [27]
Whitley Dr LUD/ILL HX2 .... 34 B4 [2]
Whitley La HIPP HX3 .... 48 D3
Whitley Rd KGHY BD21 .... 9 F1
Whitley St BFDE BD3 .... 3 G5
  BGLY BD16 .... 10 C3
Whittle Crs CLAY BD14 .... 29 E2 [2]
Whitty La LUD/ILL HX2 .... 46 A2
Whitwell St BOW BD4 .... 31 H2 [6]
Whitwood La CLECK BD19 .... 50 D1
Whytecote End
  LM/WK BD12 .... 44 D1 [19]
Wibsey Bank WBSY BD6 .... 38 A1
Wibsey Park Av WBSY BD6 .... 37 E2
Wicken Cl IDLE BD10 .... 20 B3 [4]
Wickets Cl WBSY BD6 .... 38 A2
Wickham Av WBSY BD6 .... 37 H2 [4]
Wickham St CLECK BD19 .... 45 G4
Wigan St BFD BD1 .... 2 B4
Wightman St BFDE BD3 .... 25 H2
Wignall St KGHY BD21 .... 6 C2
Wild Gv PDSY/CALV LS28 .... 27 F5
Wilfred St CLAY BD14 .... 29 G3 [7]
Wilkinson Fold LM/WK BD12 .... 44 D4 [7]
Wilkinson Ter GTHN BD7 .... 30 A1 [7]
Wilkin St KGHY BD21 .... 6 C4 [20]
William Henry St BRIC HD6 .... 50 B5 [6]
  SHPY BD18 .... 18 A1 [23]
Williamson St HFAX HX1 .... 4 C2
William St BOW BD4 .... 32 C2 [7]
  BOW BD4 .... 39 G1 [6]
  BRIG HD6 .... 52 B2
  WBSY BD6 .... 37 E3
Willow Av ECHL BD2 .... 19 H3
Willow Bank HFAX HX1 .... 4 C7
Willow Cl LUD/ILL HX2 .... 46 C2
  WBSY BD6 .... 37 H3
Willow Crs ECHL BD2 .... 19 H3
  RPDN/SBR HX6 .... 46 B3
Willow Dene Av LUD/ILL HX2 .... 46 C3
Willow Dr LUD/ILL HX2 .... 46 C2
  WBSY BD6 .... 37 H3
Willowfield Av LUD/ILL HX2 .... 46 C2
Willowfield Cl LUD/ILL HX2 .... 46 C2
Willowfield Crs IDLE BD10 .... 19 H3
  LUD/ILL HX2 .... 46 C2
Willowfield Dr LUD/ILL HX2 .... 46 C3
Willowfield Rd LUD/ILL HX2 .... 46 C3
Willowfield St GTHN BD7 .... 30 C1 [10]
Willowfield Ter LUD/ILL HX2 .... 46 C2
Willowfield Vw LUD/ILL HX2 .... 46 C2
Willow Gdns ECHL BD2 .... 19 H3
Willow Gv ECHL BD2 .... 19 H3 [1]
Willow Hall Dr RPDN/SBR HX6 .... 46 B3
Willow Hall La RPDN/SBR HX6 .... 46 B3
Willow Ri LUD/ILL HX2 .... 46 C2
Willow Rd PDSY/CALV LS28 .... 27 H2
Willow St GIR BD8 .... 24 B4
  HFAX HX1 .... 4 C4
  RPDN/SBR HX6 .... 46 B3
Willow Tree Gdns BGLY BD16 .... 11 F1
Willow Vls IDLE BD10 .... 19 H3
Wilmer Dr HTON BD9 .... 18 B4
  SHPY BD18 .... 18 B4
Wilsden Rd WIL/AL BD15 .... 22 B1

Wilson Rd BGLY BD16 .... 10 C2
  HFAX HX1 .... 4 A7
  LM/WK BD12 .... 45 E1
Wilson St GIR BD8 .... 24 D3 [18]
Wilton Av HUDN HD2 .... 53 F5
Wilton St BRIG HD6 .... 50 A5
Wimborne Dr WIL/AL BD15 .... 23 F3
Winbrooke Ter WBSY BD6 .... 37 H1 [2]
Winburg St GTHN BD7 .... 30 B2 [7]
Windermere Rd GTHN BD7 .... 29 H4
Windermere Ter GTHN BD7 .... 29 H4 [5]
Windhill Old Rd IDLE BD10 .... 13 G4
  SHPY BD18 .... 13 G5
Winding Rd HFAX HX1 .... 5 H3
Windle Royd La LUD/ILL HX2 .... 46 B1
Windmill Crs HIPP HX3 .... 42 D3
Windmill Dr HIPP HX3 .... 42 C3
Windmill Hl PDSY/CALV LS28 .... 33 H1 [1]
  WBSY BD6 .... 37 F1
Windmill La WBSY BD6 .... 37 H1 [19]
Windsor Crs HWTH BD22 .... 8 A4
  LUD/ILL HX2 .... 40 D4
Windsor Gv CUL/QBY BD13 .... 28 A1 [2]
  HWTH BD22 .... 8 A4 [3]
  SHPY BD18 .... 18 C2 [5]
Windsor St BOW BD4 .... 31 H2 [7]
  HFAX HX1 .... 5 C6 [2]
Windsor Wk BRIC HD6 .... 50 B2
Windy Bank La HIPP HX3 .... 34 C4
Windy Gv WIL/AL BD15 .... 22 A1
Winfield Gv BIRK/DRI BD11 .... 39 H4
Wingate Av HWTH BD22 .... 6 A5 [10]
Wingate Wy HWTH BD22 .... 6 A5 [10]
Wingfield Ct BGLY BD16 .... 10 D2 [10]
Wingfield Mt BFDE BD3 .... 3 J2
Wingfield St BFDE BD3 .... 3 J3
Winrose La LM/WK BD12 .... 44 D1 [20]
Winslow Rd IDLE BD10 .... 20 D5
Winston Ter GTHN BD7 .... 30 B2 [8]
Winterburn St KGHY BD21 .... 6 D3 [14]
Winter Ct WIL/AL BD15 .... 22 D1 [5]
Winter St HFAX HX1 .... 4 B7
Winterton Dr LM/WK BD12 .... 37 H5
Witchfield Hl HIPP HX3 .... 36 C4
Witham Rd SHPY BD18 .... 17 H1
Within Flds HIPP HX3 .... 48 D4
Withins Cl GTHN BD7 .... 30 C4 [13]
Woburn Ter CLAY BD14 .... 29 E3 [17]
Wold Cl CUL/QBY BD13 .... 28 A1
Wolseley St CLAY BD14 .... 29 F2 [4]
Wolston Cl BOW BD4 .... 32 D5
Womersley St HFAX HX1 .... 4 B3
Woodale Av HTON BD9 .... 23 G1 [5]
Woodbine Gv IDLE BD10 .... 20 A2
Woodbine St BFDE BD3 .... 3 G4
  HFAX HX1 .... 4 C7 [5]
Woodbine Ter IDLE BD10 .... 20 A2
Wood Bottom La BRIG HD6 .... 49 H3
Woodbury Rd GIR BD8 .... 24 C2 [3]
Wood Cl BAIL BD17 .... 12 C4
Woodcot Av BAIL BD17 .... 13 E4
Wood Cft BRIC HD6 .... 52 A2
Wood End Cl HIPP HX3 .... 47 G5
Woodend Ct WBOW BD5 .... 31 G5
Wood End Crs SHPY BD18 .... 19 E1
Woodford Av HIPP HX3 .... 48 A4 [7]
Woodford Cl WIL/AL BD15 .... 22 D4
Woodgarth Gdns BOW BD4 .... 33 E4 [2]
Woodhall Av BFDE BD3 .... 26 D4
Woodhall Cl PDSY/CALV LS28 .... 27 F2
Woodhall Ct PDSY/CALV LS28 .... 21 F4
Woodhall Cft PDSY/CALV LS28 .... 27 F2
Woodhall La PDSY/CALV LS28 .... 27 F1
Woodhall Park Av
  PDSY/CALV LS28 .... 27 F2
Woodhall Park Crs West
  PDSY/CALV LS28 .... 27 F3
Woodhall Park Cft
  PDSY/CALV LS28 .... 27 G3 [1]
Woodhall Park Dr
  PDSY/CALV LS28 .... 27 F3
Woodhall Park Gv
  PDSY/CALV LS28 .... 27 F3
Woodhall Park Mt
  PDSY/CALV LS28 .... 27 F2
Woodhall Pl BFDE BD3 .... 26 D3 [2]
Woodhall Rd BFDE BD3 .... 26 D4
  PDSY/CALV LS28 .... 21 F5
  PDSY/CALV LS28 .... 26 D1
Woodhall Ter BFDE BD3 .... 26 D4
Woodhall Vw BFDE BD3 .... 27 E3 [2]
Woodhead La BRIG HD6 .... 53 H2 [5]
Woodhead Rd GTHN BD7 .... 30 C1
Woodhead St LM/WK HX2 .... 40 D5 [11]
Woodhill Ri IDLE BD10 .... 20 D1 [2]
Woodhouse Av KGHY BD21 .... 9 H1 [5]
Woodhouse Cl KGHY BD21 .... 9 H1 [7]

Woodhouse Dr KGHY BD21 .... 9 H2
Woodhouse Gdns BRIC HD6 .... 52 D3
Woodhouse Gv KGHY BD21 .... 9 H1 [8]
Woodhouse La BRIC HD6 .... 52 C3
  HIPP HX3 .... 47 F5
Woodhouse Rd KGHY BD21 .... 9 G1
Woodhouse Ter WBSY BD6 .... 38 A2 [8]
Woodhouse Wk KGHY BD21 .... 9 H1
Woodhouse Wy KGHY BD21 .... 9 H1
Woodkirk Gv LM/WK BD12 .... 44 D4 [8]
Woodland Cl HTON BD9 .... 17 F5
Woodland Ct BGLY BD16 .... 10 A1 [1]
Woodland Crs BGLY BD16 .... 17 E5
  LUD/ILL HX2 .... 46 C3
Woodland Dr BRIC HD6 .... 50 A5
  LUD/ILL HX2 .... 46 C3
Woodlands Av HIPP HX3 .... 41 H4
  PDSY/CALV LS28 .... 27 H3 [8]
Woodlands Cl HUDN HD2 .... 53 H5
  IDLE BD10 .... 15 E5
Woodlands Dr IDLE BD10 .... 15 E5
  YEA LS19 .... 15 G4
Woodlands Gv BAIL BD17 .... 12 A4
  BGLY BD16 .... 17 E2
  CUL/QBY BD13 .... 35 H1
  HIPP HX3 .... 41 H4
  PDSY/CALV LS28 .... 27 H3 [6]
Woodlands Mt HIPP HX3 .... 41 H4 [5]
Woodlands Rd BGLY BD16 .... 11 F2
  CUL/QBY BD13 .... 35 H1 [2]
  GIR BD8 .... 24 B3 [8]
Woodlands St GIR BD8 .... 24 D4
Woodlands Ter
  PDSY/CALV LS28 .... 27 H3 [2]
Woodland Vw PDSY/CALV LS28 .... 21 F3
Wood La ECHL BD2 .... 19 H5
  HFAX HX1 .... 43 E4
  LUD/ILL HX2 .... 40 C4
  PDSY/CALV LS28 .... 21 G2
Woodlea CLAY LS19 .... 15 E1
Woodlea Dr YEA LS19 .... 15 E1 [9]
Woodleigh Av WBOW BD5 .... 38 B1
Woodlesford Crs LUD/ILL HX2 .... 40 A3
Woodman Ct WBSY BD6 .... 36 D4 [5]
Wood Nook La RPDN/SBR HX6 .... 46 B3
Wood Nook Ter PDSY/CALV LS28 .... 27 H3 [7]
Wood Pl GIR BD8 .... 24 D4 [16]
Wood Rd HTON BD9 .... 18 D5 [2]
  WBOW BD5 .... 31 F3
Woodrow Dr LM/WK BD12 .... 38 B5
Woodroyd Av WBOW BD5 .... 31 G5 [6]
Woodroyd Dr HIPP HX3 .... 40 D3
Woodroyd Rd WBOW BD5 .... 31 F4 [20]
Woodroyd Ter WBOW BD5 .... 31 G4 [5]
Woodside KGHY BD21 .... 6 B3 [2]
  SHPY BD18 .... 19 E1 [6]
Woodside Av BGLY BD16 .... 16 C2
  SHPY BD18 .... 17 H1 [5]
  HIPP HX3 .... 41 G4
Woodside Crs BGLY BD16 .... 16 C2
Woodside Dr BGLY BD16 .... 16 C2
Woodside Gv HIPP HX3 .... 41 H4 [12]
Woodside Ms HFAX HX1 .... 5 F1
Woodside Pl HIPP HX3 .... 41 G4
Woodside Rd LM/WK BD12 .... 44 D1 [11]
Woodside Ter HIPP HX3 .... 41 H4 [11]
Woodside Vw BGLY BD16 .... 16 C2
  HIPP HX3 .... 41 G4
Woodsley Rd IDLE BD10 .... 19 H3
Wood Sq HIPP HX3 .... 41 G3
Wood St BAIL BD17 .... 12 D5 [5]
  BRIC HD6 .... 52 C1
  GIR BD8 .... 24 D4 [17]
  KGHY BD21 .... 6 D5 [9]
  WIL/AL BD15 .... 23 F3
Wood St North HIPP HX3 .... 41 G3 [10]
Wood Top BRIC HD6 .... 49 H3
Woodvale Cl BOW BD4 .... 32 D2
Woodvale Crs BGLY BD16 .... 10 C1
Woodvale Gv GTHN BD7 .... 29 H2 [4]
Woodvale Rd BRIC HD6 .... 50 C4
Woodvale Wy CLAY BD14 .... 29 H2
Woodview Av BAIL BD17 .... 13 G2
Wood View Dr ECHL BD2 .... 26 C2 [3]
Wood View Gv BRIC HD6 .... 50 A4
Woodview Rd HWTH BD22 .... 9 E2 [4]
Woodville Pl HTON BD9 .... 18 A5
  HUDN HD2 .... 53 F5
Woodville Rd KGHY BD21 .... 6 C3
Woodville St HIPP HX3 .... 41 F4
  SHPY BD18 .... 19 E1 [7]
Woodville Ter WBOW BD5 .... 31 E2 [8]
Wood Vine Rd
  PDSY/CALV LS28 .... 27 H3 [6]
Woodway BGLY BD16 .... 16 C2 [2]
Woodworth Gv KGHY BD21 .... 9 G3

Wooller Rd LM/WK BD12 .... 38 A5
Woolrow La BRIC HD6 .... 50 D2
Woolshops Sq HFAX HX1 .... 5 H4
Wootton St WBOW BD5 .... 31 F3 [19]
Worcester Pl BOW BD4 .... 31 H3 [15]
Worden Gv CLAY BD14 .... 29 H3 [3]
Worsnop Buildings
  LM/WK BD12 .... 44 D1 [21]
Worsnop St LM/WK BD12 .... 38 A4
Worth Av KGHY BD21 .... 7 F2
Worth Bridge Rd KGHY BD21 .... 7 F3
Worthing Head Cl
  LM/WK BD12 .... 45 E2 [4]
Worthing Head Rd LM/WK BD12.. 44 D2 [?]
Worthing St LM/WK BD12 .... 45 E2
Worthington St BFDE BD3 .... 24 D4
Worthville Cl KGHY BD21 .... 9 H1 [10]
Worth Wy KGHY BD21 .... 6 D5
Wortley St BGLY BD16 .... 11 E3 [4]
Wren Av GTHN BD7 .... 29 H2
Wren St KGHY BD21 .... 6 D3 [15]
Wright Av HWTH BD22 .... 8 C3
Wright St HWTH BD22 .... 8 C4 [11]
Wrigley Av BOW BD4 .... 39 E1
Wroe Crs LM/WK BD12 .... 44 D2
Wroe Pl LM/WK BD12 .... 44 D2
Wroe Ter LM/WK BD12 .... 44 D2
Wrose Av ECHL BD2 .... 19 H4
  SHPY BD18 .... 19 E3
Wrose Brow Rd SHPY BD18 .... 19 E1
Wrosecliffe Gv SHPY BD18 .... 19 E3
Wrose Dr SHPY BD18 .... 19 E3
Wrose Gv ECHL BD2 .... 19 G3
  SHPY BD18 .... 19 E3
Wrose Hill Pl SHPY BD18 .... 19 E4 [3]
Wrose Mt SHPY BD18 .... 19 E3
Wrose Rd SHPY BD18 .... 19 E3
Wrose Vw SHPY BD18 .... 19 E3
Wycliffe Gdns SHPY BD18 .... 18 B1
Wycliffe Rd SHPY BD18 .... 18 B1
Wycoller Rd LM/WK BD12 .... 44 D1
Wycombe Gn BOW BD4 .... 32 D4
Wyke Crs LM/WK BD12 .... 45 E3
Wyke La LM/WK BD12 .... 45 E3
Wykelea Cl LM/WK BD12 .... 45 E3
Wyke Old La BRIG HD6 .... 50 C1
Wyncroft Ri SHPY BD18 .... 19 E4
Wyndham Av ECHL BD2 .... 25 G1
Wynford Wy WBSY BD6 .... 38 B2
Wyvern Cl GTHN BD7 .... 30 A1
Wyvern Pl LUD/ILL HX2 .... 40 D5
Wyvern Ter LUD/ILL HX2 .... 40 D5 [12]

Y

Yarborough Cft HIPP HX3 .... 42 D1
Yardley Wy LM/WK BD12 .... 38 B4 [4]
Yarwood Gv GTHN BD7 .... 29 H4 [9]
Yates Flat SHPY BD18 .... 19 E3
Yeadon Dr HIPP HX3 .... 48 D4
Ye Farre Cl BRIG HD6 .... 50 A4
Yewdall Wy IDLE BD10 .... 20 B3
Yew Tree Av GIR BD8 .... 23 G3
Yew Tree Cl SHPY BD18 .... 19 E3 [5]
Yew Tree Crs GIR BD8 .... 23 H3
Yew Tree La WIL/AL BD15 .... 22 B4
Yew Trees Av HIPP HX3 .... 42 D2
York Crs BGLY BD16 .... 10 D4 [7]
Yorkshire Wy GTHN BD7 .... 30 C4 [14]
York St BGLY BD16 .... 10 D4
  BRIG HD6 .... 52 B2
  CUL/QBY BD13 .... 35 H1 [15]
  GIR BD8 .... 23 H5
  HFAX HX1 .... 5 F5
York Ter HIPP HX3 .... 41 G4
Young St GIR BD8 .... 24 A5

Z

Zealand St BOW BD4 .... 32 C3

Aire Valley Business Centre
KGHY BD21 .... 6 D3
Aireview Business Centre
BAIL BD17 .... 18 B1
Alhambra Theatre
BFD BD1. .... 2 B6
Allerton Clinic
WIL/AL BD15 .... 23 E4
Allerton First & Middle School
WIL/AL BD15 .... 23 E3
All Saints C of E First School
WBOW BD5 .... 31 E3
Alston Retail Park
KGHY BD21 .... 7 E2
Armytage Road Industrial Estate
BRIG HD6 .... 52 D1
Ashcroft Surgery
ECHL BD2 .... 26 A2
Ashfield School
IDLE BD10 .... 14 B5
Atlas First School
GIR BD8 .... 24 D3
Aylesham Industrial Estate
LM/WK BD12 .... 38 A4
Azam & Sender Dentist Surgery
HIPP HX3 .... 36 C3
Baildon C of E First School
BAIL BD17 .... 13 E2
Baildon Recreation Centre
BAIL BD17 .... 12 C5
Bailiff Bridge Primary School
BRIG HD6 .... 50 C1
Bankfield Museum
HIPP HX3 .... 41 H4
Bankfoot First School
WBOW BD5 .... 31 E5
Barkerend First School
BFDE BD3 .... 3 H3
BBC North Studio
BFD BD1. .... 2 D6
Beacon Business Centre
HIPP HX3 .... 48 B2
Beauty Gallery
KGHY BD21 .... 6 D4
Beckfoot Upper School
BGLY BD16 .... 10 D5
Beech Hill County
Primary School
HFAX HX1 .... 4 E2
Belle Vue Boys School
HTON BD9 .... 17 G5
Belle Vue Girls Upper School
BGLY BD16 .... 17 F4
Belmont Business Centre
BFD BD1. .... 3 F4
Belmont Middle School
BAIL BD17 .... 12 C3
Benton Park School
YEA LS19 .... 15 G1
Bierley C of E First School
BOW BD4 .... 39 E1
Bilton Medical Centre
GIR BD8 .... 24 D4
Bingley Grammar School
BGLY BD16 .... 10 B2
Bingley Health Centre
BGLY BD16 .... 10 B3
Bingley Hospital
BGLY BD16 .... 10 D3
Bingley Little Theatre
BGLY BD16 .... 10 C3
Birch Lane Medical Centre
WBOW BD5 .... 31 F4
Blakehill First School
IDLE BD10 .... 19 H3
The Bolton Brow Gallery
RPDN/SBR HX6 .... 46 B4
Bolton Brow Primary School
RPDN/SBR HX6 .... 46 C4
Bolton Lane First School
ECHL BD2 .... 25 H1
Bolton Royd College of Further
Education
GIR BD8 .... 25 E2
Bolton Villas Cricket Club
IDLE BD10 .... 19 H3
Bolton Woods First School
SHPY BD18 .... 19 E4
Borough Market
HFAX HX1 .... 5 H4
Bowling Community College
BOW BD4 .... 32 A4
Bowling Park First School
WBOW BD5 .... 31 G4
Bowling Pool
BOW BD4 .... 31 H4
Bowling Special School
BOW BD4 .... 32 A4
Brackenhill First School
GTHN BD7 .... 30 A3

Bradford Area Health Authority
GTHN BD7 .... 2 B6
Bradford & Bingley Rugby Club
BGLY BD16 .... 11 E5
Bradford Business Park
BFD BD1. .... 2 D2
Bradford Business Park
BFDE BD3 .... 2 D1
Bradford City A F C (1983) Ltd
GIR BD8 .... 2 B1
Bradford Community
Health N H S Trust
BFDE BD3 .... 26 B4
Bradford Community
Health N H S Trust
GIR BD8 .... 24 A4
Bradford Girls Grammar School
GIR BD8 .... 23 H3
Bradford Grammar School
HTON BD9 .... 24 D1
Bradford & Ilkley College
BFD BD1. .... 2 B6
Bradford & Ilkley College
WBOW BD5 .... 31 E2
Bradford & Ilkley
Community College
BFD BD1. .... 2 B5
Bradford & Ilkley
Community College
GTHN BD7 .... 2 A6
Bradford & Ilkley
Community College
GTHN BD7 .... 30 C3
Bradford & Ilkley
Community College
GTHN BD7 .... 30 D1
Bradford Industrial &
Horses at Work Museum
ECHL BD2 .... 26 B1
Bradford Moor First School
BFDE BD3 .... 26 B4
Bradford Royal Infirmary
HTON BD9 .... 24 A2
Bradford Royal Infirmary
Remedial Unit
HTON BD9 .... 23 H2
Bradford Salem Rugby
Football Club
HTON BD9 .... 17 H5
The Bradford Synagogue
GIR BD8 .... 2 B2
Bradford University
GTHN BD7 .... 30 D1
Bradford University
PDSY/CALV LS28 .... 27 F3
Bradshaw School
LUD/ILL HX2 .... 34 A1
Branshaw School
HWTH BD22 .... 6 B5
Branxholme Industrial Estate
BRIG HD6 .... 50 D1
Brighouse High School
BRIG HD6 .... 50 B5
Brighouse Sports Centre
BRIG HD6 .... 50 A3
Brighouse Sports Club
BRIG HD6 .... 50 C5
Bronte House School
IDLE BD10 .... 15 E4
Bronte School
HWTH BD22 .... 8 D3
Brookfield Infant School
IDLE BD10 .... 20 D3
Broomwood Middle School
BOW BD4 .... 39 F1
Bus Station (Interchange)
BFD BD1. .... 2 D6
Butterfield Industrial Estate
BAIL BD17 .... 13 E5
Buttershaw Middle School
WBSY BD6 .... 37 E3
Buttershaw Upper School
WBSY BD6 .... 37 E2
Byron Primary School
BFDE BD3 .... 3 K3
Calderdale Business Centre
HFAX HX1 .... 4 B4
Calderdale Business Park
LUD/ILL HX2 .... 41 E2
Calderdale College
HFAX HX1 .... 4 C5
Calderdale Health Authority
HFAX HX1 .... 46 D2
Calderdale Metropolitan
Borough Council
HFAX HX1 .... 5 H3
Calderdale Metropolitan Borough
Council
HFAX HX1 .... 5 G4

Calderdale Metropolitan
Borough Council
HIPP HX3 .... 36 B4
Calderdale Metropolitan
Borough Council
LUD/ILL HX2 .... 40 D1
Calderdale Metropolitan
Borough Council
LUD/ILL HX2 .... 46 D1
Calder Industrial Estate
BRIG HD6 .... 50 C2
Calder Trading Estate
HUDN HD2 .... 53 H5
Calder Trading Estate
RPDN/SBR HX6 .... 46 B5
Calverley C of E Primary School
PDSY/CALV LS28 .... 21 G2
Calverley Medical Centre
PDSY/CALV LS28 .... 21 F3
Calverley Parkside
Junior & Infant School
PDSY/CALV LS28 .... 21 F3
Carlisle Business Centre
GIR BD8 .... 24 D3
Carlton Bolling College and
Sports Centre
BFDE BD3 .... 3 H2
Carr Green County
Primary School
BRIG HD6 .... 52 A4
Cartwright Hall Art Gallery
HTON BD9 .... 24 D1
Central Mosque
HFAX HX1 .... 4 D4
Chapel Grange Special School
GIR BD8 .... 23 F4
Chellow Dene Middle School
GIR BD8 .... 23 G4
Chesham Building
GTHN BD7 .... 30 D1
Chohan Medical Centre
WBOW BD5 .... 31 E3
Christ Church Junior &
Infant School
LUD/ILL HX2 .... 40 C5
Christ Church Junior School
RPDN/SBR HX6 .... 46 C3
Church Lane Surgery
BRIG HD6 .... 50 B5
Church School
CUL/QBY BD13 .... 28 B1
City Hall
BFD BD1. .... 2 D6
City Link Industrial Park
BOW BD4 .... 26 D5
City of Bradford Metropolitan
District Council
AIRE BD20 .... 6 C1
City of Bradford Metropolitan
District Council
BFD BD1. .... 2 D5
City of Bradford Metropolitan
District Council
BFD BD1. .... 2 D6
City of Bradford Metropolitan
District Council
BFD BD1. .... 3 F5
City of Bradford Metropolitan
District Council
BGLY BD16 .... 10 B4
City of Bradford Metropolitan
District Council
BOW BD4 .... 32 D4
City of Bradford Metropolitan
District Council
HTON BD9 .... 24 A3
City of Bradford Metropolitan
District Council
SHPY BD18 .... 18 C2
City of Bradford Metropolitan
District Council
WBOW BD5 .... 30 D3
City of Bradford Metropolitan
District Council
WBOW BD5 .... 38 D1
Civic Theatre
HFAX HX1 .... 5 H5
Clayton C of E First School
CLAY BD14 .... 29 F3
Clayton Middle School
CLAY BD14 .... 29 F3
Cliffe Avenue Surgery
BAIL BD17 .... 12 D4
Cliffe Castle Museum
KGHY BD21 .... 6 C2
Cliffe Hill School
HIPP HX3 .... 50 B2
Cliffe Middle School
BFDE BD3 .... 25 G3

Club House
BOW BD4 39
Colour Museum
BFD BD1. 2
Cooper Lane First School
WBSY BD6 36
Copthorne First School
GTHN BD7 30
Copwood Mental Health Clinic
BOW BD4 32
Coronation Business Centre
KGHY BD21 7
Cottingley Clinic
BGLY BD16 16
Cottingley First School
BGLY BD16 17
Council for Mosques
GTHN BD7 30
County Borough of Halifax
HFAX HX1 5
Cowgill House Surgery
CLAY BD14 29
Craven Art Gallery
KGHY BD21 6
Crossley Hall First and
Middle School
GIR BD8 23
Crossley Heath School
HFAX HX1 47
Crossley Retail Park
HFAX HX1 4
Cuckoo Nest Industrial Estate
GTHN BD7 24
Deanfield County
Primary School
LUD/ILL HX2 40
Delf Hill Middle School
LM/WK BD12 37
Delph End Gallery
PDSY/CALV LS28 27
Dixons City Technology College
WBOW BD5 31
Dockfield Industrial Estate
BAIL BD17 18
Drakes Industrial Estate
LUD/ILL HX2 41
Dr K Coley
BFDE BD3 3
Dr Singhs Surgery
HIPP HX3 41
Drummond Middle School
GIR BD8 24
Drummond Trading Estate
GIR BD8 2
Dudley Hill First School
BOW BD4 32
East Bierley Cricket Club
BIRK/DRI BD11 39
Eastwood First School
KGHY BD21 7
Eccleshill Clinic & Health Centre
IDLE BD10 20
Eccleshill Cricket Club
IDLE BD10 20
Eccleshill North Middle School
IDLE BD10 20
Eccleshill School
IDLE BD10 20
Eccleshill United Sports Club
ECHL BD2 20
Eldwick First School
BGLY BD16 11
Empire Business Centre
LUD/ILL HX2 41
Esholt & Aire Bronians
Sports Club
BAIL BD17 14
Essex Park Industrial Estate
BFDE BD3 3
Eureka the Museum for
Children
HIPP HX3 5
The Eye Clinic
GTHN BD7 30
Fagley First School
ECHL BD2 26
Farnham First School
GTHN BD7 30
Farrow Medical Centre
BFDE BD3 3
Farsley Community Clinic
PDSY/CALV LS28 27
Farsley Fairfield Primary School
PDSY/CALV LS28 27
Ferniehurst First School
BAIL BD17 12
Feversham College
BFDE BD3 3
Feversham Street First School
BFDE BD3 3

...wer Gallery
  BFD BD1.................................... 2 D5
...rster Square Retail Park
  BFD BD1.................................... 2 D3
...ur Lanes Business Park
  GIR BD8.................................... 24 A4
...wler Street Industrial Estate
  BOW BD4.................................... 32 A2
...xhill First School
  CUL/QBY BD13.............................. 28 A5
...ars Industrial Estate
  IDLE BD10................................. 20 A2
...zinghall First &
Middle School
  HTON BD9.................................. 18 D4
...zinghall Medical Centre
  HTON BD9.................................. 18 C5
...lford Grange Hospital
  YEA LS19.................................. 15 F3
...stead Middle School
  BGLY BD16................................. 11 F2
...rlington First School
  GIR BD8................................... 24 B3
...rlington Industrial Centre
  GIR BD8................................... 24 A4
...e Gleddings School
  HIPP HX3.................................. 47 F5
...enaire First School
  BAIL BD17................................. 12 B4
...lf Club Bungalow
  CLAY BD14................................. 29 G4
...ange Middle School
  AIRE BD20................................. 7 F2
...ange Upper School
  WBOW BD5.................................. 30 C5
...eat Horton Cricket Club
  GTHN BD7.................................. 30 B4
...eat Horton Industrial Estate
  WBSY BD6.................................. 29 G5
...eat Horton Middle School
  GTHN BD7.................................. 30 B3
...eenfield School
  BDIO BD10................................. 14 A5
...eengates First School
  IDLE BD10................................. 20 D2
...eenhead Grammar School
  AIRE BD20................................. 6 B1
...egory Middle School
  BDIO BD8.................................. 38 D1
...ove House First School
  ECHL BD2.................................. 19 H5
...aigh Hall Medical Centre
  IDLE BD10................................. 20 C2
...ainsworth Moor Junior &
Infant School
  CUL/QBY BD13.............................. 35 E2
...alifax Catholic High School
  LUD/ILL HX2............................... 34 B4
...alifax General Hospital
  HIPP HX3.................................. 47 H5
...alifax High School
  HFAX HX1.................................. 5 G6
...alifax Industrial Centre
  HFAX HX1.................................. 4 D2
...alifax Leisure Centre
  HFAX HX1.................................. 5 H5
...alifax Rugby Union
Football Club
  LUD/ILL HX2............................... 41 E1
...alifax Swimming Pool
  HFAX HX1.................................. 5 H6
...alifax Town FC
  HFAX HX1.................................. 5 H7
...alton Building
  GTHN BD7.................................. 30 D1
...ambledon First School
  BOW BD4................................... 39 E2
...anson Upper School
  ECHL BD2.................................. 19 G5
...aycliffe Special School
  WBSY BD6.................................. 30 C5
...ealth Studies School
  WBOW BD5.................................. 31 E2
...eather Grove First School
  HTON BD9.................................. 23 G1
...eath House Surgery
  HFAX HX1.................................. 47 H4
...eaton Middle School
  HTON BD9.................................. 17 G5
...eaton Royds Hospital
  HTON BD9.................................. 17 G4
...eaton Royds Special School
  SHPY BD18................................. 18 B4
...gh Crags First School
  SHPY BD18................................. 18 D3
...gh Fernley First School
  LM/WK BD12................................ 44 D2
...ghfield Middle School
  KGHY BD21................................. 6 B4

Hillfoot Surgery
  PDSY/CALV LS28............................ 27 G4
Hill Top C of E First School
  LM/WK BD12................................ 37 H4
Hipperholme Clinic
  HIPP HX3.................................. 43 G5
Hipperholme Grammar School
  HIPP HX3.................................. 43 F5
Hipperholme & Lightcliffe High
School
  HIPP HX3.................................. 50 A1
Hollingwood First School
  GTHN BD7.................................. 29 H4
Holmefield First School
  BOW BD4................................... 33 E3
Holme Middle School
  BOW BD4................................... 32 C4
Holme Wood Health Centre
  BOW BD4................................... 32 D4
Holycroft First School
  KGHY BD21................................. 6 C5
Holy Family School
  KGHY BD21................................. 6 B2
Holy Trinity C of E First School
  BGLY BD16................................. 10 D4
Holy Trinity C of E Senior School
  LUD/ILL HX2............................... 34 A4
Holy Trinity Infant School
  HFAX HX1.................................. 4 E6
Holy Trinity Junior School
  HFAX HX1.................................. 4 E6
Horton Bank Top First School
  GTHN BD7.................................. 29 H5
Horton Bank Top Surgery
  GTHN BD7.................................. 29 G5
Horton Park First School
  WBOW BD5................................. 30 C3
Hoyle Court First School
  BAIL BD17................................. 13 F3
Hutton Junior & Infant School
  IDLE BD10................................. 20 B4
Hutton Middle School
  ECHL BD2.................................. 20 B4
Idle C of E School
  IDLE BD10................................. 14 A5
Idle Cricket Club
  IDLE BD10................................. 20 A2
Idle Medical Centre
  IDLE BD10................................. 20 A1
Ingrow First & Infant School
  HWTH BD22................................. 9 F2
Inland Revenue Office
  BFD BD1................................... 2 D4
Jamia Islamia Mosque
  GTHN BD7.................................. 30 C3
John Street Market
  BFD BD1................................... 2 C4
Keighley Business Centre
  KGHY BD21................................. 9 G1
Keighley College
  KGHY BD21................................. 6 D4
Keighley College
  KGHY BD21................................. 7 E3
Keighley Cricket Club
  KGHY BD21................................. 6 D2
Keighley Industrial Park
  KGHY BD21................................. 6 D2
Keighley Leisure Centre
  KGHY BD21................................. 7 E3
Kensington Street
Health Centre
  GIR BD8................................... 24 B4
Kents Sports Club
  ECHL BD2.................................. 20 A5
Killinghall First School
  BFDE BD3.................................. 26 B3
Kilmeny Surgery
  HWTH BD22................................. 9 F2
Kings Cross Surgery
  HFAX HX1.................................. 4 C7
Kirkgate Shopping Centre &
Market
  BFD BD1................................... 2 C5
Knowle Spring Industrial Estate
  KGHY BD21................................. 9 G1
Ladderbank Middle School
  BAIL BD17................................. 13 F2
Lady Lane Park School
  BGLY BD16................................. 10 D1
Laisterdyke Clinic
  BFDE BD3.................................. 26 C5
Laisterdyke Middle School
  BFDE BD3.................................. 26 C5
Lapage Middle School
  BFDE BD3.................................. 26 B4
Laura Mitchell Health Centre
  HFAX HX1.................................. 5 G3
Law Courts
  BFD BD1................................... 2 E6

Leaventhorpe Middle School
  WIL/AL BD15............................... 23 E5
Leeds City Council
  YEA LS19.................................. 15 G1
Leeds Road Hospital
  BFDE BD3.................................. 3 J5
Lee Mount County
Primary School
  HIPP HX3.................................. 41 F4
Lidget Green First School
  GTHN BD7.................................. 30 A1
Lidget Green Middle School
  GTHN BD7.................................. 30 A1
Lightcliffe C of E
Primary School
  HIPP HX3.................................. 49 H1
Lightcliffe Preparatory School
  HIPP HX3.................................. 43 G5
Lilycroft First School
  HTON BD9.................................. 24 C2
Littlemoor County
Primary School
  YEA LS19.................................. 15 H2
Longroyde Junior School
  BRIG HD6.................................. 52 A2
Longroyde Surgery
  BRIG HD6.................................. 52 A2
Lorne First School
  BOW BD4................................... 32 A3
Low Ash First School
  SHPY BD18................................. 19 E3
Lowerfields Middle School
  BOW BD4................................... 32 B3
Lower Grange Medical Centre
  GIR BD8................................... 23 F5
Low Moor C of E First School
  LM/WK BD12............................... 38 A4
Lynfield Mount Hospital
  HTON BD9.................................. 23 G2
Mandale Middle School
  WBSY BD6.................................. 36 C2
Manningham Baths &
Sports Centre
  GIR BD8................................... 24 C3
Manningham Clinic
  GIR BD8................................... 25 E3
Manningham Middle School
  GIR BD8................................... 2 A1
Margaret Mcmillan First School
  HTON BD9.................................. 24 B2
Margram Business Centre
  HFAX HX1.................................. 4 E2
Marshfield First School
  WBOW BD5................................. 30 D4
Mental Health Service & Child
Guidance Clinic
  WBOW BD5................................. 2 B7
Mixenden Clinic
  LUD/ILL HX2............................... 40 C1
Moorfield First School
  BFDE BD3.................................. 26 B5
Moorside School
  LUD/ILL HX2............................... 41 E1
Moorside Surgery
  ECHL BD2.................................. 20 A5
Moorview Business Park
  IDLE BD10................................. 13 H5
Mosque
  BFD BD1................................... 2 B3
Mosque
  GTHN BD7.................................. 30 C2
Mosque
  KGHY BD21................................. 6 D4
Mount Pellon Junior &
Infant School
  HFAX HX1.................................. 4 A2
Municipal Baths
  BRIG HD6.................................. 52 C1
The Museum
  HIPP HX3.................................. 42 C4
Myrtle Park Primary School
  BGLY BD16................................. 10 C4
Nab Wood Grammar School
  BGLY BD16................................. 17 F2
Nab Wood Middle School
  BGLY BD16................................. 17 F2
Napoleon Business Park
  BOW BD4................................... 32 A2
National Museum of
Photography Film & Television
  GTHN BD7.................................. 2 B7
Neil Hunt Memorial Ground &
Rugby Club
  BOW BD4................................... 32 B2
Nessfield First School
  HWTH BD22................................. 9 E1
Netherleigh School
  HTON BD9.................................. 24 A2
Newbridge Industrial Estate
  KGHY BD21................................. 7 E4

Newby First School
  WBOW BD5................................. 31 E4
New Cross Street Health Centre
  WBOW BD5................................. 31 E4
New Hey Surgery
  BOW BD4................................... 32 A3
Newlands Industrial Estate
  BAIL BD17................................. 18 D1
New Line Clinic
  IDLE BD10................................. 20 D2
Newspaper Office
  BFD BD1................................... 2 E5
Norcroft Industrial Estate
  BFD BD1................................... 24 D5
North Bridge Leisure Centre
  HFAX HX1.................................. 5 H2
The North Halifax
Grammar School
  LUD/ILL HX2............................... 34 A4
Northowram Hall Hospital
  HIPP HX3.................................. 42 D1
Northowram School
  HIPP HX3.................................. 42 D2
Northowram Surgery
  HIPP HX3.................................. 42 D2
Oakbank School
  HWTH BD22................................. 9 E2
Oakdale First School
  SHPY BD18................................. 19 E3
Oakworth Health Centre
  HWTH BD22................................. 8 C4
Oakworth Junior & Infant School
  HWTH BD22................................. 8 B4
Odeon Cinema
  BFD BD1................................... 2 B6
Otley Road Medical Centre
  BFDE BD3.................................. 3 F1
Our Lady of Victories RC
Junior & Infant School
  HWTH BD22................................. 6 A4
Parkhouse Industrial Estate
  LM/WK BD12............................... 38 B4
Parkinson Lane School
  HFAX HX1.................................. 4 C6
Parkland First & Middle School
  IDLE BD10................................. 20 C2
Park Road Medical Centre
  WBOW BD5................................. 31 F2
Parkwood First School
  KGHY BD21................................. 7 E5
Parkwood Street
Industrial Estate
  KGHY BD21................................. 7 F4
Pecketwell College
  HFAX HX1.................................. 5 F3
Peel Park Surgery
  BFDE BD3.................................. 25 G3
Pellon Industrial Estate
  HFAX HX1.................................. 4 B2
Piece Hall Art Gallery
  HFAX HX1.................................. 5 J4
Plane Trees Group Practice
  LUD/ILL HX2............................... 40 C5
Playhouse & Film Theatre
  BFD BD1................................... 3 F5
Playhouse Theatre
  HFAX HX1.................................. 5 F4
Police HQ
  BFD BD1................................... 2 C6
Pollard Park Middle School
  BFDE BD3.................................. 3 K3
Poplars Farm First School
  ECHL BD2.................................. 19 F5
P O Sorting Office
  BFD BD1................................... 2 D4
Priestman Middle School
  WBOW BD5................................. 30 D5
Priestthorpe First School
  BGLY BD16................................. 10 D3
Priestthorpe Medical Centre
  BGLY BD16................................. 10 C2
Prince of Wales Business Park
  BRIG HD6.................................. 52 C1
Princeville First School
  GTHN BD7.................................. 24 C5
Princeville Road
Industrial Estate
  GIR BD8................................... 24 B5
Pudsey Tyersal Primary School
  BOW BD4................................... 33 E2
Pudsey Waterloo Junior School
  PDSY/CALV LS28........................... 27 H5
Q F Industrial Estate
  BOW BD4................................... 32 A3
Quality Foods Industrial Park
  BOW BD4................................... 32 C2
Queensbury Golf Course
  CUL/QBY BD13............................. 35 G2
Queensbury Health Centre
  CUL/QBY BD13............................. 35 E1

Page 6

D2
1. Back Ada St
2. Back Cartmel Rd
3. Back Edensor Rd
4. Back Grant St
5. Back Paget St
6. Back Simpson St
7. Back Sladen St
8. Cartmel Rd
9. Cashmere St
10. Grant St
11. Greenfield Ct
12. Lime St
13. Paget St
14. Redcliffe Gv
15. Simpson St
16. Sladen St
17. Spencer St
18. Talbot St
19. West Leeds St

D5
1. Arncliffe Av
2. Arncliffe Gv
3. Back Mannville Rd
4. Back Rydal St
5. Bath St
6. Cross Wk
7. Cross Rydal St
8. Exley St
9. Fourth Av
10. Hardwick St
11. Hive St
12. Maisis Crs
13. Mannville St
14. Mannville Rd
15. Nashville Av
16. Nashville St
17. Oxford St
18. Pentland Cl
19. Rawdon St

D4
1. Back Broomfield St
2. Back Broomfield St
3. Barlow Rd
4. Bath St
5. Broomfield St
6. Broomfield Rd
7. Broomfield St
8. Chapel La
9. Cross Leeds St
10. Gordon St
11. Highfield St
12. High St
13. Kendal Mellor Ct
14. Lark St
15. Nares Street Upper
16. Raven St
17. Rectory Rw
18. Redcliffe St
19. Roper St
20. Wilkin St

Page 7

E3
1. Aire St
2. Austin St
3. Back Compton St
4. Back Grouse St
5. Back Hyde St
6. Back Kirby St
7. Brown St
8. Caledonia Rd
9. Kirby St
10. Landor St
11. Linnet St
12. Marlborough St
13. Mitchell St
14. Mulberry St
15. Neville St
16. Pheasant St
17. Quail St
18. Spruce St
19. Swallow St
20. Thrush St
21. Victoria Park St
22. Victoria Park Vw

E5
1. Brow St
2. Carlisle St
3. Delph Croft Vw
4. Dundas St
5. Elm Tree Cl
6. Haynes St
7. St Paul's Rd

F2
1. Arnside Av
2. Athol St
3. Back Colenso Rd
4. Back Florist St
5. Cornwall Rd
6. Cross River St
7. Matthew Cl
8. Pool St

F3
1. Aireworth Cl
2. Back Rylstone St
3. Beeches Rd
4. Craven Rd
5. Grape St
6. Marlow St
7. Ribble St
8. Sussex St
9. Timber St

Page 9

G1
1. Arcadia St
2. Back Cromer Av
3. Back Cromer Gv
4. Back Foster Rd
5. Brook St
6. Broomhill Wy
7. Calton St
8. Catherine St
9. Chandos St
10. Chelsea St
11. Clarendon St
12. Cromer Rd
13. Cromer St
14. Grafton St
15. Hird St
16. Hope Pl
17. Knowle Spring Rd
18. Pickles St
19. Queens Gv
20. Tennyson St
21. Upper Calton St
22. Upper Chelsea St

H1
1. Alma St
2. Dawson Pl
3. Hainworth Wood Rd
4. Park Cl
5. Parkway
6. Woodhouse Av
7. Woodhouse Ct
8. Woodhouse St
9. Woodhouse Wk
10. Worthville Cl

Page 10

D3
1. Amy St
2. Barran St
3. Britannia St
4. Elizabeth St
5. Ellen St
6. Heath St
7. Jardine Rd
8. Kell St
9. Lund St
10. Lyndon Ter
11. Marion St
12. Myrtle St
13. Nether Moor Vw
14. Norfolk St
15. Norman St
16. Raven St
17. Sydney St

D4
1. Campbell St
2. Cooke La
3. Cooke St
4. Drill St
5. Henry St
6. Lawkholme Crs
7. Lawkholme La
8. Lord St
9. Market Pl
10. Samuel St
11. Sand St
12. Shed St
13. Towngate
14. Town Hall St

Page 14

A4
1. Ashfield Rd
2. Blenheim St
3. Booth Royd
4. Booth Royd Dr
5. Bourne St
6. Charterhouse Rd
7. Dawson St
8. Garden Ter
9. Harehill Cl
10. Harper Gv
11. Hyde St
12. Lenton Vls
13. Renshaw St
14. Sandmoor Garth
15. Sherborne Rd
16. Victoria St

Page 18

A1
1. Ada St
2. Carlton Wk
3. Clarence Rd
4. Constance St
5. Dallam Wk
6. Dove St
7. Ferncliffe Rd
8. George St
9. Glenview Ter
10. Grosvenor Av
11. Helen St
12. Higher School St
13. Jane St
14. Katherine St
15. Lockwood St
16. Lower School St
17. Mary St
18. Mawson St
19. Park Gv
20. Queens Pl
21. Richmond St
22. Richmond Pl
23. Richmond Rd
24. Shirley St
25. Upper Ada St
26. Upper Mary St
27. Whitlam St
28. William Henry St

B2
1. Alexandra St
2. Avondale Gv
3. Back Kirkgate
4. Back St Paul's Rd
5. Iver Wy
6. Marlborough Rd
7. Rossendale St
8. St Paul's Rd
9. Springwood Av
10. Springwood Gv
11. Springwood Pl
12. Wellington St
13. Wensley Av
14. Westcliffe Rd

C2
1. Bank St
2. Birklands Ter
3. Central Av
4. Dale St
5. Manor La
6. Market St
7. Sunny Bank
8. Windsor Rd

C4
1. Aireville St
2. Aireville Dr
3. Aireville Gra
4. Aireville Gv
5. Alton Gv
6. Ashfield Dr
7. Briery Fld
8. Carlton Gv
9. Carmona Av
10. Cliff Vale Rd
11. Eastbourne Rd
12. Granville Ter
13. Grove Av
14. Grove Rd
15. Hilton Gv

Page 19

G5
1. Ashbourne Cl
2. Camargue Fold
3. Flower Bank
4. Gresham Av
5. High Poplars
6. Sable Crest
7. Shetland Cl
8. Stirrup Gv

Page 20

A1
1. Calpin Cl
2. Emmeline Ct
3. Hampton Pl
4. Highdale Cft
5. Jasper St
6. Louisa St
7. Lumby St
8. Moorfield Pl
9. North Fold
10. Rawson Sq
11. Sir Wilfred Pl
12. Southcote Cft
13. Stanley St
14. Tharp Garth
15. Walter St

A2
1. Back Cavendish Rd
2. Booth St
3. Brecon Cl
4. Buckfast Ct
5. Cobden St
6. Dunkhill Cft
7. Leyton Crs
8. Leyton Gv
9. Leyton Ter
10. Wellington St

A5
1. Back Stone Hill Rd
2. Bolton Gv
3. Bromet Pl
4. Penn Cl
5. Rowanberry Cl
6. Thornbridge Ms
7. West Royd Av

C3
1. Dorian Cl
2. The Drive
3. Fir Tree Gdns
4. Riccall Nook
5. Ruswarp Crs

Page 23

F5
1. Brindley Gv
2. Dunlin Wy
3. Fulmar Ms
4. Kite Ms
5. Mallard Ct
6. Osprey Ct
7. Sanderling Ct
8. Sandpiper Ms
9. The Square
10. Swallow Fold
11. Whimbrel Cl

Page 24

C5
1. Anvil St
2. Ashwell St
3. Atlas St
4. Barden St
5. Cross Rd
6. Farcliffe Pl
7. Glenholme Rd
8. Jarratt St
9. Jarratt St (East)
10. Macturk Gv
11. Middleton St
12. St Anne's
13. St Chad's St
14. Silver St
15. White's Ter

C4
1. Belvedere Ter
2. Dalton Ter
3. Fearnsides Ter
4. Glynn Ter
5. Grandage Ter
6. Harriet St
7. Holker St
8. Hollings Sq
9. Hollings St
10. Sloan Sq
11. White's Vw

D3
1. Anderson St
2. Arnold St
3. Century Pl
4. Church St
5. Conduit St
6. Cowgill St
7. Laburnum St
8. Leyburne St
9. Lincoln Cl
10. Newport Pl
11. Newport Rd
12. Priestman Cl
13. Priestman St
14. Southfield Sq
15. Trees St
16. Wilson St

D4
1. Back Wood St
2. Denby St
3. Fraser St
4. Globe Fold
5. Hind St
6. Jasmin Ter
7. Juniper Cl
8. Lincoln Rd
9. Menstone St
10. Oxley St
11. Preston St
12. Primrose St
13. Rievaulx Av
14. Stallabrass St
15. Whetley Cl
16. Wood Pl
17. Wood St

D5
1. Back Great Russell St
2. Fieldhead St
3. Legrams Ter
4. Marion St
5. Milne St
6. Milton St
7. Monk St
8. Morpeth St
9. Musselburgh St
10. St Andrew's Vls
11. Thornton St
12. Water La

Page 25

E4
1. Darfield St
2. Eldon Ter
3. Elmsall St
4. Gaynor St
5. Hallfield Rd
6. Hamilton St
7. Hardaker St
8. Holmes St
9. Nostell Cl
10. Priory Ct
11. Roberts Pl
12. St Jude's Pl
13. Sedgewick Cl
14. Spink Pl
15. Spink St
16. Tyson St
17. Ure Crs
18. Victoria St
19. Wynne St

Page 26

A2
1. Back Dudley Hill Rd
2. Beldon Rd
3. Elbow La
4. Fletton Ter
5. Green Pl
6. Palmerston St
7. Peterborough Pl
8. Sherwood Pl
9. Sowden Buildings
10. Sturges Gv
11. Thirlmere Gdns
12. Vernon Pl
13. Wellington Gv

B2
1. Charnwood Cl
2. Charnwood Gv
3. Charnwood Rd
4. Fagley Crs
5. Intake Gv
6. Intake Ter
7. Museum Ct
8. Musgrave Gv
9. Musgrave Mt

E5
1. Akam Rd
2. Angel Wy
3. Ashton St
4. Baptist Pl
5. Blythe St
6. Butcher St
7. Chain St
8. Fulton St
9. Grattan Rd
10. Greenaire Pl
11. Hey St
12. Holmfield St
13. Infirmary St
14. Listerhills Rd
15. Longcroft Link
16. Longcroft Pl
17. Longlands St
18. Lower Grattan Rd
19. One St
20. Providence St
21. Roundhill Pl
22. St Thomas's Rd
23. Sedgfield Ter
24. Sisbridge St
25. Simes St
26. Soho St
27. Tetley St
28. Vincent St
29. Westend St

F5
1. Albion St
2. Barry St
3. Broad St
4. Charles St
5. Commerce St
6. Darley St
7. Fountain St
8. Grattan St
9. Hustlergate
10. James Ga
11. Kirkgate
12. Mawson St
13. Middle St
14. Millergate
15. New John St
16. Northgate
17. North Pole
18. Oddfellows' Ct
19. Piccadilly
20. Rawson Pl
21. Rawson Rd
22. Rawson Sq
23. Sackville St
24. St Blaise Wy
25. Southgate
26. Sunbridge Rd
27. Tyrrel St
28. Upper Piccadilly
29. Wade St

C5
1. Beswick Cl
2. Charles Av
3. Hudson St
4. Johnson St
5. Marton Ct
6. Moorside La
7. Moorside Pl
8. Moorside Rd
9. Napier St
10. Napier Ter
11. Raglan St
12. Scaley St
13. School Sq
14. Wetton St

D4
1. Barberry Av
2. Hawthorn Av
3. Hawthorn St
4. Herbert Pl
5. Melbourne Gv
6. Randolph St

Page 28

A1
1. Ackroyd St
2. Alderscholes Cl
3. Back Fld
4. Back Field Ct
5. Back High St
6. Chapel St
7. Enderley Rd
8. Fountain St
9. Friendly St
10. Henry St
11. Hugill St
12. King Edward Rd
13. Kipping La
14. Kipping Pl
15. Lane End
16. Lower Kipping La
17. Market St
18. Mary St
19. Peel St
20. Priestley St
21. Providence Ter
22. Rock Ter
23. South Sq
24. Sowden Gra
25. Vine Ter
26. Windsor Gv

B1
1. Bronte Pl
2. Commercial St
3. Corrie St
4. Craven Av
5. Green La
6. Green Mount Rd
7. Havelock St
8. Market St
9. North Cliffe Ln
10. Prospect St
11. Sandmoor Cl
12. Sapgate La
13. Springfield St

Page 29

E3
1. Alexander Sq
2. Arkwright St
3. Bright St
4. Cambridge St
5. Cranbrook St
6. Delph Crs
7. Delph Ter
8. Derby St
9. Endsleigh Pl
10. Gordon St
11. Greenwell Rw
12. Oakleigh Cl
13. Oakleigh Ter
14. Tenter Hl
15. Victoria St
16. Westfield Ter
17. Woburn Ter

F3
1. Beech Sq
2. Broomcroft
3. Chrisharben Pk
4. Cross St
5. Gaythorne Ter
6. Gregory Ct
7. Henry St
8. Pasture Side Ter (West)

H5
1. Beacon St
2. Carnaby Rd
3. Cresswell Pl
4. Cresswell Ter
5. Lea Ct
6. Whernside Mt

Page 30

A2
1. Blinns La
2. Church St
3. Green Ct
4. Lidget Av
5. Lidget Ter
6. Longford St
7. Lowell Av
8. St Wilfrid's Cl
9. St Wilfrid's Rd
10. Turner Av

A5
1. Anson Gv
2. Beldon Park Av
3. Beldon Park Cl
4. Haycliffe Ter
5. Lesmere Gv
6. Northern Cl
7. Southmere Gv

B3
1. Bakes St
2. Bartle Fold
3. Bartle St
4. Blacksmith Ct
5. Crabtree Pl
6. Crabtree St
7. Jennings Pl
8. Jennings St
9. Kingswood Pl
10. Kingswood Rd
11. Kingswood St
12. Lime St
13. Melrose St
14. Old Corn Mill La
15. Ormond St
16. Paternoster La
17. Peel Rw
18. Ramsden Ct
19. Sellars Fold
20. Town End
21. Walshaw St

C1
1. Burdale Pl
2. Cottam Av
3. Cottam Ter
4. Ireton St
5. Kirkburn Pl
6. Rilston St
7. Roslyn Pl
8. Shirley Rd
9. Staveley Rd
10. Willowfield St

C2
1. Dirkhill St
2. Kirkham Rd
3. Newburn Rd
4. Noble St
5. St Margaret's Av
6. St Margaret's Rd
7. St Margaret's Ter
8. Swinton Pl
9. Turner Pl
10. Waverley Pl
11. Waverley Ter

C4
1. Barton St
2. Basil St
3. Haycliffe Hill Rd
4. Hudson Cl
5. Keeldar Ct
6. Kettlewell Dr
7. Low Green Ter
8. Oakwell Cl
9. Rufus St
10. Smith Rd
11. Sowden St
12. Stephenson St
13. Withins Cl
14. Yorkshire Wy

D4
1. Arum St
2. Back Smith Rw
3. Bailey Walls Av
4. Centre St
5. Christopher St
6. Christopher Ter
7. Curlew St
8. Darwin St
9. Dorset Cl
10. Fox St
11. Ida St
12. Marsh Gv
13. Marten Rd
14. Mitton St
15. Murray St
16. South St
17. Spicer St
18. Tees St
19. Todwell La

D5
1. Carr Bottom Av
2. Hawes Av
3. Hawes Crs
4. Lemon St
5. Newforth Gv
6. Northdale Av
7. Smiddles La

Page 31

E1
1. Carlton St
2. Edmund St
3. Grove Ter
4. Howard St
5. Lansdowne St
6. Lower Ashgrove
7. Mannville Ter
8. Norcroft Brow
9. Sherborne Rd
10. South Brook Ter
11. Tumbling Hill St
12. Wilton St

E3
1. Belloe St
2. Bottomley St
3. Chapel St
4. Coates St
5. Coates Ter
6. Hampden Pl
7. Hampden St
8. Herbert St
9. Holme Top St
10. Jacob St
11. Launton Wy
12. Mayfair
13. Moravian Pl
14. Newstead Wk
15. Pakington St
16. Parkinson St
17. Stowell Mill St
18. Tudor St

Page 32

B4
1. Corban St
2. Crystal Ter
3. Dudley St
4. Fenby Cl
5. Fenby Gdns
6. Garth Land Wy
7. Heshbon St
8. Lilian St
9. Thornsgill Av
10. Wesleyan Ter

E4
1. Back Greaves Street
2. Baxandall St
3. Burnett Pl
4. Carlton Gv
5. Donisthorpe St
6. Ferndown Gn
7. Finchley St
8. Hastings Pl
9. Low Well Rd
10. Marshfield Pl
11. Parkside Rd
12. Ramsey St
13. Ransdale Gv
14. Rigton St
15. Stirton St

F1
1. Aldermanbury
2. Channing Wy
3. Chester St
4. Clydegate
5. Market St
6. Morley St
7. Neal St
8. Norfolk Gdns
9. Portland St
10. Prince's Wy
11. Quebec St
12. Swan St
13. William St

F2
1. Adelaide St
2. Ann Pl
3. Back Elizabeth St
4. Bower St
5. Bramley St
6. Castle St
7. Clifford St
8. Croscombe Wk
9. Duncan St
10. Elizabeth St
11. Fitzgerald St
12. Hawkshead Cl
13. Heddon Cl
14. Heddon Gv
15. Melbourne Ter
16. Radwell Dr
17. Reyner House Ms
18. St Blaise Ct
19. St George's Pl
20. St James's Gv

F3
1. Albany St
2. Baird St
3. Caulkwell Gdns
4. Clayton La
5. Garvey Vw
6. Glover Ct
7. Hillcote Dr
8. Jackie Smart Rd
9. Jesse St
10. Megraway
11. Merton Fold
12. Mitchell Sq
13. Newton Pl
14. Surrey Gv
15. Tarnhill Ms
16. Tilley Sq
17. Vere Sq

C1
1. Blanche St
2. Blucher St
3. Chapman St
4. Dewhirst Pl
5. Hetton Dr
6. Iqbal Ct
7. Latimer St
8. Lilac Gv
9. Mortimer Rw
10. Tagore Ct

D2
1. Darren St
2. Dence Gn
3. Dennison Fold
4. Dudley Gv
5. Forber Gv
6. Fremantle Gv
7. Levita Pl
8. Sutton Gv

D3
1. Andover St
2. Broadstone Wy
3. Chervana Ct
4. Farringdon Cl
5. Faversham Wk
6. Melcombe Wk
7. Stratton Vw
8. Weldon Ct

D5
1. Arlesford Rd
2. Englefield Cl
3. Felcourt Fold
4. Fontmell Cl
5. Horsham Rd
6. Knutsford Gv
7. Knutsford Ms
8. Launceston Dr
9. Leamside Wk
10. Muirhead Ct
11. Muirhead Fold
12. Purbeck Ct
13. Salcombe Pl
14. Wansford Cl
15. Wareham Cnr

Page 35

F1
1. Albert Crs
2. Alexandra St
3. Baptist Fold
4. Briggs St
5. Broomfield St
6. Cambridge Pl
7. Ewart St
8. Fountain St
9. High Cft
10. Moor St
11. Nelson Pl
12. Osbourne St
13. Queensbury Sq
14. Raglan St
15. Small Page Fold
16. Spring Garden St
17. Union St
18. York St

F4
1. Bowbridge Rd
2. Bowling Old La
3. Boynton Ter
4. Clough St
5. Cranbrook St
6. Cranbrook Pl
7. DeLarge Ct
8. Donisthorpe St
9. Ladywell Cl
10. Loughrigg St
11. Mark St
12. Moulson Ct
13. Mumford St
14. Murgatroyd St
15. Oaks Fold
16. Parsonage Rd
17. St Stephen's Ter
18. Tichborne Rd
19. Tichborne Rd West
20. Woodroyd Rd

E4
1. Galefield Gn
2. Leafsway
3. Linnve Av
4. Lochy Rd
5. Nutwood Wk
6. Poppy Ct
7. Rainbow Ms
8. Rosechapel Cl
9. Sunshine Ct
10. Wastwater Dr

F1
1. Briggs Gv
2. Briggs Pl
3. Elton Gv
4. Kilner Rd
5. Lever St
6. Mill St
7. New Laithe Rd
8. Tanglewood Ct
9. Winbrooke Ter

G2
1. Alexander St
2. Carisbrooke Crs
3. Church Rd
4. Croft House Cl
5. The Folly Hall Gdns
6. Folly Hall Wk
7. Ormond Rd
8. Prince's St
9. Purley Wk

Page 37

E4

Page 39

H1
1 Broadfield Cl
2 Broadstone Wy
3 Cordingley Cl
4 Hopkin St
5 Horsman St
6 Joseph St
7 Ladbroke Gv
8 Lister St
9 Malmesbury Cl
10 Tawny Cl

Page 41

F4
1 Ashville St
2 Batley St
3 Bracewell Gv
4 Brighton St
5 Clifton St
6 Columbus St
7 Concrete St
8 East Park Rd
9 Garfield St
10 Gilmour St
11 Inghams Ct
12 Lawrence St
13 Livingstone St
14 Melrose St
15 Ovenden Cl
16 Peabody St
17 Rushworth St
18 Ruskin Ter
19 Washington St

H4
1 All Souls' St
2 Amblers Ter
3 Brougham St
4 Church Side Cl
5 Claremount Ter
6 Laura St
7 Old Schools Gdns
8 Range Gdns
9 School Yard Vw
10 Sunny Bank Ter
11 Sunny Side St
12 Woodside Gv
13 Woodside Ter

Page 44

D1
1 Abel St
2 Back Rd
3 Barraclough Sq
4 Bell St
5 Carr House La
6 Carr House Mt
7 Courts Leet
8 Crown St
9 Crowther St
10 Garden Cl
11 High Fernley Ct
12 Lane Side Cl
13 Mary St
14 Perseverance St
15 School Pl
16 Wavertree Park Gdns
17 Wedgemoor Cl
18 Westcombe Ct
19 Whytecote End
20 Winrose Cl
21 Worsnop Buildings

Page 45

G5
1 Acer Wy
2 Ash Ct
3 Cowdray Dr
4 Green Ct
5 Industrial St
6 Lower Green Av
7 Low Fold
8 The Paddock
9 Spinners Wy
10 Upper Green Av
11 Walker St

Page 47

E1
1 Alabama St
2 Alfred St
3 Amos St
4 Back Wolsley Ter
5 Burlington St
6 Grove St South
7 Naylor St
8 Otley St
9 Ramsgate St
10 Saltburn St
11 Shalimar St
12 Soho St
13 Whitehead's Ter

E3
1 Akroyd Ter
2 Autumn St
3 Burleigh St
4 Cannon St
5 Cromer St
6 Dowker St
7 Dundas St
8 Hampton St
9 Highfield Pl
10 Hornby St
11 Knight St
12 Leadenhall St
13 Lynwood Crs
14 Maple St
15 Moorgate St
16 Norman St
17 Pohlman St
18 Raleigh St
19 Summergate St
20 Thornton St
21 Thornton Ter
22 Vaughan St
23 Winter St

F1
1 Back Cavendish Ter
2 Back Grosvenor Ter
3 Bowman Pl
4 Bowman St
5 Cavendish St
6 Cavendish Ter
7 Dombey St
8 Florence St
9 Grosvenor Ter
10 Heywood St
11 Lightowler Cl
12 Preston Pl
13 Stansfield Cl

F3
1 Bell Hall Mt
2 Bell Hall Ter
3 Constitutional St
4 Eldroth Mt
5 Elmwood St
6 Emscote Gdns
7 Green Terrace Sq
8 Hawthorn St
9 Hyde Park St
10 Laurel Mt
11 Perseverance Ter
12 Rockville Ter
13 Savile Pk
14 Thomas St West
15 Upper Haugh Shaw
16 Willow Bank
17 Woodbine St

G2
1 Clover Hill Cl
2 Daisy St
3 Hanover St
4 Henry St
5 High St
6 Hill St
7 Kent St
8 Paradise St
9 Regent St
10 St Mary St
11 Savile Grn
12 Savile Lea
13 South St
14 Stirling St
15 Swires Ter
16 Whiteley St

H1
1 Back Victoria St
2 Central St
3 Chapeltown
4 Crown St
5 John St
6 King Edward St
7 Northgate
8 Old Cock Yd
9 Old Market
10 Portland St
11 Princess St
12 St James St
13 Town Hall St East
14 Union Cross Yd
15 Victoria St
16 Waterhouse St
17 Wesley Ct
18 Westgate

Page 48

A1
1 Alfred St East
2 Berry La
3 Berwick St
4 Blackledge
5 Causeway
6 Charles St
7 Cripplegate
8 Discovery Rd
9 Dispensary Wk
10 Lower Kirkgate
11 Square Rd
12 Upper Kirkgate

Notes